AF762917

Law, Obligation, Community

Against an ever-expanding and diversifying 'rights talk', this book re-opens the question of obligation from not only legal but also ethical, sociological and political perspectives. Its premise is that obligation has a primacy ahead of rights, because rights attach to practices and modes of being that are already saturated with obligations. Obligations thus lie at the core not just of law but of community. Yet the distinctive meanings, range and situations of obligation have tended to remain under-theorised in legal scholarship. In response, this book examines the sense in which we are multiply 'bound beings', to law and legal institutions, as much as we are to place, community, memory and the various social institutions that give shape to collective life. Sharing this set of concerns, each of the international group of scholars contributing to this volume traces the specificity of the binding force of obligations, their techniques and modes of expression, as well as their centrally important role in giving form to lawful relations. Together they provide an innovative and challenging contribution to legal scholarship: one that will also be of relevance to those working in politics, philosophy and social theory.

Daniel Matthews and Scott Veitch are both based in the Faculty of Law at the University of Hong Kong.

Critical Studies in Jurisprudence

Editorial Board: Emilios Christodoulidis and Claudio Michelon (series editors, University of Glasgow and University of Edinburgh respectively), Lindsay Farmer (University of Glasgow), Lilian Moncrieff (University of Glasgow), Scott Veitch (University of Hong Kong) and Neil Walker (University of Edinburgh)

This series continues the 'Edinburgh/Glasgow Law and Society' series

Social Rights in an Age of Austerity
Edited by Stefano Civitarese Matteucci and Simon Halliday

'Integration through Law' Revisited: The Making of the European Polity
Edited by Daniel Augenstein

The Public in Law: Representations of the Political in Legal Discourse
Edited by Claudio Michelon, Gregor Clunie, Christopher McCorkindale and Haris Psarras

The Many Constitutions of Europe
Edited by Kaarlo Tuori and Suvi Sankari

Law as Institutional Normative Order
Edited by Maksymilian Del Mar and Zenon Bańkowski

Law and Agonistic Politics
Edited by Andrew Schaap

Public Law and Politics: The Scope and Limits of Constitutionalism
Edited by Emilios Christodoulidis and Stephen Tierney

Transformations of Policing
Edited by Alistair Henry and David J. Smith

The Universal and the Particular in Legal Reasoning
Edited by Zenon Bańkowski and James MacLean

Law, Obligation, Community

Edited by
Daniel Matthews and Scott Veitch

Routledge
Taylor & Francis Group
LONDON AND NEW YORK

First published 2018
by Routledge

2 Park Square, Milton Park, Abingdon, Oxfordshire OX14 4RN
52 Vanderbilt Avenue, New York, NY 10017

A GlassHouse Book

Routledge is an imprint of the Taylor & Francis Group, an informa business

First issued in paperback 2019

Copyright © 2018 selection and editorial matter, Daniel Matthews and Scott Veitch; individual chapters, the contributors

The right of Daniel Matthews and Scott Veitch to be identified as the authors of the editorial material, and of the authors for their individual chapters, has been asserted in accordance with sections 77 and 78 of the Copyright, Designs and Patents Act 1988.

All rights reserved. No part of this book may be reprinted or reproduced or utilised in any form or by any electronic, mechanical, or other means, now known or hereafter invented, including photocopying and recording, or in any information storage or retrieval system, without permission in writing from the publishers.

Notice:
Product or corporate names may be trademarks or registered trademarks, and are used only for identification and explanation without intent to infringe.

British Library Cataloguing in Publication Data
A catalogue record for this book is available from the British Library

Library of Congress Cataloging in Publication Data
A catalog record has been requested for this book

ISBN: 978-1-138-30040-8 (hbk)
ISBN: 978-0-367-86265-7 (pbk)

Typeset in Galliard
by Taylor & Francis Books

Contents

List of figures vii
List of contributors viii
Introduction ix
DANIEL MATTHEWS AND SCOTT VEITCH

PART I
The priority of obligations **1**

1 Dogma, or the deep rootedness of obligation 3
EMILIOS CHRISTODOULIDIS

2 Why should I listen to my conscience? Equity and the question of ontological obligation 18
MATT STONE

3 The origin of obligations: towards a fundamental phenomenology of legal and moral obligation 35
JOHAN VAN DER WALT

PART II
Instituting obligations **71**

4 On the company's bounded sense of social obligation 73
LILIAN MONCRIEFF

5 Duty free 101
SCOTT VEITCH

6 History, alterity and obligation: toward a genealogy of the co-operative 122
TARA MULQUEEN

7 Sovereignty, affect and being-bound 139
STACY DOUGLAS AND DANIEL MATTHEWS

PART III
The forces of obligations **161**

8 Hybrid legalities: on obligation and law's immanent materiology 163
KYLE MCGEE

9 The biographical core of law: privacy, personhood, and the bounds of obligation 183
MARCELO THOMPSON

PART IV
Civility, office and the bonds of community **217**

10 Civility, obligation and criminal law 219
LINDSAY FARMER

11 Obligations of office 234
SHAUN MCVEIGH

12 Academic freedom academic obligation 251
CARROL CLARKSON

Index 268

Figures

4.1 2013 Rana Plaza building collapse 74
4.2 Garment factories in Bangladesh 75
4.3 Tar Sands, Alberta 83
4.4 'Ice Watch' (2015) by artist Olafur Eliasson and geologist Minik Rosing 87
4.5 Drawing of the 'Unconformity' at Jedburgh, Borders 90
7.1 *Emabutfo*, 2009 154
7.2 *Europa*, 2008 155

Contributors

Emilios Christodoulidis, Professor of Jurisprudence, University of Glasgow

Carrol Clarkson, Professor of Modern English Literature, University of Amsterdam

Stacy Douglas, Assistant Professor of Law, Carleton University

Lindsay Farmer, Professor of Law, University of Glasgow

Kyle McGee, Attorney, Delaware

Shaun McVeigh, Associate Professor of Law, University of Melbourne

Daniel Matthews, Assistant Professor of Law, University of Hong Kong

Lilian Moncrieff, Lecturer in Law, University of Glasgow

Tara Mulqueen, Assistant Professor of Law, University of Warwick

Matt Stone, Senior Lecturer in Law, University of Essex

Marcelo Thompson, Assistant Professor in Law, University of Hong Kong

Scott Veitch, Paul KC Chung Professor in Jurisprudence, University of Hong Kong

Johan van der Walt, Professor of Legal Theory, University of Luxemburg

Introduction

Daniel Matthews and Scott Veitch

The starting premise for this collection is that the contemporary expansion of rights discourse has obscured the work of obligation. Obligations have a primacy ahead of rights not least because rights attach to practices and modes of being that are already saturated with obligations. The prevalence and durability of obligations are to be found in the myriad practices and more or less formal institutions that make up social life generally and on which legal organisation depends. We encounter obligations in families and friendships, practices of learning and playing, modes of address and ways of deporting oneself. Obligations thus lie at the core not just of law but of community. Yet the distinctive meanings, range and situations of obligation have tended to remain under-theorised in legal scholarship. Even where these do make some appearance, the difficult foundations and specific labours of obligations, along with their existential and political conditions and implications, are too often neglected by a focus on the regular processes that impose or legitimate particular obligations.

Positioned against an ever-expanding and diversifying 'rights talk', this collection re-opens questions of obligation from not only legal but also ethical, sociological and political perspectives. This is not, of course, to suggest that rights do not make a difference to how people's expectations are thought of and met, in law, politics and social relations generally. Clearly they do. But what is missing from this picture is the distinctive work of obligations. Obligations, in some shape or form, have a ubiquity and resilience in Western societies (as indeed they have in many non-Western societies) that simply cannot be said to be the case with rights. That there is a historical dimension to this seems clear enough. As MacIntyre points out,

> there is no expression in any ancient or medieval language correctly translated by our expression 'a right' until near the close of the middle ages: the concept lacks any means of expression in Hebrew, Greek, Latin or Arabic, classical or medieval, before about 1400, let alone in Old English, or in Japanese even as late as the mid-nineteenth century.
>
> (MacIntyre, 1981, 69)

This historical lack does not apply to obligations. And so if rights have come to dominate the contemporary imaginary, it is worth asking why, if obligations do –

at the very least – their necessarily correlative work with rights, as most legal theorists following Hohfeld would agree, they lack an equivalent articulation in contemporary legal and political discourse. The work of obligations goes far beyond, we suggest, the legal notion of correlativity with rights, and so to begin to understand this better requires bringing back into view the conceptual and social conditions within and through which obligations do their binding work.

In the Western imaginary, ever since Odysseus told his shipmates to fasten him to the mast so he could hear the sirens' song, the image of binding as at once limiting and freeing has been ever-present. This is no less true in the normative realm, as is routinely observable in the claim that good or 'free' government must be limited government. Obligations can thus be thought of, as they are experienced, in this dual mode: as both constraining and, in a way, desirable for the ends of securing goods in community. Erving Goffman observed just this when he wrote that obligations could be 'cold, entailing alternatives forgone, work to be done, service rendered, time put in, or money paid; some will be warm, requiring [an individual] to feel belongingness, identification, and emotional attachment' (Goffman 1968, p. 159). Limits to obligations were also crucial, he added, to ensure the success of their binding work, and so it was in this combination – 'the social bond and the restrictions on it' – that lay the 'classic double theme of sociology' (ibid.).

For Goffman, in Western society contract was one 'symbol of this dual theme, celebrating with one stroke of the pen the bond that ties and the acknowledged limits to what it is tied by' (ibid.). But what is intriguing for our purposes is what Goffman argued must be added to this double theme. Drawing on Durkheim's work, he writes:

> [B]ehind each contract there are non-contractual assumptions about the *character* of the participants … to enter into a contract is to assume that one is a person of a given character or being … every bond implies a broad conception of the person tied by it.
>
> (ibid., pp. 159–60, emphasis added)

It is precisely in this area 'behind' the law, in those 'non-contractual assumptions', that we might observe the operation of the ties that bind community together and uncover the work that obligations do there. This underscores the importance of the final term of the book's title: 'community'. For communities are the 'character of the participants' writ large, and they cannot be thought separately from the binding force of obligations.

The chapters in this book thus examine the sense in which we are multiply 'bound beings': to law and legal institutions, as much as we are to place, community, memory and the various social institutions that give shape to collective life. In different ways and with different objects in view, they trace the specificity of the binding force of obligations, their techniques and modes of expression as well as their centrally important role in giving form to lawful relations. Whilst the contributors share a common set of concerns, prompted by our opening premise, each has brought a unique focus to this vital and, we believe, under-developed perspective. We will say more about each of the chapters shortly. Before doing so we would like to note three features of obligations that emerge in the work that follows.

The first involves the priority of obligations. What does it mean to say that obligations have a priority? How does such a priority manifest itself and how is it known? The first three chapters (Christodoulidis, Stone, Van de Walt) address these questions directly. The very idea of priority contains a double meaning: on the one hand, it may either refer to a temporal sense – a 'before' in time – or a conceptual precedence or condition, such as an *a priori*; on the other hand, it registers an importance, even an urgency, in the sense of a primacy of concern. The opening chapters of the volume address the issue of priority in different ways, but each is dissatisfied with a straightforward, or even a complex, account of obligations as simply correlative to rights, and turns instead to the domains of ethics and ontology to assess the priority of obligations.

The second feature concerns the manner and implications of the way in which obligations are institutionalised. One can remain agnostic about the priority of obligations in the senses just noted, but one cannot ignore the fact that obligations are instituted within a number of more or less formal settings. It is specifically the consequences of legal institutionalisation that interest a number of the contributions here, including, it should be said, those already mentioned. In Parts II and III of the book, the authors are concerned, amongst other things, with how and why obligations are instantiated in legal form, how legal obligations circulate within the legal institution and beyond it, and with ascertaining some of the more or less intended consequences of these practices. Highlighting the role of obligation in this way moves the chapters beyond traditional accounts of obligations in law as being primarily the preserve of the private law of contract and tort. Instead, it is the study of the form and flow of obligations, and their subjection to opportunities and hindrances across and beyond the legal institution, that interests the authors. This is not to ignore the importance of private law, however, and several of the chapters directly address the areas of: equity (Stone), corporate law (Moncrieff), privacy (Thompson), cooperatives (Mulqueen) and trusts (Veitch). But in doing so their approach requires that attention be paid to the dynamics of institutionalisation themselves and in particular the prospects and risks attendant on these with respect to the work of obligations. One element of this must undoubtedly address the matter of the *force* of obligations, and this is something taken up explicitly, albeit in very contrasting ways, in the chapters by McGee and Thompson.

In all this it can be observed that processes of institutionalisation do not have one overarching set of conditions, purposes or effects. Nor, once institutionalised, do obligations conform neatly to the categories that law makes available. Rather, the binding (and loosing) work they are capable of can be, amongst other things, deployed, displaced, neglected or stressed in ways often unchartered in conventional scholarship. Hence, in order to grasp what is involved or at stake in these dynamics, we hope to show that there is no single, more or less authoritative, methodology for enquiry. The chapter by Douglas and Matthews, for example, utilises insights from literary and artistic resources to study the ways in which dominant concepts of sovereignty make invisible many of the problems, and possibilities, of the ties that bind our being in community. It is through such multiple modes that we are challenged to approach the particularities of institutionalisation afresh in order to better grasp the work that obligations do.

The third feature concerns the relation between obligations and identities. Obligations work in part to connect and in part to constitute identities. Some prominent aspects of the latter are commonly found in roles, and role responsibilities, where the identity of the role is inseparable from the obligations that come with it. Parental obligations are often considered in this way: one cannot understand what it is to be a parent without understanding the obligations that this role infers. Such instances formed a central component of natural law thinking. Viscount Stair, for example, described family relations as manifesting 'obediential obligations', obligations that could be neither assumed nor alienated, but just *are* by virtue of our being in certain human relationships (Stair 1981, I.i.xix).

The mutuality of the connection between identity and obligation need not take this 'natural' form for it still to be actively present across the full expanse of obligation-related activity. In law and politics, for example, role responsibilities are replete with obligations – landlord, company director, government minister, judge and so on – in ways that are partly constitutive, and hence empowering, and partly binding in terms of the limitations they put on those who fulfil a given role. So too are they present in the obligations associated with a more expansive understanding of the roles that make identities durable in modern societies. The chapters in Part IV fruitfully explore such issues with respect to, amongst other things, the obligations of office, of the 'civility' of civil society and finally, of the academic.

We now want to say something briefly about each of the chapters in terms of both their content and their engagement with the themes identified.

In Part I Emilios Christodoulidis explores the question of obligation's priority through the notion of 'dogma'. Drawing on the work of Alain Supiot, he shows why this priority exists beyond the realm of the correlativity of legal rights and obligations familiar from the Hohfeldian account. He then turns to the work of Simone Weil whose writing on 'rootedness' insisted that the practice and language of rights – like 'democracy' and 'justice' one of those concepts, as she described them, of the 'middle range' – will always be inadequate in responding to people's suffering and needs. Rights, she argued, always demand the possibility of equivalence, balance, calculation and testability, using, as they do, the form of claim and counter-claim appropriate to them. By contrast, obligation finds its priority in the call to respond to the cry 'Why am I being hurt?' This cry, said Weil, is 'infallible'; it cannot be calculated or reckoned with for it demands the attention that is due to the fragility of each human being. Obligation has then, as Christodoulidis puts it, 'the fragile as its specific vis-à-vis' and it is this, and not any notion of right, that founds and precedes the institutions of law. But if this is so, *how* these institutions engage with that priority is crucial, for they can fail to respond appropriately to the priority of obligation. The risk of institutionalisation is always therefore that it is –

or that it even makes possible and more likely – inattentive to the fragile bonds of obligation in community that alone can sustain the human as human.

Of all the areas in legal doctrine where the priority of obligation ahead of right might be thought to be traceable, arguably it is in the historical development of the private law of equity. Matthew Stone assesses this possibility through a reading of the appeal to conscience in the evolution of equity in English law. The notion that 'one is obligated in equity *by* conscience itself' as something *prior* to the law, suggests that the legal field of correlative legal rights and duties always comes *after* the recognition of this primary obligation. Stone's chapter takes up this problematic in two different, if related ways. First, it seeks to determine the nature of this primacy by exploring the ontological dimension within which obligations may be thought to be situated, and addresses what the implications for our understanding of obligations in this regard are. Second, in assessing the interrelations of law and conscience it examines the constant risk of capture posed by the legal institution and its forms of reasoning to any posited primacy of obligation and an ontological reading of community. The constant concern explored here is the vulnerability of the priority of obligation to its forceful over-determination by the law.

Johan Van der Walt's chapter directly addresses the question of how plausible it is to maintain that there is a 'priority of obligation ahead of right'. He does this by drawing initially on the work of Wesley Hohfeld whose analysis of the 'constellation of legal correlatives' precluded the independence or priority of one or other term. Van der Walt does not rely on this analysis as conclusive, however, and in the main part of the chapter offers a close reading of Marcel Mauss' influential essay *The Gift* as a way of potentially unsettling the Hohfeldian account. Gift economies, Mauss noted, involve not only reciprocal exchanges that resemble contractual performances, but are underpinned by distinct obligations. From this clue, so to speak, the chapter then turns to the works of Kant and Levinas amongst others to explore the possible roots and meaning of the priority of obligation. Here he finds that it is in the sense of a 'duty to give', and to give freely, that such priority may be given meaning. This duty, however, cannot be reduced to but can only be endangered by the equivalence, calculability and exchange that the correlativity with rights invokes. Van der Walt thus engages with, and partly critiques, Veitch's account of the 'duty free' understanding of tax avoidance offered in his chapter, by contrasting it with the 'free duty' that the notion of the 'priority of obligation ahead of right' must involve.

In Part II Lilian Moncrieff's chapter investigates the ways in which the bounded activities and conceptual design of corporations facilitate the production of and, from one perspective – that of the corporation – the invisibilisation of harms. In a critical assessment of the dominant discourses of corporate social responsibility, she argues that a new way of seeing is required to open to view what lies below the surface of corporate legal activities and the rights they deploy. The chapter opens with an account of some of the devastating effects of corporate practices in the form of cheap labour and industrial injuries and deaths in the sweatshops that feed Western consumerism. To respond to the routine and extensive harms experienced through this form of organising production, and the disappearance of responsibility for them by those who gain most from the process, requires a decisive shift in how corporations' obligations are understood. To make it, Moncrieff proposes an innovative methodology that would allow a re-viewing of corporate activities and their consequences. This requires a strong sensitivity to the layers and legacies of the material traces that constitute the wider environment within which corporations and people exist. The (sometimes very real) excavations of the lives and bodies of those who suffer the brunt of global networks of production demand, she argues, a new account of temporalities and scale, an unearthing that is geological in impetus, and global reach. Provoked into a novel combination with law, this new account may take shape in the form of a 'le-geology', a deepening and intensification of conceptual insights into the ties of obligation that would challenge the continued acceptance of the immunities of corporate right.

The global extent of tax evasion and the massive sums of money involved has become a focal concern for activists and (to some extent) governments in recent years with the publication of formerly confidential information in the Panama Papers and Paradise Papers leaks. Scott Veitch's chapter addresses this subject through an analysis of the conceptual and sociological conditions that facilitate this largely lawful practice. Using at first Hohfeld's schema, it seeks to show how tax liabilities are made to disappear through their metamorphosing into immunities. But what is key to this 'duty free' scenario is, perhaps paradoxically, the extensive deployment of practices of *obligation*. Veitch shows how obligations and the conceptual devices associated with the law of trusts combine with obligations of professional and client confidentiality to make up an immensely complex and resilient network of financial relations that disallow states from tracking the circulation of assets for the purposes of taxation. It is, he argues, precisely the complex, globalised web of legal, financial and professional obligations that makes the escape from obligations possible. He then contrasts this with how austerity measures enforced by governments hold conditionally to account the provision of social services – education, health and so on – in ways that are entirely asymmetrical with the practices of tax avoiders. Under these conditions, the problem of the 'free rider' lies not with the demonised 'welfare scrounger' but rather with the valorised wealthy who can pay to hide their assets from government accountability.

The chapter by Tara Mulqueen studies an institutional form – the cooperative – whose existence is often seen to be an exemplar of the working of ties of communal obligation. If the cooperative movement has come under immense strain in recent decades as a result of the frenzy for privatisation, then it still, for now at least, forms part of a historical memory of an alternative way of organising production, distribution and consumption on social grounds, rather than those that prioritise the extraction of profit at all costs. But that memory, argues Mulqueen, is overly nostalgic. A proper historical account that pays attention to the legal and political dynamics within which the cooperative movement and its institutional form were generated and grew will find a different reality. By offering a genealogy of the cooperative, we are obliged to face up to the ways in which cooperatives and their internal aspirations were constructed or co-opted by forces external to them. This does not negate the ideals and potential of cooperative organisation.

But it does exemplify the importance of seeing how obligations, in what Goffman might have suggested was their 'warm' sense – of attachment and solidarity – are again vulnerable to the political, economic and legal contexts within which they develop.

The relation between sovereignty and obligation is taken up by Stacy Douglas and Daniel Matthews in a way that opens out the question of community in a novel way. Drawing on a tradition of thought central to philosophy, psychoanalysis and cultural studies, they explore how an account of 'affect' – understood as a discrete of register experience, akin to the emotions – helps unpack the capacity of sovereignty to bind actors in community. Using the context of post-Apartheid South Africa as a backdrop to the analysis, sovereignty is examined through the 'affective attachments' it instals to place, community, the past and an imagined future. In seeking to challenge the affective framing of political life that sovereignty achieves, Douglas and Matthews turn to the literary and visual arts of J. M. Coetzee and Nandipha Mntambo respectively. By assessing how these two artists stage an encounter between the ontological, aesthetic and affective, Douglas and Matthews articulate possibilities for understanding the nature of our 'being-bound' in community beyond the claims of sovereignty. In particular, this turns on a renewed sensitivity to the bonds that traverse human and non-human forms of life. Relying on Raymond Williams's notion of 'structures of feeling', the sense of being-bound discerned in the artworks under consideration is 'emergent' or 'embryonic', pointing to new dispositions that might play more dominant roles in some future form of social organisation. In this way Douglas and Matthews stress the importance of the literary and artistic for legal and political scholarship, arguing that it is here that we might find resources through which we can re-imagine the obligations, bonds and responsibilities that constitute social life.

In Part III Kyle McGee, in taking up the long-standing question of law's positive normativity, develops a highly original account of the force of law and the meaning of legal obligations. In the positivist tradition, McGee sees the question of law's force too often displaced by an inquiry into legal *validity*, supplemented by an account of law's sociological *efficacy*. In order to account fully for the normative force of law, McGee argues that these issues are only part of the picture. There is, in orthodox accounts, a 'missing mass of legality' to be found in the panoply of material, spatial and architectural objects that are themselves normatively significant. Following the actor-network theory of Bruno Latour, McGee develops a theory of 'hybrid legalities' in which legal force is understood in relation to its various modes of expression. In the main we associate the law with textual and discursive modes of expression: we find law in statutes, published cases and in written and oral arguments. But McGee is keen to stress that the law takes shape in other, non-textual modalities too. In a deceptively simple illustration, McGee shows how a fence enclosing a given area of land should be understood as expressing a legal claim to property and as asserting an obligation that a walker, seeking to pass through the area unhindered, must negotiate. The fence, in this sense, must be understood as a rights/materiality/technology hybrid. The law's force, for McGee, depends on the instantiations or modes of enunciation that determine its durability and effectiveness. The technologies on which the law relies – whether a legal text or a material embodiment of a rights claim, like the fence – are never neutral and are of central importance to an account of the law's ability to modify behaviour. In lieu of an account of generalised and predictable rules that affect the lives of an abstract and stable community of persons (as we have in the positivist tradition), McGee draws our attention to the material, situated and affective courses of action that engage particular and transient publics. If we embrace McGee's materiological account of law, the objects that draw the interest of the legal scholar undergo a massive population explosion as we become sensitive to the 'legal theories' expressed in every nook and cranny of social space. So too does this account of legal hybridity challenge the transcendental affectations of the law (and legal theorists) by returning legal study to the material encounters and imbrications that constitute law's normative force.

Writing in part against what he perceives as the limitations of a Latourian account of law developed by McGee, Marcelo Thompson argues that the legal bond is situated at the heart of law's constitutive and reflexive relation with personhood. Obligation, and specifically the obligation of privacy, is that which holds together law and human subjectivity and indeed makes the dignity of humans possible. In contrast to the *modus operendi* of technology – which is that of calculation and not consideration – hesitation, the pause for thought, for reflection, for doubt, is precisely that which signals the unique space and time that legal normativity provides. Thompson offers therefore a defence of law's ability to institute reason, and thus to institute human beings as rational beings, against the collapse of normativity that technological modes of thinking precipitate. In all this, privacy, he argues, lies at the biographical core of law since it operates to recognise and protect the normative space humans need to be creative, autonomous, self-guiding, and sometimes, for sure, errant. The bonds of obligation are thus the means and measure of the institution of human dignity, the moral core of personhood that alone allows us to make sense of our place in the world and, indeed, to make sense at all.

Part IV opens with Lindsay Farmer's detailing of the relationship between civility and the criminal law. At first glance, he notes, the connection between obligations and the criminal law might appear to be tenuous. The language and conceptual work of obligations are more often associated with private law than they are with criminal law, not least since the prevailing view sees criminal law as a matter of *prohibitions* not *obligations*. Positioned against such assumptions, Farmer examines how the criminal law may be seen to impose positive obligations on citizens. The chapter turns, first, to the emergence of traffic laws in the early twentieth century, which regulated a new sphere of social life by articulating a set of obligations that drivers have towards other road users, and, second, to the contemporary phenomenon of 'responsibilisation' in criminal law. The latter refers to the ways in which criminal liability is understood by reference to positive duties rather than prohibitions: the duty to report or disclose potential criminal activity (in the context of money laundering or terrorist activity) or the duty to minimise risk (in the context of encouraging or assisting a crime). These examples aide in understanding the role that the criminal law plays in cultivating and sustaining *civility* and *civil order* in modern society. Understood as a condition of possibility for political and social life, questions of civility have become prominent in recent years, particularly in relation to an increasingly 'uncivil' public discourse. Engaging in these debates, but with a focus on the obligations articulated by the criminal law, Farmer is able offer a 'thicker' concept of civility than is usually discussed in this context. Rather than an abstract notion of civility as a 'virtue' of public life – quite distinct from legal normativity – Farmer explores how the criminal law is a crucial element in the production of a 'civil' modern society.

Through a reading of the works of Jeffery Minson and Raimond Gaita, Shaun McVeigh reflects on the obligations and forms of conduct that attach to the office of scholar and jurisprudent in Australia. Through Minson, McVeigh traces an understanding of office as it relates to civil authority and here finds a productively 'mundane' account of how to live well with plural forms of responsibility in public life. As McVeigh emphasises, an account of office in the tradition of civil prudence, on which Minson draws, has the great benefit of foregrounding the manners, styles and forms of conduct that attach to an office without ever subsuming these within a transcendental or totalising account of 'the good life'. Through Gaita, McVeigh draws out a contrasting account of office, one that attaches most explicitly to the office of philosopher, where the rhetorical capacity for eloquence is paramount. Eloquence refers not simply to a superficial stylistics that might entertain, persuade or amuse but to the capacity to articulate truthfully what it means to live well. The philosopher, in fulfilling the obligations of their office, will 'deepen the realm of meaning' and cultivate an 'ethic of answerability' to the conduct of human relations. In both Minson and Gaita, McVeigh finds a *modus vivendi* that is always in negotiation with ethical, political and legal obligations, with each sphere demanding *sui generis* forms of conduct. The crucial task, as jurisprudent and scholar, is to *live with* – and *live well* with – this plurality of obligations in public life. In the Australian context, this most explicitly involves being answerable to the colonial legacy of genocide, dispossession and racism, as well as attending to the continued existence of Indigenous peoples, their laws and traditions.

Carrol Clarkson's chapter ends the book. Its concern is with the question of academic freedom in the context of the wider community, and refers primarily to the protests, debates and critiques that are ongoing in South African universities. That academic freedom is guaranteed as an individual right in the South African Constitution does not, she argues, adequately account for the conditions in which current dialogues take place. Instead, Clarkson takes up the challenge to think about how the role and diversity of obligations better situate the problematic of academic freedom within a range of diverse communities. Through an engagement with two recent interventions from senior South African professors, she pays particular attention to the *forms* of academic production, and this question of form is enacted in the chapter itself through an alternative form of writing: a series of email exchanges. In performing writing differently, it opens to view much that is not otherwise seen, or is neglected, especially with respect to what it means to be in an academic community, and live and work amongst the, albeit contested, ties of obligation. The chapter concludes with a response by the editors, again in the form of an email address to the writer, which stands also, we hope, as a final reflection on the themes in the book as a whole.

In drawing this Introduction to a close, we have a number of acknowledgements we would like to make. The ideas and chapters in this book were first developed and discussed in two workshops held in Hong Kong and Glasgow. These were immensely productive occasions in which the exchange and challenge of ideas took place in a most collegial manner. Indeed, it seems to us that it is precisely the obligations and ties of the scholarly community, rather than any talk of rights or rankings, say, that make such collaborative working practices stimulating and worthwhile. As well as the contributors, we would also like to thank the others who attended these sessions for their participation in the discussions and Liu Jia for her help in the preparation of the text and index. These meetings required financial support and we would like to thank the Dean of the Law Faculty at the University of Hong Kong, Professor Michael Hor, and the Head of the School of Law at the University of Glasgow, Professor Iain MacNeil, for securing this. It is most of all to the contributors, however, that we wish to acknowledge our gratitude. We thank them for their commitment, time and patience in allowing us to put together what we hope will be, for the reader, a coherent and thought-provoking collection worthy of their singular contributions.

References

Goffman, E., 1968, *Asylums*, Penguin, Harmondsworth.

MacIntyre, A., 1981, *After Virtue*, Duckworth, London.

Stair, 1981 (James Dalrymple, Viscount), *The Institutions of the Law of Scotland*, [1681], Edinburgh and Glasgow University Presses.

Part I

The priority of obligations

1 Dogma, or the deep rootedness of obligation

Emilios Christodoulidis

Dogma and critique

We have been invited to reflect on the notion of *obligation* 'as the core of reciprocity, solidarity, and community'. What is key to the connection of obligation with all three of these key moral and political and, crucially also, juridical ideals is that it *precedes* – in a way that is key to its meaning – its correlation with rights. That is why the '*starting premise*' for the inquiry is that 'the expansion of rights discourse has obscured the work of obligation'. We will look at what it might mean to recover the primacy of obligation and to seek its rootedness in resources deeper than its simple correlativity with right, the surface calculus of its deployment. In his chapter in this volume, Johan van der Walt refers to this departure from correlativity (of rights and obligation) as the break with the Hohfeldian paradigm. We will seek to make sense of the 'break' in terms of the primacy of obligation as rooted in the 'dogmatic', in the way that Alain Supiot has developed it; and we will run that argument alongside the ideal of rootedness, more accurately that of 'taking root' (*enracinement*), in the work of Simone Weil.

Regarding Simone Weil: If rootedness is so cherished a property for Weil, it is because her own world was so painfully adrift. The *mediating* institutions to which she dedicated her short life never really allowed it to properly embed in the contexts of reciprocity that she desired to belong: the workplace, the union, the schools for the workers, the Durruti column in the Spanish civil war, the organisation of the Free French in London. These were all attempts to *forge* reciprocity, solidarity and community. And her *L'enracinement* (2002/1949) is a personal testimony of how these mainstays of the *human condition* – to reclaim the term from Hannah Arendt's *deracinated* worldliness – cannot be hoisted out of *any* set of givens *whatsoever*, that their recall already presupposes a certain 'thickness' on the ground. We might want to recall the notion of *obligation* to describe this thickness. We might go further to suggest that it is in the precedence of obligation, in the deep structure of its *affective* embeddedness, that Weil locates the reason why obligation precedes *rights*, if the latter are to be rescued from the banality of their generalised, indiscriminate recall. We will return to Weil in the next section to look at her account of the 'mediocrity' of the language of rights.

The main argument of this chapter is that any assumed correlation between rights and obligation misses the asymmetry that installs the former in a domain of reductive institutional thinking and the latter in the field of the inexhaustible *dogmatic* resources of legal reason. To make sense of the 'dogmatic' we return to a tradition most recently exemplified in the work of Supiot and follow him in mining a deep hermeneutics. His *Homo Juridicus* is a restatement of *law as social hermeneutic*; the *hermeneia* referred to is unique to juridical reason and sustains the dignity and autonomy of *ratio juris*, of the *nomikos logos.* Its achievement is to provide the shared symbolic medium that *binds* by 'interposing shared meaning between people' (Supiot 2007, p. xxiv). It is here that Supiot locates the anthropological function of law which marks the ambition of the work. The function is a function of *binding: the law* 'connects infinite universality to finite existence', our material to our spiritual existence. In the very same move it binds to others through sustaining a symbolic function. In this social dimension what the law achieves, across societies and history, is to generate forms of this bond, and by means of which also, a reciprocity that rests on obligations assumed. 'Binding' and 'interposing', reciprocity and obligation: words that, for Supiot, sustain at the foundational level the meaning of 'the human' and of 'the common' *in tandem.* There is a radical recuperation of juridical reason in this, as pitted against the various reductionisms of law to scientific or economic reason, and guarding against the harnessing of the juridical to historical determinisms or deconstructive undoing. Importantly the *recuperation* goes hand in hand with the radical *critique* of law, including of course the critique of rights. To see how the commitment to both recuperation and critique might be upheld, we will need to look at the concept of the *question dogmatique*, in the tradition of thought from which Supiot draws, and in which Pierre Legendre is a key figure.

As Peter Goodrich (2009, pp. 296–312) puts it in one of the few serious engagements with Legendre's vast oeuvre which is largely unknown in Anglophone scholarship,[1] Legendre takes law to be an institution that relays significant and valuable cultural goods.

> We need, we are compelled, as human beings to attach to images of identity and community that will bind us to a place, a group, an order of being while exteriorizing our fears of emptiness and non-being onto the outside and alien, the different and other. So the argument as to the anthropological significance of the norm goes and it operates across the vast corpus of Legendre's work to analyze the psychic function of scripture and Text, of word and image, of dance as a choreography of human places and social being, of rites of solemnization, of dogma as such.
>
> (ibid., p. 300)

1 'Resistant to systematization, hostile to students and disciples alike, prolific yet inaccessible or at least complicated in style, arcane and at the same time grandiose in range of reference and titles of works, Legendre is almost impossible to classify, let alone to translate' (Goodrich 2009, p. 299).

For this 'non-school or institutionally diasporic species of legal critique' (ibid., p. 302) the subjectivity is sustained in the juridical hierarchy of sites of enunciation and is mobilised though institutional roles. The emphasis on 'critique' here may appear incongruous if critique, as is customarily assumed, begins with reasons one gives oneself. It is certainly unusual to locate critique in the field of 'heteronomy' entailed by dogma, with its emphasis also on hierarchy and institution. Remember that, for Legendre at least, the hermeneutical recovery of legal meaning is pitted against the pervasive *postmodern* take of critique understood as the radical play of interpretations that cut away at the coherence of law; his argument being that such 'radicality' cuts it adrift, self-defeatingly, from its own symbolic premises, the logic of institution and identity that sustains the subject in the social. Legendre insists that the collapse of the heteronomy of the symbolic – of 'dogma as such' – will entail the loosening of the binding function of the symbolic and will engender meaninglessness.

I am not in a position to add much by way of comment to Legendre's organising insight over the psychic function of Text; instead I propose to follow Supiot along the pathways of the constitution of the dogmatic field and the function of law as a *critical* social hermeneutic. There is, to be sure, a prima facie tension in bringing together dogma and critique. Ordinarily we take *dogmatic* to mean what resists questioning; and what is taken for granted signifies and achieves closure. But for Supiot the specific kind of unquestionability that attaches to the dogmatic allows it to harbour critique. For the Legendrian that he is, for Supiot 'heteronomy' sustains the legal-hermeneutical exercise; it involves the pre-understandings that set in place the conditions for interpretation; and these conditions, for the hermeneutical enterprise to unfold, cannot be at once deployed *and* questioned. How the specific tradition relates to or differs from the grand hermeneutical endeavours of Gadamer and others, how 'dogma' relates to 'horizon', and how 'fusion' might be understood, will not concern us here. We will remain only with the dogmatic as installing an 'unquestionability' that is not merely productive but at the root of the very autonomy of juridical reason.

Why would Supiot consider such unquestionability as crucial to his normative defence of the juridical? We are best to approach this as a phenomenological argument, of how a field of hermeneutical enquiry can be disclosed and sustained. Supiot's priority is with the resources of interpretation that the dogmatic releases; dogma does the work of sustaining an interpretative plane, a discursive space. In its properly symbolic dimension heteronomy enables disclosure of a world. It is indeed disclosure that is at stake in the function of the dogmatic; the dogmatic sets the limit points that sustain the symbolic order. To question them comes at the cost of it coming undone, of collapsing it. The border, the *plus non ultra*, is set by the dogmatic in the sense implied by the term *economy* of representation. The dogmatic-juridical sustains the field of reference of human commonality. Where dogma does the work of sustaining the discursive space by setting in place the non-negotiable mainstays of the common, the work of legal hermeneutics is to unfold the dogmatic resources *as interdiction and as judgement.*

Let us take the two terms *interdiction* and *judgement* severally and in their combination.

Interdiction is a wonderful term for the equivocation it carries, as that which on the one hand *resists, stems and interrupts* and on the other mediates: *inter-dicts.* On the one hand it refers to the sense of 'diction' that *mediates* by carrying meanings 'between' ('*inter*') registers; on the other hand to the sense of *preventing* (stemming, interrupting) the subjection of the logic of one medium (law or politics) to that of another (economics). There is something profoundly urgent in this latter function of interdiction. The *non-negotiability* of the fundamental values of reciprocity, solidarity and community that underlie what it means to *belong* in a world are installed and enshrined at the level of the dogmatic as the mainsprings of obligation. They are thus vested with the unquestionability that make them conditions rather than objects of question, pre-understandings, predispositions, guiding orientation, however we might describe the hermeneutic enterprise of calling them forth in our culture's symbolic resources in renewed acts of interpretation-cum-determination.

It is at the level of this renewed instantiation that one must understand the exercise of *judgement.* We will have opportunity in the third section to look more carefully at the Thomist idea of *determinatio.* Suffice for now to describe it as the function of specification, concretisation or instantiation, of the abstract value resources in specific, particular, occasions.

In their combination interdiction and judgement attach a very particular meaning to critique understood as the *recuperation* of law as dogma that is instantiated rather than re-invented, modulated or undermined through its critical invocation in judgement. A productive tension now installs itself at the juncture of closure and under-determination, calling forth the interpretative practices that enjoin us in community. In the interstice that opens up between legal dogma and its productive deployment in interpretation, Supiot sets the opportunity-structure of legality as both limit and occasion. He says: 'The law hedges in every new beginning and at the same time assures its freedom of movement' (Supiot 2007, p. 58). If hermeneutics always depends on a horizon that cannot be transcended, the notion of the dogmatic as origin and limit is rolled out in every new interpretation. Juridical reason is deployed within the set of values it enacts as fundamental presuppositions to it, and the concept of obligation it mobilises it already presupposes as deep premise, foundation and reason.

What the dialectic of interdiction and judgement achieves is to mobilise the dogmatic resources of *ratio legis* even as the suggestion of any direct, mechanistic or deductive derivation of its requirements is clearly rejected. Since Ulpian deployed the term *auctoritatem interponere* [2] to characterise the Roman tutor's transformation of 'the external' into the internal material of law, a discussion amongst jurists has concerned precisely that traversing concept of *auctoritas*, the

2 Ulpian, 11.25, 'Pupillorum pupilllarumque tutores et ngotia gerunt et auctotitatem interponunt'.

mechanisms of legal signification that mediate the construction of legal meaning more specifically in the ways in which the general norm and the concrete decision are brought together. Amongst modern authors, as is so often the case, the incisive contribution was Carl Schmitt's (1979, pp. 41 ff.) formulation of the *auctoritatis interpositio*

> [as] justified by the specificity of the normative and arises since a concrete judgement must be made of a concrete fact, even though the only available evaluation criterion is a general principle of law. Accordingly, every decisional instance entails a transformation [...] every transformation entails an *auctoritatis interpositio* [...]; the very essence of judgement is the fact that there can never be absolute declaratory judgements. With regard to the content of the decisional norm, each constitutive and specific decisional moment entails something new and foreign. Normatively speaking, the Judgement is born out of nothingness.[3]

It is in answer to this most complex of questions over what allows the crossing of the distance between general norm and concrete judgement, one that perplexed Kelsen too, that allowed Schmitt to rebut the self-grounding gesture of law's closure and to throw legal pronouncement open as irreducibly political, not just at the level of the sovereign exception but at the level of its every application. Here we encounter the limiting function of the dogmatic. The 'inter' of interdiction marks the passage into the 'internal material of the law', as harnessed to the deeper structure of commonality and within the interpretative leeway afforded to *dogmatic* determination.

Law as social hermeneutic thus attempts to restore a proper vocabulary to reciprocity and community in a way that clearly engages the notion of obligation. 'Interdiction' returns us to the power of language not just as a tool – though of course it is that too – but as commonality, and antagonistic to the various reductionisms, whether these are of the law and economics varieties with their attendant quantifications of value, or the various forms of systemic enfolding into old and new varieties of positivism. Supiot holds on to a concept of dogma as providing the context for the hermeneutical work of the critical jurist. Context is that which cannot be transcended but also that which cannot be collapsed without a radical loss of meaning.[4] What would it mean to locate the notion of obligation at the level of dogma, as tapping the deeper resources of community and reciprocity, and deliberatively and interpretatively deployed, extended unfolded, *instantiated*, in terms of the discourse of rights, not as their correlative but as source of their proper meaning and measure of their proper deployment?

3 For an excellent analysis, see Fischer-Lescano & Christensen 2012, pp. 93–119.

4 'Critical dogmatics looks to law not as a site of prior judgments or legislated norms but rather as a field of heteronomous rules and the interpretative procedures of their elaboration' (Goodrich 2009, p. 311).

Attention, fragility and obligation

Let us now turn to Weil's critique of the discourse of rights, and her analysis of what claims of right, as a 'language of the middle range', miss. In the context of our discussion so far we might identify what they miss as what is elided in the gap that opens between what is owed as obligation and what can be delivered as right. There are a number of routes through which to approach Weil's injunction; one is through what she famously writes in the essay 'La personne et le sacré' (translated as *On Human Personality*):

> Justice consists in seeing that no harm is done to men. Whenever a man cries inwardly: 'Why am I being hurt?' harm is being done to him. He is often mistaken when he tries to define the harm, and why and by whom it is being inflicted on him. But the cry itself is infallible.
>
> (Weil 1957, p. 261)[5]

For Weil the question 'Why am I being hurt?' is in a crucial sense a question prior to and resistant to the explanatory frames and mediating structures that attempt to answer it. If one begins from a 'middle range' language – let us call it the *architecture* of justice with its distributions of rights-claims and entitlements – in order to answer Weil's question about vulnerability and humanity, one will cast it as answerable on a register that is a mirror of distortion. In the middle range, in the discourse and practice of human rights, suffering will register under a description *and* at the same time fail to invoke anything like an adequate response.

We know from Hannah Arendt, in a discussion that has raged on and on and spawned a million 'aporiae', about the dilemmas surrounding the 'right to have rights': their deprivation seen as a scandal, but its assertion a riddle. Weil has something significantly more damning in mind when she talks of the 'mediocrity' of the language of rights: 'The notion of rights, by its very mediocrity, leads on naturally to that of the person, for rights are related to personal things. They are situated at that level.'[6]

And elsewhere:

> The words of the middle region, rights, democracy, personality, are of use in that region, that of the middle institutions. The aspiration to which

5 The extract is from the 'Essay on Human Personality' that is included in the 'London Writings' published in 1957. 'La justice consiste à veiller à ce qu'il ne soit pas fait de mal aux hommes. Il est fait du mal à un être humain quand il crie intérieurement: « Pourquoi est-ce qu'on me fait du mal? » Il se trompe souvent dès qu'il essaie de se rendre compte quel mal il subit, qui le lui inflige, pourquoi on le lui inflige. Mais le cri est infaillible' (Weil 1957, p. 286).

6 'La notion de droit entraîne naturellement à sa suite, du fait même de sa médiocrité, celle de personne, car le droit est relatif aux choses personnelles. Il est situé à ce niveau' (ibid.).

> institutions are harnessed, of which they are so to speak the projection, claim a different language.[7]
>
> To put into the mouths of the afflicted words from the vocabulary of middle values like those of … rights or personhood is to offer them something that can bring them no good and will inevitably do them much harm.[8]

Why is responsiveness to the cry undone at the middle range of institutions? It is because the language of institution is a language of generalisation, of reduction and of functionality. As a language of *generalisation*, it introduces selective suppressions; classifications at once actualise and suppress possibilities. As a language of *reduction* it introduces simplification; the reality of that simplification is best captured through the idea of a reduction of *complexity* through which the language of law fashions the key concepts that have an exclusionary effect in that they stand in for the more complex environments that they displace.[9] And *functionality* introduces linkage; institutions offer possibilities of connection. Linkage-capacity[10] of concepts enables combinations and circulations that in turn provide for systemic constructions and the reproduction of expectational structures. Note how an institutional achievement emerges concisely, simply, and in the process of that emergence it walls itself against alternatives. Expectations will reproduce it and it provides its own specific register for what is given visibility and what not.

Weil does not use the language of systemic observation and exclusion, but thematises that exclusion around the reductive language of *right* and *person*, the circulation of claim and counter-claim. Rights are concepts that are linked to the logic of exchange and of measured quantity; legal personality to the comparative demand of person to person. Weil prophetically indicts the mass proliferation of rights and rights-holders whose shrillness we encounter in our Europe of optimising, of calibrating, of balancing. Against these concepts of the 'middle range' Weil interjects *attention*. The concept of attention is key to how Weil understands responsiveness. What Weil's *attention* laboriously draws into visibility, the languages of the middle range, as harnessed to function, make disappear. It is counterposed to the loud proclamation of claim and counter-claim and to the complacent vocabulary of entitlement. And although Weil, unlike Arendt, owes no explicit debt to Heidegger, I would suggest that the most incisive way to capture the function of attention is as resistance to (what Heidegger would call) the

7 'Les mots de la région moyenne, droit, démocratie, personne, sont de bon usage dans leur région, celle des institutions moyennes. L'inspiration dont toutes les institutions procèdent, dont elles sont comme la projection, réclame un autre langage' (ibid. at 43–4).

8 'Mettre dans la bouche des malheureux des mots qui appartiennent à la région moyenne des valeurs, tels que démocratie, droit ou personne, c'est leur faire un présent qui n'est susceptible de leur amener aucun bien et qui leur fait inévitablement beaucoup de mal' (ibid.).

9 See Luhmann 1995.

10 Luhmann's term is *Anschlussfahigkeit*. For the importance of the term in the general theory of autopoietic systems, see indicatively Luhmann (1995).

readiness to hand (*Zuhandenheit*) of the meaning-construction afforded by the languages of the middle range. Attention presents resistance to functionality, to generalisation and to reduction in the way that they predispose and channel expectation on the one hand, and the way that they defend them from surprises on the other. 'It might be helpful to us,' says Heidegger, 'to rid ourselves of the habit of always hearing what we already understand' (Heidegger 1971, p. 58).[11]

What are the implications of this for our discussion of obligation and right? How to begin to think beyond the order of correlativity with Weil? Let us follow her suggestion and focus on the idea of 'fragility'. With Weil, we could then argue that obligation *has the fragile as its specific vis-à-vis.* [12] The importance that this placing has for her cannot be exaggerated. Attention releases the fragile from the structures of responsibility to which the languages of the middle range confine it, and under which they subsume it, as a question of accountability and of claim of right. Thinking about justice in the middle range typically involves an architectonic of reasons, hierarchies and classifications, within which justice-claims find their proper place. Justice is the order that 'holds measured relationships between individuals and goods together'.[13] Hard cases often test these frameworks and structures of expectations, and entitlements are re-configured in the process. But the cry 'Why am I being hurt?' is not an invitation to such adjustment, given that *ex hypothesi* it has not sought its leverage in those expectational structures. Instead the cry 'Why am I being hurt?' correlates at the deeper level with the obligation invoked by fragility and realised as solidarity and as community. In contrast, in the 'mediocre' legal language of the 'middle ground' the question is posed and answered as a question of justiciability and standing. Jurisdiction draws on the institutional constituents of *ordering*. We likened these structures to Heidegger's notion of the ready-to-hand to bring this out. Institutional structures are functionally oriented, and subject positions within them are oriented and over-determined by such functional orientation. That is why they miss the fragile in the same way in which the ready-to-hand, similarly harnessed to functionality, *never appears for itself.*

Here is Weil again:

> The terms of the middle range, right, democracy, personality, are appropriate to the institutions of that range. [But] the aspiration to which institutions are harnessed, of which they are so to speak the projection, claim a different language.[14]

11 As Oren Ben Dor (2013) puts it in a profound paper comparing Wittgenstein with Heidegger, 'no way of *seeing* that precedes *seeing-as*'.

12 In relation to the concept of responsibility, see Ricoeur 1991.

13 Starting out from Aristotle's *Politics*, Rancière's *Disagreement* defines political justice 'not simply [as] the order that holds measured relationships between individuals and goods together ... [but] the order that determines the partition of what is common' (Rancière 1999, p. 5).

14 'Les mots de la région moyenne, droit, démocratie, personne, sont de bon usage dans leur région, celle des institutions moyennes. L'inspiration dont toutes les institutions

And with this we come to a claim perhaps only latent in Weil's own thought but which taps its *political* (rather than ethical) vein, in the direction of immanent critique. And it is here that that other distinction that was mentioned but left suspended – that between *law as a language of the middle range* and *law as a dogmatic resource* – might be returned to. The modality of that return is reflected in the terms 'inspiration' and 'projection' above, and the language that might reclaim aspiration must first iterate them as contradictory. Let me close this section with a mention of an argument that I have developed at length elsewhere (Christodoulidis 2017), and more briefly with respect to Weil (Christodoulidis, forthcoming).[15] The critical achievement of writing obligation, community or solidarity – in other words the dogmatic resources of juridical thought – into the languages of the middle range is that it introduces *a faultline within* the institutional language of law. The inscription of the aspiration into the mediocrity of the mediating language of rights confronts the promise of obligation, community, solidarity, with the inadequacy of that 'mediation'. Not a continuity but a tension, even, to use a more loaded term, a contradiction installs itself between dignity promised and indignity delivered; between the promise of responsibility and the denial of fragility; between the promise of solidarity and the delivery of 'shrill' contention and claim of right. I have suggested that this can be usefully thought of as the field of immanent critique.

The work of dogma as resource

Supiot looks to Weil for an argument about the dogmatic function of *value* in a way that ties usefully to our discussion of tension and contradiction. Weil writes:

> A value is something that we unconditionally accept. … [A] system of values in the instant that it orientates our life, is not accepted subject to conditions, but purely and simply accepted. … At the same time, we cannot abandon the attempt to understand them since this would mean ceasing to believe in them, which is impossible because human life cannot exist without orientation. Therein resides a contradiction which is at the very heart of human life.
>
> (Weil 1941, quoted in Supiot 2007, p. 70)

'This contradiction,' adds Supiot, 'is the driving force behind human thought' (Supiot 2007, p. 70). Weil's 'set of values', like the dogmatic, are not accepted subject to conditions, because what would it *mean*, normatively, for something to have installed itself alongside the (orienting) set of values as *their* condition? Instead, in the totalising move of internalisation the system of values subsumes all conditions that have orientation value. Thereby the set of values ascends to the meta-level, to set the conditions of intelligible normative orientation. At the same

procèdent, dont elles sont comme la projection, réclame un autre langage' (Weil 1957).

15 Christodoulidis, 'Les « mots du Droit » et le monde vécu' (forthcoming).

time this ascension places us, subjects of law, *inside* legal reason, already invested in the value set and calls for an understanding of how their requirements will be met in the midst of competing interpretations and particular dilemmas that require legal solution. Reciprocity, solidarity and obligation, as dogmatic resources, are elevated to the meta-level, furnishing normative orientation and providing the criteria to guide our interpretative choices over applications that remains underdetermined, complex and contradictory.

I understand Supiot's reference to 'contradiction' as what thus becomes productive on an internal register, suspended between the two poles of interdiction and judgement. Life requires orientation and systems of values provide that. There is no stepping outside (the system, the horizon, the dogmatic) because there is nowhere to go normatively. This we identified earlier as the function of *interdiction*. But as internalised, the 'contradiction' becomes productive to juridical thinking. The 'conditions' – that were meaningless as conditions to the 'system of value' – now become conditions of its proper instantiation. As *judgement* they inform the move from the universal to the particular that is the condition of all practical reason; they authorise actualisations and determinations of value; they allow the jurist as 'interpreter [to stand] between *lex* and judgement, between power and subject, as the guardian, curator and deliberator of *ratio legis*, or the reason of law' (Goodrich 2009, p. 297)[16] and thereby the jurist's reasoning to navigate the clashes, the impasses and the sites of sacrifice. In all this 'dogma' remains the name for that which is not lost, for that which after all its actualisations, particularisations, balancing, is, in spite of it all, never lessened.

It is perhaps more difficult for an English readership to appreciate the subtlety of the dogmatic approach in the absence of the distinction that Supiot relies on to make his argument, between *droit* and *loi* (*Recht* and *Gesetz* in German, *nomos* and *dikaio* in Greek). The non-coincidence between *loi* and *droit* subtends the reflexivity of law, both lending it *substance* and ensuring the *closure* that gives *ratio legis* its circumference and leverage, that therefore alone does the work of containing interpretations as instantiations *of law* as opposed to the open play of language. This insistence on closure relates Supiot's theory via Legendre, explicitly, to a concept of the 'mytho-logic'.[17]

We will not follow him there, to the revelatory discourses of foundation. Instead we will take the tension or 'contradiction' that Supiot borrows from Weil around the discussion of *value*, and develop it further in the direction of what with Aquinas and the Thomist tradition more generally we might identify as

16 Goodrich continues: 'the jurist is a hybrid creature … whose role was to mediate between the disciplines.'

17 Developing Legendre's theory of the 'mytho-logic' in their *Droit, Mythe et Raison*, Jacques Lenoble and François Ost argue that 'the core of the legal mythologic is the notion of a completely rational legislator. In thinking of the law *as if* such a legislator were the author of all legal norms, the jurist can conceive the law as if it were a completely rational system. In its complete rationality the law is closed, in the sense that it is supposed to be able of providing an answer to all questions' (Stewart 1987, 91).

determinatio. Values[18] express at the abstract level our human commonality. As in Aristotle, the virtues are not negotiable: they define something of the teleology of what it means to realise a life worth living, which removes from the list both arbitrariness and the need for any further or meta-level justification. They are emphatically not preferences or desires, and thus clearly to be set apart from any utilitarian or optimisation calculus. They are the normative foundations that make normative reasoning meaningful. The idea of *determination* captures the logic of instantiation, along the direction of how these principles are concretised. Institutional logic intervenes here, and the logic of reduction – the institutional achievement of reducing complexity – is a key part of it. The pragmatics of instantiation is what we come to know and practise as law. But *determinatio* in the beautiful simplicity of its pure directionality captures the connection between furnishing judgement (with content) and providing thresholds and limits as to what might count as reasonable interpretation. Direction and threshold-setting: the key moments of heteronomy that the dogmatic offers to juridical reasoning.

The aim of this chapter has been to understand obligation as a dogmatic resource and to locate it thus above the level where it is mobilised and concretised in terms of claims of right, as both setting thresholds of what can count as a valid claim of right and furnishing it with content. We can look to Supiot's analysis of *contract* to illustrate both the negative and positive function of the dogmatic: positive in terms of what is *substantively* achieved through the articulation of levels, and negative in terms of the irreducibility of obligation to the level of the articulation of rights-claims, where it would run the risk and the damage of its severing from the deeper recesses of meaning, *of contracts cutting loose from law*, so to speak. For the law of contract to perform its dogmatic function and provide closure it must first be conceived at the level of the binding form of the *pledged* word. The 'civilising mission' of the dogmatic foundation that *pacta sunt servanda*, Supiot tracks through history and across civilisations (Supiot 2007, pp. 79–109 passim). For the Western legal imaginary we might return here to the profound analyses of contract in the work of Hegel and Durkheim to capture something of the embeddedness of contract in social relationships and of its function of sustaining the social bond.[19] The important point is that with the instrumentalisation of contract comes a reversal of means and ends that hollows out the ends of law to the point where it can no longer perform the function of rationalising the field as one of human *reciprocity* – that which Supiot has invited us to think as the anthropological function.

That the dogmatic provides the institution of contract with its constitutive orientation gives us a platform to thematise the pathological. Under conditions of globalisation the constitutive orientation flounders. And contractualisation becomes an important means of de-regulation because 'globalisation applauds in

18 Or 'basic goods' according to John Finnis who provides the most influential recent restatement of the position.

19 For an important analysis, see Honneth 2014.

one and the same movement the virtues of the free market and those of the contract – flexible, egalitarian and emancipatory – in opposition to the heavy machinery of the State – rigid, unilateral and enslaving' (Supiot, 2007, p. 83). This is the distinction that displaces the older understanding (Durkheimian or Hegelian), now pitting entrepreneurial freedom against State dependence and rigidity, and at the same time, what dis-embeds contract from its dogmatic foundation. The severing of the institution of contract from its dogmatic root undercuts the framing function of law, law no longer preceding or conditioning the market economy. In the disembedding move that cuts it loose from its dogmatic function, contract is turned from 'source' to *instrument* of market operations, as accompaniment and facilitative of market transactions. The disembedding appears most obviously in the way in which the interpretative resources of the law of contract are deployed to the ends of efficiency, understood as maximisation of financial returns. 'This explains,' says Supiot (Supiot, 2007, p. 85),

> the flood of literature whose primary aim is to relate each rule of contract back to an economic law: incapacities are referred to the stable preferences of the rational actor, defects of consent such as duress to the freedom of choice of the rational actor, mistake and duties of disclosure to the transparency of market operations, and so forth.

One of its most striking expressions is the understanding of contractual responsibility as – in Justice Holmes's words – the preparedness 'to pay damages if you do not honour [a contract], and nothing more' (quoted in Supiot, 2007, p.108) which vacates the notion of obligation from contract law, and has received perhaps its more dangerous development in the doctrine of efficient breach. The *coincidence* of the meaning of contract with the remedy for its breach reflects this impoverishment of law because it removes the constitutive reference to value and hollows out the normative underpinning.

There is a parallelism, never explicitly drawn out, between Supiot's argument here and Karl Polanyi's in *The Great Transformation* (1944), although their respective approaches to the market, and the labour market too, remain distinct. Supiot's is, perhaps, more narrowly a defence of a social-democratic model against a totalising market utopia,[20] and it seeks its inspiration in law: 'The market, if it is

20 To this end it is important to renew two imperatives declared in the Declaration of Philadelphia. The first of these is the objective of social justice, which must be re-established as the unit of measure of the soundness of the juridical order in the following sense: that 'all national and international policies and measures, in particular those of an economic and financial character, should be judged in this light and accepted only in so far as they may be held to promote and not to hinder the achievement of this fundamental objective' (Declaration of Philadelphia art II, c). The second is the imperative of social democracy, which allows us to found this evaluation in the diversity of experiences, and which requires that 'the representatives of workers and employers ... [participate] in free discussion and democratic decision with a view to the promotion of the common welfare' (ibid., art I, d).

to function well, must be limited by rules and institutions that ensure the security of human, natural and monetary resources' (Supiot, 2007, p. 94). Note in this the reference to the protection of work, nature and money, Polanyi's three 'fictitious commodities'. Disembedding is not a word that is used by Supiot, but the disarticulation of law from its dogmatic anchor could be usefully captured by the term. But more interesting is the hidden reference to Polanyi's 'double movement'. Inherent tensions and resistances to marketisation abound: 'certain things resist their transformation into commodities, because they retain, e.g., the mark of the person who created them' (Supiot, 2007, p. 97) or

> the trade in 'human resources' inherent in the institution of the labour market contradicts the separation of persons and things on which the market system rests. This explains the invention of concepts – such as 'employment' or 'solidarity' – that are a hybrid of contract and status.
>
> (ibid., pp. 97–8)

Finally the hollowing-out of contract generates compensatory gestures, however transitory: 'Special domains of law have developed (labour law, social security law, [etc.]) in order to accommodate the elements that fall outside the sphere of the calculation of individual interests' (ibid., p. 100) and rational utility maximisation.

> These special areas of law prop up an ordinary law of contract that is less and less capable of mastering the complexity of the phenomenon of contractualisation. The effectiveness of such props is, moreover, constantly diminished by the progress of free trade and the opening up of national frontiers to the circulation of capital, goods and services, which obliges States to reduce these props or adapt them accordingly.
>
> (ibid.)

However we assess the link to Polanyi, and society's self-protective gesture against market exposure that is the 'double movement', there remains in the recuperation of juridical reason an urgent and important message. In the face of reductions or simplifications into generalised commodity exchange, against the collapse of juridical personality, and against the incipient Market Leninism of the neo-liberal turn in the European Union (Supiot 2008), legal reason, Supiot is keen to argue, recovers the 'sense of measure', which is above all a 'human measure'; the principle of Protagoras, 'man the measure of all things', he reminds us, is the only standard that could make sense. To rediscover this sense of measure one must place anew man's destiny at the heart of the system of evaluation of economic performances, re-orientating them to a longer temporal horizon and against the acceleration of short-termism.[21]

21 Drawing inspiration from Berque's reference to 'l'écoumène', that is man's living environment (Berque 2014), Supiot provides a number of examples against levelling quantifications that cut against the sense of measure. He writes: 'For example,

Let us keep from the dogmatic the sense of rootedness in the sources of human reciprocity; what Simone Weil called 'l'enracinement'. And let us locate there the meaning of obligation. According to the thesis of law as social hermeneutic, a community of sense is *inscribed* in dogma. We asked: If what is 'dogmatic', in ordinary language, is what we take on faith, in what sense can it underpin a social hermeneutic that informs and undergirds nothing short of the creation of meaning, the pursuit of autonomy, and the critical project? We sought the answer in an understanding of closure as necessary to context-setting, and of judgement as the manifold of its proper instantiations. This lifts *obligation* up a level, to the realm of that which provides legal thought with its circumference and meaning, and claims of right as the sphere of fallible and reversible determinations. The asymmetry between the obligation and the right installs itself as source of legal meaning and as lever of juridical reason. Any assumed Hohfeldian correlativity is here replaced by the tension generated by this asymmetry, a tension that demands and calls forth the interpretative practices that enjoin us in community.

Bibliography

Berque, Augustin, 2014, *Écoumène. Introduction à l'étude des milieux humains.* Éditions Belin, Paris.

Christodoulidis, Emilios, 2017, 'Social Rights Constitutionalism: An Antagonistic Endorsement', *Journal of Law and Society* 44(1), 123–149.

Christodoulidis, Emilios, 'Les « mots du Droit » et le monde vécu', forthcoming.

Christodoulidis, Emilios, Dukes, Ruth, Supiot, Alain, Woolfson, Charles, Ewing, K. D., Novitz, Tonia & Roedl, Florian, 2010, 'Dialogue & Debate: Labour, Constitution and *A Sense of Measure*: A Debate with Alain Supiot', *Social and Legal Studies* 19(2), 217–252.

Fischer-Lescano, Andreas & Christensen, Ralph, 2012, 'Auctoritatis Interpositio: How Systems Theory Deconstructs Decisionism', *Social & Legal Studies* 21(1), 93–119.

Goodrich, Peter, 2009, 'Law's Labour's Lost', *The Modern Law Review* 72(2), 296–312.

Heidegger, Martin, 1971, *On the Way to Language*, Harper & Row, San Francisco.

Honneth, Axel, 2014, *Freedom's Right: The Social Foundations of Democratic Life*, Polity Press, Cambridge, UK.

Luhmann, Niklas, 1995, *Social Systems*, trans. JohnBednarzJr. with Dirk Baecker, Stanford University Press, Stanford, CA.

Oren, Ben-Dor, 2013, The Gravity of Steering, the Grace of Gliding and the Primordiality of Presencing Place: Reflections on Truthfulness, Worlding, Seeing, Saying and Showing in Practical Reasoning and Law', *International Journal for the Semiotics of Law* 26(2), 341–390.

measuring land in acres loses sight of the fact that one acre is never qualitatively the same as another. This was taken into account by "archaic" units of measurement like the "journeau" or the "boisselee" of land, where measurement varied according to the quality of the soil, being linked to the number of days of labour or the quintal of grain necessary for its tender. As far as rendering to each his own and establishing justice amongst men is concerned, such a dehumanisation of units of measure cuts against such realities and has the potential to lead one to distraction' (in Christodoulidis & Dukes et al. 2010, p. 221).

Polanyi, Karl, *The Great Transformation*, Beacon Press, Boston, MA, 1944.
Rancière, Jacques, 1999, *Disagreement: Politics and Philosophy*, trans. Julie Rose, University of Minnesota Press, Minneapolis.
Ricoeur, Paul, 1991, 'Responsibility and Fragility', in Mario Valdés (ed.), *A Ricoeur Reader: Reflection and Imagination*, University of Toronto Press, Toronto.
Schmitt, Carl, 1979, *Politische Theologie: Vier capital zur Lehre von der Souveränitat*, 3rd edn, Duncker & Humblot, Berlin.
Stewart, Iain, 1987, 'Closure and the Legal Norm: An Essay in Critique of Law', *The Modern Law Review* 50(7), 908–933.
Supiot, Alain, 2007, *Homo Juridicus: On the Anthropological Function of the Law*, Verso, London; New York.
Supiot, Alain, 2008, 'Europe Won over to the "Communist Market Economy"', *Revue Permanente du Mauss* (2008), viewed 29 March 2018, www.journaldumauss.net/?L-Europe-gagnee-par-l-economie.
Weil, Simone, 1957, *ÉCRITS DE LONDRES et dernières lettres*, Éditions Gallimard, Paris.
Weil, Simone, 2002/1949, *The Need for Roots*, Routledge, London. Original *L'Enracinement*, Gallimard, Paris, 1949.

2 Why should I listen to my conscience? Equity and the question of ontological obligation

Matt Stone

Introduction

What is it about obligation that obligates us? Is it possible to answer this question whilst remaining within the sphere of obligation *as obligation*; that is, without resorting to external justifications of why it is better to obey obligations than not to? It is at the very least arguable that, for the most part, obligation is only a secondary and derivative concern for modern law. Obligations are often constructed negatively by means of proscription (I am obligated not to act dangerously). Or else they derive from the atomistic entitlement inherent in modern legal subjectivity (I am obligated to honour my freely made agreements). Or sometimes by a combination of both (I am obligated to respect others' property rights, for example).

This chapter takes up the challenge of thinking of obligation as distinct and independent of the liberal, modern articulation of individual capacity and entitlement: as 'primary obligation' and not simply the opposite side of another person's rights. The implications of this need to be sketched out. To truly isolate and purify a notion of obligation, to separate it from the egotic, formal reciprocity implicit in rights, would be to trace what Roberto Esposito understood to be the very essence of community itself, the *munus* denoting the obligatory social bond of 'debt' to others that is distinctly anterior to the protective rights-based apparatus of modernity (Esposito 2010, in particular pp. 3–6). This would be an obligation logically prior to positive law as we know it and prior to the modern subject.[1] Such a conception therefore cannot help but foreground the necessary connection between obligation and the political.

This inquiry also presents an opportunity to consider the under-theorised linkage of private law and the social bond. To find a way into this, the chapter considers the field of English equity as a possible, albeit mediated, expression of primary obligation.[2] In particular, by invoking an elementary language of 'conscience', equity – in a manner unlike any other area of English law – presents a grounded route into thinking about why and how we have duties to others. In

1 On this form of critique of modernity, see Esposito 2008, 2011.
2 For an expanded argument, see Stone 2017.

short, one is obligated in equity *by* conscience itself, as a faculty for understanding one's situated responsibility towards others. Moreover, by referring juridical obligation back to the self-evident ethical disposition of conscience, an orientation that instantiates itself in equity without an apparent need to be justified by anything other than itself, we are provoked to ask whether such duty demands ontological significance. In other words, if it is not itself derivative of some other legal or moral concept, nor represents a technical principle defined by a particular end, does conscience say something about our very *being*, placed within the ethical commitment of community? If this suggestion seems grandiose, note how easily it aligns with the enduring rhetorical idea of listening to one's inner voice, being true to one's ethical self, and so on.[3] With this in mind, this chapter will consider theoretical approaches, notably within Heideggerian and post-Heideggerian thinking, which see conscience as an important expression of our relationship with our Being and the responsibilities we therefore assume therein. If this connection proves persuasive, it becomes possible to understand the juridical deference to conscience as invoking the normative weight of precisely this sort of foundational, primary obligation. The ultimate question that this chapter will confront, therefore, is whether ontology itself really can deliver obligations, in the sense of both whether we have an obligation to listen to our conscience, and whether the substance spoken by conscience can be grasped with some level of objectivity. This is not, therefore, simply to ask of the manner that concrete obligations may be understood ontologically, but also to ask of obligation that is delivered by our relationship with Being as such. By linking this theoretical enquiry of this chapter with a field of positive law, we may see not only the manner in which primary obligation might find a form of juridical expression, but also the unavoidable contortions and difficulties in this passage from the fundament to the surface level of tangible rules and principles.

It could be asked why, other than scholastic intrigue, this line of inquiry is important. A hasty response would be to say that it outlines the way a field such as equity gives expression to resistance against the legal construction of intersubjectivity in liberal modernity. If such a foundational ethical affectivity finds a form of articulation in equity, then it may provide an avenue of critique against the excesses of a hegemonic rights-based jurisprudence. One has to be a bit careful here, however. Equitable jurisprudence, in the familiar institutional form that began to coalesce around the sixteenth and seventeenth centuries, is itself very much a product of the burgeoning modernity of the time. Equity itself cannot be romanticised as an untainted expression of a utopian social bond, and to a large extent now insinuates itself into the virulent logic of contemporary capital.[4] Nevertheless, if the rhetorical appeal to conscience can be tied to some form of vital ethical sensibility, even if as the contorted and assimilated trace, then a certain

3 On the idea of conscience as a voice of the inner self, see May 1983; Jenkins 1955.

4 Similarly, it is arguable that the modern juridical form of conscience represents a sublation of divine authority into the sovereignty of the state.

priority may be restored to its concept. A priority that elides the tired trope that equity is simply an auxiliary appendage of modern law.

Equitable obligation

Equity is at essence a mature jurisprudence of obligation in which a persistent appeal to conscience has in various ways worked to resist the sanctity of formal rights and individual entitlement in the fields of property and contract. Yet at the same time it is a repressed jurisdiction, largely absent from traditional private law theory and doctrinal jurisprudence, and commonly constructed as the exceptional supplement to the infrastructure of modern law. Of importance, here, is not so much the substance of equitable duty but the manner in which it is formulated. The centrality of conscience to the construction of obligations, particularly by reference to the defendant's own conscience being bound or affected, is not only a matter of historical significance[5] but also still vital in seminal statements of contemporary equitable reasoning.[6] A paradigmatic example occurs where a person has acquired title to an asset without any formal impropriety, yet they are capable of reflecting on contextual facts which would make it unconscionable to keep the property for themselves. In such a scenario where one's conscience has been affected, equity may charge the person with property obligations owed to others, displacing the conventional association between possession and rights.[7]

In a sense, of course, the deference to conscience is a rhetorical fudge. It allows equity, as a legal institution, to displace its justification of liability on the basis that it is already evident in a sphere of ethical intuition, outside the technical cut and thrust of conventional doctrine. This displacement is more than merely symbolic: as a tribunal of conscience, medieval equity had more in common with religious process than the application of legal reasoning as we would recognise today (Klinck 2010, pp. 23–28). Chancellors were concerned with the salvation of defendants' souls,[8] and unlike the English common law, Chancery adopted an

5 E.g. the famous words of the Lord Chancellor Thomas Egerton in *The Earl of Oxford's Case* (1615) 1 Ch Rep 485: 'The Office of the Chancellor is to correct Men's consciences' (p. 486).

6 One of the notable aspects of the place of 'conscience' in equitable reasoning is the casual context in which it is deployed, signifying its self-evident quality without providing a comprehensive definition. Its function as a porous and diffractive signifier will prove important for later parts of this chapter's argument. Nevertheless, key examples of modern cases decided with reference to the party's conscience are as follows: On the constitution of express trusts: *Choithram v Pagarani* [2001] WLR 1; on constructive trusts in commerce: *Westdeutsche Landesbank Girozentrale v Islington London Borough Council* [1996] AC 669; on constructive trusts of the family home: *Grant v Edwards* [1986] Ch 638; on fiduciary obligations: *Boardman v Phipps* [1967] 2 AC 46; on receipt of trust property in breach of trust: *BCCI v Akindele* [2001] Ch 437; on proprietary estoppel: *Gillett v Holt* [2001] Ch 210; on undue influence: *Credit Lyonnais Bank Nederland v Burch* [1997] CLC 95.

7 Most notably, via the obligations of trusteeship.

8 Klinck 2010, p. 23, referring to Metzger 1980.

inquisitorial rather than purely adversarial procedure. As J. H. Baker describes, the chief methods of gathering evidence consisted of interrogation and deposition, owed to the influence of Canon law and the *denunciato evangelica* (Baker 2002, p. 103).[9] There is little doubt that this process was predicated on the guilty introspection of the sinful party. As Dennis Klinck surmises, '[medieval] Chancery proceeded *secundum conscientam*, inquiring at large into the facts and particularly probing the consciences (bound by oaths) of the parties to make them come to terms with what they inwardly know to be the truth' (Klinck 2010, p. 29). This reflects an essential characteristic, whereby conscience is somehow intimately personal yet still determined within the structure of a legally cognisable imperative. As Alasdair Hudson has emphasised recently, this pairing of a subjective mode of individual interpretation and an objectively discoverable set of normative ideas permeates equity's model of conscience to this day.[10]

Upon the advent of modernity, in which equitable justice eventually became translated into the structure of a recognisably 'legal' form, this jurisdiction of privileged knowledge was retained. Conscience, and its corollary of unconscionability, continued to invoke a self-evident authority whilst resisting any unifying reduction to static rules.[11] And one can still recognise the same contemplative dimension of the confessional relationship after this time. For instance, in his 1760 text, *Principles of Equity*, one of the very few jurisprudential meditations on the subject, the jurist and philosopher Lord Kames talks of the way equity must achieve justice not only for those affected by one's actions, but also with respect to the duty the defendants owe themselves (Kames 2014, p. xli). Not only does this illuminate the manner in which equitable conscience describes a relationship with oneself, it also reveals how it requires a reflective element.[12] It is not that humanity simply has an intrinsic inclination towards shared, substantive moral values; rather, conscience only becomes comprehensible when the subject is capable of apprehending its own existing ethical orientation, as one's 'innate sense or conviction of a common nature' (Kames, 2014, p. xliv).

Conscience therefore foregrounds a crucial question of voice. To be obligated an obligation must be heard, if not voiced by some external command then by a movement of thinking. Indeed, it is precisely the difference from a vertical legal command that informs its distinct normative weight. Kant's categorical imperative, arguably the exemplary model of conscientious obligation in modern Western

9 The latter doctrine holds that the Church possesses its own authority to take action in the cleansing of the soul of a sinner. See also Coing 1955; Kessler 2005, s. II.

10 Alastair Hudson, 'Conscience as the Organising Concept of Equity' (2016) (2)1 *Canadian Journal of Comparative and Contemporary Law* 261–99, at 264.

11 Note Hudson's claim that this lack of definition does not prevent the development of conscience as an objective form of moral reasoning (ibid.).

12 Consider a modern example in the law of trusts: 'Unless and until the trustee is aware of the factors which give rise to the supposed trust, there is nothing which can affect his conscience', per Lord Browne-Wilkinson, *Westdeutsche v Islington*, op. cit., p. 709.

philosophy,[13] demonstrates this well. Conscience directs us inwards, impelling us to listen to ourselves as opposed to deferring unreflectively to established principles. For Kant, the voice of conscience is the voice of reason, not as the simple application of moral judgment to human actions, but as reason judging itself (Kant 1998, p. 179). Conscience is therefore a vigilance of thinking in which judgment is subjected to judgment. It is a voice that passes through the thinking subject whilst simultaneously transcending it, and which is incorporated into the very 'being' of humankind (Kant 1991, p. 233). Of course, the juridical appropriation of conscience which occurs in the courts of Chancery redoubles this question. Conscience cannot merely be the sovereign voice of positive law, but it also cannot merely be the free preferences of the subject. Ethics and authority become entwined in mutual contradiction.[14]

The next steps involve thinking further about whether, and how, the normativity of conscience can be supported philosophically as a primary obligation whilst still operating meaningfully in law. But before proceeding, it may be useful to crystallise various key positions introduced so far. First, conscience obligates via a structure of non-coincidence of self. As the frequent judicial references to being bound by one's own conscience demonstrate,[15] its symbolic work requires it to be available to the subject whilst simultaneously differentiated. It addresses the self, as a faculty of the self, yet is also received or 'heard' as somehow something other, and which can be interpreted by the court. Second, as an ethical faculty, conscience addresses people's connectedness, and puts the fate of the other directly in the self's field of concern. Equitable conscience is framed as the responsibility that flows from one's ability to reflect on the nature and impact of circumstances and actions. This is of course the condition of conscience producing a distinct obligation that is not merely derivative of aggregated individual entitlements. Third, at its most elementary, conscience presents a formal structure of ethical sensibility rather than a mere set of moral values. Conscience cannot be reduced to a charter of ascertained rights and wrongs, but instead represents the availability of thinking about rightness and wrongness. As such, equity offers no *comprehensive* definition of 'good conscience', instead insinuating its intuitive availability, and instantiating it within case law.

Obligation and ontology

Whilst one can easily accept that conscience has a vital and dynamic influence in the language of equity, we have yet to reveal any direct justification as to exactly why we should obey it – in other words, its precise normative status. This question is of particular significance for equity, as the deference to conscience relies precisely on eliding the common law dependence on the sovereign's own imperative authority. As an expression of inner self but also somehow always non-coincidental

13 'The categorical imperative, which as such only affirms what obligation is, is: Act upon a maxim that can also hold as a universal law' (Kant 1991, p. 51). On the categorical imperative as conscience, see Velleman 1999.

14 See Stone, forthcoming.

15 Supra note 6.

with self, the structure of conscience also presents norms that cannot derive from publicly deliberated principles,[16] nor from the subject's immediate personal preferences. Conscience teaches the equitable subject; but, still, why should we listen?

One immediate answer would be that conscience taps into an ethical authenticity invested in a sense of inner self. Efforts to consolidate existing philosophies of conscience emphasise how it is felt as a deeper truth of the self, such that there is an unpalatable type of existential discord in veering into inauthentic behaviours.[17] The obligation here is experienced as being produced by the real 'me' that always rests more firmly in the soul than the surface 'me' capable of distraction by corrupt and unreflective impulses. To take this approach, equity would serve to teach the subject about itself, combining ethical knowledge with institutional authority. To support this outlook, consider the jurist Christopher St German's seminal theory of early modern equity, contained in the 1518 treatise *Doctor and Student*. Here, conscience is posed as a form of grounded reasoning by which the subject seeks to interpret and apply *synderesis*, a source of divine ethical truth that inheres in people as the 'motive force of the rational soul' (St German 1974, p. 81). What obligates, in this sense, is one's own personal inner connection to this underlying ethical essence. All people are capable of apprehending *synderesis*, albeit imperfectly, and so the courts of equity are legitimated in holding individuals to account where they failed to heed its message through the work of conscience.

The idea that such a mode of normativity displays a distinctly *ontological* structure has already been observed frequently in existing literature.[18] Indeed, it seems a small step to frame *synderesis* as representing an aspect of our underlying Being, which the conscientious subject seeks to illuminate and act upon. Understood in this way, conscience is less a conventional command than it is an orientation towards an inner essence,[19] and equity would appear to speak with the weight of ontology itself. However, such an apparent connection between obligation, ontology and authority cannot be made too quickly, especially if we want to divest it of lingering theological overtones.

Here, Heidegger's work assists in unravelling this difficult question about how normativity relates to authenticity, giving us a reason why it is better to listen to conscience than not. For Heidegger, conscience is an important part of '*Dasein*', the being that is concerned with its own Being. Conscience calls *Dasein* away from the triviality of everyday life and towards an authentic connection with its

16 Contrast with Hudson 2016. The weakness in Hudson's argument is that he does not explain why, if conscience reflects objective moral expectations, it is expressed in such obfuscatory language. Hudson's argument leads to the necessary conclusion that conscience in equity is no different from, say, dishonesty in criminal law, or the duty of care in tort. And if that is the case, why are courts unable to define it with an equivalent level of precision?

17 For example, see Iredell Jenkins' analysis of our compulsion towards 'moral or psychic equilibrium': Jenkins 1955, p. 262.

18 See e.g. Beattie 2010, p. 89; Smith 1998, p. 10; Ratzinger 2010, p. 535.

19 This is reflected quite pointedly by Lord Kames, op. cit. Also, Walter Ashburner: 'the court, out of tenderness for his conscience, will deprive him, notwithstanding his resistance, of what is so heavy a burden upon it' (1933, p. 39).

potentiality.[20] The inauthentic mode of life describes the way *Dasein* may find itself distracted in the general and amorphous structures of 'manipulable rules and public norms' (Heidegger 1962, p. 334), without reflecting properly on the potentiality it has within its own situated Being. Conscience therefore draws us to a more meaningful understanding of ourselves. In this manner, Heidegger addresses the problem of how conscience can be both a general phenomenon, in that all instances of *Dasein* are capable of hearing its call, yet is rooted in the specificity of the one who questions and the answers they receive.

It is important to understand that Heidegger is not posing conscience as a conduit of determinate moral values. Such conscience does not tell us what is right and what is wrong. Instead, it describes a mode of enquiry that is necessary to properly understand rightness and wrongness as such. At its most fundamental, it addresses not a guilt for a specific wrong but a primordial guilt inherent in all of us, logically prior to any solidified conception of good and bad (ibid., p. 332). We are constitutively guilty precisely because, as *Dasein*, we are capable of confronting the relationship between our actions and our potentiality. The introspective experience of conscience is therefore, before any question of specific deeds, a taking responsibility for one's Being. Immediately, we can see certain core themes that mirror the ethereal character of conscience within the juridical matrix of equity. Both contexts invoke an orientation towards underlying self-knowledge which is not immediately present at the surface level of articulation. As considered above, equitable conscience cannot be reduced to a schema of tangible substantive rules, instead appealing to a sense of essential truth about ourselves and our situated responsibility towards others. Indeed, a core characteristic of equitable conscience lies precisely in the way it cannot be crystallised comprehensively in this manner, and therefore cannot as easily be contorted or circumvented by technical doctrinal argument (consider, for example, the way that a disingenuous obedience with the formalities of statute becomes irrelevant if the party has been deemed to have acted unconscionably[21]).

Of course, the parallels between the equitable and Heideggerian models should not be overstated. It is important to acknowledge, for instance, that whilst underdetermined as a concept, particular instantiations of conscience in equity inevitably manifest and solidify in case law. The inner voice of conscience means little in a juridical sense without being supplemented by the public voice of legal institutions. And meanwhile, although the idea of a more authentic relationship with one's being may provide us with reasons for us to listen to our conscience, Heidegger stops short of framing it as an obligation in any recognisably legal or political sense.[22] He therefore forces us to confront a distinction between conscience as structure of ontological concern and as a concrete commitment of

20 In particular, see his analysis of what he calls *Das Man* ['The They', or 'The One']: Heidegger 1962, pp. 315–16.

21 E.g. *Rochefoucauld v Boustead* [1897] 1 Ch 196.

22 On the difficulty of framing authenticity as a conventional obligation, see Crowell 2013, pp. 300–3.

political community. Heidegger does not present any necessary deduction from one sphere to the other.[23]

Such a separation of the personal and political inevitably invites critical perspectives to be taken on Heidegger's ontology and its ability to make sense of norms. Mikas Ojakangas goes as far as to say that it 'relentlessly individualizes *Dasein* down to itself', not in the sense of producing an egotic autarkic subjectivity, but in the sense of distinctly singular responsibility (Ojakangas 2013, p 18). The implications of this are put bluntly by Lambert Zuidevart: '[i]n Kantian terms, to make individual Dasein the source of its only genuine norms is to reduce moral obligations to one's pursuing idiosyncratic maxims without asking whether those maxims are right' (Zuidervart 2008, p. 32). One must also ask of the potentially ideological character – arguably both conservative and essentially humanist[24] – to such a prioritisation of something akin to *Dasein*, which may draw primary obligation away from a robust sense of a social bond. Efforts on the contrary to delineate a more prominent ethical responsiveness of the Heideggerian conscience must rely upon an emphasis of the ontological importance of the *with*. [25] In order to persevere with this line of enquiry, we therefore need to shift the frame of reference back to a more vigorous conception of community.

Sharing obligation: a categorical imperative

A crucial challenge for any idea of conscience as primary obligation is to articulate some form of social affectivity. If we accept, as suggested in the previous section, that the symbolic deployment of 'conscience' in law invokes some sort of ontological weight, we also need to understand more clearly how this imperative addresses our responsibility to others. If this should be the case, conscientious introspection must be, more profoundly, a delivery to a deeper *communal* challenge of ontology. At this point it is helpful to turn to the work of Jean-Luc Nancy as a way to bring out a more pronounced sense of community. Nancy's philosophical writing resembles in many respects a critical development of Heidegger's approach, principally through the outright prioritisation of Being-with above any conventional conception of subjectivity[26] or post-subjectivity such as *Dasein*. Being-with is therefore the basis of community; or, put otherwise, community, as the 'with', is the very expression of Being (Nancy 1991a, p. 58). For Nancy,

23 Indeed, his notion of guilt must be 'detached from relationship to any law or "ought" such that by failing to comply with it one loads himself with guilt.' (ibid., p. 328).

24 Consider the critique of the intrinsic vulnerability of Heidegger's philosophy to the political instrumentalisation of the human. E.g. Rockmore 1991; contrast with Young 2008.

25 Heidegger himself claimed that being-with, or *Mitsein*, is a component of *Dasein: Being and Time*, Part One, chapter IV. See Birmingham, 1992, pp. 109–23. Consider also the argument that Heidegger's insight is not to provide any normative theory of law, but to allow us to understand what it means to think about law: Ben-Dor 2007.

26 'In a certain way, there has never been, and never will be, a philosophy "of the subject" in the sense of the final closure in itself of a for-itself' (Nancy 2000, p. 29). See also Nancy 1991b, pp. 1–8.

Heidegger failed to take the concept of Being-with far enough, instead allowing it to inform a harmful distinction between proper and improper social formations (Nancy 2008). Nancy therefore takes up the challenge of thinking the 'with' not as a mere attribute of *Dasein*, but as the condition of possibility for Being itself. But more specifically, it is crucial to note the work he produced in the late 1970s and early 1980s on the notion of Being's obligating character ('being-obliged' (Nancy 1997, p. 51; Nancy 2003, p. 134)), and specifically in relation to his reading of the Kantian source of conscience within the domain of reason, namely the categorical imperative.

Yet it must first be noted that by Kant's time the connection of obligation and rationality was already familiar to scholars of equity. As we have already noted briefly, confounding the view of equity as discretionary justice, the work of St German in particular had posed its obligations as rooted in the co-extensive authority of both reason and God. It may be of little surprise that the correspondence between *synderesis*, a central part of St German's theory, and Kant's categorical imperative has not gone unremarked upon.[27] In the former, conscience itself is a mode of interpreting *synderesis*, an innate ethical orientation. What needs to be emphasised now is the aspect of *synderesis* that led St German to describe it as nothing less than 'the law of reason' itself (St German 1974, ch. 13). It is by appealing to the transcendental availability of conscience that it can deliver an obligation that is both recognised by and expressed within legal reasoning, whilst originating in a deeper unconditional truth about ourselves that cannot be fully presented to the graspable domain of rules and principles. Furthermore, St German argued that because our power to make positive law is granted by God, 'conscience must be ordered by the law' (Fortier 2005, p. 62). In other words, recalling his correspondence of reason and the divine, equity distinguishes itself by invoking a responsibility that runs through us all and implicates us personally in the social commitment of law. Conscience distributes a shared bond of reason that bears inextricably upon the authorship of law, and which manifests in the exceptional jurisdiction of Chancery. What both Kant and St German share in their ideas of conscience is the posing of a common responsibility for the very necessity and rationality of obligation, manifesting as an irrevocable commitment to law itself.

In his essay 'The Kategorein of Excess', Nancy similarly emphasises the connection between the categorical imperative and the movement of thinking, and draws out a further connection with freedom. Obligation is not something that can be reduced to an external demand (otherwise it is rooted in nothing more than sovereign violence), but nor is it an invention of the atomised self. At its heart, this obligation does not tell us what we should do; rather it obligates us with respect to obligation itself, by demanding that we legislate and create obligations. This is, therefore, a 'law *of making the law*', or, put alternatively, a law 'of law making' (Nancy 2003, p. 140, emphasis in original). Why must we make the law? It is, as Nancy describes, a *factum rationis* – 'it imposes itself as a fact imposes

27 See Ojakangas 2013, p. 149; Schinkel 2007. pp. 265–7; Flinn 2007, p. 179.

itself' (ibid., p. 143). In other words, it is simply not possible to take up freedom and to think without receiving the imperative, therefore without assuming responsibility for what thought produces. The rationality of the imperative means that freedom cuts across the subject, not as a possession or abstract entitlement, but as the enjoinment of the subject towards its beyond in the movement of thought. In this sense, Nancy can claim that respect for the law is 'subjectivity' itself, in which we are orientated towards a law – orientated towards the fact of reason in law (ibid., p. 147).

Nancy innovates Kant by exploring the ontological aspect of this bond, developing what Francis Raffoul has aptly termed a 'categorical imperative of being' (Raffoul 2012, pp. 65–81). The key to understanding this is found in his position on the ineluctable character of abandonment: we are abandoned to finitude, to *Being* without ground, without transcendence, and – contra Heidegger – without essence. Abandonment therefore entails that the categorical imperative to make good law (our obligation to obligate) does not arrive from somewhere, but is simply co-extensive with Being itself. The categorical imperative is nothing less than 'an absolute call, an order or command, to be' (ibid., p. 75). As such, Nancy does not present us with an imperative to withdraw into the quiet domain of solicitude with respect to Being. It is an irrecusable and social responsibility for the distribution and sharing of Being. James Gilbert-Walsh describes this complicated structure by claiming that the imperative is voiced as 'interruption' (Gilbert-Walsh 2000). This term is useful in conveying the way that Being cannot be left to settle upon an essential foundation, entailing the perpetual maintenance of the question of the sense and meaning that Being delivers. The imperative rests upon the obligatory character of the diffusion of Being through interruption itself. Interruption is structured in a paradoxical bind between its own withdrawal, its unavailability to presence, and its necessary presentation in always-inadequate instances of figuration.[28] In this sense we may understand more precisely how obligation is doubled back on itself. One is obligated to be-obligated. Or as Gilbert-Walsh puts it rather more carefully:

> 'We' do not 'have' a sense of responsibility; we are our (broken) sense of responsibility. Or, rather, the sense of responsibility which we have always relates back to and is interrupted by the sense of responsibility which we are.
> (Gilbert-Walsh 2000, p. 44)

By presenting us with a categorical imperative of Being, can we still speak within the idiom of conscience, which impels us to consider the intractable position of our own thoughts and actions with a sphere of communal reason? Or, more drastically, by tying the Kantian injunction of reason to the barest facticity of

28 Nancy here invokes the structure of Derrida's *différance*, that interruption is never present to itself. The relation of Nancy's ontology to *différance* will be considered later in the chapter.

existence do we dissolve the intelligible status of obligation? This form of ontological duty is necessarily an obligation of an order removed. It is an obligation to be obligated by Being, a fundamental responsibility laid down by our existence and freedom. Such an outlook does not regard Being as producing obligations in the sense of informing us how to act; it is only capable of aligning itself with the fundamental necessity of obligation as such; the claim that obligation is obligatory. Whilst Nancy claims that Being is taken up as a 'command' (Raffoul 2012, p. 75), he poses the 'receiving' of a command that comes from nowhere. This is of course precisely the implication of his thesis on abandonment – there is no essence, much less any form of transcendent commander, from which the obligation is issued. This reading of the categorical imperative still evokes the voice of Kantian conscience: '[t]he imperative is the proximity to self where reason hears itself' (Nancy 1997, p. 47). Yet the effect is the erasure of the gap between subject and command that one intuitively expects, leading to conclusions that are at risk of tautology or circularity.[29] As Raffoul finds in his analysis, the obligation of Being may be reduced to saying that 'being *must* come forth' (Raffoul 2012, p. 79). Or, in the words of Meurs and Devish, the imperative is simply that 'being urges us to be', without deference to anything other than the fact of Being itself (Meurs & Devisch 2015, p. 56).

Such an outlook therefore appears to present an obstacle separating primary obligation and the normative aspect of positive law. As our exploration of equity makes clear, conscience in law must be judicially interpretable and capable of delivering some sort of injunction about our responsibilities to others. If the fundamental obligation is found to be as encompassing as Being itself, how can we make sense of the difficult decisions demanded by ethics and justice? To see how far this problem can be addressed, and eventually to tie the analysis back to equity, consider Nancy's revisitation of the imperative in the question of writing. The point of connection here is found in his claim that abandonment to finitude is precisely equivalent to the notion of *différance*, as coined by Derrida. *Différance* describes the irresolvable condition of all writing, that it relies upon a differential and endless chain of signifiers with the effect of a perpetual deferral of meaning.[30] Both finitude and *différance* therefore describe the same deferral of presence: finitude is what is left in the absence of ground ('the infinity of the deferring of presence *ipso facto* constitutes ... finitude' (Nancy 1997, p. 46)). Nancy takes up Derrida's position that there is an imperative given in *différance* (ibid.).[31] Having already claimed that obligation emerges unconditionally in abandonment to finitude, Nancy can therefore draw the conclusion that

29 'The command "*Act*" does not convert itself into "You are having-to-act" [*Tu es devant-agir*]' (Nancy 1997, p. 47).

30 See Derrida 1982.

31 A similar, and extended, argument can be found in Simon Critchley's claim that there is an ethics in deconstruction: Critchley, 2014.

> *différance* obliges, that *différance* (if it had anything) has the structure and nature of an obligation, prescription, and injunction, even if these terms can no longer be understood in accordance with its ethico-metaphysical concept.
> (ibid., p. 46)

In this sense, the categorical imperative flows from our abandonment to difference, from the responsibility we have for meaning that cannot enjoy the security of a ground. The imperative commands sense whilst at the same time deferring it (ibid., p. 48).

The ethical dimension that Nancy identifies in *différance* was later developed at length by Derrida with respect to deconstruction and the imperative of justice (their relationship defined infamously as one of direct equivalence: 'Deconstruction is justice' (Derrida 1989, p. 945)). Law, like any other textual field, is marked by its incapability to complete its economy of meaning. *Différance* is therefore irrepressibly inscribed in law, which as a result is always deconstructible. The obligation that law presents therefore, to create meaning and deliver sense, is the demand of justice. Against the strictures of a law of technical doctrine, justice requires invention and responsiveness. What Nancy allows us to understand is the inescapably social dimension of this movement, in the manner that finitude 'presents itself as being-in-common' (Nancy 1991a, p. 28). As an essential point of linkage, Simon Chesterman has argued that Derrida's formulation of justice should be understood as articulated in particular through English equity. He argues that the contradiction between common law and equity in the pursuit of justice is precisely the articulation of law's deconstruction at work. It is the excess, the other, the incapability of law to be fully present to itself. The mutual dependence of common law and equity, far from simply being an awkward remnant of legal history, allows for a justice to be maintained as aporia (Chesterman 1997, p. 362). This is not to say that equity 'is' the justice that the common law is incapable of delivering. Rather, justice is invented in the impossibility of its full presence, in the irreconcilability of the contradictions between their respective idioms. Equity therefore does not reach 'just' principles; justice is pursued in the obligation we have to take responsibility for law, animated by the antinomy of equity and common law (ibid.).

Whilst Chesterman himself is cynical about his conclusions supporting 'the traditional conception of equity as a court of conscience' (ibid.), it is important to signpost the connections with the particular formulations of conscience laid out so far. To recap, Nancy redevelops the Heideggerian notion of conscience as an imperative of responsibility with respect to Being, in turn providing linkage with both the Kantian categorical imperative and the priority of Being-with. Freedom, thinking, writing – indeed, Being itself – all take place in our abandonment to finitude, and laden with the obligation that this entails. In this sense, conscience is a form of responsibility for making and remaking law; not only a responsibility for what we make of the world, but also responsibility in the sense that invention is an unconditional necessity in the exposition of the 'with'. Equity may therefore be understood as a space of interruption, in which law's fixity can be undone and in which our unconditional responsibility for obligation can be assumed effectively. Such an account may go some way to explain the enduringly nebulous language of equitable obligation – that is, the rhetorical function of 'conscience' within legal discourse. Upon this view, equity produces interpersonal obligations precisely because it gives voice to the social affectivity of community. This is, therefore, a theory of equity as articulating primary obligation, of obligations that are not derivative of rights and entitlements, but which emerge in the unconditional underlying commitment to our social Being.

Obligation and violence

The argument developed in the previous section sets out a self-consciously optimistic reading of the significance of the social bond for our understanding of the imperative of conscience. Indeed, we have seen how Nancy helps us understand how an appeal to conscience can manifest as an intuitively acceptable mode of self-understanding. And how a commitment to obligation as such, one which expresses the ethical sensitivity of community, situates itself with respect to reason and law. Equity may well be an apposite site in which such a commitment finds expression in our familiar legal landscape. Nevertheless, a somewhat more guarded and perhaps cynical conclusion to the chapter as a whole will be put forward now. The idea of ontological obligation has ultimately led us to a kind of meta-imperative, irreducible to any concrete demand other than to keep asking and responding to the question of the demand as such. It delivers an obligation which necessarily dissolves in the moment in which it is grasped. As Gilbert-Walsh interprets this question of tangibility, 'we are obliged, concretely, to maintain an open or undecided relation to our concrete end' (Gilbert-Walsh 2000, p. 41). As we have seen, obligation is therefore protected from reduction to some sort of static essence, and from the elevation of *Dasein*'s destiny to an absolute priority, for instance. Nevertheless, to end this chapter on a sceptical note, two main concerns can be put forward:

First, as already foreshadowed in the previous section, it may be claimed that the meaning of obligation is diluted by this structure. If conscience is an unconditional responsibility that is tied so tightly to Being, can we distance ourselves far enough from it to ask why it should be obeyed? Either one depicts obligation as something too abstract as to become meaningful in a normative sense (e.g. an obligation to keep open the question of obligation). Or we abandon the idea of a concrete imperative altogether, leaving us with a notion of singularities themselves constituted as living embodiments of their unconditional obligation, as *Being-obligated*, incapable of separating themselves from their responsibility. After all, freedom cannot be detached from obligation at this ontological level. The most severe risk here is that we stray into the naturalistic fallacy: claiming an analysis that we *are* provides a reason as to why are obligated *to be*. Being-with is obligatory in a descriptive sense, but this alone cannot guarantee any meaningful normativity. Without a separation from freedom, obligation manifests as a categorical commitment to the general flux of Being. Without this gap, and without the critical distance it would provide, can one say that we are any more obligated by Being than the sea is obligated to bring in the tide?

Second, the grounding of obligation in this manner, grounded precisely by the absence of grounding, risks the ideological consequences of granting obligation such a fundamental legitimacy. Such legitimacy is intensified by the claim that obligation has an effectively co-extensive relationship with freedom, and closes certain possibilities of thinking of obligation as a form of violence. It is in a similar respect that Howard Caygill comments that '[t]he view of *Mitsein* or community being at war with itself over "meaning" or the share of space and time' is rejected by Nancy, to the extent that his conception of freedom is incapable of addressing itself to historical political struggle (Caygill 1997, p. 26).

The first point relies on the idea that in order for an obligation to become properly comprehensible, it must emerge from the movement of Being to take on a tangible, comprehensible form. We have already considered how, for instance, *synderesis* would be inconsequential without the substantial and fallible work of conscientious application. In a sense, we have seen that Nancy agrees with this insofar as the always-inadequate ontical figuration of the imperative is necessary. But the point here extends further. There is a risk of thinking that the content of substantive law carries with it the unmediated normative weight of this ontological imperative, the weight of Being itself. At its most terrifying, we risk evoking a misty-eyed depiction of originary community as part of the everyday lived reality of positive law. Law may ultimately spring forth from the responsibilities of our ontological obligation, but that is very different from going so far as to say that ontology can pre-determine the norms we ultimately seek in discharging this responsibility.[32]

The second point introduces a further and related issue. That we find it hard to conceive obligation, or specifically conscience, without a sense of an externally voiced command, indicates the implicit violence in the way that such imperatives are experienced, felt and articulated. It may be the case that one can argue for an ontological level of obligation, but as soon as obligation is animated in the delivery of language, and therefore as soon as it produces meaning that is comprehensible as law, we are necessarily drawn into the realm of force. Indeed, it is only by assuming its violent character that obligation can move us as a normative phenomenon. Violence in this sense is twofold. On the one hand, there exists the irruptive nature of obligation as an unconditional responsibility that disturbs the striation of established norms. But on the other hand, on the other side of *aporia*, is obligation as a graspable phenomenon, the command of law that always somehow fails to fully capture its ethical truth whilst simultaneously accusing the legal subject of her own ethical failings. By turning obligation and freedom into such close equivalents, we risk absenting this necessary violence from obligation, such that law (even abstracted as a 'law of the law') gains a naturalistic sense of incontrovertible legitimacy in which the force of its authority becomes shrouded. To

32 Jean-Paul Martinon goes as far to say that '[Nancy's] imperative can never become law.' (Martinon 2011, p. 220).

extrapolate, if the thesis on equity, conscience and ontological obligation is accepted, then we also have to recognise the specific way in which this juridical language therefore naturalises obligation with inevitably ideological effects. Upon the analysis put forward in this chapter, equitable jurisprudence develops with an appeal to conscience, invoking the responsibility we take for judgment, and invoking the proximal sense of our own ethical Being. It presents the source of obligation as in us and cutting across us, as nothing less than the stark facticity of our freedom and our finitude. Yet, quoting Caygill again, this is a freedom that 'can neither be recognized nor mourned' (Caygill 1997, p. 25). Freedom cannot question the ontological obligation it delivers. Likewise, expressing obligations in the language of conscience risks disabling us from recognising the violence of their legal force. One should continue to be wary, therefore, of a romanticised depiction of concrete equitable jurisprudence, mythologised as the unfettered voice of ethics and distanced from the necessary and often painful exigencies of grounded institutionalised judgment.

The theoretical resources analysed in this chapter help us to understand how law demands that we keep thinking and judging. It provides a possible explanation of the persistence of the idea of conscience, an idea that never completes itself whilst nevertheless continuing to animate a desire for justice in private law. But to arrive at a critical apparatus for interrogating obligation, one perhaps should be mindful of what Simon Critchley sees as the distinct risk of Nancy's thought: the exposition of Being as a *with* that has the effect of 'flattening ... the structure of ethical experience' by dissolving any sense of intersubjective radical separateness (Critchley 2009, p. 251, original emphasis removed). Such critique counsels vigilance in understanding the necessity of violence in the obligatory nature of Being, the manner in which it impels a law of making a world in common. If Being obligates us, it nevertheless cannot tell us how to navigate the often dangerous and unforgiving terrain of the political. It is possible that conscience will not always speak the right answers.

Bibliography

Ashburner, W., 1933, *Ashburner's Principles of Equity*, 2nd edn, Butterworth, London.

Baker, J. H., 2002, *An Introduction to English Legal History*, 4th edn, Oxford University Press, Oxford.

Beattie, A. R., 2010, *Justice and Morality: Human Suffering, Natural Law and International Politics*, Ashgate, Farnham.

Ben-Dor, O., 2007, *Thinking about Law: In Silence with Heidegger*, Hart, Oxford.

Birmingham, P., 1992, 'Ever Respectfully Mine: Heidegger on Agency and Responsibility', in A. B. Dallery, C. E. Scott & P. H. Roberts (eds), *Ethics and Danger: Essays on Heidegger and Continental Thought*, pp. 109–123, State University of New York Press, Albany.

Caygill, H., 1997, 'Philosophy, Violence, Freedom', in S. Sparks (ed.), *On Jean-Luc Nancy: The Sense of Philosophy*, pp. 19–31, Routledge, London.

Chesterman, S., 1997, 'Beyond Fusion Fallacy: The Transformation of Equity and Derrida's "The Force of Law"', *Journal of Law and Society* 24(3), 350–376.

Coing, H., 1955, 'English Equity and the Denunciato Evangelica of the Canon Law', *Law Quarterly Review* 71, 223–241.
Critchley, S., 2009, *Ethics–Politics–Subjectivity: Essays on Derrida, Levinas and Contemporary French Thought*, Verso, London.
Critchley, S., 2014, *The Ethics of Deconstruction: Derrida and Levinas*, 3rd edn, Edinburgh University Press, Edinburgh.
Crowell, S., 2013, *Normativity and Phenomenology in Husserl and Heidegger*, Cambridge University Press, Cambridge.
Derrida, J., 1982, 'Différance', in *Margins of Philosophy*, pp. 1–28, Harvester Press, Brighton.
Derrida, J., 1989, 'Force of Law: The "Mystical Foundation of Authority"', *Cardozo Law Review* 11, 920–1045.
Esposito, R., 2008, *Bios: Biopolitics and Philosophy*, University of Minnesota Press, Minneapolis.
Esposito, R., 2010, *Communitas: The Origin and Destination of Community*, Stanford University Press, Stanford.
Esposito, R., 2011, *Immunitas: The Protection and Negation of Life*, Polity Press, Cambridge.
Flinn, F. K., 2007, *Encyclopedia of Catholicism*, Infobase, New York.
Fortier, M., 2005, *The Culture of Equity in Early Modern England*, Ashgate, Aldershot.
Gilbert-Walsh, J., 2000, 'Broken Imperatives: The Ethical Dimension of Nancy's Thought', *Philosophy and Social Criticism* 26(2), 29–50.
Heidegger, M., 1962, *Being and Time*, Blackwell, Oxford.
Hudson, A., 2016, 'Conscience as the Organising Concept of Equity', *Canadian Journal of Comparative and Contemporary Law* 2(1), 261–299.
Jenkins, I., 1955, 'The Significance of Conscience', *Ethics* 65(4), 261–270.
Kames, Lord (Henry Home), 2014, *Principles of Equity*, 3rd edn, Liberty Fund, Indianapolis.
Kant, I., 1991, *The Metaphysics of Morals*, Cambridge University Press, Cambridge.
Kant, I., 1998, *Religion within the Bounds of Bare Reason*, Cambridge University Press, Cambridge.
Kessler, A. D., 2005, 'Our Inquisitorial Tradition: Equity Procedure, Due Process, and the Search for an Alternative to the Adversarial', *Cornell Law Review* 90(5), 1181–1275.
Klinck, D., 2010, *Conscience, Equity and the Court of Chancery in Early Modern England*, Ashgate, Farnham.
Martinon, Jean-Paul, 2011, 'Between Freedoms: Jean-Luc Nancy's Haunting Categorical Imperative', *Mono Kurgusuz Labirent* 10–11, 216–226.
May, L., 1983, 'On Conscience', *American Philosophical Quarterly* 20(1), 57–67.
Metzger, F., 1980, 'The Last Phase of the Medieval Chancery', in A. Harding (ed.), *Law-Making and Law-Makers in British History*, pp. 79–90, Royal Historical Society, London.
Meurs, P. & Devisch, I., 2015, 'The Meaning of Sense', in T. Mulqueen & D. Matthews (eds.), *Being Social: Ontology, Law, Politics*, pp. 47–57, Counterpress, Oxford.
Nancy, Jean-Luc, 1991a, *The Inoperative Community*, University of Minnesota Press, Minneapolis.
Nancy, Jean-Luc, 1991b, 'Introduction', in E. Cadava, P. Connor & Jean-Luc Nancy (eds), *Who Comes After the Subject?*, Routledge, London.
Nancy, Jean-Luc, 1997, 'The Free Voice of Man', in Jean-Luc Nancy & P. Lacoue-Labarthe, *Retreating the Political*, pp. 32–51, Routledge, London.

Nancy, Jean-Luc, 2000, *Being Singular Plural*, Stanford University Press, Stanford.
Nancy, Jean-Luc, 2003, *A Finite Thinking*, Stanford University Press, Stanford.
Nancy, Jean-Luc, 2008, 'The Being-With of Being-There', *Continental Philosophy Review* 41(1), 1–15.
Ojakangas, M., 2013, *The Voice of Conscience: A Political Genealogy of Western Ethical Experience*, Bloomsbury, London.
Raffoul, F., 2012, 'Abandonment and the Categorical Imperative of Being', in B. Hutchens, *Jean-Luc Nancy: Justice, Legality and World*, pp. 65–81, Continuum, London.
Ratzinger, J., 2010, 'Conscience and Truth', *Communio* 37, 529–538.
Rockmore, T., 1991, *On Heidegger's Nazism and Philosophy*, University of California Press, Berkeley.
Schinkel, A., 2007, *Conscience and Conscientious Objections*, Pallas Publications, Amsterdam.
Smith, R. J., 1998, *Conscience and Catholicism: The Nature and Function of Conscience in Contemporary Roman Catholic Moral Theory*, University Press of America, Lanham, MD; Oxford.
St German, C., 1974, *St German's Doctor and Student*, ed. T. F. T. Plucknett & J. L. Barton, Selden Society, London.
Stone, M., 2017, 'Equity, Property, and the Ethical Subject' *Pólemos: Journal of Law, Literature and Culture* 11(1), 73–95.
Stone, M., forthcoming, 'The Contradictions of Conscience'.
Velleman, J. D., 1999, 'The Voice of Conscience', *Proceedings of the Aristotlian Society* 99, 57–76.
Young, J., 2008, *Heidegger, Philosophy, Nazism*, Cambridge University Press, Cambridge.
Zuidervart, L., 2008, 'Truth and Authentication: Heidegger and Adorno in Reverse', in I. MacDonald & K. Ziarek (eds.), *Adorno and Heidegger: Philosophical Questions*, pp. 22–46, Stanford University Press, Stanford.

Cases

BCCI v Akindele (2001) Ch 437
Boardman v Phipps (1967) 2 AC 46
Choithram v Pagarani (2001) WLR 1
Credit Lyonnais Bank Nederland v Burch (1997) CLC 95
The Earl of Oxford's Case (1615) 1 Ch Rep 485
Grant v Edwards (1986) Ch 638
Gillett v Holt (2001) Ch 210
Rochefoucauld v Boustead (1897) 1 Ch 196
Westdeutsche Landesbank Girozentrale v Islington London Borough Council (1996) AC 669

3 The origin of obligations: towards a fundamental phenomenology of legal and moral obligation

Johan van der Walt[1]

Introduction

This chapter explores the possibility of conceiving obligations independently of rights. In doing so, it engages with one of the key themes of this book: the nature of obligations and the possibility of contemplating the 'priority of obligation ahead of right'. The Hohfeldian perspective on the relation between rights and obligations – which one can consider paradigmatic for modern legal theory and thought – insists on the correlativity of rights and duties. This perspective evidently prompts one to doubt the possibility of any 'priority of obligation ahead of right' considering its evident implication that obligations cannot be contemplated in the absence of rights. This means that any theoretical endeavour to promote or facilitate a 'duty-oriented' conception of communal responsibility, without falling back into a rights-based conception, would have to break out of the Hohfeldian paradigm of thinking about rights and duties.

The exploration of the possibility of obligations that exist independently of rights that I present in what follows therefore scrutinises the possibility of such a break with the Hohfeldian paradigm. Key to this is an analysis of the concept of obligation that one might extract from Marcel Mauss' *Essai sur le don*. Mauss' essay expressly invokes the notion of obligations that derive from the *nature of things*, as is evident from the following key description of the *kula* ring (a Melanesian practice of gift

1 Professor of Philosophy of Law, University of Luxembourg. I am indebted to Frank Michelman and Joe Singer for many instructive discussions of Wesley Hohfeld's analysis of legal correlatives over many years, and to Chris Doude van Troostwijk and Arthur Cools for many inspiring conversations about Husserl, Levinas, Lyotard and the whole phenomenological tradition. I have learned and am still learning a lot from all of them. I thank Scott Veitch and Emilios Christodoulidis for a sustained working relationship and friendship over many years to which the thoughts developed in this chapter also owe immeasurable debt. Thanks are also due to another good friend from Glasgow, Lindsay Farmer, for pertinent comments on my reading of Mauss' *Essay on the Gift* presented in Glasgow, May 2015. I thank Pascal Ancel for directing me to the specifics of the *droit de résponsabilité* discussed in this chapter. I also thank Rachael Walsh for insightful comments on an earlier draft. And I would like to remember here also André van der Walt, who passed away in 2016, but whose influence on the thoughts developed in this chapter will always remain with me.

exchange): '[A]u fond, ce sont de méchanismes d'obligation et même d'obligation par les choses, qui jouent [dans le kula]' (Mauss 2007, p. 109)

The English translation by Ian Cunnison changes the meaning of these two lines slightly by suggesting the obligation is 'resident in the gifts' themselves, and not in the things (*les choses*), as the French text suggests.[2] This change of meaning is fortunate, for it alerts one to the specificity of the meaning of this line in the French text and invites one to scrutinise its specific invocation of 'obligation by the things' further by comparing it with the Roman law concept of *res* (English: thing; French: *chose*) from which the Romans inferred all obligations. Doing so – that is, literally reading Mauss as contemplating an obligation by things comparable to the Roman law connection between *obligatio* and *res* – allows one to read the original version of Mauss' phrase as an expression of an *ontic* and/or *ontological* conception of the nature of obligations that resonates in fundamental respects with philosophical conceptions of responsibility that one finds in the work of thinkers such as Jacques Derrida, Martin Heidegger, Emanuel Levinas and Jean-François Lyotard.

It nevertheless remains a question whether Mauss' *Essai sur le don* really offers the possibility of contemplating a duty without having to invoke a discourse of rights. Jacques Derrida insisted that Mauss' discussion of the economy of the gift is not at all a discussion about the gift in the strict sense of the word. The so-called 'gifts' circulated in the gift economy are really just counter-performances, he insisted.[3] In other words, they concern instances of compliance with pre-existing obligations in a scheme of reciprocal obligations. The asymmetrical relation between the giver and receiver of the gift that conditions the possibility of a true gift – which requires that the giver just gives and that the receiver just receives – is evidently absent from the gift economies (the institutions of the *kula* and *potlatch*) that Mauss describes with reference to an array of traditional cultures. Derrida's reading seems to be supported by a pertinent passage in Mauss' text where Mauss quotes a Maori proverb according to which the gift involves 'no risk' (2007, p. 229; 2011, p. 69). According to this proverb, the expectation that the gift will be returned in due course is so established that the one who gives at any particular moment in time need not worry about this giving, for he will be receiving again in due course.

Now, if Derrida's contention is unequivocally correct, it would effectively deprive one of any recourse to Mauss' text for purposes of finding a conception of obligation that is not *ab initio* tied to a right. This is so because the possibility of contemplating gift exchanges in terms of asymmetrical duties – that are in no way linked to a dynamics or mechanics of reciprocal rights and duties – would necessarily depend on the possibility of asymmetrical gifts that do not respond to one another. This observation therefore informs a key hypothesis of this essay: If there is no such thing as an asymmetrical gift – the only gift in the strict sense of the word, according to Derrida – there is most likely also no such thing as an asymmetrical duty, or a duty that precedes the existence of a right.

2 See Mauss 2011, p. 21.
3 See Derrida 1991, pp. 39–94.

The chapter engages with the thoughts introduced here as follows. It expounds Hohfeld's analyses of legal correlatives in Section I for purposes of clarifying the way in which duties relate to rights in standard Hohfeldian rights discourses. It then puts forward a constitutional law argument to show how the scope of rights discourses might be expanded in order to broaden the spectrum of recognised legal duties in any given society. Section I concludes with the sober observation that this expansion of rights discourses is the only way in which standard legal argument can pursue an expansion of duty discourses. This juridical expansion of rights discourses for the sake of expanding duty discourses is not insignificant, but it ultimately only underlines the reality that standard *legal* arguments and discourses will by definition or default always fall short of a call for a conception of the 'priority of obligation ahead of right'.

Section II then turns to a reading of Mauss' essay of the gift to determine whether one might at least plausibly contemplate the 'priority of obligation ahead of right' from the vantage point of a broader normative or philosophical discourse about duties. The challenge here is to determine whether Mauss' text offers one a plausible conception of an asymmetrical gift; that is, a gift that is not burdened by the exigencies of reciprocity. At stake here is the possibility of a truly *free* gift or a truly *free act* of giving that is not in any way conditioned by the *right* of another to receive a gift in view of obligations or debts created by earlier gift exchanges. To rephrase once more: at stake here is the possibility of a duty to give that is categorically and qualitatively different from the duty to pay back. The link between gifts and obligations that is put forward here is of course far from self-evident and may even strike one as rather counter-intuitive. This link would therefore have to be scrutinised incisively and Section V, below, will turn to do so. For now, let us first just note again Derrida's suggestion that Mauss' contemplation of the gift only concerns a duty to pay back, and not a duty to give. This suggestion cannot be dismissed easily and Section II indeed highlights several key elements of Mauss' text that indeed seem to confirm Derrida's assessment of it.

Section III nevertheless proceeds to qualify Derrida's assessment of Mauss' essay by pointing out another side of the essay. In other words, it highlights a certain ambiguity in Mauss' text which shows that it does create a narrow yet significant opening for contemplating a gift that is not just a matter of repayment. The text does allow one to contemplate a duty that derives, independently, from the very nature of things, as the passage cited above suggests. Section III notes further that Derrida's critique of Mauss relies substantially on Heidegger's ontological difference or divide between *Being* and *beings*, and especially the notion of *es gibt* (it gives) on which this difference or divide pivots according to Heidegger. It therefore also notes a certain resonance between Mauss' conception of a duty that derives from the nature of things and Heidegger's notion of *Being* that gives *beings*. Section IV nevertheless moves on to wrest Mauss' essay away from this very plausible Heideggerian interpretation of his text. It does so for purposes of realigning Mauss' text with a Kantian conception of moral responsibility. The aim of this shift from a Heideggerian to a Kantian reading of Mauss is to show that a duty to give that derives from the 'nature of things' can be understood better today – in modern secular environments – in terms of a Kantian regard for the moral imperative that conditions human liberty.

Section V turns to the rather conspicuous further question – already noted above – that comes to the fore when one assumes the possibility of a duty to give that is not just a duty to pay. Suppose one accepts on the basis of the arguments expounded in Section III that Mauss' text indeed contemplates a duty to give that is not just a duty to pay. Why would one still want or need to consider this 'duty' to give an obligation? Is it necessary to consider the duty to give a duty at all, and if so, why? A well-grounded positive answer to these questions is crucial for concluding the overarching argument regarding the possibility of a 'priority of obligation ahead of right' that this chapter offers. Section V endeavours to offer such an answer with reference to thoughts of Jean-François Lyotard and Emmanuel Levinas.

Section VI concludes the chapter by returning to the Hohfeldian legal discourse with which it begins. It returns to this discourse for purposes of exploring the question whether the philosophical or Maussian perspectives developed in Sections II to V may contribute to an expansion or a mutation of the Hohfeldian paradigm of reciprocal rights and duties, so as to allow for a post-Hohfeldian regard for a 'priority of obligation ahead of right' in legal discourse.

I. Expanding the scope of Hohfeldian rights–duties correlatives through constitutional law

One day, in a quite different – post-Hohfeldian – age, humanity might return to a sensibility akin to the one to which the poet gives voice in Psalm 121: 'I will raise my eyes up to the hills, where will my help come from?' A future humanity may want to return to the sensibility of these words for the purpose of recovering a sense of duty. It may come to raise its eyes to the hills again and ask: Where do our duties come from? Where does *my* duty come from? This substitution of *help* with *duty* may strike one as curious and even unfounded. Perhaps so, but it is motivated by the sense that the questions addressed in this volume demand a contemplation of an expanded concept of duty. It also turns on the conviction that a stronger or greater sense of duty – a sense not linked to any expectation of entitlement – may well be very 'helpful' (helpful in more ways than we may think).[4]

4 I am grateful to Joe Singer for checking whether this translation matches the Hebrew text well enough and also for telling me a story about how help from the heavens comes to us through people just doing their duty. The story goes like this: Some local council workers go to inform a man that the valley in which his house is standing is going to be flooded, and to help him to pack up and leave in time. No, says the man, you need not help me. If God is sending a flood, he will also send me help. The workers come back later with Jeeps when the house is already flooded knee-deep, but the man still insists: God will help me. They come back with boats when the house is almost halfway under water, but again the man refuses the help and insists that God will help him. They come back again with a helicopter when the house is already fully under water and the man is sitting on the roof. But he just keeps on saying: God will help me. After that the house gets completely submerged, the man drowns and when he gets to heaven he asks God: Why didn't you save me? Then God asks him: I sent people to help you, later I sent them again with Jeeps, boats and even a helicopter' what did you want?

Psalm 121 would seem to express an *ontological* and even *onto-theological* understanding of help or sustenance. Help comes from elsewhere. One looks to the hills for help. And as the second verse of the Psalm then asserts: Help comes from God. This onto-theological understanding of sustenance will be a key concern of this chapter. It will rely on Marcel Mauss' essay on the gift – where one finds a comparable association of God and the hills, a similar sensibility regarding the god or gods that dwells or dwell in the hills – to put forward the idea that any help that may come to us from the hills will come to us, *if* it comes, in the form of a profound sense of duty. However, we will ultimately move on from Mauss – passing briefly through Heidegger – to Kant, Levinas and Lyotard to explore the possibility of a truly *deontological* – instead of *ontological* or onto-theological – understanding of the 'priority of obligation ahead of right'. We will accordingly endeavour also to read Psalm 121 as a purely deontological poem, a poem that ultimately recognises that the arrival of sustenance – of everything that sustains us – finds its primordial form in the advent of a sense of obligation.

A future humanity may or may not return to this deontological sense of obligation that this chapter explores. It may or may not return to a sense of duty that will arrive from elsewhere – from the hills, as the poet suggests in the book of Psalms – before anything else arrives. It may or may not return to a sense of duty that arrives like a stranger who descends from the hills and brings the hills with her, so to speak. If such a future humanity were indeed to return to this primordial sense of the arrival of obligation, it would have to take leave of current understandings of obligation that are largely reduced to restrictive legal conceptions of duty. Those whose sense of duty is exhausted by these restrictive legal conceptions of obligation do not and need not raise their eyes to the hills for the sake of understanding the advent of duty or obligation. They know where duty comes from. They know, at least as far as the law and legal duties are concerned, that duties emanate from rights–duty relationships. They know this because Wesley Hohfeld tells them so in a way that appears self-evident: One has a duty because some public authority – a legislator, judge or administrative official – has endowed someone else with a right. A duty is the legal correlative of someone else's right. From a Hohfeldian perspective, any idea that a legal duty may exist in absence of a right is simply and fundamentally misconceived. This legal understanding of duty would indeed appear to have displaced, today, any other sense of duty that may precede or exceed, and eventually question, the boundaries of legal obligation.

Legal obligations or duties, it would appear then, can be determined and delimitated exhaustively by determining and delimiting the rights of others. Would anyone be burdened by a sense that contemporary societies suffer from a dearth of duties, he or she would have to consider this dearth a result of a dearth of rights. In his chapter in this book, Veitch is burdened by this sense of a dearth of duty, and he has good reasons to be thus burdened. However, he may well not be content with the idea that this dearth of duty can only be remedied by remedying a dearth of rights. He understands this 'dearth of duty' to be a result of a misconception of the way in which human beings live together. He wishes to alert us to the pervasive social reality of waves of duties (an idea drawn from Waldron) that conditions the very possibility of rights. Proper awareness of these waves of duties, he suggests, would relativize and rectify contemporary social and legal consciousness' excessive focus on rights. A due regard for these waves of duties – for the way in which people diligently do their daily duties to make things work – may well wash away this excessive concern with rights, one might say. And it may also cast new light on the way in which the law allows some individuals to *legally* opt out of these waves of duties in order to withdraw to islands of duty-free existence. This chapter is an endeavour to pay due attention to Veitch's pertinent concerns in this regard, and will engage squarely with them in its concluding section (Section VI). Let us nevertheless begin more modestly by first just posing the question of how standard legal argument may remedy a dearth of duties through remedying a dearth of rights. For this purpose, we must look closely at the essential process through which rights enter the legal world, and for that matter also enter the rest of the world in which we live.

This invocation in passing of an entry of rights 'into the legal world', that is 'for that matter also [an entry into] the rest of the world in which we live', demands more attention than one might think at first, for something very specific is at stake in the Hohfeldian paradigm of legal correlatives from which we are taking our cue here. The first thing that Hohfeld teaches us is indeed that there is no significant distinction to be drawn between the 'legal world' and 'the rest of the word in which we live'. His analysis of legal correlatives does not entertain the conception of a dualism between law and society, or between the 'legal world' and the 'rest of the world' that humans inhabit. According to Hohfeld, human beings live in one world in which different legal correlatives organise different kinds of human relationships, and the common or lay (or formalist!) distinction between a world of law, and the rest of social reality, actually concerns nothing more than a distinction between two different sets of legal correlatives – namely, the distinction between rights and duties, on the one hand, and non-rights and liberties (or privileges), on the other.[5]

The sphere of human existence that is generally – that is, in lay terms – considered the *sphere of law* concerns the sum total of rights–duties relations in any particular society at any particular time. The sphere of existence that is generally considered the *non-legal social sphere* comprises the sum total of non-rights and corresponding liberties that exist in a particular society at any particular time. It is important to stress again, however, that Hohfeld did not consider this law–society distinction of any importance for legal reasoning. The lay conception of a significant difference between the sphere of law, on the one hand, and a non-legal social sphere, on the other, becomes a formalist conception (from which follows a whole spectrum of notions regarding a sacrosanct private sphere that cannot be restructured politically) when it is adamantly sustained in legal reasoning. Hohfeld, however, was not a legal formalist. He was a legal realist that discerned no intrinsic formal division between law and society. He insisted that this distinction simply

5 See Hohfeld 1913, pp. 16–59; Singer 1982, pp. 975–1059.

emanates from political or policy decisions that turn some social relations into right/duty relations and others into non-right/liberty relations.

Let us take a closer look now at the difference between rights/duties and non-rights/liberties correlatives. How do these different correlatives come into existence? As already observed above, they are the outcome of different kinds of governmental and/or judicial decisions, but one can add to this that one is basically never sure whether one is dealing with the one set of correlatives, and not with the other, until such time as a court has decided the matter. Legislation and administrative acts can and should largely determine the nature of relations between individuals and/or groups of individuals, but legislation and governmental action often still invite significant disputes regarding the nature of the relations they establish, and then the disputing parties regularly turn to some court to settle the matter. How, then, do courts establish right/duty relations, on the one hand, and non-right/liberty relations, on the other?

A court establishes a right/duty relation between disputing parties every time that it upholds a rights-claim in a dispute. It establishes a non-right/liberty relation every time it dismisses a rights-claim. In the former case, the court tells the claimant that he has a right, and the defendant that he has a duty. In the latter case, the court tells the claimant that he does not have the right that he is claiming, while signalling to the defendant that he is free to ignore the claim of the claimant. Put in Hohfeldian terms, one can say that the latter case is one in which the court tells the claimant that the right he claims does not exist. It is not a *right*, on which his claim is based, but *a non-right*. In the same breath, the court is telling the defendant that he is free or at liberty to ignore this *non-right* of the claimant. In other words, the defendant has *the liberty* to ignore the claimant's claim.

Let us return now to Veitch's concern with the dearth of duty in the time we live. We have already indicated that any hope to remedy the dearth of duty without taking recourse to rights is doomed to be disappointed as far as legal reasoning is concerned. Legal reasoning, as we know it, cannot contemplate duties that are not correlative to rights. The best it can do is to remedy a dearth of duty by remedying a dearth of rights. How can legal reasoning accomplish this expansion of duty through an expansion of rights? A typical positivist line of legal reasoning would insist: Don't ask the courts to increase the number and scope of rights that society must honour. Go to parliament for this purpose. Another line of legal reasoning that is particularly pervasive today will take recourse to fundamental rights. It will invoke a constitutional or convention right that demands the enhancement of all ordinary legal rights for purposes of giving due effect to all constitutional or convention rights applicable to the dispute at hand. At stake, here, is the so-called horizontal effect of fundamental rights from which resulted one of the most significant transformations of judicial reasoning in the course of the twentieth century.[6] It should be noted that both lines of legal reasoning invoked here will probably be informed by a constitutional argument. In the case

6 See Van der Walt 2014.

of the horizontal effect argument, the claimant will ask the court to enhance his existing legal rights in view of the demands of some constitutional right. In the case of the positivist line, the court will basically leave or urge the claimant to engage in political action that will move parliament to bring legislation more in line with the constitution. The positivist court may even send a signal to parliament that such legislation is needed. It will just not proceed to legislate itself to improve the situation.

The constitutional argument will most likely not satisfy Veitch, for it evidently does not envisage any 'priority of obligation ahead of right'. Let us nevertheless take a look at how these constitutional arguments – cast in Hohfeldian terms – can be invoked in the case of *the disappearing assets* that Veitch targets in his chapter in this volume: A beneficiary (B) receives invisible and therefore untaxable benefits from a Trust Company (TC) based in the British Virgin Islands (BVI). Two different scenarios – both typical – can be imagined or predicted here:

1 B is resorting to legal tax minimisation practices by using applicable law of the UK (which also applies in the BVI, but somewhat differently, it seems).
2 B is resorting to illegal tax evasion practices that transgress UK law.

Considered in Hohfeldian terms, B is exploiting the *liberty* or *privilege* (synonyms as far as Hohfeld is concerned) not to be taxed in case 1. The UK does not seem to have a right to demand tax in this case. It has, instead, a *non-right*. At issue, here, is a typical case of what tax lawyers would call 'legal tax minimisation' that is made possible by some loophole or ambiguity in the law, or by some express 'tax ruling'. UK tax legislation has not imposed a clear enough duty to pay tax in this case and the UK therefore has no right to demand tax. It thus leaves tax payers free to pay or not to pay. Some pay, others don't (the smart ones don't).

In case 2, B has a clear *duty to pay* tax but fraudulently does not do so, thus violating the state's *right to receive* tax.

We can assume that Veitch is deeply vexed by both these scenarios and believes that remedial action should be taken. In case 2, he can become a whistle blower and help to put the UK's prosecuting machinery in motion. This is simple. Case 1 is more complex, but he can resort to activating one of the two lines of constitutional legal reasoning invoked above. Assuming for the sake of argument that he can meet *locus standi* requirements through recourse to public interest or class action litigation procedures, he can try to get a court to send a strong *obiter* signal to government that the constitutional (or just patriotic) duty of UK citizens and residents to pay tax demands more effective legislation. The remedy that this positivist line of argument offers may seem weak, but it is not insignificant. It may well aid any political action that Veitch, or like-minded political activists and other responsible citizens, may want to take to move the legislator to pass better tax laws.

In the UK, Veitch's legal action will probably be restricted to this positivist line of reasoning, unless he can somehow manage to translate the grievance into a human rights argument that can become actionable under the Human Rights Act.

Should he be able to do so, he can try to move a more interventionist court to demand legislative reforms on the grounds that existing UK tax legislation falls foul of the demands of the Human Rights Act.[7] The UK seems bent on removing this option from the table very soon, but it is worthwhile mentioning it while it still exists. This Human Rights Act option is interesting because the UK does not have a written constitution with a list of justiciable constitutional rights that may be invoked in an argument for legal reform. In countries with written constitutions containing a list of justiciable constitutional rights, Veitch would have been able to turn to the domestic constitution to put forward constitutional arguments demanding legal reform.

One can assume that neither of these options is likely to satisfy Veitch. The remedies they offer may well seem slight to him, and unlikely to materialise, at that. And they are light years away from any conception of the 'priority of an obligation ahead of a right'. Against this background, Veitch may well feel inclined to raise his eyes towards the hills and ask: Where may our duties come from? And when will they come? If he would be so inclined, would he just be too ahead of his time and dreaming of distant age, still to come? Or is he sensing something that is closer to us than we may think, something like a wave of duty coming our way, *always* coming our way, if we would just care to open our eyes to it? Let us turn now to Mauss' *Essai sur le don* to take a closer look at whether Veitch could be getting at something here, and at what it is that he may be getting at.

II. The possibility of the 'priority of obligation ahead of right' considered through a reading of Mauss

Can an obligation come to us, without coming to us as an obligation that is already tied to someone else's right? This is the key question that we need to address if we hope to find some way out of the Hohfeldian constellation of correlative rights and duties that underpins our current understanding of legal relationships. A duty that might be assumed without being exacted by the right of someone else would seem to be a duty assumed freely. In this section of this chapter we will engage with a careful reading of Mauss' *Essai sur le don* for purposes of scrutinising the possibility of such a free assumption of an obligation or duty.

We have already noted above how Mauss' text invokes a duty that emanates from the nature of *things – [une] obligation par les choses.* We have also shown, however, that the English translation of Mauss' text already retreats somewhat from the far-reaching meaning of this invocation of a duty that emerges from the nature of things. The English text suggests the obligation derives from the gift itself. It reads:

7 This may not look like the horizontal effect reasoning that I have invoked above, but I would like to insist that it is on the basis of extensive arguments developed elsewhere. See Van der Walt 2014.

> Pains are taken to show one's freedom and autonomy as well as one's magnanimity, yet all the time one is actuated by the mechanisms of obligation which are resident in the gifts themselves.
>
> (Mauss 2011, p. 21)

The difference that comes to the fore here between the original French text and the English translation may seem small, but it is significant. If the obligation simply derives from gifts received, and only from them, the suggestion that the duty is assumed voluntarily and freely becomes difficult to sustain. The duty that appears to be of concern in the English translation seems to be one that emanates from a gift previously received. At stake seems to be a duty that is demanded by the gift received, and not a duty that is freely assumed. The English text would indeed seem to deny the possibility of a duty freely assumed. The first part of the sentence states clearly that the pretension of freedom and autonomy is ultimately nothing but a show. In reality, the return of the gift is mandatory. This is true, however, not only of the English translation but also the original French. The latter also states clearly:

> On recherche en tout ceci à montrer de la liberté, de la liberté et de l'autonomie, en même temps que de la grandeur. Et pourtant, au fond, ce sont de mécanismes d'obligation, et même d'obligation par les choses, qui jouent.
>
> (Mauss 2007, p. 109)

To be sure, the thought that we are pursuing here through close scrutiny of Mauss' text is not linked to any suggestion that the gift exchanges of the *kula* that Mauss is discussing imply no obligation to give. Such a thought would take leave of Mauss' text all too conspicuously. Already in the first lines of his essay on the gift, Mauss invokes both the mandatory nature of the gift exchange and the tension between this mandatory nature of the gift exchange and its 'theoretical' conception. The English translations reads:

> In Scandinavian and many other civilizations contracts are fulfilled and exchanges of goods are made by means of gifts. In theory such gifts are voluntary, but in fact they are given and repaid under the obligation.
>
> (Mauss 2011, p. 1)

These opening lines of the English translation of the essay also differ slightly from the original French text. The French text seems to underline the realisation that the gift is not real. Instead of contending that contracts are fulfilled and goods exchanged 'by means of gifts', it contends that the fulfilment of contracts and exchange of goods are made in 'the form of gifts' – *sous la forme de cadeaux* (Mauss 2007, p. 65). In other words, these lines of the French text would seem to state even more clearly than the English translation that 'the gift' concerns nothing but a contractual and mandatory exchange of goods that is dressed up as an exchange of gifts.

There can therefore be little doubt that Mauss is expressly and intentionally writing about a mandatory exchange in his essay on the gift. And in some sections of his text he is talking not only about a mandatory exchange but also about a mandatory *contractual* exchange. This is especially clear where he discusses the Maori notion of the spiritual force (*hau*) of the gift that results from the fact that the giver of the material gift also gives something of himself with the material gift that will become poisonous if not returned to the giver soon enough (ibid., pp. 82–7). In this regard, Jacques Derrida's observation that Mauss' essay on the gift talks about everything except the gift – *l'Essai sur le don, de Marcel Mauss, parle de tout sauf du don* (Derrida 1991, p. 39) – is asserting something that is evidently already obvious to Mauss himself.

Derrida is undoubtedly right and risks just restating what is already abundantly clear: Mauss cannot be and is not writing about gifts that are not directly linked to contractual obligations. Any suggestion that he is must be misguided. Seen from this perspective, Mauss is offering us no escape from Hohfeld's correlative conception of rights and duties. And yet the thought that we are pursuing here is indeed that Mauss' text does provide us an opportunity to contemplate a gift, or at least an element of the gift, that exceeds whatever contractual obligation to which it is tied. One may present this thought in terms of a shift from contradiction to paradox. One can assert that the contractual obligations to which the gift is irreducibly tied simply *contradict* the notion that there is a gift at stake here. Or one can suggest that something of the gift remains real despite being irreducibly tied to contractual obligation, thus giving rise to a *paradoxical* constellation of gift and contract that sustains the tension between them and does not culminate in mere contradiction (which would necessitate the cancellation of the one or the other). The reading of Mauss' text that follows suggests that Mauss is doing, or aims to do, the latter. Mauss' text suggests that he recognises in gift exchanges a surplus or excess of giving that cannot be reduced to contract. I shall expound this claim, in what follows, notwithstanding the passages in Mauss' text that suggest he considers the gift as nothing but a form of contract, a form of contract that takes the form of a gift.

The first undeniable suggestion that the gift precedes and exceeds contractual payment and repayment can be found in Mauss' explication of the three obligations that underpin the gift economy. The duty to give back what has been received is not the only obligation. The duty to give back gifts received earlier is accompanied by two other duties, the duty to give and the duty to receive – *l'obligation de rendre les cadeaux reçus … en suppose deux autres aussi importantes: obligation d'en faire, d'une part, obligation d'en reçevoir, de l'autre.* Only a theory that attributes due importance to all three these duties – *[une] théorie complète de ces trois obligations* – can explain all the complexities of the gift exchange properly (Mauss 2007, p. 87). Why does Mauss stress the existence of three duties here, the duty to give, the duty to receive and the duty to give back? And why does he distinguish so clearly between the duty to give and the duty to gift back? The only plausible answer to these questions must be that Mauss wishes to emphasise a separate existence of the *duty to give* that cannot be reduced to *the duty to give (or pay) back*. It is important to pay specific and separate attention to this, he contends, for it could give us insight into how humans first became traders – *l'obligation de donner est non moins importante; son étude pourrait faire comprendre comment les hommes sont devenus échangistes* (ibid., p. 88).

So Mauss does seem to be contemplating an asymmetrical duty to give, after all, a duty that precedes and conditions the institutionalisation of the *kula* ring – that is, a general practice of symmetrical and reciprocal gift exchanges. He is evidently considering something like a 'first gift' – *premier don* – to which he returns later in the essay, a first gift that makes the ensuing practice of reciprocal giving possible. Remarkably, this first gift, the *vaga*, is still not quite the first gift; it has to be solicited by a prior series of gifts called the *wawoyla*. The *wawoyla* gifts solicit or court the *kula* (ibid., p. 120). The *kula* ring turns on prosaic exchanges – called the *gimwali* – between partners (*entre partenaires*) that ensues after the giving of the first gift, the *vaga*. Once the *vaga* is given, the *kula* ring is established and functions as an uninterrupted chain of supplementary giving and giving back that includes mandatory markets (*une chaîne ininterrompu de cadeaux supplémentaires, donnés et rendus, et aussi de marches obligatoires*). The *wawoyla*, however, concerns the soliciting of a future partner (*le partenaire future*) that is not yet bound by the mandatory circle of gifts known as the *kula*. The presentation of the *wawoyla* through which a future *kula* is courted thus constitutes a veritable drama of solicitation, persuasion, seduction and dazzling (*il faut donc séduire, eblouir*), and it evidently takes place under conditions in which the acceptance of the courting and the subsequent giving of the first *kula* gift, the *vaga*, are not yet certain (ibid., p. 121).

One would seem to be well on one's way towards presenting a case that Mauss is contemplating, alongside established practices of reciprocal and symmetrical gift exchanges, also an asymmetrical first gift that precedes and exceeds the duty to give back. If this is so, one could also seem well on the way towards a conception of a duty that precedes and exceeds the symmetry of Hohfeld's correlative constellation of rights and duties. The *wawoyla*, the preliminary gifts that solicit the first *kula* gift, the *vaga*, surely comes to the fore in Mauss' text as a first gift that is not yet classifiable in terms of *giving back* – that is, classifiable in terms of giving back gifts already received earlier from a partner under the auspices of an already established circle of reciprocal obligations. One indeed seems to be edging here towards a contemplation of a possibility of an asymmetrical duty to give that exceeds the Hohfeldian conception of correlative rights and duties. One must nevertheless not move too fast. At least two questions beckon one to slow down: Why is the giving of the *wawoyla*, the soliciting gift that precedes and courts the first gift, the *vaga*, a duty? And if it is a duty, where does this duty come from, considering that it does not derive from an earlier gift that must be returned?

The answer to these questions requires that we turn back to the earlier pages of the essay where Mauss distinguishes between the three duties that underpin the *kula* ring, the duty to give, to give back and to receive. Why is this first duty to give a duty and where does it come from? Mauss puts forward a remarkable explanation in this regard: The duty to give the first gift derives from the notion that the receiver of the first gift already has a right to everything that belongs to the giver – *on donne parce qu'on y est forcé, parce que le donataire a une sorte de droit de propriété sur tout ce qui appartient au donateur* (ibid., p. 89). Mauss is invoking a notion of 'right' here that Western legal thinking generally associates with Thomist natural law, namely, the right of all God's creatures to share in the fruits of the earth, a right in terms of which St Thomas expressly invokes the right of the poor to the wealth of the rich (Aquinas 1975, 2a 2ae, q.66 a.7). It is a good question, however, whether contemporary legal thinking can reverse the whole history of modern legal thought and consciousness that by and large stripped the Western legal imagination of its ability to entertain notions of natural rights that emanate from the gift of the earth that God made to all mankind.

The story is well known. Aristotelian and Thomist natural law thinking gave way to the prototype positivism of early modern social contract theories under the paradigm of which earthly sovereigns, and not God, distributed the fruits of the earth.[8] Since then, earthly sovereigns almost invariably tended to manage their distributions of the earth in terms of positive property and contractual relations until the social havoc caused by the industrial revolution moved them to reintroduce redistribution policies that were at least vaguely reminiscent of the Thomist notion of the rights of the poor to the wealth of the rich. It is also well known that the introduction of these redistribution policies – associated in the Western world with the rise of the social welfare state towards the end of the nineteenth and early twentieth century – has ever since been under pressure to cede once more to strict regimes of property and contract that allow for little or no non-contractual redistribution of property. It is the dominance of these strict regimes of property and contract in contemporary legal consciousness that explains the pervasive tax evasion practices that Veitch's chapter in this volume has in its sight. These practices are informed by the deep conviction that legal duties can only stem from the property and contractual rights of others. The idea that duties can stem from anything but property and contract is foreign to this consciousness.

Mauss' essay on the gift is evidently offered as an argument against this reduction of legal duty to correlatives of contractual and property rights. This is also how Mauss understood it himself.[9] It is nevertheless obvious that the elements of the essay that we have considered so far do not yet give us any reason to suggest that Mauss is effectively showing us a way out of the Hohfeldian constellation of correlative rights and duties. We have stressed above that Hohfeld understood his constellations of legal correlatives as outcomes of sovereign legislative or judicial decisions. Were a return to premodern natural law possible, it would not significantly alter the construction of law in terms of correlative rights and duties that we associate with Hohfeld and modern law. It would only replace the modern sovereign with the premodern sovereign – God, represented by his King – and thereby reintroduce legal correlatives that modern sovereigns no longer or rarely recognise –

8 For one of the most salient narratives of this formation of modern law, see Villey 2009.
9 See Florence Weber's introduction to Mauss (2007), pp. 50–4.

namely, the correlative rights and duties that emanate from the conviction that humans are destined to share the surface and fruits of the earth.

Mauss' essay on the gift does not contemplate a revival of Thomist or Aristotelian versions of natural law, but, as we saw above, it evidently explores premodern notions of rights and duties that emanate from the human being's common ownership of the earth, the common ownership that already gives the receiver of the first gift a property or shared-property right to everything that the giver owns – *le donataire a une sorte de droit de propriété sur tout ce qui appartient au donateur*. What Mauss is contemplating here is evidently what one might call a pagan version of St Thomas' Christian natural law. He offers us a marvellously pagan view of the world in which the first primordial correlativity of rights and duties stems from the way human beings take part in the natural order of things by giving and receiving gifts. Giving and receiving is not just a matter of exchanging material goods between the giver and receiver; it is also, and perhaps first, a matter of soliciting the favour and benevolence of the whole natural and spiritual environment – nature, gods and ancestors – that sustain the giver and receiver – *[les] échanges de cadeaux entre les hommes … incident les esprits des morts, les dieux, les choses, les animaux, la nature, à ëtte généreux envers eux* (Mauss 2007, p. 92). It all literally amounts to sustaining the most profound unity and oneness of things, a veritable mixing of souls with things and things with souls – *[on] mêle les âmes dans les choses; on mêle les choses dans les âmes* (ibid., p. 103).

It is important to note that Mauss also recognises this sense of the oneness and relatedness of things in Roman law, and specifically in the Roman law notions of the *nexum* and *res*. The *nexum* – the legal bond – derives from things as much as it derives from humans – *[le] nexum, le 'lien' de droit vient des choses autant que des hommes* (ibid., p. 184). Likewise, the word *res* – literally translatable as *the thing* – did not just denote 'inert beings' or objects, but things as they related to family relations – *plus on remonte dans l'antiquité, plus le sens du mot familia dénote les res qui en font partie* (ibid., 185). It is this sense of the word *res* that Michel Villey invokes in his contentions regarding the ancient meaning of the word *ius*. It did not signify a subjective right – the legal powers of an individual – as we know it today, insists Villey, but a *res – a thing* that determined the relations between people.[10] It is worthwhile noting here that Martin Heidegger would also point out this meaning of the word *res* in his essay *Das Ding – The Thing* – to which we return below. *Res* denoted for the Romans, he observed, that which citizens talk about to one another, that which concerns them publicly – *das in Rede stehende, das was jeden offenkundig angeht* (Heidegger 1954, p. 47).

It should now be clear why we commenced this reading of Mauss' text by insisting on the way the original French text states clearly that the duty to give does not simply stem from the gift received. The obligation is not only 'resident in the gift', as the English translation suggests, but emanates from the things themselves – *ce sont de mécanismes d'obligation, et même d'obligation par les choses, qui jouent* (Mauss 2007, p. 109). However, it should also be clear that our reading of

10 See Villey 1946, p. 217.

Mauss has thus far not brought us a single step closer to contemplating a duty that is independent of a right. It still does not seem to offer us any ground for contemplating the 'priority of obligation ahead of right' that Veitch invites us to contemplate. Mauss' text still seems to offer no respite from the correlativity of rights and duties that Hohfeld considered an essential element of modern legal consciousness. All that the text seems to offer us is a premodern conception of right/duty correlatives. It offers an extra set of correlatives in terms of which the initial gifts of the earth – the endowments that all humans receive in the first place from the gods and from nature – demand a gift in return. In this regard, the doubts that Derrida expresses regarding the notion of 'gift' in Mauss' essay still seem to hold true. There is no gift contemplated in the essay, it seems, that is not already a repayment.

The premodern conception of the correlativity of rights and duties that comes to the fore in Mauss' essay invites one to consider a certain 'natural law' expansion of modern positivist constellations of rights and duties. Whereas these modern positivist constellations of rights and duties restrict the correlativity of rights and duties to property and contractual rights, the premodern and pagan 'natural law' expansion of rights/duties correlativity contemplated by Mauss extends this correlativity to reciprocal gift exchanges. It surely offers *a vision* of a primordial sharing of the resources of the earth that disallows the reduction of rights and duties to established property and contractual rights that culminate in the tax evasion practices that vex Veitch. There is, however, no reason to believe that *this vision*, this premodern conception of expanded right/duty relations, offers a more effective expansion of right/duty relations than the constitutional law expansion considered above (in Section I). There is, in fact, much reason to believe that the language of obligations that Mauss explores and expounds in his essay on the gift is exhausted and spent today. One can hardly expect it to have more impact on the way in which contemporary law conceives of right/duty correlativity than Aristotelian or Thomist natural law has, and the impact of Aristotelian and Thomist natural law thinking on contemporary legal consciousness can already be considered negligible. Seen from this perspective, the constitutional law expansion of right/duty relations discussed above would indeed seem to offer a far more effective and credible source of resistance to the reduction of legal duties to the contractual and property rights of others.

However, we are not done with our reading of Mauss' text, for there is an aspect of his text that does seem to bring us closer to a regard for a duty that might come to us unaccompanied by any right. The elements of the text that we have covered thus far give one no reason to raise one's eyes to the hills to ask where such a duty unaccompanied by a right might come from, for they assert an all too clear knowledge regarding the origin of duties. Duties derive from the rights with which every human being is endowed in view of the common possession of the earth that God or the gods granted to all humans. But it is the language of exactly this knowledge that is by and large exhausted and spent today, and it is only when one realises this and begins to look away from it, that Mauss' text begins to point one to a duty that comes to one as if from nowhere, and unaccompanied by a right, at that. For purposes of uncovering this element of Mauss' text, we need to return once more to Derrida's observation regarding the absence of any real gift in Mauss' text.

III. The gift of time

Jacques Derrida discerns neither contradiction nor paradox in the tension between gift and obligation that comes to the fore in Mauss' essay. He discerns in it a veritable *double bind* that renders the gift *logically* impossible. On the one hand, the gift only becomes a gift when it creates an obligation – *d'une part il n'y a pas de don sans lien, sans bind ... sans obligation ... nous rapelle Mauss.* On the other hand, the gift must be freely given and must bear no relation to any obligation to be a gift in the strict sense of the word – *mais d'autre part il n'y a pas de don qui ne doive se délier de l'obligation, de la dette, du contrat, de l'échange, donc du bind* (Derrida 1991, p. 42).

This, however, does not seem to constitute an accurate reading of Mauss' text. The *Essai sur le don* surely suggests – in view of all the gift economies that it describes – that the gift *invariably* creates obligations. But there is nothing in the essay that suggests the gift *must* create an obligation to be or become a gift. Again, Mauss' text certainly considers the gift a response to and a source of obligation, but throughout the text Mauss only engages with empirical or historical observations of how gift exchanges function or functioned in practice. He never makes conceptual contestations that invoke a logic according to which they must function. As suggested above, Mauss' text surely confronts one with paradox, that is, with seemingly paradoxical phenomena, but not with the conceptual double bind that Derrida invokes. The double bind that Derrida reads into Mauss' text derives from another concern that his own text – *Donner le temps* – puts forward on the pages where he imputes a double bind to Mauss' conception of the gift. It is certainly not warranted by Mauss' text.

Why is Derrida concerned with a double bind here? The double bind that he discerns in the act of giving concerns the demand of complete anonymity with which the act of giving must comply for the gift to be a true gift, and not just a source of obligation. The giving of the gift must absolutely not reveal the identity of the giver or donor. The moment that the giver of the gift becomes recognisable, the receiver of the gift will not only be burdened by this recognition of the giver; the receiver of the gift will through this recognition also attain a reductive grasp or hold on the donor that reduces him or her to a specific or specifiable act of giving. The same applies to the valuability of the gift given. The gift must remain *invaluable.* The gift will of course always come across as 'valuable' in the sense of having 'some' or 'considerable' value. In another sense, however, it is also *invaluable* (as one often says with regard to very precious gifts). The value of the gift must remain completely unrecognisable and unknown. The moment that X is recognised as the donor of a gift with the value Y, both the giver and the act of giving become associated with a gift-transaction with a specified or specifiable exchange value. This association is inevitably reductive. The giver and the act of giving get reduced to the transaction, and to the value given, transferred or exchanged. If all of this is to be avoided, the donor and the value donated must never become known, and this means that the gift can never be known as a gift without destroying it.[11]

Elements of Derrida's concern with the anonymity and unfathomability of the gift are also evident in Mauss' essay on the gift. As we saw above, Mauss' text certainly makes it clear enough that the significance of the gift is not in the first place related to its material value, but to the unmeasurable and invaluable sentiments of friendship and sociality that it solicits. The sentiments of generosity and benevolence precipitated by the gift surely also blur the specific identity of the donor in Mauss' text. We saw above how Mauss describes the act of giving in terms of a holistic event of general generosity that involves gods, nature, animals and deceased ancestors. However, it is not from Mauss that Derrida takes his adamant concern with an anonymous and unfathomable event of giving that cannot be reflected in the value of the gifts exchanged between humans. He takes it from Martin Heidegger's notion of an *ontological difference* or *differentiation* through which *Being* (*das Sein*) allows for the emergence of *beings* (*Seienden*), not by showing itself in *beings*, but, on the contrary, through withdrawing from them. Heidegger conceived of this ontological differentiation through which *Being* allows for the existence of *beings*, by withdrawing from them, as an event of giving; an event of anonymous or impersonal giving – *es gibt* – through which *Being* gives *beings*. The insistence that *Being* does not show itself in, but withdraws from, the beings that it gives was crucial for Heidegger's endeavour to resist the metaphysical inclination to think of *Being* as another *being*, notably *a supreme being* such as God, the essential characteristic of which was its enduring and infallible *presence*.[12]

It is important to note that Heidegger himself at times describes the ontological event through which *Being* gives *beings* in terms of a holistic exchange between the four elements of the *fourfold* (*das Geviert*) – heaven and earth and mortal humans and immortal gods (Heidegger 1954, pp. 157–75). He does so in a way that is quite reminiscent of the way Mauss describes the coming together of gods, humans, nature, animals and ancestors in the exchange of gifts between humans. The poetic quality of this rehabilitation of the discernibility of *Being* in *beings* in notions such as the *fourfold* may well be debatable, but it could at least be said to be largely inoffensive as far as modern liberal democratic political and moral sensibilities are concerned. One may want to add that it is as inoffensive as it is irrelevant to these sensibilities. The offence in Heidegger's thought to modern liberal democratic sensibilities commences where his rehabilitation of the discernibility of *Being* in *beings* – through which he evidently retreated from or betrayed his own concern with an ontological withdrawal of *Being* from *beings* – begins to equate the history of *Being* with the historical destiny of the German people. It is well known today into what depths of deranged despair and personal dishonour

11 See Derrida 1991, pp. 26–7.
12 See Derrida 1991, pp. 32–8.

(notably with regard to Husserl) this equation ultimately lured him, and one need not go into this history again here.[13] Suffice it to restrict our attention to Heidegger to the very thought that he betrayed, the thought of an act or event of giving that does not enter, but withdraws from, the identifiable gifts that emerge from this act or event.

Derrida's invocation of a double bind that renders the gift impossible very clearly derives from Heidegger's contemplation of *Being that gives beings by withdrawing from them*. The gift cannot become present in the gift, argues Derrida. It cannot become a *present* or *presence* without forfeiting that what is absolutely crucial to it – namely, the irreducible and inexhaustible freedom to give; a freedom to give that necessarily includes the freedom *not to give*, the freedom to withhold the gift. And this is where Mauss' essay on the gift runs into difficulty, according to Derrida, for it turns all too evidently on the assumption that gifts previously given – concrete, material and materialised gifts – not only oblige future giving, but also seem to guarantee it. It is with regard to exactly this observation that we should note the following telling passage in Mauss' essay: 'We should come out of ourselves and regard the duty of giving as a liberty, for in it lies no risk. A fine Maori proverb runs: *Ko maru kai atu, Ko maru kai mai, Ka ngohe ngohe*: "Give as much as you receive and all is for the best."' (Mauss 2011, p. 69)

There is vast scope for slippages of meaning between the different languages – Maori, English, French – in play here. Derrida observes in his text on Mauss how the latter's rather flagrant disregard for the singularity of idiom creates the impression that the different cultural practices of gift exchanges the essay describes point to a single referent, a universal 'truth' of giving and receiving to which all cultures and societies subscribe.[14] We cannot investigate the possible slippage of meaning between the Maori text that Mauss cites and the translation of it that he provides. But it is important at least to note here another slippage of meaning that occurs between the English translation and the original French text of Mauss' essay. The French text does not simply assert the absence of risk in the act of giving, as the English translation does. It invokes the absence of the *risk to err – on ne risque pas de se tromper* (Mauss 2007, p. 229).

The slippage of meaning at issue here may seem small, but it raises a number of key concerns that are highly relevant for the search for a duty that is independent of a right on which we have embarked. It is therefore important to tease out the difference between the meaning of the French text and English translation here. The first observation is this: One does not risk *erring* in the face of risk, just like one cannot endeavour to be 'right' or take the 'right decision' in the face of risk. The essence of *risk* is the absence of information on the basis of which a decision can be 'correct' or 'incorrect'. This is why it does not make sense to suggest

13 The latest revelations regarding this increasingly unpalatable saga came with the publication of Heidegger's *Schwarze Hefte* and the letters to his brother. See Heidegger 2014; Homolka & Heidegger 2016. For an incisive discussion of this publication, see Roger 2014. For discussions of the letters, see Soboczynski & Cammann 2016; Schulte 2017.

14 See Derrida 1991, p. 41.

someone took the 'right' or 'wrong' decision in the face of risk. One can at best invoke here a fortunate or unfortunate decision. Whether a decision in the face of risk turns out felicitous, or not, is a matter of chance or luck. To invoke the 'rightness' of the decision under these circumstances is to make a mockery of the meaning of 'right' and 'rightness'.

Taking a risk is the most concrete experience of what one may want to call, with Derrida, an encounter with *the undecidable*. Derrida's reasoning in this regard is well known. It is the undecidable and only the undecidable that requires a decision, and a real decision is only possible in the face of the undecidable. A decision that is informed with regard to all crucial elements of what stands to be deliberated is not a decision but the technical application of knowledge and 'know how'.[15] The decision is the *critical* and cutting moment in a response to the unknown. Seen from the perspective of this strict conception of the words 'risk' and 'decision', one must conclude that the 'risk of making a mistake' (*risque de se tromper*) is the one thing that cannot be at issue in the face of real risk. Conversely, one can only 'risk' making a mistake when one faces no real risk. The risk invoked in the phrase 'risk making a mistake' should therefore also be seen for what it is. It cannot concern a real risk. The word 'risk' is employed incorrectly or inaccurately in this phrase to simply denote a mere 'possibility of making a mistake'.

One must conclude in view of these reflections that a significant instability of meaning becomes conspicuous when one compares the French text and English translation of Mauss' essay on the gift. When there is no risk (as the English text suggests), there is a real possibility of error (contrary to what the French text suggests). When there is no possibility of error (as the French text suggests), it must be because there is a real risk that cancels out the possibility or error (contrary to what the English text suggests).

Now, there are two ways out of this conundrum. The first is to simply attribute this instability of meaning to a mere instance of inaccurate translation that can easily be avoided by simply dismissing the translation and sticking to the French text. But this does not really help, for a closer look shows that the instability pointed out here haunts the French text without comparing it to the translation. On the one hand, Mauss invokes the absence of the risk of error: *on ne risque pas de se tromper*. On the other hand, however, his translation of the Maori text that he cites also commits him to an assertion of the absence of risk *as such*, to which the English translation of his text seems to commit him. He translates the Maori text as saying: *tout sera très bien* – everything will be very well. This '*tout sera très bien*' certainly amounts to an unequivocal assertion of the absence of risk; hence the need to conclude that the same instability of meaning that emerges from a comparison of the French and English texts also emerges from a close reading of the French text on its own.

The second way out of the conundrum is to dismiss the artful textualism deployed here for the sake of a common-sense and straightforward hermeneutic assessment of what Mauss evidently wants to say. If we do this, we may well want

15 See, for instance, Derrida 1994, pp. 52–7.

to conclude that Mauss is obviously asserting the absence of risk that the English translation puts forward and which comes to the fore in his own translation of the Maori citation. Should we indeed decide to follow this common-sense hermeneutic route, however, we ultimately run into bigger trouble, for Mauss expressly attributes the eventual shift in Semitic, Greek and Roman societies, away from economies of the gift to economies of contract, to the wish or need to avoid and terminate the uncertainty that haunted the gift economies. Two passages are especially significant in this regard. In the first Mauss refers to the Semitic, Greek and Roman distinctions between legal obligation (*l'obligation et la prestation non gratuit*), on the one hand, and the gift (*le don*), on the other, and then asks: But is this distinction not a rather recent development in the legal systems of the great civilisations (*[mais] ces distinctions ne sont-elles pas assez récentes dans les droits des grandes civilisations*)? Did they not pass through an earlier phase during which they did not have this cold calculating mentality (*[n'ont- elles] pas passé par une phase antérieure, où elles n'avaient pas cette mentalité froide et calculatrice*)? (ibid., p. 180)

By posing these questions, Mauss suggests clearly that Semitic, Greek and Roman civilisations only eventually attained a cold calculating mentality that demanded a clear distinction between enforceable legal obligations, on the one hand, and gift exchanges, on the other. Before developing this calculating mentality, these civilisations tolerated a degree of incalculability in their social exchanges that rendered a clear distinction between strictly legal relations and broader social or moral relations redundant. In other words, Mauss is clearly suggesting that the earlier economies of these societies tolerated levels of incalculability and chance that their later economies were no longer prepared to tolerate.

A second passage, a few pages further on in the essay, confirms this suggestion beyond any doubt. Here Mauss again writes how the Greeks and the Romans, perhaps following the Northern and Western Semites, separated the contract of sale from that of the gift, thus bringing about a veritable and venerable revolution (*une veritable, grande et vénérable révolution*) that broke with an outdated morality and an economy of the gift that was too exposed to chance, too wasteful and too sumptuous – *trop chanceuse, trop dispendieuse et trop somptuaire* (ibid., p. 195). It would surely not have been surprising if the English translation had resorted to the words 'too risky' to convey the French 'trop chanceuse', but it simply refers, instead, to a 'dangerous gift economy' (Mauss 2011, p. 52). We need not delve deeper into these specificities of the French text and its English translation. Suffice it to just observe, for now, that a conclusion that Mauss understood the gift economy as a risk-free contractual economy no longer seems as warranted as it may seem when Mauss' later citation of the Maori proverb, discussed above, is considered in isolation from the rest of the text. The text is far from unambiguous, but there is clearly enough evidence that it may well be less at odds with Derrida's conception of the gift than Derrida appears willing to concede.

The moment of a risk-taking decision in the midst of unfathomable circumstances is the defining element of the ethics of the gift and of hospitality that

Derrida develops in his late texts. Hospitality, he contends, is nothing but an exposure to risk – *l'hospitalité ... ne peut ni ne doit être autre chose que l'exposition au risque* (Derrida 1999, p. 137). This is of course an overstatement and therefore misstatement of the point at issue. An instance of risk taking is not as such a gift or an instance of hospitality. An act of giving and/or hospitality concerns more than just taking a risk. But taking a risk is certainly an irreducible part of giving and giving hospitality, according to Derrida. Why is this so important to him, and why is this important for our pursuit of the matter of the 'priority of obligation ahead of right'?

Risk is the pointed effect of the incalculability that conditions or preconditions the ethics of giving. It is the very sting of the incalculable. And it is the very ordeal of any duty that may come one's way *before* the security networks of rights/duties correlatives restore the comforts and consolations of calculability. It seems fair to suggest that it is this coming of duty, this arrival of duty ahead of any correlative rights claims, *this very event of duty*, that we are beckoned to consider in the call to contemplate the 'priority of obligation ahead of right'. And perhaps this arrival of duty ahead of rights does come to us like a wave, to use Waldron's image; a veritable ocean wave that puts our footholds and grips on everything that sustains us fundamentally at risk. In the face of this arrival, this approaching wave of duty, recourse to the exact scope and limits of a corresponding right for purposes of assessing and limiting one's obligation is still an option, but no longer a dutiful option. Even less so, of course, is the recourse to an absence of right – a non-right – that warrants a privileged escape from duty. The Hohfeldian discourse evidently does not apply here, for the advent of duty that we are contemplating precedes the very terms of this discourse. The Hohfeldian discourse, complete with measurability and calculability as it is, always settles in the wake of an initial arrival of an incalculable obligation, but in none of its settlements does it ever comprise a term or concept that can address the initial arrival of obligation that the ethics of the gift and hospitality has in mind. The arrival of duty contemplated in this radical ethics of hospitality always *suspends* whatever term or terms that settled legal discourses have to offer. The suspension at stake here is indeed a veritable phenomenological reduction or *epokhē*; a veritable suspension of the paradigms of understanding and knowledge that render the world measurable and manageable; a veritable suspension of natural consciousness, as Edmund Husserl might have put it.[16]

What is it that is given when something is given through such a voluntary assumption of risk? Not the material value that might be given or transferred, for that element of the gift is exactly that which forthwith attains the status of a reciprocal contractual performance. What is essentially given by voluntarily taking the risk whether one's act of giving will be reciprocated or not, is *time*, time that releases and leaves the other free to reciprocate or not reciprocate. In the final analysis, the only thing that can be given, says Derrida, is *time – [ce] qu'il y a à donner, uniquement, s'appelerait le temps* (Derrida 1991, p. 45).

16 See for instance Husserl 1992, pp. 6, 16.

The gift of time, considered in terms of an existential suspension of the secure terms of trade and transaction on which natural consciousness depends and relies for the sake of sustaining an optimally risk-free existence, opens up a *categorical divide*. It opens up a categorical difference between the secured world in which natural consciousness makes itself at home, on the one hand, and the intimation of a completely different existence that is *no longer* and *not yet* classifiable as a 'world', on the other. This different reality dawns upon consciousness whenever it is called to respond to an ethical demand that does not fit into the secured world that has become its home, the secured world on which it routinely relies as a matter of 'natural' course. The gift of time that allows the other to take his or her time suspends the regular expectations of any consciousness that has made itself at home somewhere. It exposes consciousness to a completely different reality that it cannot anticipate and measure in advance, a different reality that suspends or renders inapplicable all its available categories of anticipation, classification and measurement. Hence the invocation here of a *categorical divide*, and of '*an opening up*' of a categorical divide. It is but a short step from this *categorical divide* that opens up with the gift of time, that Derrida contemplates, to Kant's *categorical imperative*. This step must nevertheless be thought through carefully, and this is what the next section of this essay will endeavour to do.

IV. The categorical divide and the categorical imperative

The gift of time that releases and leaves the other free to reciprocate or not. This is how one might, today, articulate the arrival of a duty that is not accompanied by a sense of entitlement. Of concern, here, is the suggestion that one comes to sense what is necessary to do to let things continue as well as they might in the face of uncertainty, *before* responding to a sense of anyone's entitlement. This is also how one might rearticulate, today, the third maxim through which Kant explained the categorical imperative: Always treat every person also as an end, never as a mere means to an end – *zugleich als Zweck, niemals bloss als Mittel* (Kant 1956a, p. 61). We shall turn to Kant's categorical imperative presently. Before we do so, however, let us first take a closer look at the *categorical divide* that opens up in the gift of time that Derrida contemplates. An incisive regard for the *categorical divide* that Derrida contemplates is indeed crucial for an adequate understanding of the radical ethics that Kant envisaged with his *categorical imperative*. One of the achievements of Derrida's ethics of the gift concerns the unique way in which it invites one to reread Kant.

There simply are no terms for the ethical 'transaction' that is at stake for Derrida. One cannot come to terms with it. The only thing that is demanded here is to give, and to give unconditionally and without reserve. It is crucially important to understand the *categorical divide* between this demand to give and any obligation-limiting legal or moral discourse with which one may endeavour to render the demands of an obligation reasonable, and compliance with them 'reasonably possible'. The categorical divide is such that one may venture to call it, for a moment, an *ontological divide*. It indeed shares key features with the ontological differentiation between *Being* and *beings* that Heidegger contemplated. The wave of duty that we are contemplating can therefore, provisionally, be considered a wave of *Being* in response to which no reference to specific *beings* – or any specific circumscription of relations between them (that is, between *Being and beings*) offer adequate terms of settlement. The ontological divide that marks the withdrawal of *Being* from *beings* is the scene of an inexhaustible unsettlement. However, the categorical divide that is at stake in the arrival of duty that we are contemplating, is ultimately *not* an ontological divide. The scene of unsettlement that we are endeavouring to witness does *not* concern *Being's* release of *beings*. At stake, here, is *not* the first gift, *Being's* gift to *beings*. Heidegger's '*es gibt*' is *not* what we are contemplating. From the perspective of the arrival of duty that concerns us here, all these ontological terms are drawn from the vocabulary of an old metaphysics that Heidegger sought to renew, but in which he ultimately remained squarely stuck. This language is exhausted today. Its terms are spent. They no longer speak, in any case not to a secular, urban, liberal democratic sensibility. And it is this sensibility that we must take as the inevitable point of departure for thinking the unsettling arrival of duty 'ahead of a right' that we are contemplating. Secular, urban and, in principle (if not in reality), *liberal democratic* environments have become the home from the front porch of which the unsettling gift of time must be contemplated today. Heidegger's 'village-life' or 'pastoral' renewal of the old metaphysics of *Being* stands no chance of disrupting this world, no chance of uprooting its categories of measurement and orientation.

In contrast to the metaphysical language that pivots on the way specified *beings* emanate from unspecifiable *Being* (a language that can easily be traced to the Neo-Platonists), Kant's language of moral obligation offers a much more promising framework for thinking the arrival of duty 'ahead of right'. It was Kant's groundbreaking insight that moral responsibility is fundamentally conditioned by freedom, the freedom to assume responsibility. His practical philosophy was an epochal and definitively post-Aristotelian statement of the insight that moral obligation does not derive from nature, *Being* or any kind of ontological insight, but from the fundamental freedom to assume responsibility. It reiterated Hume's famous protest against the *naturalistic fallacy*, the idea that one can derive 'ought' from 'is' (Hume 1888, pp. 469–70). The assumption of responsibility is the sign of freedom from nature, from physical reality, from any conception of 'is', argued Kant.[17] However, Kant's language has in many respects also fallen into the staleness of an unforgiving and unimaginative moralism. It can be argued to have done so for reasons that are traceable to a fundamental incoherence in his own conception of moral obligation and practical reason (*praktische Vernunft*). On the one hand, Kant is adamant that the moral law concerns an experience of a universal imperative – you ought/*du sollst* – that cannot be fulfilled in any specified way. Any endeavour to give concrete effect to the imperative, asserted Kant, must end up contaminating the strict universality demanded by the moral law with the inevitable particularity of action. Any

17 See Kant 1956a, pp. 81–102; 1956b, p. 140.

concrete attempt to comply with and *realise* the moral law must end up contaminating the universality of the response it demands with the particularity of specific concerns. In this respect, Kant's practical philosophy also contemplates an absolute or *categorical divide* – a divide that we shall begin to call an *ethical divide* below – between the demand of the moral imperative, on the one hand, and any concrete response to it, on the other. Hence also Kant's completely consistent insistence on a strict distinction between and separation of legality (*Legalität*) and morality (*Moralität*) (Kant 1956c, p. 318).

The law, claimed Kant, is not concerned with the enforcement or promotion of moral perfection, but with the reconciliation of the external liberty of one legal subject with that of another under a general system of rules (ibid., p. 337). With this notion of the reconciliation of the external liberty of individuals, Kant evidently already contemplated the correlativity of legal relations that Hohfeld later analysed more exhaustively. For Kant, this correlativity of legal relations bore no comprehensible or knowable link to the strict and absolute demand of the moral imperative. However, Kant remained burdened by the sense that the impossibility of giving any concrete effect to the moral imperative ultimately renders the imperative meaningless; hence his postulation of the transcendental ideas of practical reason, the *summum bonum* and the *eternal life of the soul*, with recourse to which moral effort could be considered meaningful, notwithstanding its apparent futility in finite time and space. The *summum bonum* concerned the idea of an ultimate harmony between morality and nature. The idea of the *summum bonum*, contended Kant, renders thinkable the possibility of a perfectly moral existence that would also be a perfectly happy and fulfilled existence, considering that moral duty (*Pflicht*) would no longer be at odds with natural inclination (*Neigung*), but completely reconciled with it. According to him, the idea of the eternal life of the soul rendered thinkable a process of infinite moral progress that would culminate in the moral perfection and holiness (*Heiligkeit*) required to render the *summum bonum*, the reconciliation of duty and inclination, or nature and morality, possible.[18]

Hegel performed an acute analysis of these principles of Kant's moral philosophy in ten pages of the *Phänomenologie des Geistes* which he introduced under the heading *Verstellung* (dissemblance). In this analysis, he showed that Kant's notion of the *summum bonum* cannot constitute the perfection or fulfilment of the moral imperative that he contemplates, considering that the very possibility of this moral imperative turns on the impossibility of any compliance with it. The moral imperative can only be experienced as a moral *imperative* – a *demand* or *command* – as long as it remains in tension or at odds with a reality that does not comply with it. Kant's ideas of the perfection of the soul and of the *summum bonum* do not render morality possible, argued Hegel; they do exactly the opposite. They render morality impossible, given that he – Kant – himself defined morality in terms of an irreducible tension between moral duty and natural inclination (Hegel 1970, pp. 453–64). Had Kant remained consistently true to this understanding of moral obligation, he may well have been less inclined to allow

18 See Kant 1956b, pp. 238–66.

his own particular moral sentiments to lead him to facile assessments of the 'universal' moral obligations of others, as he did in the well-documented case of his advice to Maria von Herbert. Herbert had written to Kant about how her friend lost his feelings for her after she had disclosed to him a previous friendship that she had been concealing from him for too long. She had known all along that she should tell her friend about the previous friend, but struggled to do so for fear of the painful consequences to which the disclosure could lead. In his response, Kant boldly advised Herbert that all dishonesty constitutes a moral failure and justified the waning of her friend's affection for her because of her 'too late' disclosure of her previous friendship.[19]

Rigorous consistency with his own insight into the unbridgeable gap between moral duty and any finite attempt to comply with it would have exacted the insight that compliance with the categorical imperative was simply not possible under the finite circumstances that Herbert had described to Kant. It is noteworthy that Herbert's second letter to Kant (1793) already grasped well the critique of Kant's moral theory that Hegel articulated in the *Phänomenologie* (1807). She already realised well that moral duty only has significance when it competes with 'the attractiveness of sin'.[20] What she failed to realise, or realised much too late, however, is the way in which this significance of moral obligation arrives *in* and *as* moral consciousness long before the materialisation of any right of anyone else to some or other specified moral response.[21] It is this arrival of the significance of moral obligation that concerns us here, and the time has come to ask why this arrival of moral significance, prior to any identification of a right, can still be called an obligation or duty. We turn to this question in the next section of this essay. Before we do so, however, it is important that we conclude this section with a careful reflection on the significance of the third maxim through which Kant explained the categorical imperative. As already stated above, the third maxim concerns the imperative to always treat every person and yourself also as an end, never as a mere means to an end – *zugleich als Zweck, niemals bloss als Mittel* (Kant 1956a, p. 61). Had Kant contemplated the full complexity of this maxim in his advice to Herbert, he may well have responded differently to her moral predicament.

Of the three explanatory maxims of the categorical imperative that Kant offered, the third one is the least likely to fall back into Hume's naturalistic fallacy, which is

19 For the German texts of these letters, see Kant 1791, 1792, 1793. For English translations of these letters, see Langton 1994.

20 The expression 'attractiveness of sin' is taken from the English translation of the letter cited by Langton. It is a somewhat too strong rendition of the German which more literally translated only invokes a 'gereizte Sinnlichkeit' (aroused sensuality) – 'die Aufgaben der Morallität [erhaltet] ihr Ansehen … nur durch eine gereizte Sinnlichkeit'.

21 Had she done this, she may well have been able to take her friend's particular morality with a pinch of salt. The mistake Kant made here is closely related to the 'naturalistic fallacy' against which Hume argues, as I explain further in the text above, and again towards the end of this section. However, in the last part of his letter, Kant himself appears to recognise the limited morality of Herbert's friend.

ultimately the fallacy that the conduct demanded by the categorical imperative can be identified in finite and specific terms. The other two maxims through which Kant explained the categorical imperative – act in such a way that you can make the maxim of your act a universal law (*ein allgemeines Gesetz*) or a universal law of nature (*ein allgemeines Naturgesetz*) (Kant 1956b, p. 51) – both create or risk creating the impression that moral conflict can be resolved with recourse to a universal and unambiguous rule of conduct that will respect every individual's autonomy and dignity in the same way. It may well have been this fallacious conception of the moral law that prompted Kant's confident identification of moral failure in the case of Maria von Herbert. He evidently failed to realise that her dilemma could not be resolved with recourse to a single 'correct' and universal rule of conduct without either reducing her to an instrument of her friend's finite moral projections, or him to hers. Hegel grasped this well in his critique of Kant's moral philosophy. When it comes to the difficult situation that calls for a moral decision, moral consciousness always faces several moral demands, not one, and can therefore not give effect to *the* moral law – *[der] Begriff des Handelns [schliesst] eine manigfaltige Wirklichkeit und daher eine mannigfaltige moralische Beziehung in sich* (Hegel 1970, p. 448).

Kant's third maxim already begins to reflect this insight to some extent. It makes clear that the categorical imperative requires that *neither* the self *nor* the other be reduced to the one's or the other's moral projections. The humanity (*Menschheit*) of both one's own and of any other person (*sowohl in deiner Person, als in der Person eines jeden andern*) should be considered an end and not just a means to an end (Kant 1956a, p. 61). When this 'double kingdom of ends' appears impossible to realise under finite circumstances – as it always does in the case of deep moral conflict – the categorical imperative had best be articulated in terms of the freely assumed obligation to give one another time to reciprocate or not to reciprocate, and to do what is required to let things continue as well as they might *for everyone* involved. What comes out of this assumption of duty and what one might gain or lose from it are secondary questions. The relation between the moral act and whatever it achieves must simply be severed, *categorically* severed. But let us ask, now, why this *freely assumed* obligation can still be called an obligation.

V. Why is the duty to give a duty?

It is Emmanuel Levinas who first recognised that Heidegger's ontological language is still full of the language of fullness; full of the language of plenitude that characterised Western metaphysics from its beginning. Heidegger may have gone further than any metaphysician before him to de-substantialise the presupposition of full presence on which Western metaphysics turns. However, his retention of the notion of '*es gibt*' (*it gives*) as the definitional feature of his de-substantialised conception of *Being* is for Levinas the tell-tale sign of a thinking that is at best rearticulating the metaphysics of plenitude. Heidegger may have stepped back from the conception of fullness as full presence, but not from the conception of fullness itself, contends Levinas. The replacement of the conception of Being in terms of presence with a conception of Being in terms of an inexhaustible capacity to give, remains, according to Levinas, a metaphysics of generosity that is not warranted by our experience of existence. The historical record of what happened in Europe between 1933 and 1945, he writes, attests to no such generosity – *[aucune] générosité, que contiendrait, paraît-il, le terme allemand de es gibt correspondant à l'il y a ne s'y manifestait entre 1933 et 1945.* It attests, to the contrary, to a horrible neutrality of existence that only attains to meaning with the surge of *beings* – *[la] lumière et le sens ne naissent qu'avec le surgissement et la position d'existants dans cette horrible neutralité de l'il y a* (Levinas 1976, p. 435).

It is in response to this false metaphysics of generosity – false in the sense of not corresponding to one's most fundamental experience of reality – that Levinas commenced to articulate a course of thinking that turned the *ontological divide* into an *ethical divide*. For this thinking, the first encounter with existence does not entail the arrival of a gift that requires acceptance. It concerns the arrival of an obligation to respond to a void or lack, an obligation to respond that is an obligation to give – to give in whatever way that may alleviate the burden of the void or lack that determines the first experience of existence. *Being* is a dead empty lack of specification or neutrality, contends Levinas. It only attains to fullness or positivity with the arrival of an obligation in an encounter with another person; an encounter that Levinas famously describes in terms of the ethical demand that the face of the other makes upon the self (Levinas 2006, pp. 239–41). In other words, according to Levinas, the surge of *beings* from the horrible neutrality of *Being* – *le surgissement d'existants dans cette horrible neutralité de l'il y a* – takes place in an encounter with the other, and, more specifically, an encounter with the face of the other.

It is important to note, however, that the arrival of obligation in an encounter with another human being remains a primordial divide. It is no less primordial than Heidegger's ontological divide. On the contrary, it may well be said to be more primordial. The ethical divide may well be said – perhaps moving somewhat away from Levinas – to come first. It may be considered 'older' than the ontological divide. From this arrival of obligation results the fundamental parameters of the world or worlds we live in, the parameters of all *Being* and *beings*. The hills themselves only arrive, one might say, with the obligation that arrives when a stranger descends from the hills to come and knock on someone's door. Considered in this way, existence comes to us, not as wealth that commands the capacity to accept and receive. It comes to us as a need that demands a response. It does not offer, but demands a gift. And if it is a gift that is demanded here, and not some calculable contractual repayment, it is because the ethical divide tolerates no currency converter. The need that comes, the need that arrives like a wave from nowhere, tolerates none of the familiar modes of quantification that are employed on this side of the divide. That is why it demands a blank cheque, so to speak. Since no price or value is fixable here, the performance demanded inevitably takes the 'form' of a limitless gift. This is also why it is not contradictory to talk about an *obligation* or a *duty* to give freely – *a free obligation* or *free duty* – when the ethical divide is at stake. The ethical divide opens up the obligation to give, but it neither compels the response nor fixes its terms. The relation between the obligation to give and the freedom to give certainly remains irreducibly non-adequate and invariably inadequate, but it is not in the least incoherent, not in the least contradictory.

In his book *Le différend*, Jean-François Lyotard resorts to the expression '*différend*' (dispute) to name the ethical divide. The book *Le différend* is, on the one hand, a meticulous Wittgensteinian/Levinasian/Kantian study of language as an ethical response to an event. Lyotard understands the 'event' in terms of an arrival of the sense that existing language – the totality of existing phrases, sentences or idioms – is in need of an additional phrase or idiom for purposes of responding to '*what*' is happening: *dans le différend, quelque chose* '*demande*' *à être mis en phrase* (Lyotard 1983: 30). The 'what' of the '*what is happening*' cannot be named in the sense of stating '*what* is the case'. The conventions of language certainly limit sayability, as Wittgenstein instructs us. One cannot just say anything in response to the event. But language never restricts sayability sufficiently to exclude disputation – *le différend* – regarding the appropriate response to *what is happening* (Lyotard 1983, pp. 56–92). Under these circumstances – under circumstances of the sense of need that something must be said that has not been said before – the proposal of a new phrase or idiom that might ensue can never claim to name the 'what' of 'what is happening'. It cannot provide the 'what' with a referent. It can only testify to the sense 'that something is happening'. The new phrase can testify to *the case* that something (*quod*) is happening, but it cannot refer to that which (*quid*) is happening, explains Lyotard: *Le cas … serait qu'il arrive quelque chose, quod, plutôt que ce qui arrive*, quid … *le cas n'est pas ce qui est le cas. Le cas est: Il y a, Il arrive* (Lyotard 1983, pp. 120–1).

The ethical divide concerns the impossibility of a phrase that would allow for a passage from the *quod* to the *quid* of the event. The event demands a response. It demands that a response be *given* and that a new phrase be found. The new phrase will need to be selected, however, from a range of possibilities offered by the conventions of language, none among which can transcend the conventionality that determines it. No new phrase can therefore come to address the *quod* of the event on its own terms, so as to determine its *quid*. No phrase can claim the capacity to *refer* to the event. No phrase can specify its *quid or quiddity*. A certain testimony is possible here, but not one that *names* the event in the sense of saying what it is. The relation between the event and the phrase that testifies to it remains irreducibly *non-adequate*. The phrase is doomed to search for appropriateness under irreducible conditions of *non-adequacy*. Phrasing is thus never a matter of equation, but always a matter of *non-equation* and *non-adequation*.

This irreducible *non-adequation* between the event and any response to it also marks the crucial divide between the event of suffering a wrong (*tort*), on the one hand, and the damage (*dommage*) that might be claimed or awarded to compensate for the wrong suffered, on the other (ibid., pp. 18–19). This is why the duty to respond to a *wrong* – in contrast to the Hohfeldian duty to *pay* compensation to someone with a correlative right to be paid compensation – remains irreducibly linked to a duty to *give.* The duty to respond to a wrong – beyond compensation of damages – is a duty *to give* and not *to pay.* This is so because no terms of payment – and no conditions of equation or adequation that might warrant such terms – exist. The *sense of a duty* to respond to a *wrong* explodes the conventional correlativity of rights and duties that warrants specified payments and repayments.

In other words, the arrival of a sense of duty to respond to a wrong is conditioned and accompanied by a sense of irreducible non-adequacy that renders invocations of payment and repayment fundamentally inappropriate. On the other hand, the possibility of any conscious act of giving – be it to a friend, a loved one or a stranger – that is not occasioned by a sense of a wrong committed, also remains conditioned by a sense of irreducible non-adequacy (that may or may also not be a sense of inadequacy). One does not pay or repay a loved one for his or her love or a friend for friendship. One does not pay a stranger whom one perceives to be in need. No one ever comes close to a sense of what must be 'paid' under these circumstances. One simply gives, and invariably remains caught up in an inner disputation – *différend* – regarding the 'appropriateness' of a palpably non-adequate gift.

Can one still talk about a *duty* to give in these cases, a *duty* to give to a loved one or friend, or to the stranger in need? Must one talk this way? Perhaps the sense that a stranger is in need is no different from the duty that arrives from a sense that a wrong has been done. Perhaps here, too, one rather responds to a wrong, that is, to the sense that that the stranger should not have been in need in the way he or she is. But in all three these cases of giving – to the loved one, the friend, the stranger – the urge to give can hardly be imagined as unaccompanied by any sense of a *demand of appropriateness* in the face of an absolute absence of criteria of appropriateness. Perhaps people do sometimes bestow gifts unthinkingly and frivolously, without considering themselves faced with the demand of an immeasurable 'appropriateness'. Perhaps this kind of gift expresses a certain sovereignty of giving that demands further reflection, as Bataille and Derrida suggest. The focused magnanimity of the serious gift, however, invariably responds to a sense of a demand that comes to one; a demand that reaches the shore of one's consciousness like a wave of existence; a demand that brings with it an undefined sense of obligation, a sense of an ungrounded need or desire to respond appropriately.

Standard idioms and conventions of phrasing may well militate against endowing the mere sense of a need to respond appropriately – in absence of any demand to pay, repay or compensate – with the significance of an obligation. Levinas nevertheless insists that every encounter with the face of another person signals the unfathomable obligation to respond to an immeasurable 'appropriateness' that has nothing to do with any right that that person may or may not have.[22] Perhaps we have finally arrived here at a thought that appears to answer to the call to contemplate an obligation that precedes all considerations

22 See Levinas 1971, pp. 203–35.

of rights and entitlements. The question is, however, whether the pursuit of this thought has not taken us much too far away from the concrete context of political and legal responsibility that may be considered an essential ingredient of this call. Does Levinas' insistence on the obligation that stems from the encounter with the face of the other bear any concrete significance for *practical* philosophy, or must it always remain something foreign to all notions of the practical and the doable? Can one imagine it to have any meaningful bearing on concrete legal reasoning? Or does the categorical or ethical divide that conditions this unconditional obligation prevent one from doing so? These are the questions that the final section of this chapter will address.

VI. Post-Hohfeldian *legal* duties to give freely?

The work of Levinas – and of Lyotard – alerts one to the sign of an infinite obligation that has always and will always have preceded and exceeded all past and future 'correct' settlements of correlative rights and duties. This sign – the sign that signals infinite obligation before signalling existence, or signals existence as infinite obligation – is the signal that occasions all instances of standard juridical recourse to the correlativity of rights and duties. Once occasioned, however, this juridical discourse invariably, and forthwith, begins to ignore any intimation of 'the priority of duty ahead of right'. The signal of obligation precipitates the very need for juridical discourse. It is the very occasion for the juridical discourse that will forthwith begin to ignore it. The sign or signal of obligation is, in other words, the very occasion of something that is *designed* to silence or erase the sign or signal of obligation. The shelf-life of any design is indeed the period of time that it fends off and silences all signs that call for a new design. The better the design – the better the *de-sign* – the more effective the silencing of the sign. The better the law, the more unlikely the chances of escaping from its correlative constellations. It is the task of contemplating this unlikely escape from exceptionally well-designed law that Veitch considers in his chapter in this volume. He does so with an evident awareness that the hi-tech 'tax minimisation' laws that he has in his sights are not only silencing a call of duty that may come from beyond the boundaries of law. They are increasingly also hollowing out the last echoes of such a duty *within* the law. This awareness is perfectly coherent: The more rights/duties correlatives are no longer sensitive to the way in which a primordial sense of obligation allows one to make sense of existence as such, and calls one to do so, the more will all rights/duties correlatives that don't serve one's own direct interests come across as senseless burdens that had better be translated, as far as legal hi-tech would allow, into non-rights/liberties correlatives. *Voilà* the massive tax 'minimisation' practices with which Veitch engages. One cannot even invoke the pejorative term 'tax evasion' here, for the practices at issue would appear to enjoy the full blessing of exceptionally good law.

Hence, then, Veitch's call to look away from existing law and existing conceptions of rights and duties, at least for a moment; hence his call to *suspend* existing law and legal relations, as phenomenologists might instruct one to do, and to 'raise our eyes to the hills' in search of a primordial sense of duty that may come to us in advance of all existing legal rights. For the legal duties that sustain legal rights themselves ultimately evaporate when they are no longer oriented by sense of duty that we cannot measure; oriented by a sense of duty with regard to which due performance cannot be specified, a sense of duty to which one can only, and must, give oneself freely. This, then, seems to be the arduous path of thinking onto which Veitch beckons us: Away from a perfectly legal existence under which we increasingly consider ourselves *duty free*; and towards the rediscovery of the free assumption of duty – the *free duty* – that *orients* our existence in the most fundamental sense of the word conceivable.

Twentieth-century legal reasoning endeavoured to unshackle duty – to *free* it from the trappings of existing law – on a number of significant occasions, one of which was the 1932 House of Lords decision in *Donoghue v Stevenson* ([1932] UKHL 100). The essence of the *Donoghue* decision was the unshackling of a general duty of care – an *independent* duty to care – from contractual duties, on the one hand, and from the range of specific duties of care recognised in the writs of old English law, on the other.[23] This is how English law came to recognise the general legal duty for which several civil codes of Europe already provided at the time. The German civil code already invoked at the time, and still invokes today, notions of good morals – *guten Sitten* (*Bürgerliches Gesetzbuch 2002* (BGB), § 817). The French *Code Civil* invokes damage that results from unspecified negligence or unreasonable conduct – *dommage ... causé non seulement par son fait, mais encore par sa négligence ou par son imprudence* (*Code Civil 2017* (CC), art. 1383). French jurisprudence infers from this clause a common standard of social conduct – *une norme générale de conduit sociale* – that is not based on contractual obligations or any other written legal disposition – *les devoirs extra-contractuels qui ne sont explicités par aucune disposition écrite.* [24] The Dutch Civil Code refers to *ongeschreven recht* (unwritten law) in this regard (*Nieuwe Burgerlijk Wetboek 1992* (NBW), 6:162(2)). In the case of all three these codes, the clauses invoking good morals, common standards of conduct or unwritten law, serve as a basis on which any damage-causing event that can be classified as contrary to the good morals of society, can be sanctioned as a source of a legal duty to pay compensation.

The same principle was invoked in South Africa in 1975 in the case of *Minister van Polisie v Ewels* (1975) (3) SA 590 (A) for purposes of introducing into South African law a general legal duty, not only *not to cause* but also *to prevent* damage. The case was generally hailed by South African scholars of the law of civil delict as a significant breakthrough in South African judicial reasoning. *Ewels* was considered a milestone because it recognised an independent, free-standing, general legal duty to prevent harm. However, pre-*Ewels* conceptions of narrowly

23 For a discussion of the long history of the unshackling of a general duty of care in English law and its peculiar influence on South African law, see Van der Walt 2003.

24 See Viney & Jourdain 2006, p. 380.

circumscribed duties of care – drawn from old English law – persisted in the reasoning of the South African High Courts and Supreme Court of Appeal until the Constitutional Court took recourse to the horizontal effect of the South African Constitution of 1996 to put a stop to them in the case of *Carmichele v Minister of Safety and Security* (2001) (4) SA 938 (CC). Since then, the general legal duty to prevent harm appears to have been consistently recognised by South African courts.[25]

These case and legislative histories can certainly be considered narratives that tell the story of the *release* of a general legal duty to prevent harm in a number of jurisdictions of the world, and many similar histories very likely relate the development of similar narratives elsewhere. Do these narratives of release or liberation reflect a spreading recognition of a free legal duty *to give* – that is, of a legal duty to simply give oneself freely to the advent of an unfathomable sense of a *free duty*, discussed above, the *free duty* that orients one's existence in the most fundamental sense conceivable? An honest response to this question would certainly have to assess all legal systems and jurisdictions considered on and in their own terms. Both the UK and South African legal systems nevertheless suggest that the release of a general legal duty to prevent harm – as free as it might be from the specific considerations of law that used to shackle it to some or other legitimate expectation or right – does not yet constitute anything comparable to the fundamental *moral duty to give* that one may distil from the thought of Mauss, Kant, Levinas or Lyotard. Both these jurisdictions still shackle the duty to prevent harm to the condition of an acceptable *balance of interests* between the parties involved.[26]

Consider in this regard the 'text book' case with reference to which South African professors of the law of civil delict explain the general legal duty to prevent harm to their students: the case of someone who fails to save a drowning child from a river.[27] There is no legal relationship between the child and the person who fails to save him that determines a duty to act. No existing

25 See, for instance, *Minister of Safety and Security v Dirk van Duivenboden* (2002) (6) SA 431 SCA.

26 In the UK, the balancing of interests at stake here, takes place with reference to the 'foreseeability' question that the identification of a duty of care poses. See *Bolton v Stone* (1951) AC 850. In South Africa, the balancing takes place under the question of the wrongfulness of the act that caused the damage. See *Regal v African Super Slate* (1962) (3) SA 18 (A).

27 See Neethling, Potgieter & Visser 2005, p. 68. I refer here to the 5th edition of Neethling, Potgieter & Visser, *Law of Delict*, 2005, which is the only edition to which I had access at the time of writing and completing this chapter. Thanks are due to Johann Knobel for confirming that the 7th edition of 2015 still contains the example of the drowning child and passive onlooker on pages 77–8, and for refreshing my memory of the location of this passage that has become vague after many years of no longer teaching the South African law of delict. It is noteworthy that the *Ewels* case, which introduced the general legal duty to prevent harm into South African law, also invokes a 'duty to save' in the course of discussing the duty to prevent harm. See *Minister van Polisie v Ewels* (1975) (3) SA 590 (A) at 596–7.

right of the child imposes a correlative duty on the person who is witnessing the child's imminent drowning. The question is whether a legal duty can be construed or constructed under these circumstances. A prominent opinion among South African theorists of civil delict holds that this can indeed be done, by weighing up the interests of the child and the person who is witnessing the imminent drowning. This, then, is how the law or legal reasoning might construct a duty that precedes a right and indeed gives rise to one. Perhaps also not. Some theorists of the horizontal effect of fundamental rights may argue quite persuasively that the child's right to be saved does not derive from such a 'constructed' duty. They might argue, to the contrary, that the constructed duty itself derives from the horizontal effect of a constitutional or human right of the child.[28]

One may nevertheless respond that constitutional or human rights are not rights in the strict sense of the word. They are open phrases (empty signifiers) that allow for the finding of appropriate full phrases when the exigency to do so arises. Seeing things in this way allows one to recognise a certain proximity between Lyotard and Hohfeld. Hohfeld, we saw above, stresses the "legal realist" insight that an appropriate construction of correlatives is not determined in advance. It always emanates from an authoritative decision in the face of a moral or juridical exigency to find a proper constellation of correlativity. What Hohfeld is asserting here is not in the least at odds with Lyotard's invocation of 'something' that demands the finding of a phrase – *quelque chose [qui] 'demande' à être mis en phrase*. He too, ultimately exposes the finding of an appropriate constellation of correlatives to the arrival of an abyssal or groundless exigency that Lyotard denotes with the event or advent of the *différend.* [29] However, this comparison of Lyotard and Hohfeld demands that one distinguishes clearly between *the obligation to find a phrase* or a constellation of correlativity (a constellation is ultimately nothing but a phrase – that is, something said), on the one hand, and the *legal duty* that emerges from the found phrase or found constellation of correlativity, on the other. It demands that one distinguishes clearly between the *absolute and unconditional demand* that arrives with the exigency to find a phrase, on the one hand, and the *relative* and indeed *correlative duty* that emerges from the phrase found. This distinction pivots on the unbridgeable gap between the unmeasurable obligation to give that arrives with an unfathomable event, and the necessary calculability of all conceivable or recognisable legal duties that may follow in the wake of such an event.

Sustaining this distinction would be imperative for any Hohfeldian endeavour to remain faithful to Lyotard's thinking of the event as the ultimate resistance to the accountable and countable use of time – *l'ultime résistance que l'événement*

28 Judge Van Dijkhorst indeed argued this expressly in the South African case of *Jooste v Botha* (2000) (2) BCLR 187 (T) by contending that absence of a legal duty in private law due to the absence of a corresponding private law right requires the creation of a private law cause of action when a constitutional right demands that.

29 This, in any case, is what Singer is arguing when he emphasises the exercise of responsibility on which the appropriate selection of correlatives turns. See Singer 1982, p. 1058.

peut opposer à l'usage comptable du temps (Lyotard 1983, p. 15). At stake in this thinking of the event is, in other words, the resistance against a complete economic reduction of existence. To explain this, let us imagine again the person who sees a child drowning in a river, and let us impute this train of thought to him or her: 'That child has everything to lose. I have little to lose. My clothes might get wet. I have a cold and it might get worse if jump in. All things considered, I think it is reasonable that I jump in and save the child.' Or even one of these two trains of thought: 'I am not a strong swimmer and may also drown in this current, so I should not.' 'I have a serious heart condition and may very well die myself if I jump in, so I won't.' These are evidently considerations on the basis of which judicial reasoning may begin to make juridical sense of what may have come to pass, eventually, so as to attribute correlative rights and duties, or non-rights and liberties, to the parties involved in an ensuing law suit. But is it conceivable that this is indeed how someone who stares into the contorted face of mortal agony – someone who looks into *the face* of *a mortally afraid and panicking child* – would reason, without having first experienced the most simple and immediate demand to give what one has to give and even more than one has to give? Indeed, Levinas avers that the encounter with the face of the other demands that we give more than we have to give – *au-delà de ma capacité: il faut donner ce que l'on n'a pas.* [30] And this is why the arrival of the sense of a duty to give renders irrelevant, and must render irrelevant, any consideration of that which one has to give.

One might give and find that the situation ultimately did not even demand that one give much – wet clothes, possibly a cold. One may give and end up giving one's life – as some persons with serious heart conditions can be imagined doing and having done under circumstances like these. Or one may fail to give and afterwards offer correlative grounds of justification for one's failure to give. But one would like to think that it is unthinkable that any of these options, the last one included, would not have been preceded and precipitated by the sense of an arrival of an obligation of which the specific or specifiable terms were neither relevant nor available at the time. If one cannot think this thought, one will have to let go of Lyotard's endeavour to think the event as the ultimate resistance to the complete economisation of time. If one cannot think this thought, one would have to conclude that the call for a contemplation of the 'priority of obligation ahead of right' is utterly pointless. And one would begin to understand why a life that is indeed completely deprived of the sense of a *free duty to give* – a duty that remains fundamentally independent of all calculable rights – may end up as a cynical quest for a *duty-free* existence.

The law's ability to banish the arrival of a sense of obligation and responsibility is not a new concern in critical legal theory. Veitch himself has been engaging with this seemingly intrinsic irresponsibility of law for many years now.[31] The questions that he has invited us to address in this volume constitute a call to take this engagement further. His own chapter in this volume highlights the sheer social

30 See Derrida 1999, p. 141.
31 See Veitch 2007.

indecency of the sophisticated tax minimisation schemes that hi-tech law, not only makes possible, but also cultivates. It highlights the ways in which hi-tech law firms allow the rich to become the worst free riders in our societies; allow them to become and to remain casual observers of a world that is drowning before their feet. For those who have come to recognise this, the search for responsibility and obligation will increasingly prompt them to look away from the law and the legal articulation of duty; it will prompt them to raise their eyes to the hills in the hope that a deeper sense of responsibility may yet dawn upon humanity. This deeper sense of responsibility may well arrive one day, accompanied by a sober awareness that much of what is currently called law will simply have to be destroyed.

Bibliography

Literature

Aquinas, T., 1975, *Summa Theologiae*, Volume 38, Blackfriars, Cambridge.

Derrida, J., 1991, *Donner le Temps 1. La Fausse monnaie*, Galilée, Paris.

Derrida, J., 1994, *Force de loi*, Galilée, Paris.

Derrida, J., 1999, *Manifeste pour l'hospitalité*, Éditions Paroles d'Aube, Grigny.

Hegel, G. W. F., 1970 [1807], *Phänomenologie des Geistes* in *Werke in 20 Bänden, Bnd 3*, Suhrkamp Verlag, Frankfurt a. M.

Heidegger, M., 1954, *Vorträge und Aufsätze*, Günther Neske, Pfullingen.

Heidegger, M., 2014, *Schwarze Hefte, 1931–1938, 1938–1939 and 1939–1941*, in *Gesamtausgabe* 94, 95, 96, Vittorio Klostermann, Frankfurt a. M.

Hohfeld, W. N., 1913, 'Some Fundamental Legal Conceptions as Applied in Judicial Reasoning', *The Yale Law Journal* 23(1), 16–59.

Homolka, W. & Heidegger, A., 2016, *Heidegger und der Antisemitismus: Positionen im Widerstreit*, Herder Verlag, Freiburg, viewed 14 March 2018, www.zeit.de/kultur/literatur/2016-10/martin-heidegger-briefe-antisemitismus.

Hume, D., 1888, *A Treatise of Human Nature*, reprinted edn, Oxford University Press, Oxford.

Husserl, E., 1992, *Ideen zu einer reinen Phänomenologie und phänomenologischen Philosophie* in *Gesammelte Schriften 5*, Felix Meiner, Hamburg.

Kant, I., 1956a, *Grundlegung der Metaphysik der Sitten* in *Werke in 10 Bänden*, Weischedel edn., vol. 6, Wissenschaftliche Buchgesellschaft, Darmstadt.

Kant, I., 1956b, *Kritik der praktischen Vernunft* in *Werke in 10 Bänden*, Weischedel edn., vol. 6, Wissenschaftliche Buchgesellschaft, Darmstadt.

Kant, I., 1956c, *Metaphysik der Sitten* in *Werke in 10 Bänden*, Weischedel edn., vol. 7, Wissenschaftliche Buchgesellschaft, Darmstadt.

Kant, I., 1791, *Letter from Maria von Herbert to Kant of August 1791*, viewed 14 March 2018, https://korpora.zim.uni-duisburg-essen.de/kant/briefe/478.html.

Kant, I., 1792, *Letter from Kant to Maria von Herbert of early 1792*, viewed 14 March 2018 https://korpora.zim.uni-duisburg-essen.de/kant/briefe/510.html.

Kant, I., 1793, *Letter from Maria von Herbert to Kant of January 1793*, viewed 14 March 2018, https://korpora.zim.uni-duisburg-essen.de/kant/briefe/554.html.

Langton, R., 1994, 'Maria von Herbert's Challenge to Kant', in Peter Singer (ed.), *Ethics*, pp. 281–294, Oxford University Press, Oxford.

Levinas, E., 1976, *Difficile Liberté: Essais sur le judaïsme*, Albin Michel, Paris.

Levinas, E., 1971, *Totalité et Infini: Essai sur l'extériorité*, Martinus Nijhoff, Leiden.
Levinas, E., 2006, *En découvrant l'existence avec Husserl et Heidegger*, Vrin, Paris.
Lyotard, Jean-François, 1983, *Le différend*, Les Editions de Minuit, Paris.
Mauss, M., 2007 [1925], *Essai sur le Don: forme et raison de l'échange dans les sociétés archaïques*, Presses universitaires de France, Paris.
Mauss, M., 2011 [1954], *The Gift: Forms and Functions of Exchange in Archaic Societies*, reprinted edn, trans. Ian Cunnison, Martino Publishing, Mansfield Centre, CT.
Neethling, J., Potgieter, J. M. & Visser, P. J., 2005, *Law of Delict*, 5th edn, Butterworths, Durban.
Roger, P. (ed.), 2014, 'Heidegger: la boîte noire des Cahiers', *Critique* 811, December 2014.
Schulte, B., 2017, 'Martin und Fritz Heideggers Briefwechsel: Mitläufer des Seyns', *Badische Zeitung*, viewed 16 June 2017, www.badische-zeitung.de/literatur-und-vortrage/martin-und-fritz-heideggers-briefwechsel-mitlaeufer-des-seyns–128993733.html.
Singer, J. W., 1982, 'The Legal Rights Debate in Analytical Jurisprudence from Bentham to Hohfeld', *Wisconsin Law Review*, 975–1059.
Soboczynski, A. & Cammann, A., 2016, 'Ein moralisches Desaster' *Die Zeit*, 12 October 2016.
Van der Walt, J., 2014, *The Horizontal Effect Revolution and the Question of Sovereignty*, Walter de Gruyter, Berlin/Boston.
Van der Walt, J., 2003, 'Horizontal Application of Fundamental Rights and the Threshold of the Law in View of the Carmichele Saga', *South African Journal on Human Right* 19 (4), 517–540.
Van der Walt, J. C., & Midgeley, J. R., 1997, *Delict Principles and Cases*, 2nd edn, Butterworths, Durban; Michie, Charlottesville, VA.
Veitch, S., 2007, *Law and Irresponsibility: On the Legitimation of Human Suffering*, Routledge-Cavendish, Abingdon/New York.
Villey, M., 1946, 'L'idee du droit subjectif et les systèmes juridiques romains', *Revue historique de droit francais et étranger*, 201–227.
Villey, M., 2009 [1975] *La Formation de la Pensée Juridique Moderne*, Paris: Presses Universitaires de France.
Viney, G. & Jourdain, P., 2006, *La Conditions de la Responsabilité*, Librairie Générale de Droit et de Jurisprudence, Paris.

Case law

Bolton v Stone (1951) AC 850
Carmichele v Minister of Safety and Security (2001) (4) SA 938 (CC)
Donoghue v Stevenson [1932] UKHL 100
Jooste v Botha (2000) (2) BCLR 187 (T)
Minister van Polisie v Ewels (1975) (3) SA 590 (A)
Minister of Safety and Security v Dirk van Duivenboden (2002) (6) SA 431 SCA
Regal v African Super Slate (1962) (3) SA 18 (A)

Legislation

Bürgerliches Gesetzbuch 2002 (BGB)
Code Civil 2017 (CC)
Nieuwe Burgerlijk Wetboek 1992 (NBW)

Part II

Instituting obligations

4 On the company's bounded sense of social obligation

Lilian Moncrieff

Overview

The chapter routes through demise and expulsion, sweatshops and distressed ecologies, to say something about the harms, repressions, and tragedies that lurk in the recesses of corporate networks. It uncovers parts and existences that corporate costings repeatedly leave out, and that form into deposits and accumulations of neglect under the surfaces of law. A critical feature of these sub-surface deposits is that they are depleted in their ability to generate obligations, an effect traced to the company's bounded and managerial mode of interaction with the world. The chapter problematises the length of time that some existences spend in a state of disregard; governance is struggling to look after existences at the far-flung reaches of corporate networks and assemblages, it claims. But time also marks out the chapter's journey towards new methods for reaching under law's sub-surfaces. These draw together critical thinking about law and governance with thinking about the 'legacy' of corporate organisations, human and non-human accumulations of scale that reach into 'the geologic'. The chapter uses legacy and the geologic mode to give existential meaning and force back to forgotten existences, and to introduce a new formula for corporate obligation.

Recesses

Here is a picture of the Rana Plaza factory building, which collapsed on the outskirts of Dhaka, Bangladesh (Figure 4.1). More than 1,100 workers died and many more hundreds suffered injuries (Polaski 2015). The eight-storey factory was a manufacturing hub for clothing destined for retailers in Europe and the US. The tragedy was described as the 'worst industrial accident to hit South Asia since Bhopal' (Anon 2013) and 'brought worldwide attention to deathtrap workplaces' (Clean Clothes Campaign 2017).

The tragedy occurred in April 2013, but was far from an isolated incident. A decade-long pattern of comparable health and safety disasters precede the tragedy in Bangladesh (Bair 2017; Ross 2016). This pattern includes the under-built buildings and weak structures that proliferated as Bangladesh's production share of the world's cheap clothing grew (Rogers 2016; Hoskins 2015). It includes the

Figure 4.1 2013 Rana Plaza building collapse
(Rijans 007 2013)

weak oversight and regulatory curtailments, long hours, forced overtime, low pay, restricted workers' rights, and troubled histories of unionisation that extends in both directions, to before and after the tragedy (Labowitz & Baumann-Pauly 2015; Human Rights Watch 2015; Merk 2011).

A 'flattened out' map of the industry (Figure 4.2) tries to put a number on the employees and families living – or submerged – in these situations. Factories stack together in transparent layers on the map, which is interactive (on the website). We click and get details about the factories, their products and annual production capacities, local government registrations, and the number of employees at each facility. The map shows more than 7,000 ready-made garment (RMG) production factories in Bangladesh, and more than five million workers employed in the industry (Goss 2015).

Importantly, many of these factories and workers were 'invisible' to regulators and other officials before the mapping exercises (Labowitz & Baumann-Pauly 2015). It took the tragedy and the associated public outrage to cast light on the long complex chain of action, and *existence*, which stretches from the factories in Bangladesh to high-street retailers in Europe and the US. Links are now traceable on the signatory pages of the 'Accord on Fire and Building Safety in Bangladesh' (listing 200 signatories, retailers headquartered in Europe and UK) and the 'Alliance for Bangladesh Worker Safety' (29 US-based retailers).[1] These agreements

1 Details of these agreements can be found on the organisations' websites at http://bangladeshaccord.org and www.bangladeshworkersafety.org (Alliance) (sites accessed 12 July 2017).

Figure 4.2 Garment factories in Bangladesh
The site of Rana Plaza is shown at the black circle; the red circles locate factories that are signatories to the Alliance or Accord; the blue circles indicate factories that are registered with the government or trade unions. See the interactive map in colour at: http://people.stern.nyu.edu/twadhwa/bangladesh/#
Map by Anneka Goss (2015), produced in association with Stern Centre for Business and Human Rights.

are the result of the multi-stakeholder negotiations that followed the tragedy. They set out the commitments of multinational corporations in respect of workers' health and safety in the region until 2018.[2]

This chapter begins with Rana Plaza, and the revelations concerning existence that flowed from it, as a case that allows us to say something about harms, repressions and tragedies that lurk in the recesses of corporate networks. The lists and maps produced by scholars, policy makers, lawyers, trade unions, the media, reporters and activists, in the wake of the tragedy, teach us about life in and among the networked hierarchies and competitive pressures associated with corporate formations in the twenty-first century. We learn about a mass of beings (workers, managers) and things (laws, factories, beams) through which companies 'have had to pass' to make, sell and distribute their goods (Latour 2013, pp. 432–3). We learn about the anticipated and unanticipated consequences linked to corporate actions, and about existences frustrated and harmed by their entanglement with corporate projects in the RMG industry. Importantly, for the present chapter, we learn about experiences that *form at the back of the scene* in global value chains

2 For a comparison of the two agreements, see Bair (2017), Rühmkorf (2015), chapter 7, and Haar / Keune (2014).

(GVCs) and RMG, amidst the 'relentless price pressures' that their formations carry (Rogers 2016, p. 142).

This interest in *acts of unfolding* and *in what happens in the background* is a foundation for the chapter's (coming) *geologic* reassessment of corporate law, governance and social responsibility. The chapter takes an interest in the *recesses* to corporate networks and other corporate formations as a space-time with events and happenings essential to the constitution of present-day corporate obligation. Law and governance practices already contemplate as much. What we learn from each other, and from corporate constituents, NGOs, communications and social media, technology, science, or even the earth itself, informs not just our sense of how to live in the world, but also juridical practices in the present era of privatisation and globalisation (Teubner 2010). The productions about what we see and value inform public opinion, market discipline, policy making and standard setting activities across borders. They provide 'fodder' for domestic and transnational regimes of governance in the absence of (hard) law (Fransen 2017; Nolan 2014; Teubner 2012, 2010; Merk 2011; McBarnet 2009; Painter-Morland 2007).

These acts of unfolding are potentially exhilarating. Our information circuits continue to expand the vibrant amount of information that can be produced and collated, including for law. But the focus of *this* chapter is the other side to the fieldwork that surrounds unfolding or routing through the background. It concerns a simultaneous move to cut, shut down or to shroud certain parts to the picture. Because as quickly as the information pathways that attend a tragedy like Rana Plaza unfold, some of the lines of exposure also falter and cloud over. Evidence, testimony and information that flow in the short term begin to lose their rigour and contract. Millions of lives, to stress the point, remain submerged in sweatshop situations and other recesses, despite the public scandalisation surrounding tragedies like Rana Plaza (Human Rights Watch, 2015). Their persistence suggests the vulnerability of some beings and things in the information circuits to de-selection, muting and management, amidst the jostling that supports communication and exchange. And it suggests that within the immense matrix of beings and things that resource corporate action, some existences are set further back from *obligation* than others.

We see this process of de-selection, muting and management when we look closely at regulatory responsiveness to Rana Plaza, and at how communities and workers were treated and accommodated by factory owners and multinationals. The scope of the remedial programmes set out in the Accord and Alliance, for example, is limited to five years and includes less than 2,000 of the 7,000 RMG factories operating in Bangladesh (Labowitz & Baumann-Pauly 2015, p. 26). Limited funds and enforcement powers against factory owners, similarly, limit the remedial impacts; just 49 out of the 1,660 factories covered by the Accord had completed corrective action plans or were on schedule to do so by late 2016. Audits and inspections are commonly not made public or easily accessible, making effective stakeholder discipline over corporate actors difficult to raise and maintain (Kasperkevic 2016). The result is de-selection in the sense that some of the productions – about the lives of workers affected, about the conditions in the factories – are shut down in whole or part; there is a dispersal of some information and some lives into the ether. Muting or management occur, too, where companies include their 'regard' for existences harmed or frustrated by corporate action in their disclosures and policies to do with corporate social responsibility (CSR). But, as I have argued elsewhere (2015), this 'regard' aggressively manages beings and things by *taking charge of* the meaning and fulfilment of related claims and obligations.

Obligation, here, arises between discrete entities in the company's network – between companies, shareholders, workers, consumers, creditors, communities, infrastructure, materials, technology and so on.[3] It emerges in encounters and interactions, and not as an abstract or stand-alone moral or legal concept (Phillips, Freeman & Wicks 2003, pp. 489–90). Accountability of the corporation, in turn, is understood as 'a kind of contingent responsiveness to emergent stakeholder concerns and interests' in an open network of interactive relationships (Painter-Morland 2007, p. 516).[4] Directors are duty bound to consider the effect of their actions on a wider network of stakeholders as part of their responsibility to secure the 'success' of the company for the benefit of the members (Jensen 2002). They look to wider interests to ensure that the 'trust and confidence' necessary for the system to function are able to effectively develop (Painter-Morland 2007, p. 528).

The problem that the present chapter draws attention to is a material accumulation of beings and things at the back of this scene, where the traction and voice necessary to make claims, create and *impose obligations* is difficult to foster and sustain. Progress *is* made on health and safety after the tragedies in Bangladesh (International Labour Organisation 2015), as it is in other networks for transnational governance of the corporation (Fransen 2017, pp. 258–9). But, as the above examples of muting and management suggest, the practical benefits noticeably accrue to some existences and not all. It is the specific task of this chapter, then, to think about the failures in social obligation that beset this 'not all' – the 5,000 factories and millions of workers that lie outwith the negotiated agreements at Rana Plaza, and that still matter; the wider problem of sweatshops and of other existences cast to the back of the scene in the region and beyond.

How might *these parts* to a corporate network or assemblage strike forth? What tools or concepts might we use to capture submerged existences and the obligations that they potentially carry? The chapter seeks out existences that bear affect hunkered down in among the recesses of corporate constellations, and whose neglected or shrouded qualities allow for the unaccountable resourcing of corporate action (with sweatshop labour, distressed ecologies, etc.). The chapter, in its methods, takes inspiration from the hub of scholarly excitement around network analysis (Latour 2005; Callon 1998) and teachings on the inscriptive power of (socio-legal-economic) assemblages (Bennett 2010). But it draws these ideas towards a theorisation of the parts to our entrepreneurial networks and

3 On actor network theory (ANT) and the 'embedding of regulatory forces within materials and technologies' sometimes invisible to our (usual) legal sensibilities, see Cloatre and Dingwall (2013); see also Appel (2012).

4 See also McBarnet 2009.

assemblages that corporate costings iteratively leave out. The chapter looks between the (legal) scripts and frameworks that companies adhere to, to trace existences that fall into the irregular zones, places and times that come with de-selection from recognised juridical worlds.

The chapter attends to the recesses of corporate formations, like this, because of *the (long) time* that is spent by some existences in a state of disregard and dis-connection. This 'time' factor is important for the chapter in two ways. First, and most obviously, the time spent by some existences in a state of disregard suggests not only that some existences are set further back than others, but also that the popularised reversion in our institutions to governance is struggling at the far-flung reaches of corporate networks and assemblages. This standard reversion makes beings and things neglected by (legal) frameworks, and the actors that wield them, into 'an always available, ready to be mobilized reserve army capable of complicating – or rather of implicating – the economy at any moment' (Callon & Latour 2011, p. 22).[5] Like the Alliance and Accord above, this 'implication' can sparks the creation or renewal of obligations (arousing a mix of public and transnational private regulation) (Fransen 2017; Nolan 2014).[6] But being in a sweatshop is mostly not this dynamic or exciting. Many beings and things cast to the back of the scene will never, *in their time*, experience such mobilisation or implication. What of their lives and existences? Here, the 'time that passes' is a driver for the chapter's *critique* of governance and present-day institutions for corporate social obligation.

But I want to suggest that time is also important for another reason, and this has to do with the opening that the chapter seeks to create for extending engagement with responsibility questions in the epoch of the so-called 'Anthropocene' – a term that marks our entry into a geologic time period of human influence over earth's systems or processes (geologic, biospheric, atmospheric, hydrologic), a time visited upon by human actions and institutions as the agents of planetary change (Bonneuil 2015; Crutzen 2002). Crucially, for the chapter's purposes, the Anthropocene is a time where *all of the parts to all of our actions come unavoidably together, and assume geologic force*; a time, as the philosopher Timothy Morton says, of 'no away' (Morton 2013). This matters for the present chapter because beings and things *distanced* from responsibility systems take on a life of their own in this epoch (of no away). They form into high-rise or enduring

5 In Barry and Slater (2002), network theorist Michel Callon speaks of a 'struggle' that involves laboratories, experiments, restructuring activities, and processes of entanglement and dis-entanglement (Barry & Slater, 2002); and extends the invitation at 302: 'If you consider that the organization of markets is a growing concern for numerous groups, the next step is to ask: where will I go in order to participate in an experiment about the organization of markets? You could choose, depending on your habitus!' Cloatre and Dingwall (2013) make the link between the effects created in socio-technical assemblages and legal or regulatory effects.

6 Transnational private regulatory instruments emerge in a 'field of recurring political contestation about the conditions of production' for Fransen (2017, p. 257); see also Teubner (2012) and McBarnet (2009).

accumulations and (as the chapter will call such enduring matters) 'legacies', which condition existence on earth. These legacies, in the case of corporate organisations, include the entrenched inequalities of which the sweatshop is but one part, as well as other accumulations created by the processes of de-selection, from oceans of plastic and food waste to global warming.

Time, here, marks out the chapter's journey towards new methods and modes of enquiry for reaching under law's sub-surfaces to redress the problem of corporate responsibility. These methods and modes draw together critical thinking about law and governance with thinking about human and non-human *accumulations of scale* that reach into 'the geologic'; into the materials and forces that compose a world and which companies take up and transform when they make, distribute and sell. The chapter draws on the vibrant research and scholarship generated by a recent geologic turn in the humanities and social sciences, as well as law, in support of this combination (Ellsworth & Kruse 2013; Davis & Turpin 2015; Bonneuil 2015; Biber 2016).

The chapter's geologic move finds its justification in the work that the chapter does in the next part, called 'Surfaces, voids', to trace existences that fall through juridical frameworks, broadly speaking, and between the lines of corporate social obligation, in particular. The chapter sets out processes of de-selection and then traces de-selected existences to the point of their deposit and settlement; some beings or things spend so long in a state of disregard, in short, that they acquire features of sediment. Here the chapter uncovers an unpredictable and conceptually subterranean terrain to law, into which disavowed artefacts and anthropologies are regularly thrown. This terrain is shrouded, void-like, and it is antithetical to obligation.

The chapter tries to redress the void-like qualities of this sub-juridical destination or space-time in the third section, which is called 'Sediments'. It casts a geologic lens over the subterranean settlements of beings and things by refusing to confine its juridical interest to what (only) lies above, *or reaches*, the surface (achieves implication). It looks directly, instead, to an exploration of law's sub-surfaces under the neologism of 'le-geology', after some geologists and an artist arrive in boats and carve out a different angle from which we might view the meaning of the present. With this, the chapter introduces a new angle or axis for understanding corporate action, as constructed by the chapter's le-geologist. It makes this contribution in a bid to pull the different parts of corporate action together, to affirm their world-making or geologic force. The chapter uses the geologic mode, in short, to give existential meaning and force *back* to forgotten existences, using what it calls 'le-geology' and 'legacy' to institute a series of *affective* and *political* openings.

Can this really work? Isn't the complexity that exists beyond the company's sense of right difficult to organise as a meaningful horizon for worldly action? Isn't this 'chaos' the very source of the corporation's hold over us, making it a being uniquely capable of riding through complexity by framing out other worlds (Hayek 1967)? The chapter returns here to *obligation* to problematise this (now widely accepted) order of things – companies using profit and price to match the world to their sense of order, as a solution for living in a complex world. Because our sense of obligation, as Scott Veitch reminds us, comes about not only from abstract thinking about order or rules but also in the 'real, affective and sympathetic interactions we experience with others in community' (Veitch 2017, p. 416). The chapter seeks out this sense of affect in a world so animated by bounded sensibilities that even big and imposing legacies like sweatshops and plastic oceans are still being met with inertia or confined to otherly worlds. Importantly, the chapter's seeking out is necessary not just for the recovery of sense and political force for the implicated existences, though this must be the first and foremost goal (given the intense vulnerabilities involved). It is necessary, also, to understanding – and subverting ultimately – how companies relate to our present. The chapter ends with a new formula for capturing these two sides to corporate social obligation.

Surfaces, voids

The central charge that emerges in the first section 'Recesses' concerns the unaccountable resourcing of corporate actions in our present: companies make money from beings and things whose capacity to make existential claims and catalyse obligation is depleted by their situation in a network. In this section, the chapter explains how such practices are able to arise. This critical analysis is important to set out why new lines of corporate accountability need to be established, and to identify general concepts and causes that can explain the associated legacies of social and environmental neglect, injustice and harm.[7] It starts with a discussion of how companies move around, make and mend social relations.

Corporate actions draw together lots of different actors, human and non-human. Their activities make ties with classically conceived stakeholders (such as employees, consumers, investors, suppliers, distributors, creditors and communities). The company additionally draws on a body of less obvious (or less human) forces and materials, including environmental resources, infrastructure, the technosciences, bureaucratic processes and requirements, including the law. Some relations are internal to the company's governance process (employees, investors). Some are more external (nature, technoscience). 'Flattened out', the ties and intermediaries that enable the motion of corporations spread out over space and time and form a network (Latour 2005; Law 1992). Or, understood as 'trajectories that cross and engage each other to different extents over time', things aggregate and form 'assemblages' (McFarlane 2009, p. 562; Bennett 2010).[8] In both views of things, the inter-connectedness of economic action and global reach of networks ensure that ties are widely formed by companies.

On what basis, then, might we say that certain parts to the company's networks and assemblages are left out or cast towards the back of the scene? If accountability is a 'kind of contingent responsiveness to emergent stakeholder concerns and interests' (Painter-Morland 2007), how do some parts of the web of

7 A (small) selection of readings and testimonies: Sluiter (2009), Ross (2016) and Rogers (2016), Soule (2009), Murphy (2013), Banerjee (2000), Schrempf-Stirling (2014, 2011), Kantor and Streitfeld (2015); Dunkley (2016), Kolhatkar (2016).

8 On the distinction between actor-networks and assemblages, see Muller 2015.

relationships come to suffer from a lack of recognition, care and attention? We need, it would seem, to name the particular mechanisms and rationalities that make corporate constellations ***delimited***, or partial and bounded in the way that they account – and are held accountable – for the world.

Companies, as a starting point, are juridically dedicated to economic purposes, such as (to use the words of the relevant UK statute) 'to promote the success of the company for the benefit of its members as a whole' (Companies Act 2006, s. 172). This dedication, alongside separate legal personality, produces an active subject, capable of forming a legible and defensible will (Barkan 2013). The 'will' is economic in the sense that it puts the interest of the members first (Talbot 2015, p. 141) and its members are understood as self-interested and economically rational (Keay 2012; Sandberg 2011). The interchangeability of members and limited liability divest the business form of corporeal vulnerabilities, and increase its agility in sticky situations (Grear 2015; Ireland 2016). Put together, company law confers distinct organisational capacities on the corporate form, and effects 'complete instantiation of the rationalistic, accumulative, quasi-disembodied rights-bearer: homo-juridicus-economicus writ large' (Grear 2015, p. 239).

The company's sense of order is further shaped by the demands of securing 'profitability *within the law*' (Parkinson 1995, p. 42, emphasis added). This is important. If corporate law provides the company with a sense of agency and purpose, it is the wider legal system that shapes the company's journey by establishing legal standards and normative hierarchies. This net of law, which informs corporate agencies, includes social law, labour law, environmental protection, tax and securities law, and so on. Added to this are the obligations created by things like contract and property law (where the company is party), obligations imposed by delict/tort, criminal law and regulatory authorities (such as financial bodies, stock exchange, reporting and accounting bodies, etc.). Relevant obligations extend from multiple legalities, too, such as regional, national, international, trans- or supra-national, soft-law and private orderings (Zumbansen 2006).

This list is not meant to be exhaustive. The important thing about these legal frameworks, for present purposes, is not so much the detail of their substance and content. It is, rather, the way that the law *enables* the company and its overlying sense of agency. The lines drawn by overlapping legal regimes do not work by totally binding the company or preventing it from all voluntary action. They work, rather, by directing companies and directors on matters of concern while *keeping those very same actors moving* through the social landscape and time. This motion depends on the law for ordering, but exceeds it (Nedelsky 1990). It finds its energy and inscriptive capacities in negative rights, contractual paradigms and property, as per the modus of liberal political economy (Blomley 2010; Serres 1990).

Intuitively, one might think of legal structures as regulative and disciplinary – the net of law offers to shape, guide, slow or restrict the actions of its subjects – making the present emphasis on mobility counter-intuitive. The reigns are, however, only part of the company's juridical story, which also concerns the 'facilitative, productive, even constitutive functions of law for the capitalist corporation' (Tombs 2017, p. 351). Companies harness a particular force and kind of mobility from rights and liberal paradigms; these produce a subject that can use its internal governance processes to act 'in' and also 'on' the world. Regulations shape this action, yes, but themselves fall among the competitive opportunities that companies regularly dig out for their shareholders (Baars 2017; Rogers 2016; Haar & Keune 2014; McBarnet & Whelan 1999). The overlying dynamic is of legal frameworks and institutions that confer on companies the organisational capacities to navigate open terrain, and to set their acts apart from the world by *limiting* or *bounding* their responsibilities to the excess or immeasurable earth.

How does this boundedness play out, and what does it have to do with the uneven spread of obligations across a corporate network or assemblage? Is obligation not meant to come from the other side anyway (from the 'vitalism' (or not) of the actors and existences implicated in corporate projects (Bennett 2010); from encounters or interactions between discrete entities in the company's network of relations (Painter-Morland 2007))? The argument that I want to make here is about instances where this idealised or promised interaction *fails to occur* for existences entangled with corporate projects, and that the extent of this failure is apparent when we look across time. The failure occurs because companies acquire the ability to indefinitely suspend obligations (to co-construction or participation) within the legal frameworks, structures and institutions outlined above. It is important to explain these claims.

Corporate actors, entrusted with navigating between the spaces marked out by legal frameworks, select between ties and commitments according to their sense of right or purpose (profitability for the members). They do this, most simply, by not resourcing – or cutting – certain (costly) ties. This cutting is banal in one sense: it references only what it means to create the kind of closed interactional space that we associate with action, what it means to 'act' (Callon 1998). But, importantly, the demarcations enacted by the company in the pursuit of right also produce a set of lines, the other side of which concerns deficits in attention and (relatedly) obligation. Companies disconnect, in other words, the production of profit from some of the 'social, legal, political and environmental entanglements' with which their action is deeply enmeshed (Appel 2012, p. 442).[9] Some of these demarcations might be illegal, and so demand law's corrective force; some might be temporary or positive, and so generate other claims and modes of recognition in the future.[10] But others allow exiles to drift, as the beings or things that nobody wishes to claim or pay for.

9 Appel's ethnography powerfully depicts the entanglements and then disentanglements of American oil and gas companies in Equatorial Guinea, and links the latter to a series of abdications and disavowals of corporate responsibility. See Appel 2012. Appel, like the present chapter, uses disentanglement in the sense set out by Callon – e.g. 'disentanglement, implies investments and precise actions to cut certain ties, and internalize others' (Callon 1998).

10 Callon (1998) addresses the concept of 'positive externalities'. The case of the positive externalities is distinguished from the (negative) externalities under consideration in the present chapter because they are externalities that others will *wish to claim* and reap benefits from (hence 'implication' (Callon & Latour 2011) still operates).

Figure 4.3 Tar Sands, Alberta
Photo by Howl Arts Collective, Dru Oja Jay (creative commons licensed).
Beneath muskeg and forest in northern Alberta, Canada, lies a 50,000 square mile reservoir of heavy crude oil. Environmental activists continue to express concerns about the mining of this area (Taylor 2014).

The term 'negative externalities' is most famously applied to this situation, where a company 'fails to account in its calculations for the costs that it is imposing upon agents, who, despite the fact that they are penalised by its activities, remain external to the sphere of economic relationships in which the company operates' (Callon 1998, p. 245). Recent trends towards the spread of unequal burdens, low pay and inequality, tax avoidance, sweatshops, climate instability and other industrial marks on the commons and future (Figure 4.3) suggests the *patterning* that attends this drift of externalities – their forming into deposits and accumulations that mark the surfaces of the earth (Haraway 2016, p. 100; Talbot 2016, pp. 531–3; Sassen 2014; Piketty 2013; Meiville 2014; Nixon 2014). The impacts mediated by corporate entities form into longer-range lines, too, of possession and dispossession, enclosure and industrialism, empire and colonialism, ecological exploitation and decay (Grear 2015; Moore 2015; Malm 2015; Mawani 2015a, 2015b; Wark 2015; Capra & Mattei 2015; Wood 2002).

How does this happen? How do these patterns, deposits and accumulations of exile and neglect come to establish themselves underneath the legal and contractual frameworks through which companies move? How do some things come to sit far enough back to neither make their way back to the surface nor disperse?

Scott Veitch (2007) captures an important moment of establishment when he observes that legal institutions are not just involved in 'organising responsibility' but also 'irresponsibility'. Legal frameworks and norms limit the range of rights and obligations that attach to particular instances of agency, as well as deride and disavow links and obligations that fall outside these bounds. Existences live among this derision and disavowal (p. 115); unaccounted for risks, harms and effects seep across borders, jurisdictions and generations (p. 116). The dark lines that mark the Tar sands (Figure 4.3) derive not just from the drills and machinery, thus, but also from the laws that enable disavowal (land, licensing, health and safety, environmental laws, etc.). The law underwrites, too, *the distance that we keep from* incalculable wastage and loss (the muskeg and boreal forests, Figure 4.3).[11]

Iris Young (2006, 2011) captures a related experience of negative externalities disappearing down a rabbit hole in the era of corporate capitalism. Young describes how global legal regimes work by isolating responsible agents, using concepts like 'causation', 'intention' and 'control'. Her work identifies a gap between these regimes and the responsibilisation of global production strategies and GVCs. Supply chains revolve around contractual relationships, which, by their nature, bound and fragment responsibility between the contributors. The sweatshop rises up, in this context, as an assemblage of entities that is beyond the law, or beyond the contractual responsibilities of the companies and buyers involved.[12]

This chapter takes from these works the emerging outline of a shrouded space-time or void to the other side of accountability practices into which 'costly' entities and impacts are able to fall, and become 'sediment'. This void is dark because accountability practices routinely stop short of it, and because it attracts missing connections and missing times for which, increasingly, no one really knows the co-ordinates. These links are *not* missing because the company fails to make the ties – interfacing still widely occurs in the company's inter-connected worlds. They are missing, rather, because of the *multiplicity of scripts* (law, politics, economy, technology, etc.) within which the full schema of ties is never really counted out nor attended to by those who most benefit.

This bit about a 'multiplicity of scripts' is important. Because despite being cast out, there is meant to be a chance for excluded existences to get back in as part of

11 Of the lines that mark Tar sands: 'Legislation dictates that companies whose mining would disturb or destroy habitats cannot be mined unless said habitats are proven able to recover to their natural state, or be restored to an "equivalent land capability" afterwards. However, equivalent land capability has become somewhat of a loophole on the oil sands as it defines agricultural land of equal capability to arboreal land in its land use. This means that although some oil-sand mine land had been restored to wood bison pasture, the muskeg and boreal forest that was originally there had a much higher conservation significance, which is now lost' (Frontier 2017).

12 On the failure of corporate governance and CSR, as they currently stand, to address human rights concerns, environmental issues and inequality (and so create the kinds of cracks or voids Young is talking about), see also Tombs (2017), Santoso (2017), Danielson (2015), Rogers (2016), Locke (2013) and Rühmkorf (2015).

the earlier noted 'ready to be mobilized reserve army capable of complicating – or rather of implicating – the economy at any moment' (Callon & Latour 2011, p. 22). This backstop would make the fall not into a void but into a holding camp of some kind for obligation (at worst). But, against this possibility, juridical voids arise where certain scripts (financialisation, competitiveness, cheap consumer goods, fossil fuels, etc.) are (either) unyielding or totally confident about *incorporating* competing demands and demonstrating socialisation. Elements and existences externalised remain outcast insofar as they are either stunned by the totalising stability of expansive networks (Sassen 2014; Ireland 2016), or they find their claims muted and de-realised (Al-Amoudi & Varman 2016; Moncrieff 2015, 2011). The result is the dramatic *surfacing* of legal frameworks with what feels like tarmacadam. *Time* in the zone of amnesia extends to years, decades, even lifetimes for some. We are speculative, but maybe also truthful when we think of this as inducing 'sedimentation' for some existences ('the process of settling or being deposited as a sediment'[13]), and as instigating the (juridical) division of our world into above surface and subterranean zones.

There is something else to say. We must add to our understanding of the recesses set out certain additional consequences. We need to attend the further possibility that the same legal and governance structures that allow the company to push 'costly' parts of the network out of reach or focus, also, encourage the company to move on through, and make money from, the resultant voids (in accountability).

What does this mean? It means, as above, that negative externalities are routinely detached from the revenue centres of corporations, and that groups of implicated existences fall into a void somewhere below the thresholds of accountability. But, also, that wider encouragement given to corporations to self-govern and to manage responsibility questions extends their direct command over what happens on the other side of the boundary. Beings and things deposited by the corporation like this form into accumulations of scale, which are stabilised and made available to competitive logics precisely because they are made of beings and things that are *set back* from obligation. This settlement of exiles allows companies to resource their efforts with labour or affects for which no one is responsible (with sweatshop labour, sub-prime, an invisible stratosphere, etc.). This resourcing is possible because the implicated beings and entities are *processually* stripped of obligation, as above.

I have written in other pieces about the complicity of law and the governance turn, in general, and corporate governance and corporate social responsibility (CSR), in particular, with extending the company's sovereign sway like this (Moncrieff 2015, 2011).[14] CSR and the governance turn admit the company as a

13 Oxford Dictionary, https://en.oxforddictionaries.com/definition/sedimentation.

14 The sphere in which corporate decision makers try to 'integrate social, environmental, ethical, consumer, and human rights concerns into their business strategies and operations' (European Commission 2011). For a description of the concept and practice of CSR, see McBarnet (2009), Horrigan (2010); on 'integrative' practices, see Garriga and Mele (2004).

self-governing actor, capable of looking over the substrate and making decisions about future accommodations reflexively (e.g. based on its own interactions with artefacts and anthropologies). But if it is right that sub-surfaces and shrouded voids mark the other side of corporate legal thresholds, these governance prepositions begin to look seriously problematic.

Why? Because the shadow described (above) references the (growing) absence of known co-ordinates for existences disavowed and externalised by companies as they navigate open terrain. Landscapes, seas, rocks, animals and atmospheres under threat, workers and borrowers exploited, unequal burdens: the connections that could explain these things increasingly accumulate over the border, in the void where it is dark. This shadow is vital and productive for businesses in the era of corporate governance and CSR. It allows them to take charge of responsiveness, and to manage existences according to their own sense of right and profitability (Tombs 2017; Al-Amoudi & Varman 2016; Moncrieff 2015, 2011; Banerjee 2008), or to do so under the cover of law (Fortun 2014). The result is the materialisation of 'sludge' (ibid.), and of existences untethered from their moorings and congruent sense of self. Exiles lose their shape in their interactions with corporate actors due to the persistent misrecognition that befalls them in corporate management processes, or due to the continuing pressure to be flexible and 'to work' (to satisfy the company's sense of right).

This reach of the company over submerged and subterranean existences brings us back to the problems that we identified in the first section, to the failures in social obligation that beset the 'not all' – the millions of workers, communities, beings and things, which experience impacts beyond the law and beyond the reach of accountability practices. The corresponding collapse of governance narratives in respect of these same existences is also arresting. It confirms our need for new lines of interaction, which can extend obligation to the relevant modes of existence – to life in the recesses of corporate constellations, to the accumulations of scale that form amidst exposure. By thinking about this, we might begin to aim more meaningfully at establishing interactions that have in sight a better way of their being in corporate formations (than being stripped of obligation).

Sediments

Here is a piece of Anthropocene art: twelve blocks of ice are melting on the streets of Paris (Figure 4.4).[15] It is December 2015. Artist Olafur Eliasson and geologist Minik Rosing bring the ice blocks to Paris from near Nuuk, Greenland's capital, upon the Prime Minister of Greenland's boat. The blocks are free-floating icebergs from the region and consist of snow compressed over a period of time that reaches upwards of tens of thousands of years. Eliasson and Rosing arranged the works at the site in Paris for the occasion of COP21, the UN Conference on Climate Change. 'The work raises awareness,' they say, 'of climate change by providing a

15 On art in (response to) the Anthropocene, more generally, see Davis and Turpin (2015).

Figure 4.4 'Ice Watch' (2015) by artist Olafur Eliasson and geologist Minik Rosing 'The industrial revolution,' says Rosing, 'shows up in the ice as a spike in levels of CO_2'; the invention of money (by the Greeks in the sixth century BC), 'a spike in lead'.

direct and tangible experience of the reality of melting arctic ice' (Eliasson & Rosing 2015a).

Look at how the blocks are arranged in the form of a circle in the picture. The shape draws its wandering audiences among the imaginary dials of an ice clock – metaphors for the 'time that is passing' or the 'time that is running out', perhaps. But watching the ice melt with acceleration in a Western European clime is also to experience what we might call our own *legacies* – to witness the cumulative force of past actions as they 'fall forwards' into the present (Malm 2015, p. 9). 'Inside the iceberg,' says the geologist Rosing, 'you see snow layers in sequence as you go back in time. Because it is compressed, the air between the snowflakes that fell thousands of years ago is trapped in tiny bubbles' (Zarin 2015). And 'For years,' says Laurent Fabius (President of COP21) on the website for the work, 'this region [Greenland; the north pole] has been sending us signals that we cannot neglect anymore. The International Community must hear them and turn them into acts' (Eliasson & Rosing 2015b).

How might the submerged and neglected parts of a corporate network or assemblage reach us? What lines of interaction might we use to hear about the 'legacies' of action and assemblage, to search out claims, allegations and obligations that might support a meaningful change in action? Eliasson and Rosing return us to our starting questions. They hire a boat from Greenland to drag before us tangible evidence of ties and impacts dispersed over time by the actions and assemblages of industrial capitalism. And they tell us about deposits and accumulations of scale that emerge as a result: 'The industrial revolution,' Rosing says, 'shows up in the ice as a spike in levels of CO_2'; the invention of money (by the Greeks in the sixth century BC) as 'a spike in lead' (Gordon 2015).

What might we hold before the company, and ourselves, to hear about existences that fall between the lines of corporate social obligation? Where might we walk if we want to count out the legacies of neglect in corporate capitalism – the things that nobody wants to claim or pay for? For the last three decades, the voices of stakeholders (shareholders, employees, creditors, communities) and drivers for CSR (consumer patterns, reputation, technology, etc.) have been relied upon for an answer to these questions (McBarnet 2009). These groupings are regularly invited to have their say in forums like CSR, and to fill the company's immediate spatial environment with communications and demands that pertain to their state(s) or existence(s). Learning and discipline over the company are expected to flow from the resultant flurry of existential expression, according to corporate and governance scholars, and a record of the company's actual impact to develop part by part.

There are, however, problems with relying on this set of tools for learning about impact and creating obligations, which are captured in 'Surfaces, voids' above. The juridical frameworks that encourage companies to navigate open terrain allow companies to match beings and things to their sense of order, and not the other way around. This means that at least some of the voices or bodies, which might discipline corporate actors, fall into juridical voids and struggle with remaining interactive. It no longer makes sense to describe *their* participation as on the brink of governance or implication. They are, rather, exiles that take on the distressing look of *sediments* – beings and things transported and deposited into the substrate through persistent fracture – and *sludge* – parts of an action that lose their shape or moorings as the *length of time* in the zone of amnesia becomes protracted.

At the same time, there is a new arrow (pointing the way forward). We know that so-called 'voids' host claims, arguments and (potential) obligations crucial to evaluating the company's wider impact. We saw this in the lists and maps produced after Rana Plaza (in 'Surfaces, voids' above). And we (now) know that there is no road or boat to this space-time from the company's sense of order. The void outlined above pertains precisely to the wake that forms behind the company's bounded movements, meaning that we can (finally) do away with the idea that the company can resolve this problem alone (big arrow pointing forward). This is not to dispute that the beings and things affected by companies (stakeholders, the things grouped together as drivers, etc.) are the proper ones for telling us about impacts. Of course they still are. But our aim is to catalyse obligation towards existences persistently exposed to misrecognition and living as sediment in a tilted world – for example, precisely the communities already struggling with voice, and for some time now. We need, in these circumstances, an *opposing axis or tilt* for interacting around the company, and a more affective and irruptive way of gathering existential meaning and force from the submerged parts (where the company already is/acts).

Legacy, evocatively, names our interest in gathering the fragments of corporate action, like this. Defined by the Oxford Dictionary as 'something left or handed down by a predecessor',[16] it names our interest in tracing the externalities left behind by companies as they take the form of patterns, deposits or other formations above *and* below the surfaces of law. Legacy concerns the planned and unplanned, positive and negative, tangible and intangible effects created for and by corporate formations, and which 'remain longer' than the action or event itself (Gammon 2015, p. 446).[17] Importantly, the term refers not to individualised pieces or parts, but to accumulations of scale that might be linked to corporate action, and to law (because the forces involved stem from legal and contractual frameworks, as set out in the second section above). Legacy offers these things to us due to its open address of the space-time of *obligation*, the horizon inscriptive of corporate actions and right, and due to its other major source of enrichment, *time*.

'Time', said eighteenth-century geologist James Hutton (2010), 'is often deficient to our schemes ... [it] cannot be bounded by any operation that may have an end, the progress of things upon this globe' (p. 8). In 1788, Hutton set out in a boat from Dunglass in the UK to tie together his own disjointed experiences of the earth's surfaces and sub-surfaces (his thesis is sketched in Figure 4.5, the 'Unconformity') (SNH 2017). Hutton famously drags before a centuries-long audience evidence of the different layers and types of rock, which lie beneath the ground; he dates and explains different chapters in the earth's history and geological record. He investigates where the different layers and (also) times *adjoin* (Northcott 2015).

Two hundred and twenty-seven years later, Eliasson and Rosing take to their boats. In the time between their journey and Hutton's journey, the so-called Anthropocene 'happens': fossil and industrial capitalism take root, boom and bust intermittently; new markers from the agricultural, industrial and post-war (nuclear) eras enter our bodies, oceans, minerals and soil. The artist and geologist drag before us pressing signs of the legacies and inscriptions of this capitalist progress – of the 'great transformation' as Polanyi famously names it (Polanyi 2002), or 'post-1950s acceleration' (Steffen et al. 2015).

Updating Hutton's journey for this epoch of the Anthropocene, we might then say that today's geological forces likely include society/nature networks and assemblages (Bonneuil 2015; Ellsworth & Kruse 2013; Kolbert 2011; Crutzen 2002).[18] Global flows create complex and shifting entanglements of earth materials,

16 Oxford Dictionary, https://en.oxforddictionaries.com/definition/legacy.

17 Legacy is a new concept in the corporate context, to the author's knowledge. This description of legacy is thus adopted from Gammon's work, which relates to the more familiar 'sporting' or 'Olympic' legacies.

18 See Haraway (2016), Moore (2015), Malm and Hornborg (2014) and Malm (2015) on the arguably more fitting designation of the 'Capitalocene', in light of the patterns under analysis and the 'intra-species inequalities' that are part and parcel of the inscriptions generated by capitalist relations. These relations make 'anthropos' a controversial subject of action and/or responsibilisation for the present age.

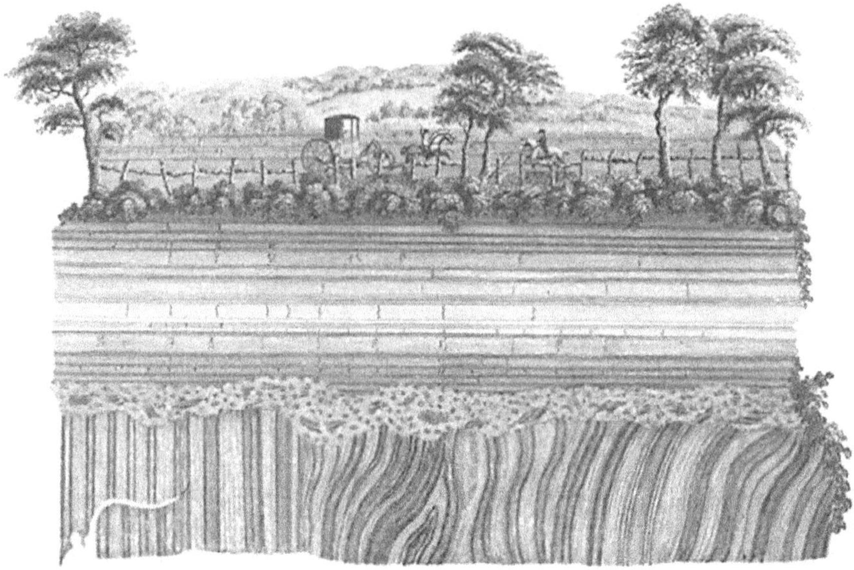

Figure 4.5 Drawing of the 'Unconformity' at Jedburgh, Borders
The drawing featured in Volume I of James Hutton's *Theory of the Earth* (1788); the section drawn illustrates where rock formations created at different times and by different forces adjoin.
John Clerk of Eldin (1787)

technologies, infrastructure, chemicals, weather, information, people and objects; the 'geologic' forms into a 'teeming assemblage of exchange and interaction among the bio, geo, cosmo, socio, political, legal, economic, strategic, and imaginary' (Ellsworth & Kruse 2013, p. 23). Corporate networks command our attention as a source of some of the most 'brutal inscriptions': 'it is not the products of ***humanity*** that come to be stratified but the externalities of Monsanto and DuPont, the radiation of nuclear bombs, and the oil spills of Exxon Mobile' (Davis & Turpin 2015, p. 7, emphasis in original). Their presence among the geologic, applying Hutton's formula for time above, opens up new chances to vouch for the existence of those neglected by the present order of things and to expand redress.

How so? It is so because even forgotten existences still express presence and changes in condition where there is no possibility of their going anywhere but into our bodies, air, seas, rocks and soil. Carbon deposits, debris in the ocean, human and non-human lives wasted and dispensed with as part of the everyday: all these things mark and condition life on earth in a time of 'no away' (Morton 2013, p. 94). Their parts linger and express themselves underneath the surface of daily actions and intentions; they gather new meaning and force over time, as they aggregate and form into tangible or high-rise accumulations of scale. The chapter calls these accumulations legacies, a new axis or object that it presents for juridical evaluation of the company and its obligations; a slice through the world and time that could capture the rigour and shape of corporate impacts over time as big or 'hyper' objects (Morton 2013), which straddle human and non-human, bios and geos, above and below surface.[19]

Could a legacy view present us with new ways forward for relating existence and crossing worlds in the case of corporate action and assemblage? Could it transform the 'tremendous inertia' towards distressed ecologies and sweatshops that falls on the side of the modern, with its political ontology of 'away' (Morton 2013, p. 94)? Practically speaking, we might say that investigations and (eventually) obligations, which attend a longer temporal frame to those entwined with the 'success' of the company, could help us to reach under (laws') surfaces. We cross check the company's words with new rulers and instruments, which bring us into contact with forgotten worlds. We detect changes in the condition of (even) submerged beings and things by accounting over a longer period of time.[20]

If we add a *le-* for 'legal' to our entry into this new geologic mode, we might also express commitment to grappling with the legacies that stem from legal and contractual frameworks, more specifically. We attend the sub-surface le-geologies of our present by tracing the life-changing and geologic forces that flow from liberal legal frameworks and corporate legal institutions for so many. Importantly, we do so not (only) by waiting to see what of existence reaches the surface, as the mantras of governance suggest. We refuse in the Anthropocene to confine our juridical interest to only 'what works' in this sense (Morton 2017; Fortun 2014; Haraway 2016). Le-geology requires, in addition, that we look directly under law's surfaces and create new lines of interaction with parts or existences struggling with the company's bounded sense of purpose over time; that we make new pathways for the discovery of law's own *unconformities*, accumulations that form at unorthodox angles to the surfaces of our accountability practices (their apparent normative success). These engagements are for recognising the responsibility that we have for the institutions through which we try to live together; and for recognising when and where these institutions frustrate or mis-manage existences that still matter (in 'Recesses' and 'Surfaces, voids' above). Constructing accountability practices that can address the *actual state* of our world, like this, we might see Hutton in his boat and before the newly formed Royal Society of Edinburgh in 1785, underscoring for us the importance of relating or interposing surface and (irruptive) sub-surface developments.[21]

19 There is considerably more to be said about what legacy is – e.g. axis, object, hyper-object – but too little room in the present chapter; I will shortly return to this, to what kind of object or thing a 'legacy' is, and at how it might press on the claims and schemas of responsibility. I accept that more explanation might be needed for the reader to accept this statement in this publication at this time.

20 Lyell 1997, p. 356, for the geologists' classic view.

21 The chapter's interest in the Royal Society of Edinburgh Meeting at which Hutton presented his Theory of the Earth for the first time, in 1785, is not in the immediate success of his claims, as the 'founder of modern geology', but in the difficulties he faced – illness in anticipation, a dismissive and hostile reception for radical and potentially *subversive* ideas about the earth's systems and processes in 1785. See Dean (1992). The irruptive dimensions to what we cannot see in Hutton (e.g. heat) are important to the present analysis and its concern with the voice of submerged

We need something else, as well: a new scene for making sense of this new juridical object, legacy, and mode of engagement, le-geology. It might be difficult for readers to understand what either mean without a mode for making sense of the obligations that the two together potentially carry (towards companies, towards wider society). This sense making is also critical given the vast uncertainty that accompanies any sight of the world beyond the scripts and institutions that we rely on for order in our present (Hayek 1967). However, this new scene is already with us. It is the figure of 'the section' (the slice through the world in Figure 4.5).

The sectional view of things takes us from the pictures of Rana Plaza and the Tar Sands in Alberta (Figures 4.1 and 4.3) where we look upon beings and things, the earth itself, as cast into chaos. We have no idea of where to focus. We look, then, upon a map of the company's network laid out 'flat' (Figure 4.2). We have no reliable way of accounting for what lies between the company's (or the ethnographers') words (what is not said, what is still submerged in the negotiations or disclosures). But as we arrive at 'Ice Watch' (Figure 4.4) and 'the geological section' (Figure 4.5), by contrast, we are thrown among submerged layers, atmospheres and legacies, which lie deep under the earth's (physical, juridical) surfaces. We are surprised by their patterning and by the difference that our experience of these legacies makes: 'I thought,' said the artist, Eliasson, in Paris, '"I know what ice looks like" … But, when I opened the truck … I put my hand to it and suddenly I drew my hand back! I said to myself, "The ice is really cold"' (Zarin 2015).

The encounters that legacy and le-geology bring us could be affective, like this. If they renew and extend presence for submerged parts of the company's network. If they make up the spectrum of interactions (claims, arguments, allegations) that pertain to the actual state in which companies leave the present. To catalyse this opening for interaction and (importantly) obligation, however, this sense of presence needs to be *curated* on a plane or topography that is distinct from the company's bounded sense of right. This is important to avoid processes of de-selection, muting and management, starting all over again (in case legacy, too, is transformed into only 'capitalizable expression' (Pavoni 2015)). We need to *curate* legacy, in other words, with a sense of time and topography that can avoid any additional exposure and that can check or *cut across* the reflexive picture. We relativise the bounds and limits of our open interactive networks by placing them in correspondence with the legacies to which they *adjoin*. The section is a tool for capturing the *vertical rise* of people and things that form into accumulations *over time*, and so adds to our collective toolkit for understanding structure and enclosure.[22]

existences; new lines of interaction form around the irruptive claims and allegations of submerged existences in legacy.

22 Again, more research must follow on this. Law could carry important tensions here, as a system for the curation of our collective and political interactions. But it also has difficulties with openness (bounded systems, etc.), clearly in 'Surfaces, voids' above. Time, the chapter argues, offers new opportunities to relativise and test the bounds of these systems, to produce 'cut across' tensions or hold collective shapes; but only if these shapes are supported (and themselves tested) with vital, collectivist and political work.

What might this involve? In an earlier version of this chapter, I thought about the rigour and the shape of legacy in terms of the *evidential* demands of the encounter that the chapter imagines, and of how we might 'link seemingly disparate events across the globe'; of examining 'the ways in which human and non-human realities emerge together in a variety of co-productions and surprising interplays' (Biemann 2015, pp. 117, 129). I stressed how these links might be captured within a legal apparatus, or sit alongside more routinely projected sensory, spatial, temporal and legal severances that exist between sites of cause and effect. And I said something about new concepts and tools to support the practical development of links between the company and its more amorphous impacts; we need, I said, new ways of making the 'points of contact' show up (Moncrieff 2016).

But as I continue to think about the world in which we live, and all of our places in it, I realise that these evidential questions are not the only or first frontier for making the difference, essential though they are as areas for advancing interactions around legacy. We need also to be really careful not to look at new objects (legacy) with old models or tools (e.g. the liability model and its history of disavowals). We need, as well, to come to grips with the precise nature and scale of the challenges that face us in a time of profound interconnection and accelerated flows, and to observe the limits and complicities of our institutions, structures and systems of liability when tackling things that concatenate past, present and future.

Scholars of the geologic turn talk about reinventing '"what we know" from an entirely different angle (the vertical accelerating rise)' (Ellsworth & Kruse 2013, p. 8) and about 'capturing the new unconformities' (Baker & Gordon 2013). This is close to what the chapter proposes. The chapter says something about the harms, repressions and tragedies that lurk in the recesses of corporate networks and assemblages. But – and this 'but' is really important – the aim of this work is not so much to air more grievances as to create arguments for *why and how we might turn the world on its side* to look for the vertical rise (in abandonment). The chapter fulfils this goal by reconfiguring law's understanding of the world (as geologic), enhancing our ability to find force among the existences that crisscross worlds (by creating interactions around legacy). And, importantly, where this interaction projects a rise (in abandonment), over time it interrupts and subverts the company's capacity to match beings and things to its (economic) sense of order by *taking the flat earth away from it* (the section).

There is a formula for this double aspect to corporate social obligation and it turns on legacy. Legacy is a means for gathering the remains of corporate action: patterns of externalities dispersed through time and the company's gifts to other generations. But as we trace how the world takes its shape over time, like this, legacy also marks the company itself out as a benefactor of delegated functions, a 'body sent out on a mission' (from the word's medieval Latin origins in *legatia* and old French *legatie*).

How so? It is so because legacy traces a longer-range relationship of affect between companies and the communities of beings and things that resource corporate activities. And it is so because the gifts that corporate organisations bestow on the world must pass, on account of this relation, through a 'legacy test': a slice through the world that looks for the vertical rise in abandonment, and registers the length of time that some existences spend in a particular location or state. Obligation passes, with this, from a site or ability that lies mainly with companies (to match the world to their sense of order) to a community of beings and things that *put a bend* in the company's bounded sense of right. This bend, or double turn to corporate 'social' obligation, pushes forth in a juridical that is inescapably geologic.

Conclusion

This chapter has spent its time exploring the space-time of corporate obligation, thinking about the immense matrix of beings and things that resource corporate projects. It deconstructs the presumptive claims of governance to these matrices, and to the associated bodies and voices that it imagines as leaning on corporate actors (through governance and CSR). Serious problems set in, the chapter argues, in the governance vision when the bodies and voices of this immense matrix are assumed to be regular and disciplinary to the corporation. This assumption underestimates an unpredictable and conceptually subterranean terrain upon which disavowed artefacts and anthropologies regularly find themselves. This terrain is volatile, shrouded, and it is antithetical to obligation.

The chapter's geologic view of corporate obligation demands that we cross the threshold, from here, to look past governance processes for beings and things struggling with the boundedness of corporate obligation over time. The aim is to give meaning and force back to forgotten existents, as they show up in enduring accumulations of scale and legacies of the corporation. It is so because the *rise* and *affect* of these legacies is fundamental to understanding the impact of corporate institutions, and to evaluating the present distribution of obligations. They allow us, in sum, 'to *judge* of those operations by which a world, so wisely ordered, goes into decay' (Hutton 2010, p. 10, emphasis added). Assuming that we can agree on the worth of this, and that there is more to our communities than the company's sense of right, we need now to turn our attention to it.

Bibliography

Al-Amoudi, I. & Varman, R., 2016, 'Accumulation through Derealisation: How Corporate Violence Remains Unchecked', *Human Relations* 69(10), 1909–1935.

Anon, 2013, 'Corporate Social Responsibility: Disaster at Rana Plaza', *The Economist*, 4 May, viewed 20 November 2017, www.economist.com/news/leaders/21577067-grue some-accident-should-make-all-bosses-think-harder-about-what-behaving-responsibly.

Appel, H., 2012, 'Walls and White Elephants: Oil Extraction, Responsibility and Infrastructural Violence in Equatorial Guinea', *Ethnography* 13(4), 439–465.

Baars, G., 2017, 'Capital, Corporate Citizenship and Legitimacy: The Ideological Force of Corporate Crime in International Law', in G. Baars & A. Spicer (eds), *The Corporation: A Critical, Multi-Disciplinary Handbook*, pp. 419–433, Cambridge University Press, Cambridge.

Bair, J., 2017, 'The Corporation and Global Value Chains', in G. Baars & A. Spicer (eds), *The Corporation: A Critical, Multi-Disciplinary Handbook*, pp. 326–335, Cambridge University Press, Cambridge.

Baker, M. & Gordon, J., 2013, 'Unconformities, Schisms and Sutures: Geology and the Art of Mythology in Scotland', in E. Ellsworth & J. Kruse (eds), *Making the Geologic Now: Responses to Material Conditions of Contemporary Life*, pp.163–169, Punctum Books, New York.

Banerjee, B., 2000, 'Whose Land is it Anyway? National Interest, Indigenous Stakeholders, and Colonial Discourses', *Organization & Environment* 13(1), 3–38.

Banerjee, B., 2008, 'Corporate Social Responsibility: The Good, the Bad and the Ugly', *Critical Sociology* 34(1), 51–79.

Barry, A. & Slater, D., 2002, 'Technology, Politics and the Market: An Interview with Michel Callon', *Economy and Society* 31(2), 285–306.

Barkan, J., 2013, *Corporate Sovereignty: Law and Government Under Capitalism*, University of Minnesota Press, Minneapolis.

Bennett, J., 2010, *Vibrant Matter: A Political Ecology of Things*, Duke University Press, Durham.

Biber, E., 2016, 'Law in the Anthropocene Epoch', UC Berkeley Public Law Research Paper No. 2834037, viewed 20 November 2017, https://papers.ssrn.com/sol3/papers.cfm?abstract_id=2834037.

Biemann, U., 2015, 'Geochemistry and Other Planetary Perspectives', in H. Davis & E. Turpin (eds), *Art in the Anthropocene: Encounters Among Aesthetics, Politics, Environment and Epistemologies*, pp. 117–130, Open Humanities Press, London.

Blomley, N., 2010, 'The Right to Pass Freely: Circulation, Begging and the Bounded Self', *Social and Legal Studies* 19(3), 331–350.

Bonneuil, C., 2015, 'The Geological Turn: Narratives of the Anthropocene', in C. Hamilton, C. Bonneuil & F. Gemenne (eds), *The Anthropocene and the Global Environmental Crisis: Rethinking Modernity in a New Epoch*, pp. 15–31, Routledge, Oxon.

Callon, M., 1998, 'An essay on Framing and Overflowing: Economic Externalities Revisited by Sociology', in M. Callon (ed.), *Laws of the Markets*, pp. 244–269, Wiley-Blackwell, London.

Callon, M. & Latour, B., 2011, 'Thou Shall Not Calculate! Or How to Symmetricalize Gift and Capital', *Athenea Digital: Revista De Pensamiento e Investigacion Social* 11(1), 171–192.

Capra, F. & Mattei, U., 2015, *The Ecology of Law: Toward a Legal System in Tune with Nature and Community*, Berrett-Koehler Publishers, Oakland, CA.

Clean Clothes Campaign, 2017, *Rana Plaza*, viewed 2 April 2017, https://cleanclothes.org/safety/ranaplaza.

Cloatre, E. & Dingwall, R., 2013, '"Embedded Regulation:" The Migration of Objects, Scripts and Governance', *Regulation & Governance* 7(3), 365–386.

Crutzen, P., 2002, 'Geology of Mankind', *Nature* 415(6867), 23.

Danielson, D., 2015, 'Beyond Corporate Governance: Why a New Approach to The study of Corporate Law is Needed to Address Global Inequality and Economic Development', in U. Mattei & J. Haskell (eds), *Research Handbook on Political Economy and Law*, pp. 195–204, Edward Elgar Press, Cheltenham.

Davis, H. & Turpin, E. (eds.), 2015, *Art in the Anthropocene: Encounters Among Aesthetics, Politics, Environments and Epistemologies*, Open Humanities Press, London.

Dean, D., 1992, *James Hutton and the History of Geology*, Cornell University Press, Ithaca.

Dunkley, E., 2016, 'Ten Biggest Bank Scandals Have Cost £53bn in Fines', *Financial Times*, April 11.
Eliasson, O. & Rosing, M., 2015, *Ice Watch*, archive and record of the artwork, viewed 20 November 2017, http://olafureliasson.net/archive/artwork/WEK109190/ice-watch.
Eliasson, O. & Rosing, M., 2015, *Ice Watch Paris*, exhibition website and narrative, viewed 20 November 2017, http://icewatchparis.com.
Ellsworth, E. & Kruse, J., 2013, *Making the Geologic Now: Responses to Material Conditions of Contemporary Life*, Punctum Books, New York.
European Commission, 2011, 'Communication from the Commission to the European Parliament, the Council, the European Economic and Social Committee and the Committee of the Regions on a Renewed EU Strategy 2011–2014 for Corporate Social Responsibility', COM/2011/681 final, viewed 20 November 2017, www.europarl.europa.eu/meetdocs/2009_2014/documents/com/com_com(2011)0681_/com_com(2011)0681_en.pdf.
Fortun, K., 2014, 'From Latour to Late Industrialism', *HAU: Journal of Ethnographic Theory* 4(1), 309–329.
Fransen, L., 2017, 'Embedding the Multinational Corporation in Transnational Sustainability Governance', in G. Baars & A. Spicer (eds), *The Corporation: A Critical, Multi-Disciplinary Handbook*, pp. 257–267, Cambridge University Press, Cambridge.
Frontier, 2017, 'The Alberta Tar Sands: What Are They?' Blog and video, *Huffington Post*, viewed 20 November 2017, www.huffingtonpost.co.uk/-frontier/the-alberta-tar-sands-wha_b_15581512.html.
Gammon, S., 2015, 'A Legacy of Legacies: Limitations of the Future Perfect', *Annals of Leisure Research* 18(4), 445–449.
Garriga, E. & Mele, D., 2004, 'Corporate Social Responsibility Theories: Mapping the Territory', *Journal of Business Ethics* 53(1), 51–71.
Gordon, H., 2015, 'Olafur Eliasson's rallying cry', *The Economist: 1843 Magazine*, 9 December, viewed 20 November 2017, www.1843magazine.com/culture/the-daily/olafur-eliassons-rallying-cry.
Goss, A., 2015, 'Beyond the Tip of the Iceberg: Bangladesh's forgotten apparel workers', viewed 2 April 2018, http://people.stern.nyu.edu/twadhwa/bangladesh.
Grear, A., 2015, 'Deconstructing Anthropos: A Critical Legal Reflection on "Anthropocentric" Law and Anthropocene "Humanity"', *Law and Critique* 26(3): 225–249.
Greenpeace, 2017, 'Fracking's Environmental Impacts: Water', viewed 20 November 2017, www.greenpeace.org/usa/global-warming/issues/fracking/environmental-impacts-water.
Haar, B. & Keune, M., 2014, 'One Step Forward or More Window-dressing? A Legal Analysis of Recent CSR Initiatives in the Garment Industry in Bangladesh', *International Journal of Comparative Labour Law and Industrial Relations* 30(1), 5–25.
Haraway, D., 2016, *Staying with the Trouble: Making Kin in the Chthulucene*, Duke University Press, Durham.
Hayek, F., 1955, *The Road to Serfdom*, Routledge Classics, London.
Hayek, F., 1967, 'The Corporation in a Democratic Society: In Whose Interests Ought It and Will It Be Run?', in F. Hayek, *Studies in Philosophy, Politics and Economics*, pp. 300–312, Routledge Press, London.
Horrigan, B., 2010, *Corporate Social Responsibility in the Twenty-First Century: Debates, Models and Practices across Government, Law and Business*, Edward Elgar Press, London.

Hoskins, T., 2015, 'Reliving the Rana Plaza Factory Collapse: A History of Cities in 50 Buildings, Day 22', *The Guardian*, 23 April, viewed 20 November 2017, www.theguardian.com/cities/2015/apr/23/rana-plaza-factory-collapse-history-cities-50-buildings.

Human Rights Watch, 2015, 'Whoever Raises Their Head Suffers the Most: Workers' Rights in Bangladeshi Garment Factories', viewed 20 November 2017, http://features.hrw.org/features/HRW_2015_reports/Bangladesh_Garment_Factories/index.html.

Hutton, J., 2010, *Theory of the Earth (1788)*, Classic Books International, New York.

International Labour Organisation, 2015, *Strengthening workplace safety and labour rights in the Bangladesh Ready-Made Garment Sector*, viewed 20 November 2017, www.ilo.org/dhaka/Whatwedo/Publications/WCMS_474048/lang–en/index.htm.

Ireland, P., 2016, 'Corporate Schizophrenia: The Corporation as a Separate Legal Person and an Object of Property', Working Paper, viewed 20 November 2017, https://research-information.bristol.ac.uk/en/publications/corporate-schizophrenia%2841587955-7dba-45d1-948a-ed5363848254%29/export.html.

Jensen, M., 2002, 'Value Maximisation, Stakeholder Theory, and the Corporate Objective Function', *Business Ethics Quarterly* 12(2), 235–256.

Kantor, J. & Streitfeld, D., 2015, 'Inside Amazon: Wrestling Big Ideas in a Bruising Workplace', *New York Times*, August 15, viewed 20 November 2017, www.nytimes.com/2015/08/16/technology/inside-amazon-wrestling-big-ideas-in-a-bruising-workplace.html.

Kasperkevic, J., 2016, 'Rana Plaza Collapse: Workplace Dangers Persist Three Years Later, Reports Find', *The Guardian*, 31 May, viewed 20 November 2017, www.theguardian.com/business/2016/may/31/rana-plaza-bangladesh-collapse-fashion-working-conditions.

Keay, A., 2012, 'The duty to promote the success of the company: is it fit for purpose in a post-financial crisis world?', in J. Loughrey (ed.), *Directors' Duties and Shareholder Litigation in the Wake of the Financial Crisis*, pp. 50–96, Edward Elgar Press, Cheltenham.

Kolbert, E., 2011, 'Age of Man', *National Geographic*, March 2011, viewed 20 November 2017, http://ngm.nationalgeographic.com/2011/03/age-of-man/anthropocene-photography.

Kolhatkar, S., 2016, 'Wells Fargo and a New Age of Banking Scandals', *The New Yorker*, 4 October, viewed 20 November 2017, www.newyorker.com/business/currency/wells-fargo-and-a-new-age-of-banking-scandals.

Labowitz, S. & Baumann-Pauly, D., 2015, 'Beyond the Tip of the Iceberg: Bangladesh's Forgotten Apparel Workers', Stern Centre for Business and Human Rights, viewed 20 November 2017, http://people.stern.nyu.edu/twadhwa/bangladesh.

Latour, B., 2005, *Reassembling the Social: An Introduction to Actor-Network-Theory*, Oxford University Press, Oxford.

Latour, B., 2011, 'Networks, Societies, Spheres – Reflections of an Actor-Network Theorist', *International Journal of Communication* 5(1), 796–810.

Latour, B., 2013, *An Inquiry into Modes of Existence*, Harvard University Press, Cambridge, MA.

Law, J., 1992, 'Notes on the Theory of the Actor Network: Ordering, Strategy, and Heterogeneity', *Systems Practice* 5(4), 379–393.

Levy, D. & Palpacuer, F., 2017, 'Global Production Networks and the Changing Corporation', in G. Baars & A. Spicer (eds), *The Corporation: A Critical, Multi-Disciplinary Handbook*, pp. 336–345, Cambridge University Press, Cambridge.

Locke, R., 2013, *The Promise and Limits of Private Power: Promoting Labor Standards in a Global Economy*, Cambridge University Press, New York.

Lyell, C., 1997, *Principles of Geology*, ed., J. Secord, Penguin Classics, London.
McBarnet, D., 2009, 'Corporate Social Responsibility beyond Law, through Law, for Law: The New Corporate Accountability', in D. McBarnet, A. Voiculescu & T. Campbell (eds), *The New Corporate Accountability: Corporate Social Responsibility and the Law*, pp. 9–58, Oxford University Press, Oxford.
McBarnet, D. & Whelan, C., 1999, *Creative Accounting and the Cross-Eyed Javelin Thrower*, Wiley, Chichester.
McFarlane, C., 2009, 'Translocal Assemblages: Space, Power and Social Movements', *Geoforum* 40, 561–567.
Malm, A., 2015, *Fossil Capital: The Rise of Steam Power and the Roots of Global Warming*, Verso Press, London.
Malm, A. & Hornborg, A., 2014, 'The Geology of Mankind? A Critique of the Anthropocene Narrative', *The Anthropocene Review* 1(1), 62–69.
Mawani, R., 2015a, 'Bee Workers and the Expanding Edges of Capitalism', *The Funambulist Papers* 60, viewed 20 November 2017, https://thefunambulist.net/philosophy/the-funambulist-papers-60-bee-workers-and-the-expanding-edges-of-capitalism-by-renisa-mawani.
Mawani, R., 2015b, 'Law and Colonialism: Legacies and Lineages', in A. Sarat & P. Ewick (eds), *The Handbook of Law and Society*, pp. 417–432, Wiley, Malden.
Meiville, C., 2014, 'The Limits of Utopia', *Salvage* 1, viewed 20 November 2017, http://salvage.zone/mieville_all.html.
Merk, J., 2011, 'Production beyond the Horizon of Consumption: Spatial Fixes and Anti-sweatshop Struggles in the Global Athletic Footwear Industry', *Global Society* 25(1), 73–95.
Moncrieff, L., 2011, 'The Molotov Milkshake: Corporate Social Responsibility and the Market', *Law and Critique* 22(3), 273–293.
Moncrieff, L., 2015, 'Karl Polanyi and the Problem of Corporate Social Responsibility', *Journal of Law and Society* 42(3), 435–459.
Moncrieff, L., 2016, 'Law, Scale, Anti-zooming, and Corporate Short-termism', *Law, Culture and the Humanities*, 1–24.
Moncrieff, L., 2017, 'Trumpism and Being in Worlds that Fall between Worlds', *Law and Critique* 28(2), 127–133.
Moore, J., 2015, *Capitalism in the Web of Life: Ecology and the Accumulation of Capital*, Verso, London.
Morton, T., 2013, *Hyperobjects: Philosophy and Ecology after the End of the World*, University of Minnesota Press, Minneapolis.
Morton, T., 2017, *Humankind: Solidarity with Non-Human People*, Verso, London.
Muller, M., 2015, 'Assemblages and Actor-networks: Rethinking Socio-material Power, Politics and Space', *Geography Compass* 9(1), 27–41.
Murphy, R., 2013, *Over Here and Under-taxed: Multinationals, Tax Avoidance and You*, Vintage Press, London.
Nedelsky, J., 1990, 'Law, Boundaries, and the Bounded Self', *Representations* 30, 162–189.
Nixon, R., 2014, *Slow Violence and the Environmentalism of the Poor*, Harvard University Press, Cambridge, MA.
Nolan, J., 2014, 'Refining the Rules of the Game: The Corporate Responsibility to Respect Human Rights', *Utrecht Journal of International and European Law* 30(78), 7–23.
Northcott, M., 2015, 'Eschatology in the Anthropocene: From the Chronos of Deep Time to the Kairos of the Age of Humans', in C. Hamilton, C. Bonneuil & F. Gemenne (eds), *The Anthropocene and the Global Environmental Crisis: Rethinking Modernity in a New Epoch*, pp. 100–111, Routledge, Oxon.

O'Connor, C., 2014, 'These Retailers Involved In Bangladesh Factory Disaster Have Yet To Compensate Victims', *Forbes*, 26 April, viewed 20 November 2017, www.forbes.com/sites/clareoconnor/2014/04/26/these-retailers-involved-in-bangladesh-factory-disaster-have-yet-to-compensate-victims/?.

Painter-Morland, M., 2007, 'Redefining Accountability in a Network Society', *Ethics Quarterly* 17(3), 515–534.

Parkinson, J., 1995, *Corporate Power and Responsibility: Issues in the Theory of Company Law*, Oxford University Press, Oxford.

Pavoni, A., 2015, 'Resistant Legacies', *Annals of Leisure Research* 18(4), 470–490.

Phillips, R., Freeman, E. & Wicks, A., 2003, 'What Stakeholder Theory is Not', *Business Ethics Quarterly* 13(4), 479–502.

Piketty, T., 2013, *Capital in the Twenty-First Century*, trans. A. Goldhammer, The Belknap Press of Harvard University Press, Cambridge, Mass.

Polanyi, K., 2002, *The Great Transformation*, 2nd edn, Beacon Press, Boston, MA.

Polaski, S., 2015, 'Remembering Rana Plaza: The Road Ahead', remarks made by the ILO Deputy Director General for Policy, at multi-stakeholder event, European Parliament, Brussels, 22 April, viewed 20 November 2017, www.ilo.org/global/about-the-ilo/newsroom/statements-and-speeches/WCMS_363015/lang–en/index.htm.

Rogers, B., 2016, 'Law and the Global Sweatshop Problem', in R. Appelbaum & N. Lichtenstein (eds), *Achieving Workers' Rights in the Global Economy*, pp. 137–151, Cornell University Press, New York.

Ross, R., 2016, 'The Twilight of CSR: Life and Death Illuminated by Fire', in R. Appelbaum & N. Lichtenstein (eds), *Achieving Workers' Rights in the Global Economy*, pp. 70–92, Cornell University Press, New York.

Rühmkorf, A., 2015, *Corporate Social Responsibility, Private Law and Global Value Chains*, Edward Elgar Press, Northampton.

Sandberg, J., 2011, 'Socially Responsible Investment and Fiduciary Duty: Putting the Freshfields Report into Perspective', *Journal of Business Ethics* 101(1), 143–162.

Santoso, B., 2017, '"Just Business" – Is the Current Regulatory Framework an Adequate Solution to Human Rights Abuses by Transnational Corporations?', *German Law Journal* 18(3), 533–558.

Sassen, S., 2014, *Expulsions: Brutality and Complexity in the Global Economy*, The Belknap Press of Harvard University Press, Cambridge, MA.

Schrempf-Stirling, J., 2011, 'Nokia Siemens Networks: Just Doing Business – or Supporting an Oppressive Regime?', *Journal of Business Ethics* 103(1), 95–110.

Schrempf-Stirling, J., 2014, 'A Social Connection Approach to Corporate Responsibility: The Case of the Fast Food Industry and Obesity', *Business & Society* 53(2), 300–332.

Serres, M., 1990, *The Natural Contract*, trans. E. MacArthur & W. Paulson, MIT Press, Cambridge, MA.

Sluiter, L., 2009, *Clean Clothes: A Global Movement to End Sweatshops*, Pluto Press, London.

Scottish Natural Heritage (SNH), 2017, 'Hutton's Unconformity – Siccar Point', viewed 20 November 2017, www.snh.org.uk/publications/on-line/geology/elothian_borders/hutton.asp.

Soule, S., 2009, *Contention and Corporate Social Responsibility*, Cambridge University Press, New York.

Steffen, W., Broadgate, W., Deutsch, L., Gaffney, O., & Ludwig, C., 2015, 'The Trajectory of the Anthropocene: The Great Acceleration', *The Anthropocene Review* 2(1), 81–98.

Talbot, L., 2015, *Critical Company Law*, 2nd edn, Routledge, Oxon & New York.

Talbot, L., 2016, 'Trying to Save the World with Company Law? Some Problems', *Legal Studies* 36(3), 513–534
Taylor, A., 2014, 'The Alberta Tar Sands', *The Atlantic*, 25 September, article and more photos, viewed 20 November 2017, www.theatlantic.com/photo/2014/09/the-alberta-tar-sands/100820.
Teubner, G., 2010, 'Fragmented Foundations: Constitutionalism Beyond the State', in P. Dobner & M. Loughlin (eds), *The Twilight of Constitutionalism*, pp. 327–342, Oxford University Press, Oxford.
Teubner, G., 2012, *Constitutional Fragments: Societal Constitutionalism and Globalisation*, Oxford University Press, Oxford.
Tombs, S., 2017, 'The Functions and Dysfunctions of Corporate Social Responsibility', in G. Baars & A. Spicer (eds), *The Corporation: A Critical, Multi-Disciplinary Handbook*, pp. 347–359, Cambridge University Press, Cambridge.
Veitch, S., 2007, *Law and Irresponsibility: On the Legitimation of Human Suffering*, Routledge-Cavendish, Oxon.
Veitch, S., 2017, 'The Sense of Obligation', *Jurisprudence* 8(3), 415–434.
Wark, M., 2015, 'Climate and Colonialism', Public Seminar, viewed 20 November 2017, www.publicseminar.org/2015/11/climate-colonialism.
Wood, E., 2002, *The Origin of Capitalism: A Longer View*, Verso Press, London.
Young, I. M., 2006, 'Responsibility and Global Justice: A Social Connection Model', *Social Philosophy and Policy* 23(1), 102–130.
Young, I. M., 2011, *Responsibility for Justice*, Oxford University Press, New York.
Zarin, C., 2015, 'The Artist Who is Bringing Icebergs to Paris', *The New Yorker*, 5 December, viewed 20 November 2017, www.newyorker.com/culture/culture-desk/the-artist-who-is-bringing-icebergs-to-paris.
Zumbansen, P., 2006, 'The Conundrum of Corporate Social Responsibility: Reflections on the Changing Nature of Firms and States', in R. Bratspies & R. Miller (eds), *Transboundary Harm: Lessons from the Trail Smelter Arbitration*, pp. 240–253, Cambridge University Press, New York.

5 Duty free

Scott Veitch[1]

I want to speak about bodies changed into new forms.

Ovid

Introduction

The Panama Papers exposé went some way to revealing the mechanisms and magnitude of global asset distribution as a way of circumventing state accountability techniques (Obermayer & Obermaier 2016). Two things stand out about this: one is the exposure to publicity of that which had hitherto been secret, and the other, that despite such secrecy much of what was exposed was legal. In the following, I attempt to understand the interplay of legal concepts and practices that make people, assets and obligations disappear from the radar of state and public accountability. I argue that the work of obligations and regulation is, ironically, key to this. I then consider how this 'duty free' scenario reveals the asymmetrical treatment of property rights and social rights, the conceptual labour that underpins this and some implications with respect to austerity and free riders.

Follow the money: now you see it, now you don't

The state has a general power to impose taxes via legislation and the citizen (or other legal person, such as a corporation) is liable to be subject to duties of taxation. Schematically, we can use Hohfeld's correlatives:

Power (of state) ⟵⟶ Liability (of citizen) [i]

In Hohfeld's terms, the state's power is a '(legal) power to effect [a] particular change of legal relations', while the citizen's liability is 'a liability to have a duty created' (Hohfeld 1964, pp. 51, 59).

Once a taxation scheme is specified through legislation, and the amount owed calculated and communicated, the power–liability relation produces a concrete

1 I am grateful to Lusina Ho, Daniel Matthews, Kyle McGee and Johan Van der Walt for their help with this chapter. The usual disclaimer applies.

right–duty relation. Now, in other words, the state has a legal right to collect the amount due and the citizen has a legal duty to pay it:

> Right (of state to collect amount owed) ←→ Duty (of citizen to pay amount due) [ii]

Powers operate, it could be said, at a different level from rights: what the power does is give the legal capacity to create the right; that right may or may not be created. And likewise the imposition of a specific duty is based on a general liability to have duties created.

This is not, of course, the only relevant correlative relation involved. A 'power to change legal relations' can refer, among other things, to the 'legal relation' a citizen may have when legally gaining income. When wages are acquired through an employment relation, for example, an employment contract may be restricted by the interposition of other legal standards: no contracting below the minimum wage, no discrimination on grounds of gender, etc. A number of duties may also ensue correlative to earnings. These will include a duty of others not to interfere unwarrantedly with a person's entitlement, but will also crucially include one deriving from a state's power to assign such economic gain within legislative categories that attract tax obligations (income tax, say). In this way, the right to income legally generated can be made to correlate with a duty to pay taxation as set out in legislation:

> Right (to income) ←→ Duty (to pay taxation) [iii]

This is a very elementary formulation of a basic model of tax obligation. What is interesting is now to consider how in certain instances some (but not all) of these relations are changed into others. Such transformations are achieved through the productive deployment of private law devices in complex chains of legal structuring. We will discover that while [i] remains, [ii] disappears and [iii] is transformed through such deployment. The result is the disappearance of a citizen's tax obligations, significantly not through exemptions made within existing tax legislation, but rather through dynamic transformations best captured by introducing another two of Hohfeld's correlatives.

Let us flesh this out a little bit by considering, again, in a highly simplified manner, how offshore trusts operate. A settlor (X) puts assets (shares, money, land titles, etc.) in a trust company (TC) set up in, for example, the British Virgin Islands (BVI).[2] X no longer owns these assets or any liabilities that may attach to them. The legal ownership of these assets is transferred to the TC who, as trustee, has certain obligations, among which are fiduciary obligations to those who are

2 Alternatively, X transfers assets to a domestic holding company which in turn becomes owned by a BVI holding company; this can then be put into a TC. (The chain of corporate holdings will likely be far more labyrinthine than this.) Either way, the process is internationalised, and foreign exchange controls circumvented, through complex legal (re)structuring of asset holding.

the beneficiaries of the trust. In terms of visibility and accountability, from the point of view of anyone outside looking into the question of ownership (including the state [S] in which X or the beneficiary resides), it is TC that is now the legal owner of the assets. But such legal ownership is not the sole form of property holding now in existence; the beneficiaries (B) established by the trust have equitable ownership. *They*, however, are not visible to anyone looking from the outside (including the state in which X or B resides). Because of non-disclosure agreements made in the BVI, the identity of B, the value of the assets in the trust and B's beneficial entitlement are all shielded from outsiders. Anonymity and invisibility of assets are now legally guaranteed.

But there is a two-way-mirror effect here. What is not visible from the point of view of a state's jurisdiction is the identity of and disbursement value to the beneficiary; the state, so to speak, tries to look for B's economic gains but can see nothing but its own reflection. However from the point of view of B in S's jurisdiction, the link to value is perfectly transparent: the *trustee* knows an identity to whom the benefit is to be transferred (even if that is a holding company rather than a named person) and, of course, B knows who they themselves are, even though the state does not. From this perspective the connections between trustee, beneficiary and benefit is unbroken, visible, known and secure; there is no invisibility or anonymity here.

Now B can receive their benefit (shares, money, etc.) in such a way that they do not attract tax obligations, in conformity with the particular legal conditions of the domestic jurisdiction (S): for example, payments may be made below the tax threshold or be made in such a form that they are not liable to capital gains taxes and so on. One legal device that may be utilised here (again depending on the domestic jurisdiction) is that of the gift. While gifts might be thought to attract obligations of gratitude on a beneficiary, they will not, if done 'correctly', attract obligations of taxation from the state.

What has happened here? An array of private law techniques – law of trusts, equity, corporate structuring, gifts – are hedged in by fiduciary obligations, obligations of non-disclosure and privacy, and distributed across international jurisdictions in complex legal webs, in order that assets and benefits can simultaneously be made to appear and disappear.[3] More prosaically, tax obligations are avoided on unaccountable amounts of economic gain. Most important of all, all this is perfectly legal.[4] Economic gain that might otherwise have been potentially liable for duty imposition has now become, literally, duty free.

So what has changed? In Hohfeld's terms, [i] still holds true. The state (S) has the power and the citizen (or corporation) a liability to be subject to duties of taxation. At a general level such power has not been relinquished; it continues to exist, as it were, in a constant state of potential. To understand what *has* changed,

3 The old saying that the law is like a spider's web that catches the poor and weak while the rich break through is inverted here; the latter do not break the web, but maintain it.

4 Other kinds of economic gain may also be shielded from the view of the state, though not necessarily from its taxation laws. For example, money acquired from illegal activities, such as drug dealing or human trafficking, may deploy such devices in order to be shielded from criminal law liability.

we need to introduce two other correlative pairings from Hohfeld. One involves privilege and the other immunity. Here is Stone's succinct description: 'whereas a privilege is freedom from a duty, an immunity (on Hohfeld's definition) would be freedom from the liability to have a duty created' (Stone 1964, p. 147).

Again we have two levels: just as a power may be used to create a right, an immunity can operate to prevent the creation of a duty. In Hohfeld's terms, 'a power is one's affirmative "control" over a given legal relation as against another; whereas an immunity is one's freedom from the legal power or "control" of another as regards some legal relation'. (Hohfeld 1964, p. 60) There may be many ways of using immunities and many reasons for doing so. A state, for example, may ratify an international human rights treaty that grants citizens an immunity from the liability of being made a slave. By doing so the state is 'disabled' from creating (the severe) duties associated with slavery. In Hohfeld's terms, the correlative is expressed as this:

Immunity ←→ Disability [iv]

Immunities may also be achieved through a process more akin to accretion than to the either/or format which is the result of legal ratification. It is this kind we are dealing with here.

To return to our example: if B is resident in S, [iii] no longer applies. That is, where in the basic model the right to income was liable to duties of taxation, that link is broken. B still legally acquires economic gain; but it no longer correlates to a duty to pay taxation. Instead, B's position has now assumed what in Hohfeld's terms is a privilege: 'one's freedom from the right or claim of another' (ibid.). So acquiring a privilege means that the other has a 'no-right' as against him/her. The correlative in [iii] has therefore transformed into this correlative:

Privilege ←→ No-right [v]

Thus when it comes to B's relation to S, while B has the right to receive benefits disbursed under the trust, S has a 'no-right' as against this same gain since it counts as privileged vis-à-vis the state. In other words, what would ordinarily be S's right to impose duties of taxation on legally acquired gain and to collect money due under the basic model has now become a 'no-right' of S; and what would ordinarily be a duty on the citizen cannot now register since B's right to income has become privileged vis-à-vis S. Hence:

Right (to income) ←→ Duty (to pay taxation) [iii]

has become:

Privilege (of beneficiary to duty free income) ←→ No-right (of state to tax income) [vi]

This also means that [ii] has disappeared, as S is unable to concretise a right to any amount of tax owed because of the two-way-mirror effect which ensures anonymity and invisibility of economic gain. The meaning of this is important: B is *not* in breach of a duty to pay a sum owed (as they would be if they breached [ii]) precisely because there *is* no legal sum owed.

There is one other level to note here: the security of B's privilege is further enhanced by a second level of protection. This is the *disability* of the state to 'change the relation' back the way; that is, to go from [vi] to [iii]. B's freedom *from* the state's power of potential intervention in the legal relation (legally gained money disbursed from the trust, say) is secured through the disabling of S's power to intervene (as expressed in the form of [iv]). Such disability is, as it were, more powerful than a concrete privilege since it blocks the *possibility* of legal intervention.

Whereas [iii] depended on the power in [i] being operationalised to intervene in a legal relation (an employment contract, say), such operationalisation is now barred due to the transformation [iv] effects on [iii].

It is important to understand why this intervention is barred. These are *not* tax exemptions granted by the state. Hohfeld claimed the 'best synonym' for 'immunity' is 'exemption'. Yet he also noted there is 'a subtle distinction between an immunity and an exemption' (ibid., pp. 62–3), and the distinction is, here, of the greatest consequence. Consider, by analogy, that in states that have compulsory military service, citizens have a duty to complete such service unless they are exempted from doing so. To be exempted, some personal identification and knowledge is necessary from both sides – citizen and state – such that the citizen is explicitly warranted an exemption. (The citizen may be medically unfit, say, and, with this knowledge, the state exempts him/her from carrying out the duties attached to military service.) This is different from the 'duty free' scenario. Here the state cannot ascertain the identity of the citizen in the first place in order to exempt them (or not) from liability to tax duties. The *difference* between an immunity and an exemption is that in the former someone 'is free, rather than freed, from such tax'[5] (Hohfeld 1964, p. 63, fn. 97, quoting a judicial opinion).

But this immunity is gained, as it were, indirectly. It is the result of the operation of a combination of (private) laws of general application – property, trusts, equity and so on – which, working together, achieve the condition of B's immunity and S's disability. A straightforward granting of a tax 'exemption' by S would create a privilege, but this would, no doubt, given the vast sums involved, be publicly and politically objectionable in most states. By contrast, establishing everything lawfully by deploying legal processes of immense complexity within and across national jurisdictions – the BVI trust mechanism (or the series of holding

5 Compare the situation of Queen Elizabeth II who is exempted from paying taxes on her personal income in the UK. Since 1992, however, she has 'volunteered' to pay tax. One might doubt if this is really a tax; more like *noblesse oblige*, still alive and well in the highest echelon of the UK's aristocracy.

company transfers that will take assets offshore), hedged in through appending other legal devices (non-disclosure, commercial confidentiality, lawyer–client privileges, etc.) – means that what is going on here is neither illegal nor blatant. Indeed, in a final act of security, it is not just that beneficiaries do not have tax liabilities or duties to states: because of the legality of these complex structures, *states have duties to beneficiaries* (whoever they are) not to enquire too closely into their economic gains. In other words, the *disappearance* of certain obligations – primarily taxation, but also potentially well-established civic obligations – is entirely dependent upon a series of legal rights *and* obligations, prominent among which is the law of obligations.[6] The maintenance of legal security for beneficiaries' property therefore may rely ultimately on the capacity of *state* legal systems to protect these legal entitlements and expectations *from* the state. Indeed, in a final irony, it may even rely on the institutions of the very state that is being deprived from access to assets. As Stiglitz and Pieth observe, 'after the United States invaded Panama (making investors nervous), Mossack Fonseca shifted its main operations to the British Virgin Islands. BVI soon became its biggest jurisdiction of operation. BVI also had the added advantage of a legal system answerable to British courts, offering a great deal of security to investors'[7] (Stiglitz & Pieth 2016, p. 6, fn. 10).

There is an added dimension to this that we have not yet touched on. To see this it is helpful to depart from (or perhaps augment) Hohfeld's strictly analytical account of correlative rights and duties (and their various transformations) by paying more attention to the institutional conditions within which they are situated. When we do so, we note that the work of obligations may in fact be more significant than that of rights. This is because of what Jeremy Waldron calls the existence of 'waves of duty'.[8] That is, if rights are to be taken seriously, then attention must be paid to the range of duties on others required to uphold them. But such duties are far more various than the correlative model would suggest. For example, the right to property may impose correlative duties of non-interference on multiple actors. A right *in rem*, say – a right 'against the world' – means that countless people have a correlative duty not to interfere unwarrantedly with this right. In this rather trite sense there are far more obligations than rights. But in a more complex conceptual sense, even within apparently simple cases of property exchange – contract law, say – duties multiply within the law. For example, Peter Birks draws attention to what he terms the 'packages of obligation inherent in transactions' that come with simple agreements between parties in a

6 Roger Cotterrell makes a related point with respect to moral obligations, noting also the shared terminology in law and morality with respect to 'trust': 'The trust-form, concentrating and guaranteeing property-power, not only fails to impose moral obligations on the powerful, but actually encourages us to think of *moral obligations owed to them* because of their beneficial entitlements' (Cotterrell 1987, p. 88, emphasis in original).

7 You would be hard-pressed to make this up; the more or less invisible hand of genius is here present!

8 See Waldron 1989, pp. 503–19.

contract of sale. These '*natura contractus*' may include all kinds of terms set into the contract that may never be agreed – about the quality of goods, distribution of liabilities and so on. As he puts it: 'The seller who says no more than "Yes" is genuinely opting into a complex *bundle of obligations*' (Birks 2014, p. 29, emphasis added).

If we now broaden this account to the context of institutional conditions and requirements, we find that there are inevitably multiple levels and instances of obligations that go beyond the conceptual senses just mentioned. Consider two examples. The first deals with what may be termed a positive right (or a 'social right', of a kind we will return to later), while the second is a 'negative right' (or a first-generation, political right).

As a positive right, the right to education can only be secured equally throughout a large society by the positive action of many others. Typically, this will involve assigning duties to a range of actors, individuals and institutions. So an individual's right to education will require for its protection duties on government and local authorities to assign adequate resources to fund schools at various levels. Schools and teachers will in turn have a wide range of duties imposed on them by state and professional bodies. There will then be further duties to establish everything from assessment schemes to student safety procedures, and so on. The right to education therefore produces these multiple levels and instances (or 'waves', as Waldron calls them) of obligation, without the existence of which the right would in practice likely be meaningless.

This same pattern is also true for negative rights, even if it is at first glance less obvious. Consider, then, a second example: the right to freedom of assembly. On one level this correlates to a duty not to interfere with those who exercise their right by assembling. Such a duty may attach to countless other actors (other citizens, and importantly the government and its agents) producing (as we saw earlier) many more obligations than rights. While in one sense these duties may be adequately performed by doing nothing – not interfering – that is not, however, the only kind of duties involved if the right to freedom of assembly is to be secured. Here too there are further duties that require *positive* action if the right is to be adequately protected. These include, for example, duties on the government to provide adequate resources to secure the safety of those exercising their right: duties of police officers to protect, for example, protesters in a demonstration from interference by third parties; duties on the police force as an institution to train officers adequately in being able dealing with such situations; duties to teach officers the relevant laws within which they are bound to act, and so on. In addition, if the right to freedom of assembly is alleged to have been breached, procedural and other duties come into play: duties of investigation and proof, ultimately perhaps the whole array of court procedures, and so on. The right to freedom of assembly is therefore not simply correlative to a single duty *not* to interfere, but requires a plethora of levels and types of obligation to carry out positive acts if it is to be taken seriously. This complex field of conceptual and pragmatic institutional activity is captured well by MacCormick (2007, p. 133):

> The instruments that confer or protect [rights] are themselves complex and polysemous, and the business of practically guaranteeing implementation of or respect for the rights calls for a substantial body of interpretative decision-making by appropriate courts or other authorities. In terms of the simple, perhaps 'atomic', person-to-person right-duty relationship these appear as large complex molecules, where a single 'right' may imply a myriad of rights-and-duties, and indeed other legal relations or positions.

What is the relevance of these observations to the 'duty free' scenario? Part of the answer is that the protection of B's entitlements and expectations (more accurately described as privileges and immunities rather than rights, as we have seen) requires precisely the same sorts of positive institutional activities just identified. At various levels and in various forms it is the actions of multiple duty holders which shore up the security of their assets and guarantee their anonymity. This will take the form predominantly of role responsibilities including the duties of several different types of office holders. For example, the duties imposed on trustees require a legal and institutional framework within which assets are reliably protected for the sake of those who establish trusts (X) and their beneficiaries (B). Again, these may incorporate different levels of protection, from statutory to professional and procedural obligations. Without the assurances made available through such regulatory institutional practices, along with the complex 'packages of obligation' (as Birks put it) involved in multiple private law transactions, the likelihood of those who desire to hide themselves and their assets getting involved in the practice would be small.

'Waves' of obligation may be necessary and desirable to protect all rights, including, as we have seen, those that are important to modern political communities, such as rights to education and freedom of assembly. But the same kind of waves, in their conceptual and pragmatic aspects, are also necessary in the washing away (so to speak) of traces of identities and assets such that they cannot be seen by state authorities. Whether and for whom *this* is desirable is, of course, a different matter.

There's no such thing as a 'free' market

The dynamic – or accretion-like – quality of the achievement of immunity is significant in itself and in its implications. In itself the complexity of the structuring of legal relations with respect to offshore trusts makes it extremely difficult to smash the two-way mirror. In one sense this is hardly surprising: anonymity and invisibility of assets are precisely what X and B want, and they are hardly likely to get them directly from their government. Rather, they have to pay privately for them. Paying for the services of the intermediaries – lawyers, accountants, financial advisors and so on – necessary to set up, secure and care for assets over potentially lengthy periods of time requires a lot of money. The more 'caring' and trustworthy the intermediaries are, the more attention they give to assets and potential threats to them, the more attentive to their obligations and considerate to legal niceties they are, the better paid they will be.

This observation also signals something else: this a highly regulated form of market activity. The idea that these practices amount to a free market – a kind of unfettered Smithian 'natural liberty' in action – is simply not true. An 'unregulated' global free market would be extremely problematic for such business. In part this is because without regulation these assets and their mobility would be nothing. Often literally, nothing: many of the assets simply would not exist without complex institutional normative ordering.[9] Moreover, the legal conduits being utilised are of a highly technical and specialised nature. (The dry quality of their reformulation in the present analysis gives the tiniest glimpse of the massive – Sahara-like – scale of dryness in the complexity of offshore trust funds.) The obvious truth is that the lawyers, accountants and other intermediaries would not be paid the fees they are, by the highly money-conscious people employing them, if they were merely occasionally greasing the wheels of financial transactions carried out by the principals themselves.[10] Indeed, the amount paid to such 'middle men' is a valuable index of all this *as* regulatory activity.

Hence the public 'debate' where an opposition is posed between regulation (bad) and deregulation (good) is misleading. So too is the claim that deregulation is now gaining the upper hand as the welfare state recedes under the liberalising transformations associated with globalisation. Welfare states may well be receding as modes of organising social relations and protections, but that is not the same as deregulation. As David Graeber has argued, the contrary is in fact true: ours is not an era of deregulation but of hyper-regulation. The fusion of public and private power, techniques and mentalities across governments and corporations has now assumed proportions, Graeber (2015, pp. 18, 9) claims, of 'total bureaucratization':

> [A]ny market reform, any government initiative intended to reduce red tape and promote market forces will have the ultimate effect of increasing the total number of regulations, the total amount of paperwork, and the total number of bureaucrats the government employs.[11]

9 For an account of this with respect to financial derivatives see, for example, Campbell & Picciotto 2000.

10 Mossack Fonseca, subject of the Panama Papers leak, is only the fourth largest 'off-shoring' firm. Plausible estimates (given the secrecy involved, that is all they can be) of the amount of economic gains being kept secret from state tax jurisdictions is 'in the trillions of dollars' (Stiglitz & Pieth 2016, pp. 6–7).

11 He calls this the 'Iron Law of Liberalism'. The hyper-bureaucratisation that has resulted from the marketisation of universities is another example with which some readers will have familiarity. As Graeber observes: 'There was a time when academia was society's refuge for the eccentric, brilliant, and impractical. No longer. It is now the domain of professional self-marketers' (Graeber 2015, pp. 134–5). Consonant with the wider culture of audit, accounting and quantification, he adds, importantly, 'Not only is this [wider] world ultimately a product of financialization, it's really just a *continuation* of it' (ibid., p. 42, emphasis added).

One need only think of the regulatory force required to establish a 'free market' (the European Union is exemplary) to see that such bureaucratisation is a reality with which we have become all too familiar as we are required to make our accommodations to it across the spectrum of routine activities, from work to leisure.

What is too readily perceived then as the sole form of interference in the market – that which is associated with certain kinds of redistributive state activities – downplays or ignores the enormous amount of regulatory activity across legal and corporate practices, including those of 'offshoring'. (These latter activities are of course equally redistributive in their intent and effect, just in different ways; they distribute wealth up the way, as it were, into fewer hands.) But it is intense, expensive and often constitutive regulatory activity that is necessary to sustain what appears as the unfettered liberty of market transactions. Hence another irony surfaces: the unaccountability of trillions of dollars to states globally has only become possible in an age of generalised institutional hyper-regulation. Perhaps this shouldn't be too surprising. There is historical precedent for the basic principle; comparing the regulations that were eventually enacted to counter the devastating social effects of the free market mentality in nineteenth century England, Karl Polanyi had already noted this paradox: 'While *laissez-fare* economy was the product of deliberate state action, subsequent restrictions on *laissez-faire* started in a spontaneous way. *Laissez-faire* was planned. Planning was not' (Polanyi 1957, p. 141).

What are some of the implications of this dynamic achievement of immunities? One of the most significant is this: that it is the settlors and beneficiaries that decide whether and how much will be their liability for taxation.[12] This is a remarkable power, one that differentiates one class of people from the rest of a state's citizens. If immunity is a relational achievement vis-à-vis the state, it produces a *de facto* differential *status* with respect to regular taxpayers. In replacing [iii] with [vi] they – at least as they are advised by their lawyers, financial advisors, etc. – assume the status whereby payment of taxes is a matter of *their* choice, no longer that of the state seeking to impose a duty equally on all.

In this sense it is also a direct attack on a fundamental principle – equality of all before the law – of the doctrine of the rule of law.[13] Unlike Queen Elizabeth II volunteering to pay an amount of the profit from her private income to the state (see footnote 5), no hint of *noblesse oblige* emerges here. (Charity does not count; it does not alleviate injustices, it merely confirms them.) Quite the opposite, in fact. Besides, if the Queen's status as immune is constitutionally grounded, it is not so for those in the 'duty free' class. Rather, this status is achieved not by design but, as I have called it, accretion, and the final assurance of this is what it

12 Sometimes states may be complicit in this, making secret deals as in the case of Ireland and Apple. These deals are nonetheless almost entirely dictated by the large market players: hence while Ireland was 'willing to rob their so-called European partners of billions of euros in tax revenues … Apple's effective tax rate [was] 0.005 percent' (Stiglitz & Pieth 2016, p. 21).

13 See also Harrington (2017).

takes to attain it: the acquisition of sufficient wealth to be able to buy into this position.[14]

The role of money has been mentioned a couple of times, and it is worth remembering that its function is not straightforwardly that of buying out of duties that may otherwise be owed. That indeed is why these practices do not amount to bribery, tax evasion or fraud; they are legalised. In the kind of activities we have been discussing, money itself is not identical with the legal mechanisms invoked and paid for. Still, money does have a catalytic capacity that can be drawn on to aid the transformations we are observing, and this remains highly important. Marx noted this capacity in his early manuscripts when he asked, 'Does not my money thus change all my incapacities into their opposite?' Through money, may not the weak become strong, the stupid wise, the unloved loved, he asked. The power of money – this 'visible god', he quotes Shakespeare[15] – is in reality immense in its capacity to transform: 'What I cannot do as a man, thus what my individual faculties cannot do, this I can do through money.' Such capacity has, however, a dual use; it can facilitate one thing ***and*** its opposite. This is crucial in our context. 'If money,' Marx continues, 'is the bond that binds me to all human life, that binds society to me and me to nature and men, is not money the bond of all bonds? Can it not tie and untie all bonds? Is it not, therefore, also the universal means of separation?' (Marx 2000, p. 110)

It is precisely this kind of operation we have endeavoured to trace in the previous section. But we have also seen that money is not sufficient on its own to do all the necessary work of 'tying and untying' obligations. It is, however, the means through which legal concepts, categories and institutions are set in motion, for it is these latter that secure the anonymity and invisibility of asset-holders and holdings. If money is, as Marx put it, 'the true agent both of separation and of union, the galvano-chemical power of society' (ibid.), then it is its structural complicity with legal doctrine and practice that explains the disappearing effects we have seen here. As a form of complicity, law needs money and money needs lawful forms to do its work. It is a form of legal aid, we might say, for the wealthy.

Immunity and its implications

The term Hohfeld uses – immunity – is instructive in ways that take us beyond its technical use in his analysis of correlative legal relations. Etymologically,

14 Of course, this is what the monarch, and her predecessors, needed, and had, too: wealth. In gaining their tax immunity and constitutionalising it, they were merely ahead of the game. It is only the sustained operation of historical amnesia that allows it to appear otherwise. As Bob Dylan (1983) put it: 'Steal a little and they throw you in jail, steal a lot and they make you a king.'

15 It 'will make black white, foul fair/ Wrong right, base noble, old young, coward valiant …Will knit and break religions … place thieves/ And give them title, knee and approbation/ With senators on the bench'; 'thou visible god/ That solder'st close impossibilities/ And makest them kiss! that speak'st with every tongue/ To every purpose!' (*Timon of Athens*, 4.3)

'immunity' has its Latin root in *munus. Munus* has a double signification: one aspect refers to the duties that come with public office. These are responsibilities formed in the state – the *municipality* – to be carried out by those citizens whose honour it is to have been selected as holders of official positions. In this sense *munus* involves an assignation of responsibility or obligation, and it is one such obligation that explains its other signification. Conceived of as an honour, taking up civic office is understood as a gift bestowed on a citizen. But with gifts come responsibilities. 'In nominating somebody as a magistrate,' writes Benveniste, 'one confers on him honour and certain advantages. This obliges him in turn to counter-service in the form of expenditure, especially for games and spectacles' (Benveniste 1973, p. 79). In this second form the notion of exchange or reciprocity is expressed as the obligation to offer gifts in return for gifts received. This is not corruption, but carries the sense of public 'munificence' (the root is shared) which registers a

> favour received and the obligation to reciprocate. This explains both the sense of 'administrative duty', 'official function', and that of 'a favour shown to somebody', because what is concerned is 'public service', that is to say an office conferred on somebody who honours it by keeping it within limits.
>
> (ibid., p. 150)

From here we see that 'community' carries that double too: as com-*munis*, it is a form of binding association rooted in duty and service among citizens in a reciprocal manner. It is not, says Benveniste, '"he who shares the duties" but really "he who has munia in common". Now if the system of compensation is active within one and the same circle, this determines a "community", a group of persons united by this bond of reciprocity' (ibid., 79). It is the achievement of this *unity* through reciprocities of mutual compensation that thus marks the identity of a group as *a* community, something that is expressed well in the variant reading of *communis* as com-*unis*; united, as one.[16]

What then of 'immunity'? There are again two aspects to pay attention to here. The first is as a simple negation of what has just been described. Here is how a recent writer on the subject expresses the point:

> If the members of the *communitas* are bound by the same law, by the same duty, or gift to give (the meanings of *munus), immunis* is he or she who is exempt or exonerated from these. *Immunis* is he or she who has no obligations toward the other and can therefore conserve his or her essence intact as a subject and owner of him or herself.
>
> (Esposito 2013, p. 39)

Here the author seems to be indirectly acknowledging something of significance. Immunity is the negation of community. But while community is clearly

16 See Williams 1988, p. 70.

understandable as a noun (the '*communitas*'), its equivalent in negation is more difficult to identify as such and the author turns to the adjective – *immunis* – which describes the individual 'who has no obligations'. Such an individual has burst apart or failed to acknowledge any ties of reciprocity and no longer sees him or herself as bound within the group.

And this points us to the second, linguistic, connection that has important political bearings. According to Benveniste (1973, p. 79),

> [the] archaic sense of *immunis* [is] as 'ingratus' (that is to say one who fails to make return for a benefit). If *munus* is a gift carrying the obligation of an exchange, *immunis* is he who does not fulfil his obligation to make due return.

The one who sees or thinks him or herself as *immunis* is the ingrate, the one who is ungrateful, who cannot reciprocate gratitude, or indeed anything at all, for what s/he has been given. It is crucial to note the structure of this latter point. For although the one who is *immunis* has broken or failed to recognise the bond of obligation in one sense, s/he has not departed the *communitas* entirely. Why not? Precisely because s/he has *benefitted* from something the community made available. That is why s/he is ungrateful *for* something – the benefit, the gift bestowed on her/him.

This simultaneous connection and disconnection is another way of thinking about the two-way mirror. B's privilege is precisely that of a *beneficiary*, one who benefits in terms of anonymity and asset-holding from the complex web of legal instruments and relations made available to them by others, including the apparatuses of state jurisdictions, which are the product of enormous amounts of *collective* regulatory activity. A beneficiary's immunity – their failure to 'make return for a benefit' – captures precisely both their dependency on others *and* their disavowal of obligations that are otherwise necessary to maintain the community of which they are still in one sense a part. It is doubtful whether a subjective sense of 'ingratitude' would register on those who become so immune. If anything, it is more likely, one suspects, to be feelings of entitlement that are present. But the *secrecy* of such activities indicates a structural manifestation of an awareness that these practices are far from honourable – even from the point of view of those engaging in them.

Before leaving this, we might note in passing that this is also a good way of thinking about a problem taken up elsewhere in (mainly analytical) political theory, that of the free rider. The 'free rider problem' is one which emerges when it is possible and desirable for one or more individuals to benefit from others' collective efforts without making one's own contribution to these. In so far as this problem has been translated into the popular imagination it is a mark of how successful a political slant it has been given that attention is normally directed to issues of 'welfare state dependency'; those who 'take something for nothing' has attracted the opprobrium of those who moralise against 'dole scroungers' and 'benefit cheats'.

When this problem is put in an alternative, more factually accurate perspective, it becomes clear that the real 'free rider' problem lies elsewhere. Aside from the fact that it has always been the middle classes that benefit most from the welfare state,[17] and remembering that the Mossack Fonseca revelations only expose one among a far greater set of such activities, the 'offshoring' of *trillions* of dollars of assets as a way of avoiding state duties vastly dwarfs anything that might be gained by 'cheating on social security'. In a sense, the Panama Papers merely revealed details of something that was widely known to be occurring, and which was taken for granted as the normal working of offshoring practices. The fact that Donald Trump, in his election debates with Hillary Clinton, could point out (rightly) that if he paid zero federal income tax it was due to the rules available in the United States which allowed him to do so merely confirms the existence of such an expectation among the wealthy and super-wealthy. (That he was publicly so proud of this while standing for public office – 'That makes me smart,' he said – is the only thing that possibly differentiated him from others in his class.) Contrary to those who would have it seen otherwise, free riding is largely the province of the wealthy in the global economy.

The asymmetries of austerity

The achievement of immunisation of economic gain as against taxation duties has another kind of implication. This is, in a sense, a result of the mixture of legal and policy practices. In terms of resources available to the state, the implication is a serious one.

Following on from the previous observations about immunities resulting from dynamic accretions of complex legal transactions, the question of whether the state can *afford* tax privileges or endure immunities is not addressable. The question (like the assets) is, so to speak, off the table; its disappearance appears merely as the collateral damage of the legitimate working of private law mechanisms. Yet this is not as unintentional as might first appear. This becomes clear when we consider what happens in the case of social rights which, by contrast, are *not* so immunised; they, in other words, *are* subject to the question of affordability.[18] In times of austerity (it is just clearer then, not qualitatively different from 'normal' times) the question of affordability *is* raisable and it is answered by making the capacity to address citizens' welfare needs subject to a test of affordability. That is, needs, and the social rights which protect them, are made commensurate with money.

At one level such commensuration is impossible. Social *needs* – which social rights protect: to health, education, welfare and so on – cannot be made the subject of economic calculation without misrepresenting and misunderstanding what these are. Fulfilling the need for the well-being achievable through education, for example, cannot simply be addressed by paying for it. Otherwise one could go

17 See e.g. Garland 2016.
18 See also Christodoulidis 2017.

into a shop, pay and come out educated. That education involves attaining certain standards *internal* to a particular practice – learning to read well or play a musical instrument, or how to reason with rules and principles – means there is an incommensurability between the practice of learning these standards and paying money to be able to learn them. One might have to pay to be educated, but one cannot be educated (in reading, playing a musical instrument or reasoning or anything else) by buying it like you would buy a piano or a set of textbooks. Such constitutive incommensurabilities are an essential element in appreciating the differences between an institution (such as a music school that one may pay to attend, which needs to buy instruments and pay staff) and a practice (like learning how to play music) (MacIntyre 1985). Hence that someone may have to pay for an education does not reduce what education is to a money form, and if you thought it did, you would not understand what it means to be educated.

However, to the extent that *de facto* commensurability *is* introduced, then it damages the meaning of education, just as it 'short-changes' the one who seeks education. To see how this might occur, consider the following objection: that it is not the *need* – to be educated or healthy and so on – that is being made commensurate with money, but rather the delivery of services required to meet the need (i.e. institutions such as schools, hospitals, etc.). But this objection is mistaken. If people have rights, it is perfectly reasonable to assert that without financed institutional support for them they become worthless. We have already seen how the security of rights depends upon conceptually and institutionally formulated 'waves of duties' requiring (even in the case of 'negative' rights) positive actions on behalf of numerous actors. A citizen's right to vote in a large democracy, for example, where the state provides no resources to organise, collate and count votes would severely reduce the meaningfulness of the right. The value of equal citizenship that the right to vote protects and promotes would be undermined by making it subject to economic calculations of affordability. Likewise with needs: the value of education is undermined when the costs of meeting these needs becomes the measure of access to education, since it is now possible that the costs may be deemed unaffordable. Analogously to the funding required for the right to vote to be meaningful, if there is said to be insufficient tax revenue in the government fund to properly support education or health as a universal right, then financial calculations which lead to cuts in services mean the needs and values protected by that right are likewise vulnerable to the negative impact of 'austerity measures'. (This has been the case, post-financial crash, in the United Kingdom, particularly, though not solely, with respect to health.) Hence the *de facto* introduction of commensurabilities can override constitutive incommensurabilities to the detriment of needs and the rights protecting them. Such is one effect of setting social rights on the scales of 'affordability'.

It is the exact opposite with the 'duty free' situation. The immunisation we have detailed achieves a *de facto* incommensurability between liability to taxation and assets and economic gain, despite the fact that these assets and gains *are* commensurate with (taxable) money. They may indeed just *be* money. The disability of the state to create tax duties is sustained not because commensurability is impossible; in fact, those who seek anonymity and invisibility of assets do what they do precisely because it *is* possible. Unlike the needs that socio-economic rights protect, there are no needs here to be met such that, were they not met, it would put the wealthy in a position of vulnerability. On the contrary: should taxation be levelled on them, it would achieve equality, not hardship.

But in times of austerity, though again not just then, unlike welfare needs and the rights that seek to protect them, X's or B's assets are *not* put on a scale of 'affordability'. They are made unamenable to the question of whether they should be measured; they are immunised against an enquiry into whether or not the state can afford their disappearance. In short, private assets are protected from tax calculations in a way that citizens' welfare needs are not, and it is precisely the *asymmetry* of commensurating practices that is central to this.

Conclusion

There are two readings of the 'duty free' scenario that we might conclude from this analysis. First, that those paying for the legal and financial instruments and labour necessary to disappear themselves and their assets from state accountability mechanisms do no more than draw on the resources available to them. In doing so they objectively treat states and legal orders as just one among many business factors to be taken into account in their financial calculations. They treat, in other words, the market mechanisms of exchange as covering the whole field of their operations, refusing to see any difference between public and private interests. One can treat this as either a form of global ordering beyond the state, as a whole new network of more or less subterranean *lex mercatoria* whose function is to generate and sustain wealth for those who would want to secure as much as they can to themselves. Or one can see it as merely a continuation of a far older pattern, one that with respect to the law of trusts goes back centuries, and with which states have been and remain complicit, preserving and protecting the immunities and privileges of those with assets to shield from public view. This would confirm the primacy and durability of Locke's dictum in his *Two Treatises* that 'The great and chief end therefore of men's uniting into commonwealths and putting themselves under government is the preservation of their property'. Such an account *would* offer a formulation of the 'public' as qualitatively different from the realm of private interest. But this formulation could be seen as both ideological and pragmatic. Ideological since the claim that rich and poor are equally 'all in it together' requires some legitimating narrative about 'the public' or 'commonwealth' of shared interests that transcends all individual interests, when the reality is always otherwise: that it is the interests of the wealthy that are really being served. Pragmatic since it points to the fact that asset-holding and a 'free' market cannot rely solely on their own devices and momentum to achieve the desired security of property. As Locke in his wisdom saw, without settled rules, impartial judges and organised coercive force – that is, without law and government – private property would remain insecure.

A second, more critical reading of this situation commonly turns to moral or civic critique, and/or to state sovereignty as a means of redress. On the moral or civic account, normative standards against which to judge this behaviour are reasonably clear and largely uncontroversial. That one should pay one's taxes as a citizen is a condition and expression of equal reciprocal duty in community. As just noted, failing to respect such a principle of equality prioritises an instrumental mentality but one that still relies on institutions and fellow citizens as resources for realising individuals' strategic self-interests. In treating others as means to their enjoyment of benefits and not as equals, this form of free riding is a bit like the person who doesn't buy their round in the pub: they're happy to be there and enjoy the company and contributions of others but refuse to contribute when it's their turn. Someone who acts in this way, when they are perfectly capable of paying, is usually thought socially suspect.[19]

Likewise, normatively speaking, with the tax avoider. They are, to use our earlier term, *ingratus*, deploying what Shaxson calls an '*inverted morality* that holds tax, democracy and society to be bad, and tax havens, tax avoidance and secrecy to be good' (Shaxson 2012, p. 31, emphasis added). Ordinarily, those who do not like the use to which taxes are put, nor the ways in which they are currently defined or rates set, cannot just refuse to pay. They may seek to replace, if they can, those representatives who make the policy decisions with others whose views reflect their own. Occasionally, as a last resort, on deep moral or political grounds some group might withhold a portion of their taxes to make, and make widely known, an important objection. But as civil disobedients attempting to persuade others in the community of the injustice they perceive current policies to be perpetrating, they know they are breaking the law and they will do so with as much publicity as possible, and accept the legal consequences.[20]

None of these features applies, however, to those who are the 'duty free'. They are, by contrast, secretive; they pay others to hide themselves and their wealth from public view; and they have no obvious moral or civic justification for their position; otherwise, putting their case publicly would not be such a problem. Most significantly, they do not see themselves as the equals of their fellow citizens. They see themselves as *immunis*, somehow special, elevated, different from the rest. Yet they are willing to accept the benefits of the structures of wealth generation –

19 I am all too aware that countries vary in their expectations of appropriate behaviour in this social setting. But where the practice does exist as described, I would also resist a claim that others always have a correlative individual right; insisting on any such claim would be immensely prissy (and almost as bad as *not* buying your round!). As with most social practices, a sense of appropriateness is important. But if rights do seem out of place here, still, the obligation remains.

20 The 'Peace Tax Seven' were one such group in the UK. As Quakers, they conscientiously objected to their 'financial conscription' through taxation in paying for military hardware that was being deployed, at that point, in the killings resulting from the UK state's invasion of Iraq. The courts agreed with the tax office, however, that there was no exception in law available to them: they must still pay their taxes. For a reading of this, see Veitch, 2007, pp. 136–144. On conditions of civil disobedience, see Rawls 1999.

including, among many other things, the legally regulated (and taxed) productive labour of their fellow citizens – and the security provided to them by the publicly funded legal institutions they rely on. Since they refuse to contribute as others do by buying their privileges and immunities, *evaluatively* speaking, there would not be much more by way of fine-grained analysis to be carried out with respect to such attitudes. Since their 'thirst for money'[21] appears unquenchable, 'greed' would be a perfectly sufficient evaluation.

But such an approach, while understandable, may overly psychologise the diagnosis and veer towards a condemnatory moralism that merely targets the usual suspects for opprobrium. Besides, efforts at shaming are unlikely to gain any purchase in the shameless province of an inverted morality. Yet it may form part of an impetus for a more sophisticated political response that does have some promise. On this view, it is the exercise of sovereignty and political will that is required to intervene to break the cycle of tax avoidance.[22] Legislation could be enacted to plug the holes through which assets currently slip, making them henceforth liable to taxation. On this view, there is nothing intrinsic to the law as it stands, including private law doctrines, that makes it immune from legislative change in a way that would improve tax collection. If change is currently blocked, then it is due to a *lack* of political will, not because of anything in the nature of legal ordering as such. There may be various reasons why such a lack exists, not least the coincidence of the interests of the wealthy with those of the political class in many states. But if political will is lacking in a particular national jurisdiction, then it is also possible to try to deal with the problem at the supra-state level, as the European Union has recently tried to do. This, of course, makes it more difficult to broker agreements and co-ordinate action, but again this is a matter of political will or its failure. Besides, if this is a global issue, then like addressing global warming, it needs global solutions, and these cannot be enacted by sovereign states on their own.

This is a view with which I have a good deal of sympathy. The practice of offshoring may be technically complex, but an alternative, more rigorous set of legislative enactments could surely make some improvements on the current situation, particularly if national and supra-national action were carried out in tandem.[23] But I would like to press for a little caution here, and it follows directly from the analysis of the problem offered in the earlier parts of this chapter. The nature, complexity and scale of the 'duty free' situation in both its conceptual and sociological density suggest that legislation will run up against certain limits. Even if these are contingent within the law as it currently stands, they are significant in terms of thinking about redressing the situation. Contingencies come in different

21 This is Obermayer and Obermaier's (2016, p. 231) description of the Chinese politicians and their relatives whose names were found in the Mossack Fonseca files. That they are supposedly *communist* politicians is either tragedy or farce, depending on your point of view.

22 This view, summarised briefly here, is the position taken by Johan van der Walt in his chapter.

23 See e.g. Stiglitz & Pieth 2016; Pogge & Mehta 2016.

forms, with different weights attached to them, and some are easier to remove than others.

In concluding this chapter, I therefore note the following three reasons to be cautious about the capacity of legislative reform. First, the spread and speed of mobility of assets within an extensive globally linked capitalist network means that efforts at reform are limited in part because a global system of accountability is only as strong as its weakest link. But because there are financial incentives to *be* the weakest link, states or territories, or at least certain groups therein, can benefit from playing this role in the network, and use their sovereignty to remain beyond the reach of the jurisdiction of other states. Second, there is a technological aspect to this activity that is new and throws up novel kinds of regulatory challenges. That money and assets are moveable globally at the click of a mouse, and that they can be stored online in electronic forms and cryptocurrencies that ensure anonymity, constitute significant difficulties in addressing the traceability problem. This may seem like a relatively small, pragmatic issue, easily solved by political will and the better deployment of technological means. But the note of caution sounding here is also one of realism. Consider a final example: if one of the most powerful states in the world – China – a one-party authoritarian state, with firm and largely uncontested centralised political will, and with a technical surveillance capacity that would be the envy of any investigative regulator (assuming they were happy to sideline basic human rights) – if such a state cannot easily succeed in stopping assets leaking into the global system unaccountably, then one can appreciate why democratic states might face greater challenges. The virtual dimension to the global economy now undoubtedly plays a major part in adding to any state's difficulties with respect to the prospects of success for legislative reform.

And this leads to the third and final reason for caution. The problem faced by China, and other states, is not merely technological. It is legal. China is instructive then for another reason. That is, the rise of tax avoidance coincides in China with the release of private property rights into the economic and legal systems over the last 30 years, and the freeing up of market activities and importation of legal forms (corporations, trusts, etc.) to establish what is essentially now a capitalist market. As this system develops in sophistication and wealth generation and is hooked up to global financial markets and their legal and accounting techniques, then powerful economic actors can get round the strong state and its tax demands by using the same legal conduits available internationally that we identified earlier. But in so far as the structuring of exchange, wealth, investment, profit and their protection rely on rules of *general* application, it is far from obvious that new tax-specific legislation can stop these activities without re-working aspects of the *whole* legal edifice. The generalised protection of private property *does* put brakes on what the state can legally do, as Locke noted, and different forms of property rights will play a central part in this. But it also *releases* the brake on a range of other activities and interests.

It has been the purpose of this chapter to highlight how a plethora of obligation-related activities – those 'waves of duty' to be found in private law and in banking, accountancy and professional legal practice, and ranging from property forms to duties of client confidentiality – together make up the global network within which the 'duty free' situation now flourishes. This vast network depends not only on the correlative role that rights and obligations play, but also on the transformations that are achievable within this schema that make identities and assets disappear. But more than this, I have suggested, rights come with what Birks called 'packages of obligation' and it is these, when thought of in their plurality of places and styles, not just in law, that make up the dense weave of the network. To change it requires a subtlety of understanding and action at different places that will not easily be translated into gap-filling tax legislation. That even aspects of professional ethics – doing the right thing by clients in keeping their activities confidential – may be a component in this situation should give a small indication of the full extent and complexity of the non-taxation-specific problems requiring attention.

It is not fatalistic therefore to see that sovereign legislation may have its limits. The legal tools involved in offshoring may well be contingent. But they are only part of the problem, and it is only by starting from a realistic appreciation of the whole legal, professional and technological mechanisms at work that the situation might come to be understood and addressed differently.

Bibliography

Benveniste, E., 1973, *Indo-European Language and Society*, Faber & Faber, London.

Birks, P., 2014, *The Roman Law of Obligations*, Oxford University Press, Oxford.

Campbell, D. & Piccioto, S., 2000, 'The Justification of Financial Futures Exchanges', in A. Hudson (ed.), *Modern Financial Techniques, Derivatives and Law*, pp. 121–133, Kluwer Law International, The Hague.

Christodoulidis, E., 2017, 'Social Rights Constitutionalism: An Antagonistic Endorsement', *Journal of Law and Society* 44(1), 123–149.

Cotterrell, R., 1987, 'Power, Property and the Law of Trusts: A Partial Agenda for Critical Legal Scholarship', *Journal of Law and Society* 14(1).

Dylan, B., 1983, 'Sweetheart Like You', Columbia Records, New York.

Esposito, R., 2013, *Terms of the Political*, Fordham University Press, New York.

Garland, D., 2016, *The Welfare State: A Very Short Introduction*, Oxford University Press, Oxford.

Graeber, D., 2015, *The Utopia of Rules: On Technology, Stupidity, and the Secret Joys of Bureaucracy*, Melville House, Brooklyn, NY.

Harrington, B., 2017, 'Trusts and Financialization', *Socio-Economic Review* 15, 31–63.

Hohfeld, W. N., 1964, *Fundamental Legal Conceptions as Applied in Judicial Reasoning*, ed. W. W. Cook, Yale University Press, New Haven, CT.

MacCormick, N., 2007, *Institutions of Law: An Essay in Legal Theory*, Oxford University Press, Oxford.

MacIntyre, A., 1985, *After Virtue: A Study in Moral Theory*, 2nd edn, Duckworth, London.

Marx, K., 2000, 'Economic and Philosophical Manuscripts', in D. McLellan (ed.), *Marx: Selected Writings*, 2nd edn, pp. 83–121, Oxford University Press, Oxford.

Obermayer, B. & Obermaier, F., 2016, *The Panama Papers: Breaking the Story of How the Rich & Powerful Hide Their Money*, Oneworld, London.

Pogge, T. & Mehta, K., (eds.), 2016, *Global Tax Fairness*, Oxford University Press, Oxford.
Polanyi, K., 1957, *The Great Transformation: The Political and Economic Origins of Our Time*, Beacon Press, Boston, MA.
Rawls, J., 1999, *A Theory of Justice*, rev. edn, Belknap Press of Harvard University Press, Cambridge, MA.
Shaxson, N., 2012, *Treasure Islands: Tax Havens and the Men Who Stole the World*, Vintage, London.
StiglitzJ., & Pieth, M., 2016, *Overcoming the Shadow Economy*, Friedrich-Ebert-Stiftung, Global Policy and Development, Berlin.
Stone, J., 1964, *Legal System and Lawyers' Reasoning*, Stevens, London.
Veitch, S., 2007, *Law and Irresponsibility: On the Legitimation of Human Suffering*, Routledge, Abingdon.
Waldron, J., 1989, 'Rights in Conflict', *Ethics* 99(3), 503–519.
Williams, R., 1988, *Keywords: A Vocabulary of Culture and Society*, Fontana Press, London.

6 History, alterity and obligation: toward a genealogy of the co-operative

Tara Mulqueen

The concept of obligation, particularly when counterposed to that of right, suggests an alternative way of relating to one another that exceeds the commodified and depersonalised modes of relation that are often thought to characterise modernity. This sense of alterity is often located in a past that seems all but lost or forgotten, supplanted and displaced, and in need of retrieval. This deep sentiment permeates Simone Weil's *The Need for Roots*, where she elaborates the idea of rootedness as a fundamental human obligation (Weil, 2002). Obligations for Weil, unlike rights, correspond to needs and exist regardless of whether or not they are recognised. However, coupled with a longing for the past, this presents a paradoxical framework in which obligations, which had no need for recognition, nonetheless suffer for having been forgotten and supplanted by relations mediated by the state and the economy. Jean-Luc Nancy warns us against this longing for 'a lost community' that constitutes the modern experience (Nancy 1991, p. 9). Such narratives essentialise the modes of relation associated with obligation, locating them in a past that never existed as such. In so doing, they may also take for granted that what is perceived of as alternative in the present may already be mediated by relations of state and economy.

This chapter explores these dynamics of history, alterity and obligation in relation to the co-operative movement in England. Co-operatives are often regarded as an alternative to capitalist modes of organisation, with values of mutuality and solidarity prevailing over those of self-interest and profit-seeking. However, the alterity of the co-operative is often taken for granted as an inherent part of the form of organisation itself, which is thought to embody a set of timeless values and a 'spirit of association' (Webb 1907, p. 2). However, as I will show, this way of understanding co-operation serves to remove it from its history, taking for granted the ways in which the very idea of the co-operative is already part of the system to which it would be an alternative. In contrast to this approach, this chapter makes some initial gestures toward the possibility of a genealogy of the co-operative, drawing on the work of Michel Foucault. I will argue that the co-operative, as it is understood in the present, was constituted in part through a process of legal recognition in the mid-nineteenth century. Legal recognition has often been perceived as enabling for the co-operative movement; however, legal recognition also served to temper working-class politics by subjecting them to the market, and subordinating them to the state. This latter disciplinary and constitutive function of legal recognition has been obscured by the normalisation of law that occurred in the nineteenth century, by which rights granted by the state came to be perceived as real freedoms. More broadly, the experience of the co-operative movement in England demonstrates that even when we relate in ways that appear alternative, or when we emphasise ideas such as obligation, we may be already operating within a framework that is circumscribed by a discourse of right.

A genealogy of the co-operative allows us to see the ways in which it is not the manifestation of a timeless set of values, but rather that it is the outcome of contingent historical circumstances. These historical circumstances determine, to a considerable extent, what we understand to be 'alternative' in the first place. A genealogical perspective also allows us to see the ways in which co-operatives may indeed be alternative in spite of their articulation within the system that they are meant to replace. That co-operatives exist at all demonstrates the persistence of alternative modes of relationality and an ever-present possibility of being otherwise. By moving away from essentialised notions of alternative values, a different sense of alterity emerges.

Co-operation, community and history

In England, the idea of mutual co-operation is thought to have found its clearest and most enduring expression in the founding of the Rochdale Society of Equitable Pioneers in 1844 by 28 impoverished weavers, influenced by nothing but the hardship of their own circumstances. The Rochdale Society is often regarded as the first modern co-operative. The Pioneers both created the business model that would see the widespread growth of the co-operative movement and articulated a set of principles that would define and guide co-operatives internationally until the present day. While the Rochdale Society certainly did exist, and has been very influential in the domestic as well as the international co-operative movement (albeit largely for reasons quite unrelated to its founding), much of the story around it is a myth. It was not opened by starving weavers devoid of outside influence, nor was it the first successful co-operative (Fairbairn 1994, p. 1). Although ostensibly a story about origins, the myth of the Rochdale Pioneers serves to remove co-operation from its history. Co-operation is a concept which can be taken so generally as to seem without history, meaning simply to work [*operari*] together for some shared end. This end need not necessarily be 'good' by any measure;[1] yet many of the strongest advocates of co-operatives over the past two centuries have figured it as part of a fundamental human nature; a biological necessity and predisposition, which is at once both necessary (for survival)

1 As when Karl Marx discusses the centrality of co-operation in the development of capitalist industry, by which he refers to the concentration of labour that forms the basis of capitalist exploitation, in Chapter 13 of the first volume of *Capital* (Marx 1990, pp. 439–54). See Gurney 1994 for a discussion of the roots of the use of the term 'co-operation' in Owenism.

and laudable.[2] In the Rochdale Pioneers narrative, this immutable and timeless value of co-operation is married to an exceptional historical event. The story, from that point, is largely told as one of success which serves to reinforce the integrity of the founding, and the fidelity of the movement to its immutable values and principles, which themselves exist somewhere outside of history, in our very biology. As Catherine Webb wrote in an early history of the movement,

> The Co-operative Movement is but a modern development of that spirit of association which may be traced all through our social history, as is seen in many features of the life of the early English village communities in Saxon and Norman times.
>
> (Webb 1907, p. 2)

This way of reading the history of co-operation, which conflates a romanticised conception of relationality with a specific organisational history, is but one instance of a much broader tendency in modernity. I will return in more detail shortly to the co-operative movement in England, but it is worth exploring a little further what this general tendency is. As Nancy suggests, it is the experience of the loss of community that is constitutive of modernity as such; it is 'the gravest and most painful testimony of the modern world' (Nancy 1991, p. 1). This pervasive sense of loss influences both how we read history and how we understand our present. As Nancy describes, '[u]ntil this day, history has been thought on the basis of a lost community – one to be regained or reconstituted' (ibid., p. 9). This community has been figured in many different ways: fraternity or brotherhood, corporations and guilds; and 'always it is a matter of a lost age in which community was woven of tight, harmonious, and infrangible bonds' (ibid.).

This sense of loss and longing can be read in what Simone Weil at once advocates and mourns as 'the need for roots'. This need is the most important in her enumerated set of fundamental human obligations, which she wrote in response to an invitation given toward the end of her life to imagine a new, just society for postwar France. Human obligations would be the foundation of this new society, undoing the culture of right that had predominated since the French Revolution. Obligations, unlike rights, did not require any form of recognition and

2 This kind of view has been articulated by wide range of authors. Peter Kropotkin, for instance, describes mutual aid as 'a feeling infinitely wider than love or personal sympathy – an instinct that has been slowly developed among animals and men in the course of an extremely long evolution, and which has taught animals and men alike the force they can borrow from the practice of mutual aid and support, and the joys they can find in social life' (Kropotkin 2012, p. xvi). Much more recently, Richard Sennett has provided a similar reading of co-operation. While suggesting that co-operation is something desirable, he also provides the following definition: '[c]ooperation can be defined, drily, as an exchange in which the participants benefit from the encounter. This behaviour is instantly recognisable in chimpanzees grooming one other, children building a sandcastle, or men and women laying sandbags against an impending flood. Instantly recognisable, because mutual support is built into the genes of all social animals; they cooperate to accomplish what they can't do alone' (Sennett 2012, p. 5).

corresponded to fundamental human needs, both physical and spiritual. While most of these needs and corresponding obligations are relatively straightforward, the need for roots is more elusive. Weil offers the following by way of brief definition:

> A human being has roots by virtue of his real, active and natural participation in the life of a community which preserves in living shape certain particular treasures of the past and certain particular expectations for the future.
>
> (Weil 2002, p. 40)

For further elaboration, Weil looks to the past – not only to historical examples of uprootedness (of which there are many) but also to a prior rootedness that is all but lost to us in the present. The modern condition for Weil is one in which the relations of community and obligation have been supplanted by the state and the economy, an event linked to the disappearance of the medieval trades corporations and guilds. As she laments, 'in our age, money and the State have come to replace all other bonds of attachment' (ibid., p. 96).

Nancy suggests that we should be sceptical of such narratives, not only because they project an essentialised vision of community into the past, but also because they sustain particularly totalising forms of politics in the present. They make regaining or realising such a community the presupposition of politics, from the formation of the nation-state to the unsurpassable horizon of communism. While there are real historical successions and shifts, these cannot be cast simply as the loss of community. As Nancy explains,

> *Society* was not built on the ruins of a *community*. It emerged from the disappearance or the conservation of something – tribes or empires – perhaps just as unrelated to what we call 'community' as to what we call 'society'.
>
> (Nancy 1991, p. 11)

Community, in this sense, exists in an idealised form that bears no relation to social forms. In contrast to this, Nancy articulates a conception of community that cannot be circumscribed by these historical and essentialising designations. Community, for Nancy, is not something that we have lost, because we are always-already in community: it predicates our very being. Being, for Nancy, is always 'being with,' bound up in an inoperative (*dèsoeuvrement*) 'originary or ontological "sociality"' (Nancy 1991, p. 28). Community 'is not a project to be realised, it does not occur as a series of social practices, and it is not a value or an idea – rather, it *is* only as shared finite existence' (James 2005, p. 186). In this ontological reading of community, it is not something that can be appropriated for political ends; it *is* the political (*le politique*), or the condition of possibility for any other form of relation we might create.

Co-operatives, in the historical narrative briefly recounted above, become the pure manifestation of a sense of community and association that is traced back to the medieval guilds. This vision of co-operation, and the belief that a communality associated with a distant and even timeless past, could be manifested in the present does precisely what Michel Foucault suggests that we often want history to do for us: 'confirm our belief that the present rests upon profound intentions and immutable necessities' (Foucault 1994, p. 381). It also has the effect of naturalising the present order, of which co-operatives form a part, by *naturalising* the conditions of its own constitution. Imagining co-operation largely in terms of a set of values and an ethos that then manifest in a particular organisational form takes for granted the ways in those values reflect historically specific realities.

Yet whatever we may say about the benefits or virtue of 'co-operation', it is not given to us without historical content. A failure to address this is indicative of a broader tendency in accounts of co-operation which emphasise a vision of alterity and an ethos of mutuality and solidarity that often animate co-operative projects but only at the expense of reckoning with the ways in which co-operatives may be limited or shaped by both the forms they take, as well as their own history. Historian Stephen Yeo, for instance, suggests that co-operatives are inappropriately seen as functioning within a system which it is 'their project to replace' (Yeo 1988, p. 27). However, while it may sometimes be their project to replace that system, they also *do* operate within it, and they have been shaped by this inclusion.

A genealogical approach

In order to understand the emergence of the co-operative historically, not as the manifestation of a timeless set of values, but as a historically specific form of organisation, I turn to Foucault's notion of genealogy. Genealogy has been described by Foucault and his many interlocutors as a 'history of the present' (Foucault 1995, p. 31)[3] and the opposite of any gesture which would attempt to locate the present in the past. The search for the origin or essence of ideas endows the present with a stability that it does not possess. The search for origins 'assumes the existence of immobile forms that precede the external world of accident and succession' (ibid.). Genealogy, by contrast, resists 'the metahistorical deployment of ideal significations and indefinite teleologies' (ibid., p. 370). It is the very things we assume to be without history, taken to be transcendent and immutable values, rooted in a fundamental nature or principle, that are the products of often 'arcane and ignoble' histories (May 1993, p. 56). Genealogy designates a different positionality in relation to history, one in which, as Nietzsche would have it, 'a new demand becomes audible', a demand to question 'the value of … values themselves' which requires 'a knowledge of the conditions and circumstances in which they grew, under which they evolved and changed…' (Nietzsche 1989, p. 20).

Genealogy and the ontological reading of community introduced above may at first seem like unlikely bedfellows.[4] The very idea that there could be an essential

3 See also Brown 2001, ch. 6.

4 The connections between Foucault and Nancy no doubt run more deeply than can be explored here, particularly given the importance of Martin Heidegger for both thinkers. Even if Foucault, perhaps inadvertently, precludes a Heideggerian solution to the

content to being that would be the object of an ontology is undermined by genealogy's commitment to the rejection of such ideal and ahistorical notions. However, what Nancy proposes is not a reading of community as positivity, but rather as a fundamental sharing and an excess that makes history possible in the first place. History is not the 'succession of events' but rather it is their 'common dimension' (ibid., pp. 156–7). From an ontological perspective, it is the very presence of 'the present' that cannot be taken for granted. The present, as such, can never properly 'happen', as it is only a mechanism by which we present ourselves to ourselves (Nancy 1994, p. 151). In order for history to be possible at all, it is necessary that the world not be completely determined by the categories which we use to give it meaning, however totalising they may seem. The genealogical study of the creation of objects of discourse or regulation presumes, even requires, that these objects do not completely determine the world: there is a necessary separation between words and things without which genealogy would not be possible. If words had a complete identity with the world, there would be no need to question their history, nor would there be any scope for changing meaning, as the entirety of possible meaning would already be present in the word itself. The legally constituted idea of a 'co-operative' would already include all its possible manifestations. As Foucault notes '[i]f language was as rich as being it would be the useless and mute double of things; it would not exist' (quoted in Han 2002, p. 53). This might be described as the constitutive insufficiency of discourse.[5] It is echoed by Nancy when he suggests that

> [i]f there is an illusion from which one must protect oneself today more than ever, it is the illusion that consists in getting hung up on words (history, philosophy, politics, art…) as if they were immediately to be equated with things.
> (Nancy 1997, p. 6)

The first step in a genealogical inquiry then is to recognise how discourse functions constitutively to create objects about which truth claims can be made, rather than reflecting a purely given reality. Genealogy, as Foucault describes in an early treatment of it,

> applies … where discourse is effectively formed: it tries to grasp it in its power of affirmation, by which I mean not so much a power which would be

questions he poses, the amenability of a Heideggerian ontology to Foucault's project remains (see Han 2002, pp. 54–60). Making no pretension to philosophical mastery, I have brought these two strands of thought together for the sake of their practical confluences. As far as I am aware, there has been very little work drawing together the thought of Foucault and Nancy.

5 The phrase 'constitutive insufficiency' is borrowed from Golder and Fitzpatrick (2009, p. 65). They use it in relation to Foucault's idea of disciplinary power, rather than discourse.

> opposed to that of denying, but rather the power to constitute domains of objects, in respect of which one can affirm or deny true or false propositions.
> (Foucault 1981, p. 73)

Discourse creates objects which mediate the relationship between language and the world: objects of discourse, in turn, do not correspond directly and completely to things in the world. In his work on sexuality, for instance, Foucault asserts that 'it is precisely this idea of sex *in itself* … that we cannot accept without examination' (Foucault 1990, p. 152, emphasis in original). Although 'sex' would often be equated with biology, and situated as part of an objective material reality, he insists that we must avoid this assumption and recognise that 'sexuality is a very real historical formation; it is what gave rise to the notion of sex, as a speculative element necessary to its operation' (ibid., p. 157). In this formulation, the word 'sex' does not designate an isolated object in the world; it is rather 'the most speculative, most ideal, and most internal element in a deployment of sexuality organized by power in its grip on bodies and their materiality' (ibid., p. 155).

By analogy, it is the very idea of the co-operative, insofar as it is taken to be the manifestation of a transcendent and immutable set of values, that needs to be questioned. The historical narrative and normative reading of co-operation presented in idealised readings of the co-operative conflates a very general sense of co-operation with the specific history of a modern organisational form, effectively inverting the relationship to create an ahistorical object in the co-operative. But in order to understand how the co-operative was constituted as such, we need to reverse the relation and see the history of the organisational form as that which produces values which are then taken to be without history. Rather than existing outside of history and manifesting in the Rochdale Pioneers, the idea of co-operation was itself formed and constituted by the historical experience leading up to the founding of that society, and indeed well beyond it.

Constituting the co-operative

Many of the practices and ideas that we would associate with co-operatives long precede the Rochdale Pioneers and can be traced back to what E. P. Thompson called 'the moral economy of the crowd' in the eighteenth century (Thompson 1971). From at least the sixteenth century, riots and other forms of popular direct action were relatively commonplace amongst the poor in England. Lamenting a tendency amongst historians to read these actions as spasmodic reactions to changes in price, Thompson articulated the idea of the moral economy as a way of recognising the framework in which these actions were carried out, given meaning and legitimised. The moral economy of the crowd stresses the presence and importance of how common people thought and felt, and how traditions and beliefs shaped their responses, in ways that eluded the prevailing and often pejorative designation of 'riot'. As Thompson explains, '[t]he food riot in the eighteenth century was a highly complex form of direct popular action, disciplined and with clear objectives' (ibid., p. 78). The common people who participated in these riots, often led by women, were not simply motivated by their hunger; they 'were informed by the belief that they were defending traditional rights or customs; and, in general, that they were supported by the wider consensus of the community' (ibid.). The rioters were effectively 'taking the law into their own hands', sometimes with the implicit support of authorities who were known to welcome the 'popular hubbub' against forestallers (ibid., p. 95). It was in this context, often as an extension of the activities of rioters, that the earliest 'flour and bread' societies, the forebears of co-operatives, were formed.[6]

From these disparate 'beginnings', the question of how the co-operative was constituted in the mid-nineteenth century could be approached from any number of angles (Brown 2001, p. 101).[7] The remainder of this chapter will focus on the particular role of law and legal recognition. The co-operative emerges in the mid-nineteenth century as a distinct organisational form in part through a process of legal recognition. While law is not the only factor contributing to the constitution of the 'object' of the co-operative, it is important insofar as this created a replicable model, the legal origins of which are often taken for granted. This legally constituted idea of the co-operative shapes how we understand the limits and possibilities of co-operation as an alternative form of organisation and association. Legal recognition is usually seen as key to the success of the co-operative movement, giving it a basis of legitimacy on which to grow and expand. This view can be traced back to J. M. Ludlow and Lloyd Jones; two prominent nineteenth-century Christian Socialists who were themselves largely responsible for the legal recognition of co-operatives. They observed that legislation created for building societies and co-operatives (the Regulation of Benefit Building Societies Act of 1836 and Industrial and Provident Societies Act of 1852, respectively) was 'anticipated by the spontaneous efforts of the working class' (Ludlow & Jones 1867, p. 96). These forms of organisation were 'not the creature of Parliament, but the working man's own creation' (ibid.). However, far from being just an expression of the working-class project of co-operation, legal recognition actively served to discipline working-class politics. This discipline, as I will detail below, is evident in the explicit intentions of those who advocated for the legal recognition of co-operatives. However, it also occurs through what Foucault refers to as a 'normalization' of law in the nineteenth century, in which rights granted by the state come to be perceived as real freedoms (Foucault 1990, p. 144).

Legal recognition and market discipline

There can be little doubt that the intention of legal recognition for co-operatives was to discipline working-class politics. This becomes particularly apparent through an examination of the views of the Christian Socialists, who were the

6 See Bamfield 1998, p. 16. These societies did not have any particular legal form, although they were sometimes set up as Friendly Societies, at least after the first Friendly Societies Act in 1795.

7 Beginnings, in this sense, are conceptually distinct from 'origins'.

main proponents of the Industrial and Provident Societies Act in the mid-nineteenth century. At this time, co-operation was an important site of ideological struggle. It was thought by some, and particularly middle-class reformers, that co-operation could ameliorate the growing tensions between capital and labour brought about by industrialisation.[8] The demand for political rights for the working classes and the relative success of the Chartist movement were palpable threats to existing hierarchies.[9] In this context, co-operation seemed like a viable alternative: instead of political rights, represented by the franchise, the working classes could be given what were effectively regarded as economic rights, enabling them to participate more fully in the market. These economic rights, in turn, would have the effect of teaching the working classes about the natural laws of the market, which it was thought would result in the acceptance of the inevitability of these laws. Charles Kingsley, another prominent Christian Socialist, provides an indicative example of this view in his pamphlet *Who are the Friends of Order?*, written in response to critics who claimed that the Christian Socialists were fomenting a revolutionary spirit amongst the working classes by advocating co-operation.

> We tell people simply to do their duty in that state of life to which God has called them … [the results of our work have been] to make ardent and discontented spirits among the working classes more patient and contented; more respectful of those institutions of which they have never been taught the value, and of which they have too little experienced the benefit; to turn their minds from those frantic and suicidal dreams of revolution …
>
> (quoted in Saville 1954, p. 151)

These political views about the best way to manage the working classes motivated the Christian Socialists' support for the legal recognition of co-operatives.

The idea that the market could serve this disciplinary function was relatively new in the nineteenth century, and reflects the increasing influence of the discourse of political economy. Political economy, as Foucault describes, cast the market as being governed by a set of natural, immutable laws that operated independently of state intervention (Foucault 2008, p. 13–17). However, the meaning of these laws and their relationship to morality and religion shifted considerably over the course of the early and mid-nineteenth century. In the early nineteenth century, approaches to the morality of the market were dominated by evangelism. In the evangelical view, the market functioned in a retributive fashion: failure to conform to the demands of the market, which required particular forms of moral restraint, led to punishment and failure. In turn, hard work was to be rewarded: '[e]ffort and

8 See Loftus 2002.

9 While the Chartists ostensibly 'failed' in the short term, the latent threat of the struggle for the franchise exercised a considerable influence on the imagination of middle classes. John Saville (1954) traces the development of Christian Socialism to the 1848 demonstration at Kennington Common, which had been feared would lead to revolution.

enterprise were rewarded with high wages and profit; idleness and inattention punished with poverty and the bankruptcy court' (Johnson 2005, p. 12). In order to facilitate this, investors needed to bear the full responsibility of their actions. Consequently, there was a reluctance to adopt regulatory measures that would provide protection in the event of business failure, such as limited liability.

The shift in attitude away from the retributive, evangelical view was precipitated by a range of factors. Amongst these, the desire to maximise the public benefits associated with profit-seeking was particularly important (Hilton 1991, p. 265). In addition, as more people from the middle class began to invest, it was difficult to justify holding them accountable for the sins and failures of more powerful businessmen. Instead of retribution, liberals advocated the importance of a 'reputation for honesty' in order to enable success on the market (ibid., p. 259). This reputation, along with a system of registration and accounting to foster transparency and public scrutiny, would determine whether or not a business could be successful. The market was still endowed with 'providential design', but with greater protections in place, it became a site for the development of good character (Searle 1998, p. 19). In order to be successful, it was necessary to demonstrate integrity.

This new morality was perhaps most important for the working classes, who it was feared did not believe in the laws of political economy (ibid., p. 37). In the early nineteenth century, it was thought that the working classes should not be taught the laws of political economy, only that their characters might be improved in anticipation of their judgment by the market. However, the political success of Chartism precipitated the shift in thinking described above: working men *should* learn the laws of the market. The sooner they could see that the workings of the market were beyond their control, the sooner they would abandon their revolutionary impulses. It is not that men will be educated in political economy, but that the *experience* of the market will teach them the laws of political economy. As James Ludlow claimed in his Select Committee interview concerning the creation of a legal form for co-operatives, even if their experiments failed, they would have this beneficial effect. When Robert Slaney MP (the chair of the Select Committee) asked if their disappointment would 'show that they were wrong in the idea that any injustice so far had been done to them' (Slaney 1850, p. 105), Ludlow responds, 'yes; it would promote their submission to things as they are' (Ludlow 1850, p. 105). Moreover, as indicated by an exchange in the same committee with E. V. Neale, legal recognition and the opportunity to try their experiments would rid them of their political utopianism more generally, and resolve them to accepting the present order.

> I think it would enable them to ascertain by trial whether the ideas which they have, and I believe they are very extensively entertained, as the real means of bettering their condition, can be carried out, or whether they cannot be. At present they may fancy that there is a paradise which would be very delightful if they could get into it, and if they think that it can only be done by overturning the laws, they may be disposed to endeavour to do so.
>
> (Neale 1850, p. 200)

In light of this reasoning, it would be 'politic' to let them try their experiment. The discipline of the market would be a moral one as well as a political one for the working classes, diverting their attention from dreams of revolution and shaping them into responsible subjects. Would 'facilities', as Slaney asked, 'given for such purposes, within the law ... tend to foster habits of forethought and providence?' (Slaney 1850, p. 101). To which Ludlow responded, 'I cannot say that I know of any more powerful means of increasing the security of the country' (Ludlow 1850, p. 101).

Incorporation and enclosure

The disciplinary character of legal recognition is also apparent in the legal form itself as a means of regulatory intervention. Initially, co-operatives were recognised as a form of society that closely resembled an older model of Friendly Society, introduced in the late eighteenth century. An amendment to the Industrial and Provident Societies Act in 1862 recognised co-operatives as bodies corporate, gave them limited liability and the ability to federate. Both the fact of regulation itself and the provision of the body corporate form indicate another dimension of the discipline entailed by legal recognition. 'Discipline,' as Foucault explains, 'sometimes requires *enclosure*, the specification of a place heterogeneous to all others and closed in upon itself. It is the protected place of disciplinary monotony' (Foucault 1995, p. 141). While Foucault was referring to the physical spaces of the prison, the school and the barracks, the body corporate may be seen analogously as a form of metaphysical enclosure that functions in a similarly disciplinary manner. In order to understand this, it is important to have a grasp of both the history of the body corporate and how it came to be used in the nineteenth century in the construction of the ostensibly free market.

The body corporate, as a legal form, has its roots in the medieval Church.[10] The fundamental structure of the body corporate, as it comes to us from the medieval Church, is one in which the unity of the earthly collective of the Church is derived from the unity of Christ in heaven.[11] This is a transcendent metaphysical structure in which the unity of Christ, and thereby the unity of the collective, is an abstraction that can only be maintained by being 'beyond' the world. As the form is secularised and adopted by the state in the early modern period, this transcendent metaphysical structure is retained. However, instead of Christ, it is the figure of the sovereign that provides the transcendent reference. This figure is no longer 'beyond' the world, but within it. In this respect, the sovereign becomes one of what Peter Fitzpatrick refers to as 'deific substitutes' (Fitzpatrick 2007, p. 162). While the state had to obscure its origins in order to maintain its deific status, corporations that were subordinate to the state were clearly understood to derive their unity from the state (as opposed to generating it themselves). This is clearly reflected in laws regarding incorporation in the early modern period. Incorporation was a narrow, public affair. Incorporation could only be done through the

10 See Kantorowicz 1997.
11 Ernst Kantorowicz 1997, p. 200.

grant of a Royal Charter, and later by a specific Act of Parliament. The first clear articulation of the corporation in English law is widely regarded to have come from Sir Edward Coke in the *Sutton's Hospital* [1612] case. There he wrote that 'a corporation aggregate of many is invisible, immortal, and rests only in intendment and consideration of the law' (Coke 1826, p. 303). Corporations, as Blackstone indicates, were formed for the public benefit and had to be authorised by the Crown: 'the King's consent is absolutely necessary' (Blackstone 1765, p. 472).

This dynamic between state and corporation changed considerably in the nineteenth century, with the provision of general incorporation by registration through the Joint Stock Companies Act 1844. As part of what has frequently been described as a wider process of juridification, incorporation became available by a simple process of registration (Habermas 1987, p. 375).[12] This was in keeping with shifting dynamics around the morality of the market described above: the process of registration brought joint stock companies within the fold of regulation, and made their accounts accessible for public and regulatory scrutiny.[13] The provision of general incorporation by registration exemplifies one of the key tensions of political economy and liberal governmentality in the nineteenth century: increased state intervention through regulation as a means of 'freeing' the market. The market, as noted above, was understood to be ordered by a set of fundamental laws. It was, in Foucault's description, a 'site of truth' (Foucault 2008, p. 38). In relation to the market, law had to function so as to allow that truth to express itself. Government interventions could not be regarded as ends in themselves or as concerned with the expansion of the state (ibid., p. 203). However, this does not mean that government no longer intervenes or that the level of intervention decreases. The limitation of government prescribed by political economy is not, in other words, a 'negative boundary' (Foucault 2007, 352). Instead, as Foucault writes:

> [a]n entire domain of possible and necessary interventions appears within the field thus delimited, but these interventions will not necessarily, or not as a general rule, and very often not at all take the form of rules and regulations. It will be necessary to arouse, to facilitate, and to *laisser faire*, in other words to manage and no longer to control through rules and regulations. The essential objective of this management will be not so much to prevent things as to ensure that the necessary and natural regulations work, or even to create regulations that enable natural regulations to work.
>
> (ibid., 352–3)

In this sense, the provision of general incorporation and the subsequent legal recognition of co-operatives was about *exposing* them to the market, as opposed to simply regulating them.

12 See also Veitch, Christodoulidis & Farmer 2012, pp. 255–64.
13 See Taylor 2014, p. 139.

Although this entailed greater involvement of law in company affairs, it was not necessarily perceived as an increase in regulation. One effect of the extended provision of incorporation by registration was that it came to be seen increasingly as a private right, rather than the narrow privilege it had been in the early modern period. 'The reform', as James Taylor argues, 'was also facilitated by, and helped to perpetuate, a reconceptualisation of corporate privileges as private rights, and of joint-stock companies as private bodies' (Taylor 2014, p. 136). As a right, it was perceived of as 'natural' and a reflection of the self-perception of the group, rather than law. This perception of incorporation as a right masks the fact that its provision in fact marked a greater penetration of law in everyday life. Insofar as the legal fiction of incorporation is forgotten through its naturalisation as right, this is, in Foucault's terms, a 'normalization' of the law (Foucault 1990, p. 144). This perception of incorporation as a right also has the effect of immanentising the transcendent metaphysical structure: while incorporation remains a fiction of law, it nonetheless comes to have an identity with life, as if arising from the collectivity itself. The immanent legal form then comes to supplant other modes of relation, effecting a form of closure on the collectivity that now understands itself to be truly united, or made into one.

In this sense, incorporation can be seen to function as a form of metaphysical enclosure, not unlike the enclosures of land, through which the commons were privatised throughout the seventeenth and eighteenth centuries. In relation to associational life, incorporation functions as a way of channelling the disparate actions and modes of relation of the 'moral economy of the crowd' into a discrete organisational form, the co-operative. Incorporation constitutes that which is recognised through this form as an object of regulation, infinitely replicable, making them 'interchangeable' as 'elements of discipline' (Foucault 1995, p. 145). They become knowable, predictable entities with their articles of association and their annual accounts; they are, at least in form, delocalised. Enclosure creates a discernible order, yet remains invisible as long as it is perceived as natural. And so despite transparency in one sense, in another sense enclosure functions, like the prison, to prevent those within it from lateral perception that could be a source of disorder and danger. It is the lack of lateral perception and invisibility that function as 'a guarantee of order' (ibid. p. 200). As Foucault explains in relation to physical means of enclosure,

> [i]f the inmates are convicts, there is no danger of a plot, an attempt at collective escape, the planning of new crimes for the future, bad reciprocal influences … if they are workers, there are no disorders, no theft, no coalitions, none of those distractions that slow down the rate of work, make it less perfect or cause accidents. The crowd, a compact mass, a locus of multiple exchanges, individualities merging together, a collective effect, is abolished and replaced by a collection of separated individualities.
>
> (ibid., p. 201)

Insofar as legal recognition through the co-operative form is meant to discourage and prevent other, malicious or seditious forms of political organisation amongst the workers, it has a similar effect. Preoccupied with their own self-sufficient co-operative associations, potentially competing with other such associations, concerned more with their own vertical ascent in the market than their lateral or horizontal growth as a movement, legal recognition prevents or limits the multiplicity of forms of action required for more radical political change. The market makes it such that 'there is no need for common aims' (Angelis 2002, p. 308). In the market as in the panopticon, 'a real subjection is born mechanically from a fictitious relation. So it is not necessary to use force to constrain' (Foucault 1995, p. 202). Like the 'enslaved sovereign' in Foucault's *The Order of Things*, the body corporate, and with it the co-operative, is bound by forces that it cannot see, and by its own perceived immanence in the world. In a more practical sense, this metaphysical enclosure and normalisation of the law translates into the perceived technical neutrality of the law (Brown & Halley 2002, p. 5). Instead of imposing a form of order on working-class organisations, the law is merely seen to supply a means of expression for them, granting them a legitimacy and some protections that enable their operation, without fundamentally altering them or adding anything to them.

Conclusion

The argument that legal recognition had a specifically constitutive and disciplinary effect on working-class politics in the mid-nineteenth century does not mean that co-operatives, so constituted, offer no meaningful sense of alterity. Nor, more broadly, does it mean that narratives of associational obligation are always necessarily compromised by a discourse of right. Perhaps the main consequence of the normalisation of law described above is to mask historical contingency, such that the emergence of the co-operative as an organisational and legal form of association can be regarded as the manifestation of a timeless set of values. Yet values are never timeless, as Nietzsche warned, nor are the various means through which people organise themselves in order to achieve particular ends. The reintroduction of historical contingency allows for a more careful discernment of both the limits and the possibilities of alternatives such as co-operatives.

When E. P. Thompson described the moral economy of the English crowd and early forms of co-operative direct action, he attributed them with asking 'the simple question: "Why not?"' (Thompson 1963, p. 874). This question, more so than any timeless and universalised set of values, gestures toward the possibility of alterity. The early societies were motivated by a certain creative potentiality: in the context of the failure of existing structures to meet needs, it was possible to create new modes of relation and new structures to meet those needs. The absence of a predetermined legal framework meant that such initiatives could exist without having to correspond to or fit within dominant categories or structures. The constitutive and disciplinary effects of these structures, when they emerged in the mid-nineteenth century, meant that whatever capacity for alterity there might be in such organisations, they would not be able to fundamentally challenge the established order as long as the terms of this constitution are taken for granted. It is not a question of romanticising these early societies, nor advocating for a return to them, but rather acknowledging the greater scope for alterity that existed in the absence of juridification. The possibility of alterity, of being-otherwise, requires, at the very least, some distance from dominant structures, or a recognition that the world is always in excess of these structures. The possibility of distance is diminished by the normalisation of law and the naturalisation of forms of organisation, as no such distance is possible where the categories of law and right appear to have an identity with life itself. In masking and obscuring the historical contingency of these terms, the possibility of alterity as such is diminished.

When it comes to alternative modes of relation, be they of obligation or mutuality or solidarity, it is not necessarily to the past that we must look in order to give them value. A romanticised reading of the past offers little to contemporary concerns, and risks entrenching present power relations. However, this does not mean that we have no recourse to values, or that we cannot advocate for obligation as a mode of relation. A more generous reading of Weil might suggest that her conception of obligation and its integral connection to human need merely expressed a truism: without somehow respecting the obligation to meet fundamental human needs, there is no life. This does not require any form of recognition. But when these obligations are ignored, the quality of life diminishes in proportion to the neglect, until it eventually ceases altogether. To this end, obligation, like community, is not part of a lost past in need of retrieval but rather an ontological concomitant of life itself. The same might ultimately be said for co-operation, but only once we have done the careful work of tracing its genealogy.

Bibliography

de Angelis, Massimo, 2002, 'The Market as Disciplinary Order: A Comparative Analysis of Hayek and Bentham', *Research in Political Economy* 20, 293–317.

Bamfield, J., 1998, 'Consumer-Owned Community Flour and Bread Societies in the Eighteenth and Early Nineteenth Centuries', *Business History* 40(4), 16–36.

Blackstone, W., 1765, *Commentaries on the Laws of England Volume 1*, Clarendon Press, Oxford.

Brown, W., 2001, *Politics Out of History*, Princeton University Press, Princeton, NJ.

Brown, W. & Halley, J., 2002, 'Introduction', in W. Brown & J. Halley (eds) *Left Legalism/Left Critique*, pp. 1–37, Duke University Press, Durham, NC.

Coke, E., 1826, *The Reports of Sir Edward Coke Vol. 5*, ed. J. Farquhar, John Butterworth and Son, London.

Fairbairn, B., 1994, 'The Meaning of Rochdale: The Rochdale Pioneers and the Co-operative Principles', Occasional Paper, Center for the Study of Cooperatives, University of Wisconsin.

Fitzpatrick, P., 2007, 'What Are the Gods to Us Now? Secular Theology and the Modernity of Law', *Theoretical Inquiries in Law* 8(1), 161–190.

Foucault, M., 1981, 'The Order of Discourse', in R. Young (ed.), *Untying the Text: A Post-Structuralist Reader*, Routledge, Boston.

Foucault, M., 1990, *The History of Sexuality Volume 1: An Introduction*, trans. R. Hurley, Vintage Books, New York.

Foucault, M., 1994, 'Nietzsche, Genealogy, History', in J. D. Faubion (ed.), *Essential Works of Foucault, Volume 2: Aesthetics, Method and Epistemology*, Penguin, London.
Foucault, M., 1995, *Discipline and Punish: The Birth of the Prison*, trans. A. Sheridan, Vintage Books, New York.
Foucault, M. 2007, *Security, Territory, Population: Lectures at the College de France 1977–1978*, ed. M. Sellenart, trans. G. Burchell, Palgrave Macmillan, Basingstoke.
Foucault, M., 2008, *The Birth of Biopolitics: Lectures at the College de France 1978–1979*, ed. M. Sellenart, trans. G. Burchell, Palgrave Macmillan, Basingstoke.
Golder, B. & Fitzpatrick, P., 2009, *Foucault's Law*, Routledge, Abingdon.
Gurney, P., 1994, 'The Middle-Class Embrace: Language, Representation and the Contest Over Co-operative Forms in Britain, c. 1860–1914', *Victorian Studies* 37(2), 253–286.
Habermas, J., 1987. *The Theory of Communicative Action, Volume 2: Lifeworld and System: A Critique of Functionalist Reason*, Polity Press, Cambridge.
Han, B., 2002, *Foucault's Critical Project: Between the Transcendental and the Historical*, trans. E. Pile, Stanford University Press, Stanford, CA.
Hilton, B., 1991, *The Age of Atonement: The Influence of Evangelicalism on Social and Economic Thought 1785–1865*, Clarendon Press, Oxford.
James, I., 2005, *The Fragmentary Demand: An Introduction to the Philosophy of Jean-Luc Nancy*, Stanford University Press, Palo Alto, CA.
Johnson, P., 2005, 'Market Disciplines in Victorian Britain', Working Papers on the Nature of Evidence: How Well Do 'Facts' Travel? No. 06/05. Department of Economic History, London School of Economics.
Kantorowicz, E., 1997, *The King's Two Bodies: A Study in Mediaeval Political Theology*, Princeton University Press, Princeton, NJ.
Kropotkin, P., 2012, *Mutual Aid: A Factor of Evolution*, Dover Publications, Mineola, NY.
Loftus, D., 2002, 'Capital and Community: Limited Liability and Attempts to Democratize the Market in Mid-Nineteenth-Century England', *Victorian Studies* 45(1), 93–120.
Ludlow, J., 1850, *Report from the Select Committee on Investments for the Savings of the Middle and Working Classes*, The House of Commons, London.
Ludlow, J. M. & Jones, L., 1867, *Progress of the Working Class 1832–1867*, Alexander Strahan, London.
Marx, K., 1990, *Capital, Vol. 1*, Penguin, London.
May, T., 1993, *Between Genealogy and Epistemology: Psychology, Politics and Knowledge in the Philosophy of Michel Foucault*, University of Pennsylvania Press, University Park.
Nancy, Jean-Luc, 1991, *Inoperative Community*, University of Minnesota Press, Minneapolis.
Nancy, Jean-Luc, 1994, *The Birth to Presence*, Stanford University Press, Palo Alto, CA.
Nancy, Jean-Luc, 1997, *Sense of the World*, University of Minnesota Press, Minneapolis.
Neale, E. V., 1850, *Report from the Select Committee on Investments for the Savings of the Middle and Working Classes*. The House of Commons, London.
Nietzsche, F., 1989, *On the Genealogy of Morals*, ed. W. Kaufmann, Random House, New York.
Saville, J., 1954, 'The Christian Socialists of 1848', in J. Saville (ed.), *Democracy and the Labour Movement: Essays in Honour of Dona Torr*, Lawrence & Wishart, London.
Searle, G. R. 1998, *Morality and the Market in Victorian Britain*, Oxford University Press, Oxford.
Sennett, R., 2012, *Together: The Rituals, Pleasures and Politics of Cooperation*, Yale University Press, New Haven, CT.
Slaney, R., 1850, *Report from the Select Committee on Investments for the Savings of the Middle and Working Classes*, The House of Commons, London.

Taylor, J., 2014, *Creating Capitalism: Joint-Stock Enterprise in British Politics and Culture, 1800–1870*, The Boydell Press, London.

Thompson, E. P., 1963, *The Making of the English Working Class*, Vintage Books, New York.

Thompson, E. P., 1971, 'The Moral Economy of the English Crowd in the Eighteenth Century', *Past and Present* 50, 76–136.

Veitch, S., Christodoulidis, E. & Farmer, L., 2012. *Jurisprudence: Themes and Concepts*, Routledge, Oxford.

Webb, C., 1907, *Industrial Co-operation: The Story of a Peaceful Revolution*, Co-operative Union Limited, Manchester.

Weil, S., 2002, *The Need for Roots: Prelude to a Declaration of Duties towards Mankind*, trans. A. Wills, Routledge, London.

Yeo, S. (ed.), 1988, 'Introduction' in *New Views of Co-operation*, Routledge, London.

7 Sovereignty, affect and being-bound

Stacy Douglas and Daniel Matthews

If ever it left us, sovereignty has returned. The protectionist and nativist instincts that helped propel Donald Trump into office have been felt throughout the Western world as new nationalisms have forced themselves into the political mainstream. The promise of post-national identities, global flows of people and capital, and the weakening of the 'bright lines' of state control have been met by a forceful resistance that foregrounds local interests and concerns, often depends on ethnically defined notions of identity and clings fervently to nationalistic histories and modes of belonging. Whilst we might dismiss some of these movements as being motivated by atavistic fears of difference, there is a powerful sense that the events of 2016 represent the high watermark for the form of turbo-charged globalisation let loose as the Berlin Wall fell and the 'new world order' took hold in the early 1990s. As Kyle McGee argues, the West is suffering from a loss of both 'place' and 'land' as the dual forces of globalisation and global warming put extant forms of attachment to locale and community under erasure (McGee 2017). In such conditions, the allure of sovereignty with its promise to 'take back control', as the Brexit campaign had it, is quite understandable. If 'waning sovereignty' (Brown 2014) has accompanied these 'twin vertigoes of placelessness and landlessness' (McGee 2017, p. 128), its recent revival offers – some would believe – a line of defence against the forces of globalisation and the increasing precarity this brings.

Against this background we engage with the theme of obligation in two ways. First, we explore the ways in which juridically enforceable obligations installed and defended by modern constitutional sovereignty are crucial to giving shape to the affective life of a community. We approach sovereignty through the sentiments that it produces – or claims to produce – and the particular effect that it has in enframing the world and giving scope to a sense of our political attachments and modes of belonging. We dwell on the *sensibilities* associated with sovereignty and on how the mobilisation of the rights and duties associated with the protection of sovereignty affectively enframes the way a political community attaches to place, past and an imagined future. Second, continuing our emphasis on the register of affect, we explore a sense of 'being-bound' that both *precedes* and *exceeds* juridically defined obligations. The binding quality of obligations – evidenced in the root word *ligare*, which we find in ligature, ligament, allegiance and religion – evokes a set of values and practices that range beyond the more limited notion of an obligation at law. It is this more expansive sense of 'being-bound' that we explore in what follows, underscoring the affective, political and existential dimensions to the bonds that give form to collective life. Ultimately, we are interested in unsettling the affective life of sovereignty, in revealing and attuning our selves to a sense of 'being-bound' that challenges sovereignty's power to re-centre an autonomous legal subject, and its attendant national community, within an anthropocentric horizon. Such a horizon is today increasingly compromised. In particular, the 'twin vertigoes' of globalisation and climatic change ought to attune us to a set of relations that transcend the assumed bifurcation between human and non-human life, ushering in a sensitivity to the bonds that sustain habitability beyond the limited set of relations honoured by modern sovereignty.

We find possibilities for such an unsettling of sovereignty's affective force in artistic practices coming out of South Africa, namely in the work of J. M. Coetzee and Nandipha Mntambo, and explore the implications of their work for rethinking what it means to 'be-bound' beyond the juridical proscriptions associated with sovereignty. The complex challenges associated with the constitutional settlement in South Africa is not our central concern. Rather, by attending to the practices of two artists working within this context we hope to shed light on a broader problematic. The oldest questions of legal and political theory – the nature of the body politic, the territorial limits of political power and the aspirations of the common good – are today being reposed with a renewed urgency. It is our contention that turning to art and literature helps unseat the predominant affective disposition installed by contemporary juridico-political techniques. We think that the South African case, as it has been tumultuously unfolding for the past nearly 25 years, can offer some important insights here, especially as it demonstrates how the affective force of sovereignty reaffirms a deeply held anthropocentricism that we must today begin to challenge if we are to avoid an eternal return of well-worn scripts that equate constitutional sovereignty with justice. We begin by unpacking our approach to affect before moving to discuss sovereignty, South Africa, Coetzee and Mntambo.

Affective attachments

Affect has been a matter of concern for philosophers and cultural theorists for generations – from Baruch Spinoza to Giles Deleuze, Eve Sedgwick to Brian Massumi – but in the context of legal studies, participation in what Patricia Clough has called the 'affective turn' in the humanities and social sciences (2007) has been less than enthusiastic. The reasons for this are clear. Normative power is traditionally understood as the capacity to shape the *reasons* one has for acting. By constructing a set of rules that call for either rule-following or rule-breaking behaviour, the law's power to coerce is predicated on the ability for all actors to make considered, putatively rational – and at least conscious – choices. Legal culpability is assigned on this basis, with judges and juries acting as the ultimate arbiters of the 'reasonableness' of one's actions. Central to the law's own account of its justification to pass judgment and to forcefully coerce is its unique form of *rationality* that is said to be untroubled by other less predictable forces such as morality, religion or politics. As Edward Coke famously argued more than 400 years ago, the common law depends on an 'artificial reason', cultivated through lengthy study and an immersion in legal texts that is quite distinct from the 'natural reason' to which any individual may lay claim (1658). This distinct form of rationality has been central to the history of modern law.

To speak of affect is to evoke a different and murkier terrain. Affect refers to that dark hinterland between instinct and emotion, the ungraspable 'feelings' associated with a beautiful place, a moment of terror, an atmosphere of joyful abandon or stoical defiance. Studies of affect invite an engagement with the non-cognitive, the non-representational and the non-rational, paying close attention to those forces that are 'beneath, alongside or generally *other than* conscious knowing' (Seigworth & Gregg 2010, p. 1). To be affected by an encounter, an artwork, place or event is to be 'gripped' or 'moved' in a way that we often struggle to explain. Is it any wonder, then, that law and legal theory has generally avoided affect?[1] If the great achievement of modern law has been to define itself as a distinct form of rationality, predicated on the assumption that subjects are capable of making considered choices about rule-following behaviour, a focus on affect troubles the very basis on which the law claims its authority to judge. Moreover, to equate the law's normativity with an affective force would be to reject the focus of most orthodox *and* critical accounts of law's normativity by pointing to something other than the law's (either 'compromised' or 'successful') mode of reason-giving (Matthews & Veitch 2016). Although we are not alone in exploring the relation between law and affect, given that this represents an unorthodox approach to legal study, let us begin by unpacking this concept a little and explaining the form of analysis that a focus on affect allows us to make.

We start with a rather bald definition that nonetheless helps orientate our thinking: *studies of affect examine the capacity that bodies have to affect and to be affected* (Anderson 2014, pp. 79–84; Seigworth & Gregg 2010, pp. 1–25). A *body* could be anything: human or non-human animals, material objects, landscapes, artworks, a bank of memories, a set of institutions, an oeuvre of written texts. In this sense, studies of affect embrace a post-human landscape in which human agency is neither the necessary measure nor the point of entry for any given study (Braidotti 2013). Attention to networks and assemblages that 'cross-hatch' the human and non-human, and in which affects are traced across these divides, is perhaps the *sine qua non* of the literature associated with the affective turn. The *capacity to affect* refers to the force of a body *in potential*. An oft-cited passage from Deleuze, whose work is central to one of the most prominent strands of

1 A happy counter-example can be found in Sharon Krause's *Civil Passions: Moral Sentiment and Democratic Deliberations* (2008) where she argues that, despite canonical legal and political theorists' attempt to do so, reason cannot be unlinked from affect. Similarly, Andreas Philippopoulos-Mihalopoulos explores the normative force of affect in *Spatial Justice* (2015).

affect theory, illustrates the point: 'you do not know beforehand what good or bad you are capable of; you do not know beforehand what a body or mind can do, in a given encounter, a given arrangement, a given combination' (Deleuze 1988, p. 125). In this sense affect can describe a force that is understood as an open *potentia* within a body and its entanglement with others. It is this that makes affect so elusive; it is either latent, and therefore in potential, or it is exuberant and excessive, ranging beyond the particular categories or contexts in which it appears. To put it another way, if we know precisely what an 'affect' is, then it ceases to be such and becomes something else: a concept, an emotion, a thought, a memory, an idea.[2] Affect, then, is something sensed at the fringes of these more definite determinations. To speak of a capacity *to be affected* is a testament to the necessary mediation of affective life, asserting that we always find affect *in medias res*; bodies are always already in relation with other bodies. The forces that affect a body are multifarious: biological and physical, cultural and institutional, geographic and material. The excessive quality that is often associated with affect, then, should not obscure the ways in which we are affected by any number of habitual, material, social and bodily constraints. Affects testify to the fact that bodies are bound up, one with another, and thereby both produce and are the repository of a set of forces which are beyond the control of any one body in isolation.

In what follows we are less concerned with elaborating a definition of affect than we are with exploring what thinking with and through an affective register allows us to explore in the context of constitutionalism. Our particular concern in this regard is to examine the tension between two aspects of affective life, briefly outlined above. On the one side, we are concerned with the juridico-political techniques, institutions and practices that mediate affective life by delimiting and enframing the capacity that bodies have to be affected. We are concerned with how a constitution allows a set of affects to appear, register and be given value, with how a constitution produces a set of *affective attachments* or *affective bonds*

2 By distinguishing between *affect* and *emotion* we suggest that the former refers to signifying forces that tend to be articulated in non-narrative forms whilst the latter refers to more concrete semantic determinations that are more easily defined and their experience more easily narrated across time (Anderson 2014, p. 12). An emotion is tied to a subjective experience and can be more or less easily delimited, whereas affect refers to something that is unexpected and elusive. As Anderson and Ash have argued, the full force of an '*affective* atmosphere', for instance, is usually only approachable in retrospect (2015), whereas the nature of an emotion is, in a more definitive sense, knowable at the time of its occurrence. Notwithstanding this distinction, much of the literature on affect moves easily between 'emotions' and 'affects', describing both as part of the same discourse and area of study. Sara Ahmed's study of the 'politics of *emotion*', for instance, traces the political feelings and sensibilities that are often unarticulated, instinctive and connected to bodily sensations, traits that are often more readily associated with *affect* than *emotion* (Ahmed 2004). Elaborating the nice conceptual distinctions between 'emotion' and 'affect' is not central to our concerns here. For clarity, however, we will retain the division, using affect to refer to a broader and more nebulous set of feelings and attachments that arise in an unexpected way and that defy easy codification.

to community and place, to the past and future.[3] On the other side, we are concerned with a more refractory sense of affect, with an eruptive and unexpected *potentia* that breaches a given disposition by affirming an alternative set of affective attachments and dispositions, ushering in and allowing to be felt something beyond the frame that the constitution installs – something that we explore below in relation to artistic practices. In both registers, then, we are concerned with a particular form of *binding*, of understanding how a set of bonds are fashioned and implemented and, too, whether they can be made plastic; perhaps, even, broken and reformed. It is our contention that the bonds of sovereignty consign the aspirations of political community to a narrowed horizon that obscures a broader set of allegiances – particularly bonds to non-human animal life – that are imperative in the current conjuncture. Through a reading of artistic practices, we suggest that the importance of bonds and allegiances that transcend those of sovereignty can be sensed and articulated.

In foregrounding questions of sensibility and affect, we follow Jacques Rancière in tying an account of the *political* to an understanding of the *aesthetic* in that our focus is on the 'frames' or 'filters' that give shape to the social field.[4] However, here we are concerned less with the specificities of political speech or with the conditions of in/visibility within the *polis* (Rancière 2004b) than we are with a more nebulous, but nonetheless related, set of concerns that we bracket under the notion of 'affect'. It is perhaps Raymond Williams's (1985, pp. 128–35) 'structures of feeling' that comes closest to our own thinking. In lieu of focusing on fixed social forms – like class or the institutions of government – Williams draws attention to 'a kind of feeling and thinking which is indeed social and material but ... in an embryonic phase' (ibid., p. 131). If a political or constitutional settlement deliberately allows a set of questions and concerns to appear or 'register' within the *polis* – effecting what Rancière calls a 'distribution of the sensible' – there are also a set of more elusive forces that are nonetheless significant in constituting our sense of the present. These 'emergent' feelings condition the experience of everyday life (Williams 1985, p. 132). Whilst we wish to examine the role that constitutional discourse plays in enframing affective life, we take from Williams a due attention to those 'embryonic' or 'emergent' forces that can be traced in artistic and cultural forms. Art – and here we discuss both the literary and visual arts – offers an 'impression' or a 'sense' of those affective forces and attachments

3 It is clear that the South African constitution addresses itself quite explicitly to *past* injustices but perhaps more important, in our reading, is the force of the constitution's affective attachments in determining the co-ordinates for *future* transformation. As we discuss, it is the emergent possibilities of transformation, reconciliation and a more just settlement that are themselves circumscribed, at the level of affect, by the form of the constitution itself.

4 In a series of influential texts Rancière has explored the aesthetic delimitation of political life, seeking to account for the way in which politics is engaged in a particular 'distribution of the sensible' in which divisions between seen and unseen, heard and unheard are reproduced (2004a, 2004b, 2010).

that push against or experiment with the limits of an established aesthetico-political order.

The limits of sovereignty

Constitutions seek to enframe affective life. The promise of civil and political rights organised as a set of normative expectations can supply populations that feel entitled to draw on and deploy such protections with a sense of security, ownership and belonging. New constitutions, written after extreme domestic conflict, legacies of colonialism or imperialism, or transformations from monarchical, parliamentary or dictatorial sovereignty, often elicit feelings of great hope and change, as they promise better futures for individuals, especially those historically excluded from the political or legal landscape. The 1996 *Constitution of the Republic of South Africa* is an apt example with such affective investments, and one that provides an important backdrop for our argument. After almost 50 years of legally instantiated apartheid, the once 'new' South African Constitution promises more than mere civil and political rights. It goes so far as to guarantee justiciable socio-economic and third-generation rights. Undertaking to protect and provide for the flourishing of every individual in South Africa, the Preamble to the 1996 document declares that it will 'improve the quality of life of all citizens and free the potential of each person'. The new code includes environmental and water protection as part and parcel of the bounded legal community; it re-draws the boundaries of who is within and who is without in many radical ways to affect a 'transformative constitutionalism' that has been since described as 'post-liberal' (Klare 1998). And this has been greatly celebrated, with good reason. The promises of political and legal transformation, beyond a mere extension of voting rights to the previously disenfranchised majority, were necessary for real change to occur in a country with such long and deep roots of legally instantiated racism and concomitant injustices.

However, these promises also carry with them inherent limitations to what is imaginable as transformative. Whilst the Constitution's assurances contain affective attachments to a hopeful future of prosperity and belonging, they also have a disciplining effect on the boundaries of that future; in other words, as the Constitution deploys laudable and lofty aspirations, it also delimits the kinds of feelings appropriate for the new, post-apartheid nation. Indeed, the Constitution establishes, at an affective register, a project of national identity that links the people to a new legal code and circumscribes feelings of belonging and boundedness within the framework of sovereignty. Whilst this is true of every national constitution, we want to briefly examine how this was achieved in the South African context before turning to explore how contemporary South African artistic practices seek to make space for alternative affective attachments.

The critique of the assimilative properties of the Truth and Reconciliation Commission (TRC) in South Africa, established by the Promotion of National Unity and Reconciliation Act in 1995, with hearings conducted in 1997/8, is well known. Mahmood Mamdani, one of the process's most forthright critics, has powerfully argued that the TRC 'individualized the victims of apartheid … was unable to highlight the bifurcated nature of apartheid as a form of power that governed natives differently from non-natives … [and] extended impunity to most perpetrators of apartheid' (Mamdani 2002, pp. 33–4). In particular, he claims that the TRC was unable to account for the role of the rule of law in creating and sustaining apartheid; in this sense the law, as an instrument of repression, was simply left 'off-stage'. In a similar vein, Emilios Christodoulidis and Scott Veitch claim that the TRC and the new Constitution both proceeded on the basis of a compromised division between the political and economic realms. The false distinction between political and economic claims of injustice meant that some considerations – namely those of property rights and sovereignty – were side-lined from the conversation about the future of democracy in South Africa: 'whilst the political constituency is democratised, the economic constituency is not. Responsibility for the latter is hived off to the market, in such a way that suffering consequent on economic immiserisation does not register as a matter of political choice' (Christodoulidis & Veitch 2008, p. 18).

The post-apartheid transition deployed a political-legal framework that illuminated some considerations, whilst dissimulating others.[5] However, where Christodoulidis and Veitch, in keeping with scholars such as Tshepho Madlingozi, critique the bracketing of economic considerations, we want to highlight the erasure of an affective landscape.[6] As the reconciliation project was bound up with feelings of reunification, ultimately aspiring to create a sense of belonging for a once (legally) divided nation, contrasting feelings of anger, disgust and dissociation were structurally suspended. The project of national sovereignty, beginning in 1994 with the election of the African National Congress, needed to conjure a set of affective attachments to a closed and delimited identity to ensure the supremacy of its juridical power.

This dynamic can be seen in *AZAPO & Others v President of the Republic of South Africa & Others*, 1996 (*AZAPO*). Here it was argued that the TRC, in violation of the Constitution, took otherwise justiciable claims outside the normal parameters of law by dispensing amnesty and thereby contravening citizens' rights to have criminal violations settled by a court of law.[7] The Constitutional Court did not agree with this argument and held that amnesty for such violations was permitted by the Constitution, by international norms, and indeed was pivotal to the negotiated transition from apartheid, perhaps even for the creation of the new Constitution itself. Where the applicants attempted to contest the hegemonic turn to reconciliation for national unity, the court denied it, in the name of

5 Christodoulidis and Veitch also ask the important and oft overlooked question: why reconcile? They argue in this text that the possibility of not reconciling was never up for consideration: 'was it not also analogously the case that at the institutional level the risk of reconciliation meant countenancing the possibility that it might not occur?' (2008, p. 17).

6 See, for example, Madlingozi 2007.

7 The appellants' case turned on the interpretation of s. 20(7) of the Promotion of National Unity and Reconciliation Act 1995.

constitutional sovereignty. The court made clear that this transitional framework was required for the security of a national sense of belonging and for the maintenance of the law's own authority. The *AZAPO* decision, then, was not simply concerned with questions of justiciability and the rule of law; it was also invested in policing the boundaries of a community's affective responses to long-standing injustice by relying on the logics of sovereignty. Feelings of disgust, anger and instincts for revenge were filtered through the framework of sovereignty and effectively silenced, and a sense of national identity and belonging achieved supremacy over these rival claims. The closed, operative and juridically delimited political community involved side-lining other affective claims and attachments.

The sense of the world that sovereignty produces is one concerned with legal parameters that keep central a clear and autonomous legal subject, linear temporality and delineated disputes, all subject to state justiciability. Our contention is that the deep problems facing South Africa, but also the globe, are beyond such narrow proscriptions. In this sense, we suggest that the limitations associated with the constitutional enframing of affective life in South Africa also gesture towards a larger set of issues that confront sovereignty today: issues of globalisation, a warming Earth, mass migration and ecological degradation. The modes of thinking and, most significantly, *feeling* that sovereignty installs limits the range of what registers in political life. Our thought here is that moving beyond sovereignty will take more than a set of legal changes in the direction of globalised cosmopolitanism or the expansion or re-imagining of rights. Indeed, the expansion of rights, central to the South African constitutional innovations, should be salutary in this context. As the present collection underscores, the proliferation of rights discourse has tended to undervalue the register of obligation. And it is precisely a critical attention to the work of obligation that might unsettle the affective power of sovereignty.

Obligations are often simply understood as a correlate to rights – to have a right to something means that someone else has a corresponding obligation, and vice versa – but as Scott Veitch has argued, this approach misapprehends the more expansive and dynamic register of obligation which precedes rights, allows for their institutional implementation and provides the means for securing for their content (Veitch 2017). Our interest in privileging obligation ahead of right is related to the more general effort of this chapter to move away from a thinking of the political that is predetermined by the framework of modern constitutionalism. The history of rights is unthinkable apart from the history and theory of modern sovereignty. As Martin Loughlin suggests, the culmination of modern political rationality holds that 'rights-bearers do not possess rights either because they are inscribed by nature or because they can be understood to be expression of human reason, but only because they have been conferred as a product of the legalisation of the sovereign' (Loughlin 2006, p. 72). Rights, therefore, are inextricably tied to the form of modern law that presupposes a natural correlation between rights and the sovereignty of the state.

A distinct set of ethical, political and ontological concerns are too easily disregarded if we favour a 'rights talk' that is amenable to the forms of authority instantiated by the state. The binding quality of obligations, in contrast to rights, attunes us to modes of attachment that precede the juridical register in which rights move. As Simone Weil reminds us, 'the notion of obligations comes before that of rights, which is subordinate and relative to the former' (1952, p. 3). The sense of the 'rootedness' of the human condition that Weil found within the language of obligation, should be our guide here. Obligations – with its evocation of ties, bonds, ligaments and allegiances – are situated, relational, affective and material in a way that rights seldom are. On this point, it is worth recalling that pre-modern understandings of law's normativity did pay proper attention to the obligations that arise out of a given place and a network of situated and affective relations. As Sir Edward Coke articulates it in *Calvin's Case* (1608), the law's capacity to bind subjects emerges from the '*ligaments* that connect minds and souls to one another' that both exceed and precede the positive law.[8] Similarly Sir John Fortescue, writing in the fifteenth century, found the etymological origins of law in *ligando* (binding), rather than *legendo* (reading), and analogised the ligaments of law with the nerves that unify the physical body (1942).[9] It is this notion of the bonds that emerge out of the primary situatedness of human life and the web of relations through which it can sustain, institutionalise and protect habitability that are lost from view with emergence of modern legal and political forms.

This notion of primary obligations that bind us in community, ahead of the articulation of right, signals a mode of thinking that might attune us to the ligaments that extend beyond the limited sphere of modern constitutional sovereignty. In an effort to remain sensitive to these bonds, perhaps it is a re-articulation of our very nature as *bound-beings* that we need to undertake. And this, we argue, is an affective and aesthetic task perhaps more than it is a political or juridical one. As we set out below, one way to stimulate a confrontation with this reality is through the experience of and openness to the affective force of art and literature.[10]

Being-bound/becoming-minor

South Africa's new Constitution took effect in February 1997. Eight months later J. M. Coetzee delivered the Tanner Lectures on Human Values at Princeton University, (subsequently published as *The Lives of Animals* (1999)). What could be more fitting than inviting a leading South African author to speak to the question of 'human values' in the context of one of, if not *the*, most potent political transformation since 1945, a transformation that testified to the enduring force of the values associated with enlightenment and its concomitant humanism?

8 *Calvin's Case* (1608) 7 Co Rep 1a, 77 E. R. 377.
9 Quoted in McGee, 2017, p. 124.
10 Karin van Marle argues that it is the legal register that is in part to blame here. Law is too generalising, too wedded to its own institutional preservation and too quick to make decisions; she sees these characteristics as central to law's function and, therefore, looks to art for ways to navigate the confounding problems of violence, transition, and reconciliation (van Marle 2007).

The Constitution's Preamble champions law's positivity – that the law is *made* and therefore can be *re-made* through human agency – and owes its heritage to the intellectual ambitions of the eighteenth and nineteenth centuries where the capacity for reason directed an ongoing quest for human progress, civilisation and freedom. The 1996 Constitution serves as a shorthand for anthropogenic supremacy over any supposed 'natural order' and evinces the human capacity for self-rule. Given this context, both the form and content of Coetzee's Tanner Lectures was, on first blush, decidedly odd. Coetzee spoke on the nature of human obligations to animal life, in the form of a fictional story about an aging Australian novelist called Elizabeth Costello. What of the rights of revolution and resistance? The democratic and egalitarian values that might shape South Africa's future? Or the values of forgiveness and reconciliation, so hotly debated at the time? How does fictional speculation about human responsibilities to animals address any of this?

In what follows we read Coetzee's lectures alongside his celebrated novel *Disgrace*, published shortly after the Tanner Lectures.[11] We argue that it is precisely the nature and limits of political community that preoccupies Coetzee in these two texts. As we observe below, Coetzee stages a complex encounter between the affective, the aesthetic and the ontological in *The Lives of Animals* and *Disgrace* that speaks directly to the constitutional settlement in his native South Africa. He thinks through what it means to belong to a polity and seeks to show the forms of life that are occluded by 'the people' that grounds the political community's authority. Coetzee, we suggest, asks what it might mean to take seriously, and quite literally, the promise that political community belongs to *all who live in it*,[12] despite presumed demarcations across species divisions.

The Lives of Animals opens with Coetzee's fictional Costello taking aim at the supposed supremacy of 'reason' in determining the differential responsibilities that attach to human and non-human life; something to which Descartes and Kant (amongst others) have confidently subscribed. As Costello suggests: 'seen from the outside, from a being who is alien to it, reason is simply a vast tautology. Of course, reason will validate reason as the first principle of the universe – what else should it do? Dethrone itself?' (1999, p. 25). Instead of pursuing a 'reasoned' argument on her subject, Costello turns to the literary in order to evoke a set of values and sensibilities that are irreducible to the 'vast tautology' of reason. It is literature that allows us to approach the animal *as an animal*, rather simply an object of argumentation. Costello examines this notion in relation to Ted Hughes's poem 'The Jaguar': 'By bodying forth the jaguar, Hughes shows us that we too can embody animals – by the process called poetic invention that mingles breath and sense in a way that no one has explained and no one ever will' (*LA*, p. 53). The imaginative realm is where new solidarities might be fostered, new

11 The lectures and the novel were both first published in 1999. For ease, quotations will use the abbreviation 'D', followed by page number for references to *Disgrace* (2000) and 'LA' for *The Lives of Animals* (1999).

12 It is these terms that are used in the Preamble to the 1996 Constitution.

assemblages between the human and non-human given voice, and where our sensibility to new bonds and duties might emerge. As her son John rightly points out, argumentation is 'not her métier' (*LA*, p. 36); it is not even the appropriate register for her subject. The bonds that tie us to animal life are not reasoned out, Costello insists, but are something that we can only encounter if we adopt an appropriate aesthetic sensibility.

Attuning ourselves to an altered aesthetic sensibility is for Coetzee something embedded within the affective *potentia* of a literary event. In this sense, the form of Coetzee's lectures is crucial to understanding their impact. From the opening sentence, without preamble or introduction, the audience is thrown into a fictional world (*LA*, p. 15; Attridge 2004, pp. 192–3).[13] As Majorie Garber rightly argues, Coetzee's choice to write a fictional story for his lectures foregrounds the question of literature itself and its role in elucidating the chosen topic; as Garber ponders: 'in these two elegant lectures we thought John Coetzee was talking about animals. Could it be, however, that all along he was really asking, "What is the value of literature?"' (*LA*, p. 84). The question of the value of the literary is itself the subject of Costello's own interventions, particularly in a heated debate with Coetzee's fictional philosophy professor, Thomas O'Hearne (*LA*, pp. 59–67). And this theme is similarly taken up in *Disgrace* as David Lurie seeks to justify the continued study of the romantic poets in the time of a 'great rationalisation' that sees the study of literature being replaced by a set of instrumental courses on 'communication skills' (*D*, p. 3). The key insight here is that Coetzee positions literature as a privileged domain in which we can experiment with new political dispositions and sensibilities, where counter-hegemonic affective attachments might be worked through. In an important sense, it is the 'métier' of his own intervention that is crucial because it is within the literary that the affective register can be acutely stimulated and it is this domain which provides a powerful critique of the limits of political life in South Africa.

Let us expand this point by turning to *Disgrace*. In the latter stages of the novel, Lurie feels unexpectedly moved by his encounters with animals whilst staying at his daughter's smallholding. He is inexplicably affected by his engagements with the dogs in a local animal clinic where strays are cared for or, more often, put down: his 'whole being' is gripped by his work and in the aftermath of an afternoon of euthanizing 'tears flow down his face' though 'he does not understand

13 This fictional world, nonetheless, uncannily mirrors the context of Coetzee's own appearance. Our narrator, we soon find out, shares the same first name as the author (John). With him as our guide, we follow Elizabeth Costello – who, like Coetzee, is a southern hemisphere novelist of some renown – on a trip to an American university where she delivers a lecture on the topic of obligations to animal life. Costello and Coetzee not only share the same first letter to their surnames, but, as Garber points out, Coetzee, 'like Elizabeth Costello, is a novelist addressing an audience of college students and faculty. Costello herself, like Coetzee, the author of *Foe*, is celebrated for her rewriting of a classic – in her case Joyce's *Ulysses*' (*LA*, p. 75.) The *mise en abîme* staging of Coetzee's intervention is central to understanding its effectiveness. Author, narrator and principle character move within a Trinitarian economy, with audience and reader encouraged to revel in the slipperiness of each constructed persona.

what is happening to him' (*D*, p. 143). This response evidences the growing significance of a bond that is first introduced when David discoverers two Persian sheep tethered outside a neighbouring house, ready for slaughter:

> A bond seems to have come into existence between himself and the two Persians, he does not know how. The bond is not one of affection. It is not even a bond with these two in particular, whom he could not pick out from a mob in a field. Nevertheless, suddenly and without reason, their lot has become important to him.
>
> (*D*, p. 126)

As Paul Patton (2004, p. 104) argues, this encounter sets Lurie off on a deterritorialised line of flight, where he is – in Deleuze's terms – 'becoming-minor', a trajectory that refers to any divergence from, or resistance to, 'the standard or norm in terms of which the majoritarian identity is defined'. As Patton's reading of the novel shows, Lurie's transformation is operative at an ontological register. His very sense of *being* is gripped and re-cast through his affective attachment to these animals. This reminds us that 'to be' is to 'be-bound' in a given constellation or assemblage. It is the possibility of testing or re-configuring such bonds that Lurie experiences in his encounters with animal life. And, significantly, this altered sense of being is co-terminus with a new set of duties or obligations, something Lurie realises as he seeks to explain why he has taken on the job of disposing of the euthanized strays from the clinic, something he insists on doing on his own terms:

> Why has he taken on this job? To lighten the burden on Bev Shaw [manager at the clinic]? For that it would be enough to drop off the bags at the dump and drive away. For the sake of the dogs? But the dogs are dead; and what do dogs know of honour and dishonour anyway? For himself, then. For his idea of the world, a world in which men do not use shovels to beat corpses into a more convenient shape for processing.
>
> (*D*, pp. 145–6)

Perhaps the obligation that David feels towards the dogs is best described in aesthetic terms: he is bound – not in order to ease the workload of another, nor by virtue of the dogs themselves, their value or dignity – but because of a certain *sense of the world* that such an obligation implies and the *ugliness* of a world in which such obligations are not honoured. Or perhaps David's sense of obligation comes as a result of him seeing his own reflection in the dogs; he is an 'old dog' himself, one that had a place in the old South Africa, but which is now being obliterated by the likes of the young black intruders that come to Lucy's house. Here too, however, it is the affective register (even if a somewhat selfish impulse) that propels David into action and care for another. In this interpretation, it is his unspoken attachment to a sense of the world and his privileged place in it that drive his new-found sympathies for animals. In either case, Lurie is gripped by an affective attachment, which he cannot rationally grasp, that re-orientates his position within a network of relations. He becomes newly aware of how he affects and is affected by a set of relations he once dismissed, and through this he begins to assume a disposition in which the privileged, and largely isolated, position he once held becomes friable.

If Lurie's newly formed bonds evidence his 'becoming-minor', what sense of obligation is 'majoritarian' in this context? Lurie's 'minor' obligations to animal life are contrasted in the novel by a form of thinking that reduces all bonds and duties to a matter of cost/benefit, calculation and debt. As Derek Attridge (2004, pp. 162–91) has argued, it is the 'great rationalisation' that Coetzee attacks in this novel. This 'rationalisation' is as much a part of the neoliberal economy as it is lying behind a certain form of constitutionalism and memorialisation that seeks to put to work or render *operative* and *useful* any and all resources at its disposal in an effort to build national unity. It is this rationalising impulse, in which all are united in a kind of communal accounting exercise, that Coetzee challenges. Perhaps the most striking, and troubling, account of this form of thinking is in Lucy's own 'rationalisation' of the vicious sexual assault she suffers:

> But isn't there another way of looking at it? What if ... what if *that* is the price one has to pay for staying on? Perhaps that is how they look at it; perhaps that is how I should look at it too. They see me as owing something. They see themselves as debt collectors, tax collectors. Why should I be allowed to live here without paying? Perhaps that is what they tell themselves.
>
> (*D*, p. 158)

There is a sense conjured here of a debt to the past, the obligations owing by virtue of historic injustice. Evoked too is the fact of taxation as the fundamental obligation owed to political community, the just contribution required to building and maintaining a state. In one interpretation, there is a disturbing acceptance of a kind of accounting where the cost of remaining in South Africa is measured in terms of sexual violence and female submission to male sexual desire. In another sense, it is Lurie who is deeply attached to the bond of a debt-obligation that needs to be worked out in the ledger books of public life. Indeed, it is Lurie himself who is so keen on going to the police, to have his justice carried out by a familiar institution, one that maintains the landscape of law and order that he is used to in the old South Africa. It is Lurie who stubbornly adheres to the easy-to-hand narrative of 'Lucy as victim', needing recompense and recognition from the state even as she refuses it.[14] Tellingly, Lucy avoids this 'national accounting exercise' by refusing to make her rape public, favouring the curation of a localised sense of belonging that ultimately involves giving up 'her' land 'in order to preserve a sense of home' and personal integrity (Motha 2013, p. 107).

14 Of course, Lurie misses the irony of valorising the state's prosecutorial competencies when it comes to Lucy, whilst he conspicuously fails to acknowledge that his own actions against his student, Melanie Isaacs, constitute assault at all.

We might read these 'minor' bonds of attachment as bearing witness to the utter failure of the public sphere or a wilful turning away from the challenges of civic reconciliation. But in a nation where the public was formerly defined by the exclusion of the majority, such affective attachments to 'minor' concerns have their own power and piquancy. The point that we wish to stress here is that Coetzee – through Lucy – allows his readers to sense a 'universe of discourse' (*D*, p. 58) beyond the calculating impulses of the tax and debt collector, beyond the regime of secular tribunals and a narrowed 'national unity', towards a sense of being-bound that exceeds the anthropo- and state-centric discourses of constitutionalism that are as rife today as they were in 1996. Similarly, the bonds and attachments that come to dominate Lurie's life as *Disgrace* closes – to the dogs at the clinic, to his incompleteable and unperformable opera, to the prospect of grandfatherhood – reflect the dwindling affective attachments of a man that had a privileged place in a nation that is rapidly changing. The novel does not close with a complete transformation of Lurie, nor could it. Nonetheless, Lurie's 'rights of desire', associated with the domination and patriarchy of the 'old' South Africa become increasingly fragile in the novel's final chapters.[15] And it is through these newly formed bonds that we glimpse the possibility that Lurie's allegiances to the former regime might wither away.

Through an examination of Lurie's affective transformation, the depiction of Lucy's 'minor obligations' to place and privacy, and the depiction of Costello's sensitivity to the duties and allegiances humans owe to animals, Coetzee allows us witness the possibility of an altered set of affective attachments to those installed by the 'post-liberal' constitution in South Africa. Coetzee evokes a set of bonds that must be approached through both ontological and aesthetic registers. Such bonds, most prominently, allow us to sense that our very being is bound up and affected by non-human life. Such an expanded sense of political community, and the obligations that it might infer, is 'emergent' or 'embryonic' – in Raymond Williams's terms – and therefore approachable only at the outer limit of what can be thought within the current disposition. But the bonds that Coetzee foregrounds can be *felt* or *sensed*. In this way, Coetzee points to the deep grip that sovereignty has on our affective and aesthetic regimes, in turn exposing the limits of legal transformation. But so too does his writing show that it is the register of affect, rather the putative 'rationality' of law and politics, that is integral to how we

15 Of course, this is in no way a redemptive novel. There is a powerful sense that Lurie remains bound by a set of affective attachments to the 'old order' as he nonetheless shows signs of transformation. His anger at Lucy, his vehement conviction that she has chosen to live 'like a dog', shows not only his deeply harboured attachment to the formal, familiar institution of the police – a potent symbol of the old South Africa – but also his lauding of the distinction between human reason and capacity over the disdainful passivity of the animal. Coetzee allows us to witness the tragedy of being caught within and between competing claims.

might challenge the bonds of the constitution and through which we might glimpse the possibilities of 'being-bound', otherwise.

Being-bound/becoming-undone

Coetzee, although globally celebrated as the literary voice of caution and critique during South Africa's Truth and Reconciliation Commission and transition from apartheid to democratic constitutionalism, is of course not the only artist that asks his audience to consider the role of affect in thinking about what it means to live together differently. Another such voice that offers provocative contemplations on the slippery relationships between human and animal, birth and death, and other overly drawn dualisms, is that of artist Nandipha Mntambo. Mntambo works in the realms of sculpture, painting, drawing and photography, and is most well known for her fascinating use of cowhide to create ghost-like casts of bodies (sometimes specific and sometimes abstract) evocatively arranged in exhibition spaces.

This, as well as her other work, which blends the use of cow hair, paint and bronze, has attracted international attention and much speculation regarding her commentary on gender, race and South African tradition.[16] However, speaking about her own work, Mntambo rejects simple interpretations that re-cast the centrality of these dualisms.[17] She insists that, as these binaries are alluded to in criticism about her work, critics re-deploy the very boundaries they refer to – boundaries circumscribing ideas of gender, race, the human and indigeneity. Years after Coetzee's acclaimed novel was published, Mntambo continues to ask similar questions about community and belonging in South Africa – but also beyond these national boundaries – by using provocatively produced materials that offer unique insight into the role of aesthetics in ontic and ontological questions of community.

Mntambo's work challenges the anthropocentric supremacy that lies at the heart of our legal and political world by presenting visceral, object-focused and trans-species-inspired art. But more than de-centralising the human subject, Mnatmbo's work also blurs the very distinction between animal and human. In her work, there is rarely the presence of any one clearly distinct body; instead she

16 Reviewers of Mntambo's work place a strong emphasis on her reclamation of the feminine, rejection of the heteronormative gaze, connection to South African tradition, and embracing of hybridity. For example, see Geryvenstein (2014) and Makhubu (2012).

17 Mntambo explicitly distances herself from any easily identifiable identity or artistic category. She cites her time at Michaelis School of Fine Art in Cape Town as formative in negotiating a set of stereotypes, especially as they relate to 'African-ness'. She claims: 'I was one of very few black students on the campus and I guess because of the history of South Africa and the way that people understood blackness or even art history in the contest of where we live, there was a push to try and make me interested in certain materials. Materials such as a wood or clay, which were typically materials that black people would use, I guess because they were easily accessible. I found myself not really interested in those things' (Mntambo 2016, p. 119).

Figure 7.1 Emabutfo, 2009
Cowhide, resin, polyester mesh, waxed cord.
© Nandipha Mntambo. Courtesy of Stevenson, Cape Town and Johannesburg.

explores the 'cross-hatching' of species relations. In *Europa*, the artist herself dons the horns of a bull, transforming her body into an indeterminate form *between* the animal and human. In her haunting sculptures, she uses animal skin – cowhide – to reproduce empty, abstract figures that sometimes resemble human form, and other times do not. She uses her own body for these casts. The result is a refusal to inscribe either the human or the animal in any simplistic binary. As A. Moret suggests, 'while the human form is absent in Nandipha Mntambo's sculptures, the vestiges of its curves and lines remain in the fibrous memory of the cowhide' (Moret 2013).

This mere trace of the human and animal, a challenge to the representational capacities of art, encourages a confrontation with anthropocentrism, but also with the bonds that persist across life forms. The cowhide in ghostly form simultaneously reminds us of both cow and human, as well as death and life, and the uncertain borders between the two. Interestingly, Mntambo's exploration of this theme is not only limited to her art exhibits; the very process of art-making forces her to reflect on the way our sense of being is bound up with and traverses any staid opposition between human/animal, organic/inorganic: 'When I first started working, I didn't have a handle on the chemical process and how to control it so there was a lot of decay and rot and flies and maggots' (Mntambo 2016, p. 120). Mntambo's process conjures an interstitial space between living and dying, ruled by the forces of rot and decay that are themselves strangely fecund. A related theme arises in the very practice of sculpting her materials. She tells us that,

Figure 7.2 Europa, 2008
Archival ink on cotton rag paper.
© Nandipha Mntambo. Courtesy of Stevenson, Cape Town and Johannesburg.

yet again, the process of her art production disrupts any illusions of human mastery over the cowhide, because the material actively resists her intentions:

> I was thinking about material memory and the fact that cowhide, as much as I try to control it through chemical processes or stretching it over mould, if I were to re-wet it, it would continue to remember a particular shape. So, the control that I think I have isn't a reality because the material functions in a way that it remembers and even chooses to remember.
>
> (Mntambo 2016, p. 127)

Here the supposedly lifeless cowhide continues to act against the sovereignty of the artist, taking positions that speak to its own history and memory, rather than bending to the ultimate will of its new-found sculptor. And this is not the only element of her work that disrupts and unsettles the myth of the sovereign human and its concomitant horizon of law and politics. She also actively interrogates the strict division of gender between male and female. Mntambo claims about her work ***Europa*** that 'no one speaks about the female body, the animal-human; how we understand sexuality, how we understand the border between the male and the female … and that, for me, is what the work is about' (Mntambo 2011, p. 19).[18]

Mntambo's art evokes an ontology or sense of being-bound that disrupts assumed borders between animal and human, female and male, life and death. Hers is a practice that renders legible the non-autonomy and non-sovereignty of our being in community, thereby actively interrupting the hegemonic distribution of the sensible. She represents, through her painting and sculpture work, the complicated relations that exist between frequently deployed categories, and in doing so, disrupts their presumed dualisms. However, her solution is not to endorse a straightforward programme of illumination but, rather, to analyse 'the things that you don't necessarily hear or understand immediately … that underlying unclear, complicated space that you can't really articulate' (Mntambo 2016, p. 125). In this sense, Mntambo's work operates at an affective register that challenges the dualisms that structure our experience. Her art intervenes in these fictions to thwart our attempts to sterilize and simplify them (Mntambo 2016, p. 128). Surfacing within the messiness of a life radically bound up with others, and otherness, Mntambo forces us to reconsider the question of what matters and, indeed, what matter *is*. Her sculpture, in its very performance and embodiment of a materiality that crosses human and non-human, questions the anthropocentric horizon of being and inspires a confrontation with an expanded network of obligations. Mntambo's sculptures trouble the centralisation of the human subject, a necessary strategy for a culture set on ensuring protections for *all that live in it*, helping us recognise that the bonds that shape our being in the world traverse the ethnic, national or anthropocentric.

In this sense, Mntambo's work is directly resonant with, but also extends, Rancière's account of the politics of aesthetics. It too makes an incisive critique of the way in which the organisation and delimitation of 'what is valuable' constitutes the *polis*. Mntambo, like Rancière and Coetzee, wants to challenge not only subjects that are deemed to be authorised members of political community, but also how, and crucially in what manner, politics are enacted; for all three, the role of the aesthetic in constituting – but also disrupting – the sensible is central, even though it has been largely side-lined by the gatekeepers of the political-juridical world. Mntambo's art practice forces open the frameworks that determine 'what counts'. Her refusal of individual and national sovereignty therefore speaks to the limits of the juridical and quasi-juridical processes of redress that dominated the

18 Mntambo extends the issue of gender to contemplate her reception as an androgynous but ultimately female-identified artist: 'I've always been interested in that space of how one understands male versus female. In my personal life … being seen to be androgynous … it's something that always been there. And in art, men are the ones that generally become successful sculptors. I think there's a very gendered understanding of who can take what role within the artistic space' (Mntambo 2016, p. 117).

South African transition and its aftermath. Through exhibition art, Mntambo demonstrates how affect can both be introduced as something that 'counts' in the political-juridical world, and something that sends ripples of uncertainty into the self-assured, anthropocentric parameters of legal subjectivities.

Conclusion

A return to Williams's 'structures of feeling' is apt for understanding the significance of Mntambo's and Coetzee's work. Like Rancière, Williams is concerned not only with predominantly accepted beliefs and the ways in which they shape horizons of intelligibility, but also those emergent feelings and inclinations that exist in the peripheries of hegemonic culture. For Williams, there is a gap, and perhaps more importantly a competitive struggle, between the sentiments espoused in official policy and those found in other places, especially in the field of art. For example, he compares the difference in thinking about poverty, debt and illegitimacy between dominant Victorian ideology, which attributed these things to individual failings or deviancy, to the emerging counter-explanations explored in the work of Charles Dickens and Emily Brontë, which situated poverty, debt and illegitimacy as general conditions of the social order (Williams 1985, p. 134). Williams uses this example to illustrate the way in which a dominant framework of thinking gave way to an emergent, yet for a long-time suppressed, alternative through the semantics of artistic practice. Whilst this alternative structure of feeling would eventually be institutionalised as the new standardised paradigm, it too would be susceptible to challenge and change through yet another emergent and informal set of beliefs. Mntambo's and Coetzee's artwork, then, may function like that of Dickens and Brontë, tapping into an embryonic feeling about the inherent relationality of our lives and the need to reject the logic and form of sovereignty, whether in South Africa or elsewhere.

As the affective force of sovereignty returns in the contemporary moment, we believe that literary and visual art can offer resources for unsettling claims to nation, place and identity that continue to act as a barrier to cosmopolitan and environmental transformation. For as long as these scripts of seclusion continue to circulate, the privileging of the individual subject and its attendant community will continue to dominate how we understand the bonds that constitute social life. As we have explored through Mntambo and Coetzee, we are bound-beings – bound to others through our very existence but also bound to earth, water, air and a panoply of non-human life forms. The case of legal transformation in South Africa, as analysed by many South African legal and political theorists but also, and crucially, artists such as Coetzee and Mntambo, offers critical insight into the compromised project of constitutionalism that remains tied to an anthropocentric horizon, undergirded by a modern sovereignty that translates all political claims into the language of rights. Our reading of the artworks considered in this chapter seeks instead to emphasise the affective, existential and political inferences of our 'being-bound' that precedes and exceeds the rights and obligations that sovereignty installs.

Of course, formal legal and political change can and does make important contributions to social transformation. But affective change is the greater challenge because it is woven into – indeed, it constitutes – the nature of our bonds to place, past and others. There is an urgent need to recognise these affective attachments if we are to do justice to our being-bound in the face of vital political challenges that so often revert to well-worn scripts of autonomy and isolationism. As legal scholars, we must confront the role of affect in law and politics and look to non-legal sources for ways to undo and unsettle its deep-seated hold on our collective imaginations.

Bibliography

Ahmed, S., 2004, *The Cultural Politics of Emotion*, Edinburgh University Press, Edinburgh.

Anderson, B., 2014, *Encountering Affect: Capacities, Apparatuses, Conditions*, Ashgate, Farnham.

Anderson, B., & Ash, J., 2015, 'Atmospheric Methods', in P. Vannini (ed.), *Non-Representational Methodologies: Re-Envisioning Research*, pp. 34–51, Routledge, New York.

Attridge, D., 2004, *J. M. Coetzee and the Ethics of Reading: Literature in the Event*. Chicago University Press, Chicago, IL.

Braidotti, R., 2013, *The Posthuman*, Polity, London.

Brown, W., 2014, *Walled States, Waning Sovereignty*, Zone Books, New York.

Christodoulidis, E. & Veitch, S., 2008, 'Reconciliation as Surrender: Configurations of Responsibility and Memory', in F. Du Bois & A. du Bois-Pedain (eds), *Justice and Reconciliation in Post-Apartheid South Africa*, pp. 9–36, Cambridge University Press, Cambridge.

Clarkson, C., 2014, *Drawing the Line: Towards an Aesthetics of Transitional Justice*, Fordham University Press, New York.

Clough, P., 2007, *The Affective Turn: Theorizing the Social*, Duke University Press, Durham, NC.

Coetzee, J. M., 1999, *The Lives of Animals*, Princeton University Press, Princeton, NJ.

Coetzee, J. M., 2000, *Disgrace*, Vintage, London.

Coke, E., 1658, *Prohibitions del Roy*, 12 Co. Rep, 65.

Deleuze, G., 1988, *Spinoza: Practical Philosophy*, City Light Books, San Francisco, CA.

Geryvenstein, L., 2014, 'Steven Cohen, Nandipha Mntambo: Neo-Baroque Hybrid Forms', *NKA Journal of Contemporary African Art* 2014(35), 64–73.

Elliott, D., 2011, 'The Silence that No One Talks About', in S. Perryer (ed.), *Nandipha Mntambo: Standard Bank Young Artist Award 2011*, pp. 25–32, Stevenson Gallery, Cape Town.

Fortescue, J., 1942, *De Laudibus Legum Anglie* [*The Commendation of the Laws of England*], trans. and ed. S. B. Chrimes, Cambridge University Press, Cambridge.

Klare, K., 1998, 'Legal Culture and Transformative Constitutionalism', *South African Journal on Human Rights* 14(1), 146–188.

Krause, S., 2008, *Civil Passions: Moral Sentiment and Democratic Deliberation*, Princeton University Press, Princeton, NJ.

Loughlin, M., 2006, 'Ten Tenets of Sovereignty' in N. Walker (ed.) *Sovereignty in Transition*, pp. 55–86, Hart, Oxford.

McGee, K., 2017, *Heathen Earth: Trumpism and Political Ecology*, Punctum Books, New York.

Madlingozi, T., 2007, 'Post-Apartheid Social Movements and the Quest for the Elusive "New" South Africa', *Journal of Law and Society* 34(1), 77–98.

Makhubu, N., 2012, 'The Peculiar Language of Material: Nandipha Mntambo's Work Signals a Complex Relationship between Metaphor and Material', *Art South Africa*, 38–43.

Mamdani, M., 2002, 'Amnesty or Impunity? A Preliminary Critique of the Report of the Truth and Reconciliation Commission of South Africa (TRC)', *Diacritics* 32(3–4), 33–59.

van Marle, K., 2007, 'The Spectacle of Post-Apartheid Constitutionalism', *Griffiths Law Review* 16(2), 411–429.

Matthews, D., & Veitch, S., 2016, 'The Limits of Critique and the Forces of Law', *Law and Critique* 27(3), 349–361.

MntamboN., 2011, 'A Sense of Pause', in R. Simbao, *Nandipha Mntambo: Standard Bank Young Artist Award 2011*, pp. 9–24, Stevenson Gallery, Cape Town, viewed 4 January 2017, https://issuu.com/stevensonctandjhb/docs/nandi_sbya_2011_issuu.

Mntambo, N., 2016, 'Nandipha Mntambo', in H. Momodu-Gordon, *9 Weeks*, pp. 115–130, Stevenson Gallery, Cape Town, viewed 4 January 2017, https://issuu.com/stevensonctandjhb/docs/9_weeks_book_issuu?e=9663888/33358781.

Moret, A., 2013, 'Nandipha Mntambo: In Her Skin', *Installation* 23, viewed 4 January 2017, http://installationmag.com/nandipha-mntambo-in-her-skin.

Motha, S., 2013, 'As If: Constitutional Narratives and "Forms of Life"' in S. Motha & K. van Marle (eds), *Genres of Critique: Law, Aesthetics and Liminality*, pp. 91–108, Sun Press, Stellenbosch.

Patton, P., 2004, 'Becoming-animal and Pure Life in Coetzee's Disgrace', *Ariel: A Review of International English Literature* 35(1–2), 101–119.

Philippopoulos-Mihalopoulos, A., 2015, *Spatial Justice: Body, Lawscape, Atmosphere*, Routledge, Abingdon, Oxon.

Rancière, J., 1999, *Disagreement: Politics and Philosophy*, University of Minnesota Press, Minneapolis.

Rancière, J., 2004a, *The Flesh of Words: The Politics of Writing*, Stanford University Press, Stanford, CA.

Rancière, J., 2004b, *The Politics of Aesthetics: The Distribution of the Sensible*, trans. G. Rockhill, Continuum, London.

Rancière, J., 2010, *Dissensus: On Politics and Aesthetics*, Continuum, London.

Rockhill, G., 2004, 'Translator's Introduction: Jacques Rancière's Politics of Perception', in J. Rancière, *The Politics of Aesthetics: The Distribution of the Sensible*, Continuum, London.

Seigworth, G. J. & Gregg, M., 2010, 'An inventory of Shimmers', in M. Gregg & G. J. Seigworth (eds), *The Affect Theory Reader*, pp. 1–25, Duke University Press, Durham, NC.

Shorkend, D., 2015, 'Nandipha Mntambo's Underworld Grapples with Duality', *Cape Times*, 10 September, p. 34.

Thurman, C., 2015, 'Supplements to Support the Spirit', *Business Day*, 11 September.

Veitch, S., 2017, 'The Sense of Obligation', *Jurisprudence* 8(3), 415–434.

Weil, S., 1952, *The Need for Roots*, Routledge and Kegan Paul, London.

Williams, R., 1985, *Marxism and Literature*, Oxford University Press, Oxford.

Part III

The forces of obligations

8 Hybrid legalities: on obligation and law's immanent materiology

Kyle McGee

Untimely mediations

The theme drawing this book's contributors together is untimely. What could be less in sync with contemporary liberal political and legal cultures than a sustained interrogation into the multiple connections among *law, obligation, and community*? These are precisely the public values that the rapacity of neoliberal capitalism has outpaced and rendered obsolete, supplanting them in turn by regimes of flexible, 'consensual' management and instrumentalized techniques of behavioural optimization; systematic detachment and the privatized narcissism of individual self-interest; and a wholesale retreat into a solipsistic simulacrum of community in the form of closed enclaves, digital and physical, of mutually reinforcing prejudice and identical perspective. They are, unmistakably, also the values to which the nativist and nationalist politics of Nigel Farage, Donald Trump, Marine Le Pen, and others have cynically appealed in promising, in no uncertain terms, to *restore* what has been lost through the globalization of liberal political economy, national identity chief among them. A certain vision of law trading on its neoliberal evisceration is a central pillar: borders define the Nation, and borders are policed by law. Immigration reform, amped-up border patrol units, and a shift in law enforcement priorities to aggressively target street crime (drugs and theft, but also the failure to carry proper identity and residency documents) constitute the other side of the rapid deregulation of criminal enterprises in the financial, pharmaceutical, and oil and gas industries. The narcissistic atomism and closed communication circuits of neoliberal politics likewise find their complement in the homogenizing totality of the Nation. Each of these political transformations generates tension within the global market structures to which they respond, but even if they restrict the flow of capital, they cannot be mistaken for an overcoming of those structures. At best, they represent a kind of authoritarian repurposing of markets to stimulate growth within the national borders of the most powerful industrialized countries, on the back of the (domestic and international) poor. The challenge is to rethink and to reclaim law, obligation, and community from the darkness of neoliberal nationalism and the wretched conjugation of intensifying economic inequality, geocide, and the host of nativist phobias this fusion entails.

Elsewhere, I have argued that Trumpism and related political movements emerge from the chaos of globalization and global warming: confronted by the disorienting, overwhelming existential threats of placelessness and landlessness, the certainty afforded by ethnonationalist identity politics and strong borders, coupled with the promise of untrammelled economic growth within those borders predicated on the outright denial of the reality of climate science, can seem quite *rational.* [1] Rationality is itself a means of securing refuge from uncertainty: it consists largely in the habit of furnishing reasons in order to justify or explain, or at least make sense of, perplexing and potentially threatening realities. But as the twin vertigoes of placelessness and landlessness readily attest, reality under neoliberalism is constantly falling apart.

Actor-network theory (ANT), which is sometimes accused of 'complicity' with neoliberalism, grasps quite well that reality is incurably unstable and must be reproduced, re-enacted, in order to continue in existence. For ANT, a series of substitutions, mediations, and displacements is needed to sustain a society (or, for that matter, a nature), since it targets generative events (translations, associations, becomings) rather than discrete, well-defined, bounded entities possessed of durable, continuous identities. Identity, definition, durability, continuity, stability, and other metaphysical properties must constantly be achieved, locally and at some cost, since the courses of action they purport to explain are constantly fragmenting, splitting off, detaching, scattering, and running into new ones. Preservation is a consequence of successive transformation. Everywhere action fractures in the dispatch, in continual interlaced movements of invention, transmission, parasitic disruption, and transformative reception and renewal. The key actors are not humans in intersubjective communication striving for rational consensus but chains of translations expanding through the interventions of human and nonhuman mediators.

This view contrasts starkly with the presumptions that lie beneath the surface of liberal legal theory, and which are regularly exposed in critical approaches to law: that the law is a set of social conventions founded on a fictional or mythological consensus and the shared belief in authoritative institutions, where the authority of such institutions is secured in reflexive fashion by the very fiction of consensus. The material *things* scaffolding this artificial consensus – paper bills and tickets, gates and fences, painted lines and coloured lights, iron bars and barbed wire – can be said to generate effects due only to the implicit collective recognition and delegation to them of a capacity to act by human subjects: they reflect, in a derivative and passive fashion, a system of values that transcends them. And, likewise, the scope of those effects is strictly limited to the scope of that stipulated recognition. Accordingly, their effects are contained, predictable, and unsurprising. They introduce no novelty because they enjoy a merely factual, corporeal existence. If they relate at all to legal categories, rules, standards, doctrines, or other

1 This deterritorialization of the Globe and reterritorialization on the Nation leaves entirely out of account the Earth that both presuppose (and disavow); this is the guiding thread of the argument in McGee 2017.

constructs – which on such a view necessarily pre-exist any such relation – it is only as a mute, passive, cold, hard, meaningless lump of matter relates to a supple, active, meaningful system of ideas. This bifurcation, distinguishing a formal-ideal legal plane from a material-corporeal factual plane and subordinating the latter to the former,[2] causes the structure of law to replicate the structure of reading (or writing), and sets its economy of force upon purely discursive foundations. It is the operational ground of the enormously influential tradition of legal thinking drawing law from *legendo* (reading), rather than *ligando* (binding).

It would be too simplistic to argue that philosophies of law can be firmly divided into different schools depending on whether they associate law with one or the other of these roots. The competing etymologies of *lex*, which mirror the disputes concerning the origin of *religio*, are both conceptually and historically undecidable. And this is not the place to interrogate that undecidability. But what is crucial is that the stress laid on one or the other dimension of the genealogy and the concept of law has substantial consequences. This is not obvious. Consider the introductory discussion of the issue in George Dawson's 1694 *Origo legum*:

> *Lex*, which we render *Law*, is derived, as some think, *a Legendo* from reading, because Laws are to be writ and made publick, that so they may be read by the people. But *Cicero* in his first book of Laws [i.e. *De legibus*] derives it *a legendo* taken in another sense, *viz.* for *choosing*, because they to whom the Legislative Power belongs, ought to *choose* that which is most profitable and advantageous for the Commonwealth, and enact it into a Law: The *Grecians*, saith he, call Law by the word [*nomos*], which signifies a distributing to every man his own: and I will derive it in our Roman Tongue *a Legendo* from *choosing*; for as they have placed Equity and Justice, so do we a power of Choice and Election in every Law. And some there are in the third place, that derive it *a Ligando* from *binding*, because a Law doth bind and lay an obligation upon all those it is impos'd on. And thus it is left uncertain from whence the word *Lex* is derived, and it matters not much if it be.
>
> (Dawson 1694, p. 1)

'It matters not much' because all of these dimensions belong to law properly conceived. But it matters a great deal to how the binding force of law is grasped: according to the symbolic reductionism of a consensual public order for which this force is nothing more than a psycho-linguistic phenomenon of social obedience, or according to the immanent materiology of the primordial beings of law for which it is a generative and constructive phenomenon of collective interdependence. And by refusing to trouble ourselves with this matter, because after all there is truth in both accounts, we lose the thread of the problem of legal force. Instead of force, the respectable philosophical problem becomes *legal validity*. But this is only so because the problematic of force has been dissolved into this poorly

2 This operation, as applied in particular to the legal *persona*, is studied in great detail in Esposito 2015.

constructed notion of validity and its merely 'sociological' counterpart, legal efficacy. Efficacy is not equivalent to force; rather, elements of what is called validity and elements of what is called efficacy each belong to the concept of force that interests us here.

To distinguish the validity of law from the efficacy of law requires prioritizing *legendo*: the positivity of the norm and the normative order to which it belongs, founded on social convention or consensus, must eclipse and in a way negate the positivity of the generative force of attachment more closely associated with *ligando*. The understanding of the binding force of law that emerges from this dichotomy consists in the limited, mechanical value of mere coercion (which, in most accounts, is not even properly a subject for jurisprudential thought[3]). Where this validity/efficacy complex operates, law's normative force (*ligare*) must be accounted as a phenomenon of legal validity (*legere*) traceable ultimately to the democratic legitimation of law, a move that requires law be taken as an epiphenomenon of politics. As Kelsen (2006, p. 30) explains, 'To say that a norm is valid is to say that we assume its existence or – what amounts to the same thing – we assume that it has "binding force" for those whose behaviour it regulates.' This declaration, cast in Kelsen's characteristically self-assured rhetoric, is fraught with peril: it is an admission that, like astronomy, legal theory has its own 'missing mass' problem.[4] We know law binds, but we can't know how without accessing the dark matter of legal normativity. And we can't do that with legal theory's ordinary tools, like the concept of validity or the technique of outsourcing law's bindingness to the sphere of politics by way of the concept of legitimacy.

There is something strange, even perverse in proposing today, as I will, to loosen the ties of legal discourse to its ground in consensus, to reject the very terms in which the problem of democratic legitimation demands to be cast. Is this not precisely what Trumpism, with its vulgar instrumentalization and indeed open disdain for legality, proposes: to replace public consensus and shared meaning, and their cumbersome norms of verification, with the efficient authoritarian will of the despot? In this condition of what we might call 'actually-existing surrealism',[5] alternative facts subvert consensus. But that is the point: the centre has fallen out,

3 There are exceptions. Hans Kelsen, of course, made coercion a keystone in the architecture of his conceptual jurisprudence, and, more recently, Frederick Schauer has argued that coercion and sanction are integral to not only the empirical or sociological but also the philosophical understanding of law. See Schauer 2015.

4 Kelsen's (2006, p.116) own solution, the theory of the basic norm, is no solution at all. It is a transcendental foundation for legal validity: 'The basic norm is not created in a legal procedure by a law-creating organ. It is not – as a positive legal norm is – valid because it is created in a certain way by a legal act, but it is valid because it is presupposed to be valid; and it is presupposed to be valid because without this presupposition no human act could be interpreted as a legal, especially as a norm-creating, act.' Accordingly, this theory conflates validity and force at a still deeper level of analysis.

5 I lift this felicitous term from Seltzer 2016, pp. 75, 190. Seltzer's use gestures not toward Trumpism per se, of course, or the jointly articulated problems of placelessness and landlessness to which Trumpism is merely a response, but toward the disorienting

not only of modern political and legal discourse in general and of the democratic logic of political representation in particular, but of the very semantic and other social structures of the world they presupposed. Nothing short of a new ontology of truth in the broadest sense is required to respond to this vertiginous condition of post-consensualism and, perhaps, to advance the project however slightly of reclaiming law, community, and obligation. It is toward that broader end that this chapter's argument in favour of an alternative thinking of the force of law drives.

The missing mass of legality

To recast the force of law as a genuine problem, however, it is not sufficient merely to acknowledge or to look more closely at material things and practices, so long as we continue to think of them as things and practices that serve conventionally legal categories and rules: the traffic signal that instructs drivers when to stop and go pursuant to the traffic code, the pharmaceutical drug that incarnates the invention protected by the patent, the document that conveys the land consistent with private law rules. This re-examination must be accompanied by a more profound shift in principle, or it can succeed only in vindicating, with greater detail, the simplistic narrative that the existence of the legal category is independent of and invulnerable to, and takes conceptual precedence over, the actors that therefore merely instantiate it. That relationship between actor and category is the first obstacle to locating the missing mass of legality. Ordinarily, it is taken to be linear and unilateral, but it is neither. Instead of determination (i.e. an active form determining a passive matter), the relationship is one of expression: the interlacing of multiple formed matters and material forms, which generates something new – a normative effect – that exceeds its immediate conditions of production.[6]

This expressive relation is not solely the province of artefactual embodiments or enactments of law; it does not demand that legal scholarship abandon texts, interpretative practices, and chains of reasoning in favour a hodgepodge of other objects, like fences, databases, and film images. It can be discerned clearly in conventional legal texts. The primary challenge in doing so is overcoming the ingrained prejudice that conflates the text with the law. Blurring the edges of textual and legal beings was, for a time, a powerful critical strategy, undercutting as it does the spurious referentiality of legal utterances while foregrounding – and so problematizing – their conditions of (im)possibility. But it has become a mere habit and has led, if not to the simple identification of law with language, at least to the conviction that law as such is a creature of language.[7] To disturb the habit, it would be necessary to redistribute textuality and to localize the global domain of language it occupies, to call into focus writing and text not as pervasive or

experience of an archivally and bureaucratically doubled world, in which to enact is always to re-enact.

6 This argument is developed in McGee 2014, pp. 123–84.

7 A recent defence of this theorem is Constable 2014. Clearly, this is the radical conclusion of a thinking of law that unduly prioritizes *legendo*.

universal structures of agency but as agents among others. If we grasp text as the technology of the written word, as one medium or one kind of expressive substance in and through which legal beings may circulate, we do nothing to undo the complexity or interest of the relationship of law and text, but begin to sense the myriad *other* technologies that may perform the law in their own distinctive ways, but which were previously discounted for no other reason than that they were implicitly submitted to the domain of language or the structure of writing, and thus deprived of any unique agency. Likewise, we give ourselves grounds for contrasting the textual expression of law against those unique to other media, sharpening their differences and thus becoming better equipped to trace their movements.

We have no access to these strange beings of law without mediation, textual or otherwise. Indeed, they have no access to one another, or to anything else, without mediation. So it is not the case that recognition of the ontological specificity of legal beings requires the positing of a pure 'heaven of legal concepts' in which rights, duties, and other categorial relations would subsist independently of their terrestrial mediators, strung together in accordance with an ethereal autonomous logic of forms. On the contrary (and paradoxically, if we assume that the differentiation of law from non-law is inscribed in its concept), it is only in the earthly practices of legal mediation and their witnessable construction of local orders that the singularity of law and legal form emerges. To appreciate what this entails, and what it does not entail, it may be useful for illustrative purposes to tentatively invoke the language of cybernetics and distinguish the material event and its formal registration. If every communicative act is decomposable into its occurrence and its repetition, where the repetition enters into the occurrence as a necessary ingredient (i.e. to render it the act that it is), every act of legal mediation would be composed of its material performance and its formal repetition, its empirical occurrence and its higher-order categorial significance. This has the important advantage of showing clearly that legal relations (such as rights, duties, privileges, powers) require but are not reducible to the mediators that instantiate and disseminate them. According to this schema, matter and form, or event and significance, or doing and meaning, mutually presuppose and so condition one another. But the plane of form would constitute the 'properly legal' facet of any act: the doing is what it is (here, a *legal* doing) through the meaning it obtains by virtue of its place in a social system of meanings. For purposes of legal theory, this amounts to vesting agency in (social, meaningful) form, eliding the material entanglements generative of legal relationality.

The notion of *hybrid legalities* corrects this distribution of agency. The account glimpsed above suggests that a legal text (a contract, a statute, a legal brief, a judicial opinion) has material ('textual') and formal ('legal') aspects that should be distinguished to observe how the legal meaning shapes the textual occurrence, how the category informs the actor. What should attract our attention, however, is how the materiality of the text individuates a legal category. This requires relativizing the matter/form distinction. The signs included in the text already signify (to speak like a cybernetic theorist: they already incorporate the unity of a prior matter/form distinction in the language system), but this is obviously insufficient to acquire the quality of legality. Those signs (substances, i.e. formed matters) become, in their turn, matter for their successors, which adopt or appropriate their properties for themselves. The words composing the text signify, but the text becomes a legal theory when it is tested in an *ordeal* by other actors. An ordeal is a more or less rigid, more or less ritualized process in which multiple actors sort and evaluate the values at stake in different, often competing legal theories. Various forms of ordeal have been developed in the common law and civil law traditions and still other forms have developed in other traditions, while vernacular legal practices are responsible for the invention of a multitude of informal ordeals; legal anthropology and ethnography are uniquely valuable for decoding these. Where the ordeal is a formalized proceeding, such as those held by tribunals (a motion hearing or a trial, for example), the outcome of the ordeal is itself reduced to a new text that will subsequently enter into the composition of new legal theories to be tested in new ordeals. The 'formal structures' of law are in this way produced and institutionalized by the substances that express and modify them. And if that is so, there are, strictly speaking, as many legalit*ies* as there are ordeals, since the generation of legal forms (categories, rules, etc.) in one ordeal has no necessary connection to any other. Familiar notions of legality and of a stable legal system obscure the fact that ordeals must be attached to one another in some fashion, in unavoidably local, costly, and risky conditions, to constitute a coherent legal regime or order or tradition – which is why we speak of hybrid *legalities*.

Why, then, do we speak of *hybrid* legalities? We have remained with the law/text relation that is so familiar to lawyers that the answer may not be obvious. The text orders the flow of values constituting the legal theory tested in the ordeal, so it is a substance of expression fusing at least two dimensions: one technological (the written word) and one legal (the values circulating in it). Consider in this light the notion of *black-letter law*. Doctrine, broadly conceived, is the progressively blackened and progressively ossified hybridization of legal beings and the technology of text. As legal value-objects and legal theories are repeated in diverse ordeals and successively re-translated in a series of otherwise unrelated texts that cite one another in order to construct new legalities, they take on greater reality, greater solidity, greater fixity. Opaque, they resist inquiry into their 'foundations', the theories and the actors animating them, in favour of a certain deference to the expression, to the letter, the text. We speak of hybridity, then, not because there are two autonomous regimes or dimensions (here, law and technology or text) but *because there are not*: hybridity is a basic, not a founded, condition. If black-letter law is the paradigm case of the black-boxing of law and text, licensing their effortless conflation as well as the premature unification or systematization of disparate legalities, the theory of hybrid legalities may serve as a wedge with which to pry this box open.

Although there is no denying that the beings of law thrive in the media of text (as well as interlocution, where human speech replaces the technology of text), it has never been clearer that they also thrive elsewhere, in diverse media ecologies absolutely irreducible to discourse. If that is so, many of the qualities we take for essential properties belonging to law's nature or concept are nothing of the sort; instead, they must arise quite contingently from the historical encounter of legal beings and the technology of the written word, with the beings of law acquiring quite different properties in other expressive milieus. Among these sacred properties are the law's systematic nature, enabled not by any intrinsic quality of law but by the organizational possibilities afforded by the printing press. This is not to say that legal beings cannot organize themselves in something like a systematic fashion; on the contrary, it is to affirm that they can, and do, but only in conjunction with a particular technological expressive ballast. In Mireille Hildebrandt's terms, the principle at work here can be formulated as follows: *the law is not technologically neutral.* [8] But neither is it neutral in any other way. When non-legal beings prehend legal ones, a transient exchange of properties, a mutual borrowing of material traits, occurs. The written word translates and so alters the legal beings represented on the page (for example, a state's preferred value-objects and legal theories reflected in a code or judicial opinion), and the alteration consists in the law's acquisition of systematicity and the other properties traceable to the technology's affordances, giving rise to an apparent self-positing of a state legal system which is nothing of the sort.

Already we begin to see the 'binding force' of law in a new way. It is a strictly local phenomenon confined to the locus of an ordeal; an indexical phenomenon or event, defined by its in-courseness or being-just-where-it-occurred, not a general feature of valid law or of legitimate legal orders; it is an achievement contingently produced, not predestined or automatically given; it is not a property or an effect of rules, but belongs to a much broader distribution of agents; it is sensitive and relative to its media – xenomorphic – rather than rigid or unchanging; it is connective, and, as it were, circulatory. It may, but need not, take the forms of obedience, coercion, sanction.[9] In all cases, it is the normative effect of a legality – that is, the effect peculiar to the beings of law mobilized in a particular ordeal.

That normative effect materializes only in the generative trajectory that I, following Bruno Latour's work on law, call a chain of obligations.[10] 'Obligation', here, has the sense not simply of one person's duty to another or to many others,

8 See Hildebrandt 2015; for a review essay unpacking this thesis in connection with the theory of legal expression and the problem of techno-regulation, see McGee 2016.

9 To witness the production of coercion in the law/text relation requires extending the chains of obligations assembled in an ordeal to the legal relations enabling or compelling a repressive apparatus (e.g. a sheriff, a military) to act according to a judgment, where a judgment and a repressive apparatus exist. Where they do not, as in, for example, many vernacular or popular legal ordeals, or certain international legal ordeals, the remedy may take the form of ostracism, blood feud, vengeance, self-help, etc. But such a focus is still too restrictive: by force we understand not merely coercion specifically but the generation and transformation of legal relations generally.

10 A generative trajectory is a semiotic device introduced by Algirdas Greimas. For Greimas, it is a processual (i.e. multi-phased, synaptic), non-discursive, semantic being serving to account for discursive production; however, as my usage indicates, it is a quite useful addition to a descriptive juridical infra-language targeting the processes, expressions, and interactions we call the force of law.

but of one value-object's bond to another and to the longer series of transformations in which it is embedded. To be clear, a chain of obligations *is* also a series of transformations constituting a legal relation between or among persons, such as a duty or a privilege. But such a relation is only an outcome; if we descend to the perspective of the enunciation, as the theory of hybrid legalities requires, the problem is how that relation, which compresses and so conceals a whole series of bonds among legal beings, like an accordion, is produced. A chain of obligations rearranges the value-objects in circulation, absorbing the material affordances that they convey, in order to terminate the ordeal or (in science and technology studies terminology) to close the controversy. Among the clearest examples of a textual chain of obligations – *because* it is written, and written according to a certain style – is a common law judicial opinion (McGee 2015), but Latour's ethnography witnesses the assembly of interlocutory chains of obligations in the debates of French administrative law judges (Latour 2010), and there is no shortage of examples composed in media other than the textual or the interlocutory.

Value-objects seem to do a lot of work in this account and we have not yet accounted for them. In his ethnography, Latour identifies ten of them that seem to guide the process of adjudication he observed at the *Conseil d'État* – most of which can be seen as considerations or factors quite endogenous to the legal institution, such as the rate of progression of the case, the relative authority of interlocutors, the coherence and limits of law[11] – but it is a mistake to conclude that the range of value-objects circulating in any ordeal is narrowly limited to the legal institution's recognized factors of reproduction. In this connection, I take quite seriously and indeed elevate to the level of principle a remark made almost in passing in Latour's (2010, p. 195) study: let us not hurry to distinguish which elements or actors 'characterize pure law' and which others can be 'relegate[d] … to the role of mere intermediaries, additives, servants, or baggage', which are 'too trivial to mention'. In general, legal theory is rather too quick to decide how law is transmitted. Latour can be read (uncharitably) to fall victim to this same problem, precisely because he flags institutionalized value-objects. A better reading of Latour's argument is that the ten objects he traces cause the global construct of a legal system itself to pass into the local trajectory of the ordeal, rendering the system one cluster of objects among others, a 'whole' smaller than its 'parts'. In any event, the theory of hybrid legalities clarifies that the range of possible value-objects is endless or open-ended.

But they do not simply appear on the scene, fully formed; they must be made, and made to act, in each ordeal. To be sure, in formal proceedings, *scripts* often seem to help guide lawyers' and judges' arguments (the established elements of a cause of action, the requirements of a statutory rule, etc.) and, in that sense, also guide and domesticate the formation of value-objects. But scripts, or rules-as-scripts, in themselves explain nothing of consequence because they only act, and thus obtain meaning, when they are *made* to act and to obtain meaning; and they are made to act and obtain meaning by the value-objects that enrol them,

11 See Latour 2010, pp. 194–5.

interpret them, and speak them through the lawyers' or judges' arguments. As ethnomethodologists delight in demonstrating (as did writers like Mills and Wittgenstein), rules are not 'followed' – their application cannot be specified in advance – but are said to be followed, based on a bewildering variety of local order-producing methods enacted *in situ* that do not resemble rule-following, like (in Garfinkel's discussion of the act of following instructions to build a chair) 'tallying parts [and] matching-in-order-to-be-finished-with-each-next-thing-tallied' (Garfinkel 2002, p. 200). Such unruly methods produce rules as rules. Which is to say that such methods improvisationally transform what seem to be predetermined, inert, given scripts into concrete, mobile, responsive actors. This is not exactly how legal value-objects are made, but it provides us with a clue.

Value-objects are objections demanding to be taken into account in the chain of obligations they themselves compose. This kind of reflexivity, or infra-reflexivity, is an ordinary feature of not only legal trajectories but of any sequence or course of action, and yet for legal trajectories it works in a special way. Where other trajectories continually detach and scatter the subject-positions and enunciative strata that compose them, with little regard for their recollection or consistency (after a scientific fact is stabilized, after a technological innovation is cast in durable media, after a political collective is gathered), the legal trajectory ceaselessly reprises these other trajectories. Not for the purpose of, for example, extending the referential chains concealed in the scientific fact, but for specifically legal purposes: to terminate the ordeal. The objections demanding to be taken into account to shape the chain of obligations are the successors of the subject-positions and enunciative strata composing the trajectory or course of action reprised in the ordeal. Here, the demand is oriented toward the actualization or objectification of a bond or tie (*vinculum*) attaching an action to an actor, where both are themselves specified only in the ongoing legal trajectory. Each-next-thing is taken into account in order to stabilize the chain, quiet the objection, and so actualize the legal bond realizing the action as the actor's action. What is called 'legal reason' is then not a detached set of methodological precepts, but the concrete art of establishing continuity out of the radically discontinuous levels of enunciation that proliferate elsewhere and detach or fragment in the dispatch, such that attributions can be made, statuses can be constructed, relations can be stabilized. In this way, by weaving its invisible threads, 'law brings off the miracle of proceeding as though, by particular linkages, we were held to what we say and what we do', despite that 'in fact there is neither real continuity of courses of action nor stability of subjects' (Latour 2013, p. 370).

Not all ordeals are disputes about past events. Wholly prospective ordeals about the legal effect of an otherwise non-legal course of action abound. An oil and gas company's design and installation of an extraction facility asserts various legal theories tested in internal memos: the company's theories of ownership tested against the (virtual) claims of third parties, such as nearby residents, indigenous communities, etc.; theories of environmental regulation tested against possible interpretations of state legal theories contained in regulatory texts; theories of employee rights tested against possible interpretations of wage and safety standards (virtually) advanced by workers, unions, or state regulators; and so on. Instead of an oil and gas company's extraction facility, we could point to a biotechnology company's genetic modification techniques, a software company's web query algorithms, a property owner's fenced enclosure of a particular lot, a filmmaker's assembly of a montage. In each case, demanding legal value-objects and contestable legal theories find expression in technical or aesthetic artefacts, and in such a way that they can be said to have observably performed some role in shaping those artefacts. It is in this sense that the latter materially incorporate a whole chain of obligations constituting a composite legal relationship or status directed outside themselves (ownership relations, employment relations, regulatory relations, gender relations, affective relations, etc.) – a chain that is normally quite invisible, but which becomes strikingly visible in, for example, legal discovery, where the principal object is to reconstruct and reprise this chain to specify *other* attributions, relations, or statuses, or in the critical/interdisciplinary analysis of law's relations with technology, the arts, and other practices. In short, the beings of law demand, in the tone appropriate to their media, that all those affected by the consequences of a course of action must be taken into account in carrying out the course of action. Within this 'must' is concentrated the whole binding force of law, the missing mass of legality. Formal state legal organs can only limit or restrict this force, domesticate and channel it, but cannot be credited with its origination.

But it is essential to consider also the progression of quotidian ordeals from another perspective, namely of one encountering the materialization of a legal theory in, for example, the body of an extraction facility, a technique for splicing genes, software code, a fence, a film image, etc. There is an important sense in which these beings may enforce the law in concrete ordeals, but it is not simply that they overtake or supplant legality, rendering legal relations superfluous as in the techno-regulatory dream of a fully automated world of behavioural optimization. Neither is it that law is simply ubiquitous and incapable of being specified or differentiated, as new materialists argue.[12] It is that the legal and other dimensions of these beings cross into and interfere with one another, producing a complex normative effect; but only this effect allows us to detect the ontological interference that is its ground. Stated differently, for the theory of hybrid legalities, law is not a self-subsisting reality or superordinate plane of organization that would enter into relations with equally self-subsisting non-legal realities, but is generated in the crossing: not as an abstract category but as a mode of relation or connection, a *direction* or *current* folded into countercurrents. Law *is* the ontological interference that it both presupposes and overcomes.

Materialism rightly argues that legality is '…a matter of performativity and the production of spaces, that it is not separable from corporeality and relationality…,' but from this it concludes that law is boundless. Boundaries and forms only cut off

12 A view of this kind is defended in Andreas Philippopoulos-Mihalopoulos's account of lawscapes; see 2014; see also Davies 2017. For a further discussion of new materialist legal theory, see McGee, forthcoming b. For a broader overview of this 'panlegalist' variant of legal-pluralist theorizing, see Melissaris & Croce 2017.

relations; law is a sprawling complex of pathways.[13] But there is another turn of the screw that materialism obscures, which is that law binds in a particular way, that its pathways traverse and are traversed by counterpaths, and to specify it requires *more* connections, not less. So law's differentiation consists in more, not less, heterogeneity, entanglement, and interference. The specificity of its peculiar distribution of agency is eclipsed unless this hybridity is pushed as far as it will go, to the point at which its mode of making bonds, though enriched by others, resists conflation with them.

Let's take a simple example – a kind of exploded view of these relations as they appear in all their banality – picking up expressly on the metaphor of the border that new materialism rejects. If I am impeded by an inconvenient fence enclosing an area I meant to pass through, and I walk around it, conferring on it a power to direct my movement, my intention has been diverted in a precise, normatively significant way; but in addition, the legal theory of ownership it expresses has at the same time become an obligation I must negotiate. That is, in addition to the diversion or disruption of intention, there is a corporeal assertion about the makeup of the web of legal relations in which I am caught, here in connection with the absent owner of the lot. As a result, I am involuntarily and incorporeally transformed in at least two ways: individualized, but also displaced into an anonymous aggregate of others similarly excluded. Moreover, the sorts of tactics or methods I can use to negotiate the obligation imposed on me are constrained by the material and architectural traits of expression confronting me: in this ordeal, the compulsive force of the obligation is as strong, and as weak, as the traits of the wood, iron, or steel standing in the place of (as *lieu-tenant*) the right of exclusion.

In the moment of encounter, the fence seems to have been placed for me and me alone, like Kafka's gate, which is to say: as a techno-legal mediator, it *positions* me, unifying and objectifying me for its own purposes, transforming me into a being it excludes and to which it stands opposed. I am made to occupy a particular enunciative position defined by a set of prescribed qualities derived from the affordances and limitations of the mediator. I am *figured and shaped* by the enclosure's circum-spection. The position I am made to occupy in this assemblage thus contains a measure of concrete abstraction insofar as this obligation defines an act as *my* act, yet makes no distinction between me and others. And so it nevertheless shifts me out of my experiential here-and-now, displacing me into the anonymity of the crowd of those excluded by the enclosure. As a unit, I am at once contained and grouped with all the other excludable units.[14] This techno-

13 To illustrate, Davies 2017, p. 156, suggests that the metaphor of the border should give way to that of the pathway as the guiding metaphor for legality itself.

14 There is a hint here of what Roberto Esposito calls immunization, insofar as '[w]hat unifies the immunized community is common separation, resulting from the law's general protection of individuals' possessive capacity'. The liberal legal theory of personhood, entangled as it is with theories of ownership, finds a material ground in this common separation. See Stone 2015, p. 388. In this light, one could further extend the dominion of the small enclosure to that of the border wall to detect new transformations in personhood, identity, community, etc.

legal encounter is a scene that is irreducibly technological and juridical. The legal – here, a theory of property ownership – enters into the thing itself; a whole network of legal transformations is embedded within it. This local 'face-to-face' encounter is thus massively mediated. Yet there are limits to this: the fence, a corporeal ownership proposition, is constitutive of the identity of the property owner on whose behalf it acts, *but only for me*. This is one of the key implications of the argument sketched above. Because there is no more universal or general plane of legality than the event in its in-courseness or the indexicality of the legal force generated at the site of the ordeal itself, just there, the property owner is only a property owner for me – and yet in the perfectly 'objective' sense that this aggregate relation is the outcome of a specific legal reality test (the ordeal), the result of a variety of contemporary and historic struggles that have shaped it.

In a very elementary way, this example demonstrates the lived production of the force of law. Although the example is painfully mundane, it has illustrative value since any street corner, any home, office, or classroom – indeed, nearly any lived space – is teeming with legal theories and is thus a frequent site of ordeals testing them, unremarked-upon but not unremarkable. So, as we noted above, the law is not technologically neutral; it exchanges properties with text, artefacts, images, and other media that prehend it. It becomes sturdier, more durable, more incontestable, more spatialized, perhaps – and generally, the greater the number and variety of mediators, the denser is the bond they co-produce – but also quite frail, not only in that these media may be prone to corrosion but also because the law must give up any pretension to transcendence, universality, sovereignty. It's not a transcendent 'legal form' but a knot of fragile jurimorphs, no more universal or sovereign than the beings that successively translate it. And it's sensitive to their shortcomings in every way. Not only 'as a practical matter' but in its ontological makeup.

But let us linger here another moment. In either respecting or subverting the enclosure, my act also projects a legal theory about the obligations of non-owners. This theory is not drawn from or grounded in a pre-constituted intersubjective community or norms of consensus about the rights and duties attendant to the institution of property, but from the situation itself – that is, its ensemble of relations. The critical effect of pragmatically crediting or discrediting the theory of ownership is that it becomes *modalized*, either positively or negatively, in the unfolding ordeal.[15] If the theory is credited, if my action confers a power of normative reorientation on the technical object (i.e. my action allowing the thing to reorient my action), it is positively modalized: it becomes ever so slightly more difficult to contest *elsewhere* because it has been performatively sanctioned, and the black box of property ownership blackens a little bit more – like the repetition of a piece of textbook physics or chemistry on its way to becoming common-sense matter-of-fact. If the theory is discredited, however – if I dismantle the fence, or stage a protest because I contend that the enclosed area belongs to someone else

15 On positive and negative modalization in the context of the scientific construction of facts, see Latour 1988.

or is sacred or ecologically important – I do a little bit to crack the black box open. If the box doesn't pop right open, and I'm arrested (a state legal theory of crime) or sued (a civil tort theory), or, in America, shot (an owner's legal theory of trespass or self-defence/defence of property), it's not because a pre-existing system of norms is acting on me, or because I implicitly conceded to a social contract. It's that those legal theories have more, and more heterogeneous, and more deeply connected allies than the theory I mobilize. *But that can always change.* My positive modalization performatively enrols me, even if reluctantly, in support of the owner's theory of ownership; my negative modalization does not, but comes with its own costs. The boundaries of techno-legal order are negotiated and renegotiated in each such 'interobjective' ordeal.

This mundane example shows how 'local' we must be prepared to go to register the beings of law-in-action. So the force of law can be quite frail, and quite bounded. But this is not the end of the story. From a slightly different vantage point, the legal effect does not turn out to be so radically local. The legal theory on which our owner's fence relies is deeply historical, even mythological (think only of Rousseau's second discourse), and thoroughly entwined with ancient and modern notions of property, the things owners can do and the obligations of non-owners: a vast archive of legal utterances (*corpus juris*) that is contained in no book, no code, no database, and certainly not in a heaven of legal concepts, but in the very universe of things in its ongoingness. On this score we are unapologetically Nietzschean (2003, p. 16): '"Thus and thus it shall be" – that stands at the beginning: later, often after a long series of generations, it becomes a "thus it is."' Law's materiology is inherently critical of the 'thus it is' and refuses to lose hold of the 'thus and thus it shall be', which continues to operate in even the most familiar legal institutions and quotidian interactions.

This generality is not grafted onto the ownership theory from without; it is built into it from the start, if opaquely, and it shows that this theory has countless semblances, ancestors and contemporaries alike. This is crucial because the logic of expression cannot be understood on the basis of a single example. Although an obligation or other legal being cannot subsist outside of the fleeting trajectory giving rise to it, it is possible and instructive to compare similar encounters in entirely different media ecologies. And if we do so, a new dimension of expression surfaces. We can see the obligation to refrain from entering an enclosed space expressed not just in a set of writings or in a barrier or other technology, but also in the market manipulation of a price-fixing cartel which makes it impossible for a new competitor to enter a particular market space, or in a close-up cinematic image displaying a husband's jealousy which transmits to spectators a particular affective or emotional model. By connecting many disparate forms of expression it becomes possible to construct not a legal system made of norms and rules or a transcendent legal form enclosing an autonomous legal reality – call it a state science of law, or royal jurisprudence – but an element of the law's unique ontology, an ontology grounded not in an inside/outside dichotomy or the purity of the norm but in multiplicity, hybridity, and interference – a roving nomadological jurisprudence, what could be called a 'minor jurisprudence' had not the copyright already been conferred.

To be clear, the same kind of work would have to be done if we wanted to 'rationally reconstruct' a legal system. If I am right about the irreducible hybridity of law, then what is achieved in any ordeal, whether it is in everyday experience or in formal court proceedings, is only ever a local and fragile stabilization. The mirage of a pre-given, stable legal system or institutional normative order emerges only through the theoretical act of neglecting the essential labour necessary to *connect* these trajectories. They do not connect or resonate unless *made* to do so. Lawyers and judges – in their actual deeds if not their reflective words – prove this point with their copious citations to prior legal texts and utterances in their legal memoranda and in judicial opinions. These citations are not there to boast of the author's erudition but to establish connections between disparate ordeals or encounters – to achieve the provisional systematization of law. Is it any more unreasonable to compare a maritime dispute from 1875 about a bill of lading in order to explain why Mrs Wilson has no cause of action against her credit card company than it is to draw a line of affiliation between an encounter with a fence or wall and a cartel's price-fixing or a film's depiction of adultery? In all cases, the work of comparison is being carried out to fix and stabilize a connection that does not otherwise exist. What has changed is the expressive milieu or the media ecology.

To explain legal normativity with reference to, for example, my implicit recognition of an owner's rights, as one may be tempted to do, is to presuppose the agency of an already-constituted legal community of intersubjective relationships, when in fact the techno-legal mediator, which is a relation and not an individual, is itself *performing* the 'recognition' for which this explanation searches, and so participating in the ongoing constitution of a legal collective – a collective that can only *subsequently* be re-translated and rationalized as a stable community of subjects voluntarily recognizing one another's rights in pursuit of some shared objective. To insist on the social, political, or institutional context of property relations in which it is meaningful, or possible, to engage in fence-building as a form of property-claiming, is to miss the point of the hybridization move I advocate: that a global or systemic context doesn't do any work at all,[16] but is only an amalgamation of agencies that hasn't yet been disentangled. And what we've done by closing in on the ownership theory at issue is to have drawn one from the indistinct mass called 'context' – precisely in order to show that the context, the structure, the system of relations, is not something other than the performances of the agents we can descriptively draw out, and must draw out in practice. The next step in unpacking this 'context' would be to inquire into the ways the hybrid ensembles or assemblages sustaining the ownership relation connect up with other ordeals, other passages of law: an ordeal is a small, fabricated, reduced world that must be threaded together with other little worlds, always locally and bearing all

16 Thus Garfinkel (1991, p. 10): '[N]ot only does no concept of context-in-general exist, but every use of "context" without exception is itself essentially indexical.'

the costs, to account for the seemingly stable, permanent, generalized legal relations that otherwise appear to circulate freely throughout society. So long as that remains to be done, the illusion of an already-given, totalized, metadispatching legal system will continue to haunt legal and socio-legal theory, occluding any understanding of the ontological originality of law and its force.[17]

Democracy and materiology

The beings of law do not need a democratic foundation. That they act, circulate, and transform other relations – that they exist – among nondemocratic collectives is evident. But if our account cannot envisage their democratic *bona fides*, we risk a fatal misunderstanding on political grounds. So we must ask: in shifting the inquiry from validity and legitimacy to the force of law, have we ruled out the possibility of specifying any democratic grounds of law or the relation of law and democracy more broadly? For several reasons, we have not.

First, the argument above unearthed a democratic or proto-democratic kernel at the core of the problem of the force of law. That it belongs to a 'minor' tradition in democratic theory – that which runs, beautifully but inconsistently and unpredictably, from Lucretius to Dewey and Whitehead – rather than the discursive theories of liberal democracy that still largely dominate the field or to the radical-democratic post-Marxist alternative is no basis for rejecting its democratic credentials. Second, it is important to note the perspective from which we sketched this account of legality: that of the *law's immanent materiology* rather than a general political theory or philosophy of law. To a degree, this account fails to enter into an extended dialogue with other legal theories, including those organized around the question of validity, simply because it foregrounds what the latter reject out of hand. This sketch may thus be understood as a step toward a new kind of dialogue with them – in a key that is, perhaps, somewhat liberated from their gravitational pull. And third, although there is a sense in which the rejection of the big legal animal (the legal system, the institutional normative order, etc.) and the confinement of law to the local ordeal may be seen to result in a kind of might-is-right dynamic – since, in general, prevailing legal theories prevail by recruiting allies to amplify their expressive power, not by virtue of their greater rationality or coherence, as determined by some imaginary, self-subsistent scheme of rationality and coherence – we should consider that *democracy* is itself a messy, antagonistic, often illogical affair in which might and right are not cleanly distinguishable and in which they are, in fact, little more than labels that seem to designate qualitatively different methods or strategies only as a result of the

17 The example of the physical enclosure has obvious limits, but it is hoped that the description is suggestive enough to partly demonstrate how certain nonphysical enclosures and other incorporeal expressive media (e.g. market devices such as the wage standard or interest rates) may operate.

purification of a universalizing discourse. I will conclude by drawing these three points together.

Above, I conferred a propositional form on the impossible democratic kernel embedded in the problem of legal force: all those affected by the consequences of a course of action must be taken into account in carrying out the course of action. This may recall the Habermasian discourse principle (those rules of action are valid which all affected persons could agree to) but critically deviates from it in several important ways. It proposes an obligation, not a criterion of validity; it proposes that obligation as material expression, in asignifying techniques, performative practices, and collective ensembles of heterogeneous and often unpredictable actors, not as communication; it is oriented toward particular, observable courses of action, not general, hypothesized rules of action; it projects a risky, provisional public ('those affected'), rather than presupposing a stable community of persons; it prioritizes attachment and materiality over consensus and rational speech, Lucretius's *ligando* over Cicero's *legendo.* [18]

This obligation, which crystallizes the intensive quanta of the force of law, localizes and multiplies publics – a different public is involuntarily gathered for a different course of action – while grasping the emergent nature of those publics. It is not *this* public that claims to have issued any legal declaration or norm that is now in question; if there is a norm at stake, it is one to be *invented* in the ordeal. After all, what is a consequence of a course of action is a question of who and what is affected: a perspectival judgment requiring a lengthy concatenation of mediations and translations to have been assembled. We are no longer (purely) in discourse, but we are in law: a kind of experimental jurisprudence. And so it is this public obligation that most clearly shows the legal trajectory, or chain of obligations, whatever its makeup in a particular ordeal, to be oriented around a matter or mass (*res*) that is at the same time unifying and divisive, collective and contentious. For this reason, the theory of hybrid legalities and the expressive force of law belong to what I have called the law's immanent *materiology* (from *res* for matter or mass).

The term does little to explain itself, and to understand it adequately, we would need to contrast it against the other *topoi* with which it intersects to constitute the

18 To justify the association of Lucretius with *ligando* in the relevant sense would require a separate essay, but this association is important enough to merit a comment. For a signpost, see Lactantius 2003, p. 277: '[T]he word religion comes from the bond of piety because God has bound man to him and tied him with piety: we simply have to serve him as master and obey him as father. Lucretius interpreted the word much better [than the superstitious pagans] when he said he was "untying religious knots."' The phrase in *De rerum natura* (I, 932) is '*religionum nodis animum exsolvere pergo*', free the soul from the bonds of religion (or superstition). Curiously, in his discussion of *legere* and *ligare* as possible roots of 'religion,' Derrida overlooks Lucretius entirely (Derrida 2002, p. 71). This is probably owing to the erroneous contention of Benveniste, whom Derrida follows, that Christians like Lactantius and not pagans like Lucretius are the originators of the etymological links grounding law and religion in *ligando*.

practical metalanguage of law-in-action.[19] Where law's materiology describes the processes by which diverse raw materials are fashioned into value-objects and chains of obligations, its *anthropology* provides techniques of personation that this materiology presupposes, while its *sociology of action* provides rituals and criteria of actionability the other dimensions cannot themselves specify. I cannot begin to untangle this knot for lack of space, but it suffices to note that my project here has not been to pronounce on the essence of law, but to redistribute legal materiality, taking from the validity/efficacy dyad and giving back to the generative force it obscures.

One criticism of the approach outlined here may be that, for it, the law withdraws from justice, moral truth, the good, and still other pricey values, in favour of the much less costly value of brute strength.[20] Putting aside which of those two kinds of values is in fact more difficult to sustain, this criticism misses the mark in two ways.

First, nothing prevents a successor from reifying, reducing, and otherwise translating a particular legal trajectory – by, for example, seizing on to a 'rule' or a *ratio decidendi* that may be drawn from it and discarding the remainder – for the successor's own purposes in some new course of action, including a moral or political one in which this instance of legality could become a principle of constitutional politics or of moral action, held up as a standard, or denounced, critiqued, derided. (Courts do this to one another with extreme regularity: reification and reduction are ordinary judicial tools. So do lawyers, journalists, policymakers, politicians, academics, and so on.) In other words, the presumed existence of stable 'legal rights' to which a person is entitled (reproductive rights, free speech, etc.) or stable 'legal duties' owed by a person (to refrain from interfering with another's property, to honour freely made agreements, etc.) as represented *outside of any particular ordeal* continue to do the rhetorical, political, moral, economic, and other kinds of work we regularly make them do. In this respect, the account sketched here arguably renders the relations of law to justice, the good, and so forth *more* transparent than those traditions of legal thought that loudly proclaim their affinity for this problem.

Second, the alleged withdrawal of law from justice in the process of constructing a (formal, judicial) chain of obligations simply never materializes, because the avatars of justice – whether construed as principles, narratives, attachments – can and do enter into circulation as legal value-objects in concrete ordeals. Not without losing their character as law-transcending figures, it is true; but if the criticism is that our approach loses sight of what transcends, and so does not act to make a difference in, the making of law, this is no criticism at all. On the contrary, it is a

19 Tracing this metalanguage is my current preoccupation, but few results have yet been published. Further commentary appears in McGee 2017 chapters 1, 4. See also McGee, forthcoming a, and McGee, forthcoming b.

20 Many thanks to Marcelo Thompson for raising this concern, in more articulate terms than are reflected here, in discussion following the workshop in Glasgow.

vindication, because the law's immanent materiology is concerned with precisely what makes a difference in the making of law.

Thus, it is not the dominance of might over right to which we are committed, but their reciprocal subsumption. Where the allies enrolled are reasons, principles, rules, and so on, right is said to prevail; where the allies are technological, architectural, imagistic, political-economic, and so forth, might is said to prevail. But reasons can be quite as violent or coercive as technologies, which can themselves be just as rational as any reason. In all events, it is a question of recruiting diverse allies (reasons, and principles, and market devices, and technologies, and images ...) to shape a world; and in that, the beings of law provide potential grounds *for* democracy, rather than requiring a foundation *in* democracy.

Bibliography

Constable, Marianne, 2014, *Our Word is Our Bond: How Legal Speech Acts*, Stanford University Press, Stanford, CA.

Davies, Margaret, 2017, *Law Unlimited: Materialism, Pluralism, and Legal Theory*, Routledge, Abingdon, Oxon.

Dawson, George, 1694, *Origo legum, or A Treatise of the Origin of Laws and Their Obliging Power*, Richard Chiswell, London.

Derrida, Jacques, 2002, 'Faith and knowledge: The Two Sources of "Religion" at the Limits of Reason Alone', in Gil Anidjar (ed.), *Acts of Religion*, pp. 40–101, Routledge, New York; London.

Esposito, Roberto, 2015, *Two: The Machine of Political Theology and the Place of Thought*, trans. Zakiya Hanafi, Fordham University Press, New York.

Garfinkel, Harold, 1991, *Studies in Ethnomethodology*, Polity, Cambridge, UK; Malden, MA.

Garfinkel, Harold, 2002, *Ethnomethodology's Program: Working out Durkheim's Aphorism*, ed. Anne Warfield Rawls, Rowman & Littlefield Publishers, Lanham, MD.

Hildebrandt, Mireille, 2015, *Smart Technologies and the End(s) of Law*, Edward Elgar Publishing, Cheltenham, UK.

Kelsen, Hans, 2006, *General Theory of Law and State*, Transaction Publishers, New Brunswick, NJ.

Lactantius, 2003, *Divine Institutes*, trans. Anthony Bowen & Peter Garnsey, Liverpool University Press, Liverpool.

Latour, Bruno, 1988, *Science in Action: How to Follow Scientists and Engineers through Society*, Harvard University Press, Cambridge, MA.

Latour, Bruno, 2010, *The Making of Law: An Ethnography of the Conseil d'État*, trans. Marina Brilman & Alain Pottage, Polity, Cambridge, UK; Malden, MA.

Latour, Bruno, 2013, *An Inquiry into Modes of Existence: Anthropology of the Moderns*, trans. Catherine Porter, Harvard University Press, Cambridge, MA.

Lucretius, *De rerum natura, The Latin Library*, last viewed 27 April 2017, www.thelatinlibrary.com/lucretius/lucretius1.shtml.

McGee, Kyle, 2014, *Bruno Latour: The Normativity of Networks*, Routledge, Abingdon, Oxon.

McGee, Kyle, 2015, 'On Devices and Logics of Legal Sense: Toward Socio-technical Legal Analysis,' in Kyle McGee (ed.), *Latour and the Passage of Law*, pp. 61–92, Edinburgh University Press, Edinburgh.

McGee, Kyle, 2016, 'On Legal Replicants', *Jurimetrics: The Journal of Law, Science, and Technology* 56(3): 305–318.

McGee, Kyle, 2017, *Heathen Earth: Trumpism and Political Ecology*, Punctum Books, California.

McGee, Kyle, forthcoming a, 'Actor-Network Theory and the Critique of Law', in Thanos Zartaloudis (ed.), *Law and Philosophy: Critical Intersections*, Rowman & Littlefield International, London; New York.

McGee, Kyle, forthcoming b, 'Law in the Mirror of Critique: A Report to an Academy', in Emilios Christodoulidis*et al.* (eds), *Handbook of Critical Legal Theory*, Edward Elgar Publishing, Cheltenham, UK.

Nietzsche, Friedrich, 2003, *Writings from the Late Notebooks*, ed. Rüdiger Bittner, trans. Kate Sturge, Cambridge University Press, Cambridge; New York.

Philippopoulos-Mihalopoulos, Andreas, 2014, *Spatial Justice: Body, Lawscape, Atmosphere*, Routledge, Abingdon, Oxon.

Melissaris, Emmanuel & Croce, Mariano, 2017, "A Pluralism of Legal Pluralisms", *Oxford Handbooks Online*, last viewed 27 April 2017, www.oxfordhandbooks.com/view/10.1093/oxfordhb/9780199935352.001.0001/oxfordhb-9780199935352-e-22?rskey=jSiU9Y&result=1.

Schauer, Frederick, 2015, *The Force of Law*, Harvard University Press, Cambridge, MA.

Seltzer, Mark, 2016, *The Official World*, Duke University Press, Durham, NC; London.

Stone, Matthew, 2015, 'Roberto Esposito and the Biopolitics of Property Rights', *Social & Legal Studies* 24(3): 381–398.

9 The biographical core of law: privacy, personhood, and the bounds of obligation

Marcelo Thompson

Law's drawing hands

What is the origin of the force of privacy obligations? That privacy obligations *are* legal obligations and obligations endowed with a certain force is indisputable. The daily news appears intent on convincing us of the contrary, so insistent and pervasive are the privacy violations it portrays. There is also a great deal of normative indeterminacy in the expectations on which privacy rests. Yet it is clear that, in a vast number of circumstances, people can expect others to be *bound* by an obligation to respect their privacy.

For all their seeming fragility, these expectations are immensely powerful. So much so that the whole edifice of the law rests on them. The visible face of privacy expectations may be that of their pervasive disappointment. Much more prevalent, however, are those less visible situations where the boundaries of access obtain, where privacy is preserved and, with it, the spaces for the development of human subjectivity. It is only through the discreet workings of such boundaries that law can exist – that law can pass[1] – as a normative order. For law, thus, protecting privacy is an existential affair.

Privacy, human subjectivity, and the law hold, in other words, a relationship of reciprocal necessitation; a relationship so profound it might be said that, like space, time, and the universe, none of these ideas would be able to exist without the others. Together, they form a biographical core of legal normativity.[2] Understanding how they intertwine has important implications for how we approach

1 On the 'passage' of law, see Latour 2010, pp. 127ff, and, more systematically, in the light of the idea of passage more generally, Latour 2013, pp. 33ff., 357ff. Elaborating on Latour's analysis of law, see the series of essays in McGee 2015a, in particular, for our purposes here, the chapters by McGee (McGee 2015b) and Gutwirth (Gutwirth 2015), as well as Latour's response, at pp. 61ff, 122ff and 331ff. See also McGee 2014, pp. 128ff and McGee 2015a, pp. 467, 469ff. These works are engaged with incidentally throughout the paper and Latour's in particular, in more detail, at pp. 199ff. In ways that will become clear below, however, the reference here turns the argument in those works on its head.

2 I engage with the notion of 'biographical core' as a term of art in (Canadian) privacy jurisprudence, from where I borrow the term, in the concluding section. The discussion presented here is wider.

each of them as a concept. Pursuing such an understanding is the chief aim of the pages that follow.

There are immediate theoretical reasons for pursuing this inquiry. On privacy, it provides an answer to the question at the beginning of this paper, enabling us to observe how the origin of the force of privacy is bound with that of law itself. On law, it not only addresses contemporary social theories that see law emerging in non-human realms,[3] but also highlights how law and morality are intertwined, before any interpretive enterprise, at the very genesis of the interpreter. On human subjectivity, it invites us to revisit theories according to which law exists to address certain normative defects[4] or perform certain functions,[5] but which refrain from fully acknowledging the human dimension of such tasks.

Beyond situated theoretical gains, however, carrying out this inquiry is, I believe, an existential task for jurisprudence. It is so as it highlights how pursuing and institutionalizing the best normative interpretation of human subjectivity and its boundaries might, in the end, be the central task of any legal system, and a task on which the very existence of law depends. One could think here of an allegory in which, through the looking glass, law seeks to interpret human subjectivity, while human subjectivity conducts the same interpretive survey regarding the law. But that could raise the question of whether the relationship between law and human subjectivity is then purely one of mutual reflexivity and interaction between beings that display episodic curiosity about but otherwise remain external to each other. A better illustration would be M. C. Escher's lithograph of two hands drawing each other in a strange loop.[6] Law and human subjectivity, in effect, constitute each other. Their origin and their boundaries, their fate and their force are intrinsically and reciprocally intertwined.

Privacy is the quintessential realm where this relationship takes place. It is here that law probes the reasonableness of the boundaries between human subjects, and between these and the world around them, institutionally recognizing such boundaries, and lending thus some fixity to them. Those are also the boundaries from within which human subjectivity, like the hand in Escher's drawing, emerges to further constitute the law. Yet human subjectivity does not arise casually. It calls

3 See infra pp. 199ff. for discussion.
4 See e.g. Hart 2012, pp. 92ff, and infra n. 29 and accompanying text.
5 See Luhmann 2004, pp. 142ff, and discussion at p. 201 infra.
6 See Hofstadter 1979, p. 10 (famously introducing the idea of a strange loop, which he describes as a 'phenomenon [that] occurs whenever, by moving upwards (or downwards) through the levels of some hierarchical system, we unexpectedly find ourselves right back where we started'). The idea is further developed in Hofstadter 2007. Hofstadter's work is ultimately an exploration of the self-referentiality of human consciousness, the idea of an 'I' emerging from how our experience of the complexity of symbols and meaning tends to turn back upon itself. Oren Perez discusses Hofstadter's work in 'Law as a Strange Loop', though Perez does so from the perspective of Luhmann's and Teubner's views on the autopoiesis of social systems, which is significantly different from (if not antithetical to) the perspective I am coming from. See Perez 2009.

for institutional membership in the community of legal beings. It needs recognition from the law before it can, in turn, shape the law. Such a recognition is given, and queried in each raise of hands, through personhood. Personhood, the institutional face of human subjectivity, defines membership within the law.

This membership comes with certain capacities, which in turn are differentiated on the grounds of certain statuses. But all these are laid out in fairly general and non-negotiable terms, attaching to whoever falls into a certain legal position. Privacy, instead, contains as much objectivity as subjectivity; it follows, traces, and further enables the development of human subjectivity as it unfolds. In doing so, it extends and individuates the institutional contours of human personhood, in the light of expectations that are recognized as reasonable in the law. Law exists through these expectations, as they enable the rational exercise of the capacities, faculties, and powers – whilst addressing the shortcomings and vicissitudes – of the beings on whose existence law depends; that is, human beings, beings through and for the sake of whom law exists.

Before we take this exploration further, a note is due on the usefulness of our inquiry. It may seem obvious to affirm that law cannot exist without the recognition of human subjectivity and the consequent enablement of the conditions for its development. Indeed, if human flourishing is not seen as an end of the law, to what end, then, does law provide people with reasons for action; to what end does law mediate 'between people and the right reasons that apply to them'?[7] For however maligned the very thought of what 'right reasons' might be, there would be something profoundly inconsistent, delirious even, in denying that the value of human subjectivity is one such reason. The recognition of human subjectivity and its boundaries is, at the same time, end and condition of the very idea of normativity – or at least of forms of normativity whose reflective, central-case viewpoint is that of human beings. And the institutional order of the law is one such form.[8, 9]

It follows that thinking about law commands a certain degree of conservatism, of boundedness, in identifying law's subjects. Saying so bears no inconsistency with the progressive opening of personhood as a category. It does not speak against affirming the equality between – or indeed across – genders, races, ethnicities, and religions. Nor does it mean that the boundaries of personhood should

7 See Raz 1994, p. 214 (terming this conception, within which the authority of law rests in its legitimacy to perform such a mediating role, the 'service conception of authority'). For a recent restatement of the theory, see Raz 2006.

8 Thus, Neil MacCormick notes that understanding human beings as norm-users, and how they use norms, 'precedes understanding any possibility of deliberately creating relevant norms that are to become patterns for behavior' (MacCormick 2007, p. 20).

9 See Finnis 2011, p. 15 (noting how law, in its central-case viewpoint, is treated as an aspect of practical reasonableness, and thus 'attentive to all aspects of human opportunity and flourishing' and 'concerned to remedy deficiencies and breakdowns, and aware of their roots in the various aspects of human personality' – and criticizing descriptive theories like Hart's and Raz's for, all the while appealing to practical reason, not adopting themselves a practically reasonable viewpoint).

develop without concern for the profound ecological crisis devastating the earth.[10] But it does mean that the expansion of such boundaries ought to be a reflective enterprise, with its content and limits circumscribed by some measure of practical rationality. There are reasons in personhood, and these are also reasons of the law.

For a significant body of literature, however, the turn of the millennium delivered a remarkably different diagnosis.[11] With mounting evidence of the drastic impacts of human action upon the environment – signalling the emergence of a new geological epoch, which came to be known as the Anthropocene – the thought that people could be at the normative centre of anything suddenly sounded absurd.[12] How could we, our hands so soiled, continue to imagine ourselves on the high ground? Rather, it was precisely this idea of our conceptual purity, this proclaimed separation of ourselves from other forms of being, which delivered the world to the current state of affairs. Monumental though the environmental crisis is, thus, it would be but a symptom of a larger problem of design – namely, a problem with how we have been programming the devices through which we represent and constitute social reality to overlook the interminglings between nature and culture, fact and value, the hybrid, cyborg nature of being in the world.[13]

In effect, at the root of all forms of violence and inequality would be our attempt to introduce and legalize artificial forms of alterity based on a distilled, 'transcendental' image of human subjectivity – of which all other instances of being are imagined as countercategories.[14] The undoing of such a mystification of

10 Nor does the argument here imply, to any extent, that law does not – or should not – ascribe legal personhood to categories of beings other than human persons. For an excellent exploration of the ways and reasons why law *does* so, see Teubner 2006. As Teubner explains, drawing on Luhmann, the personification of non-human entities reflects a strategy of coping with uncertainty – which, in turn, is but an instantiation of the broader, normatively stabilizing function Luhmann ascribes to law itself (ibid., pp. 503, 505). All this is very fine. What cannot be overlooked, however, is how the very need to cope with normative uncertainty is a profoundly *human* need, how it is only from the vantage point of human subjectivity that any legal strategy can make sense (including personification). See infra pp. 189ff. and 197ff. for discussion.

11 See supra n.1 and discussions at pp. 199ff. and 207ff.

12 See e.g. Purdy 2015, p. 271 (explaining the move towards 'post-humanism' or 'eco-centrism' in recent political thought as, in part, a call 'for leveling the hierarchical divide between human and nonhuman by blurring that boundary', in recognition that '[w]e are less distinct from the rest of nature than we often imagine'). See also Grusin 2015, p. vii (highlighting approaches in the humanities and social sciences engaged in 'decentering the human in favor of a turn toward and concern for the nonhuman'). Grusin notes that 'almost every problem of note that we face in the twenty-first century entails engagement with nonhumans' (ibid.). Though it should perhaps be said that, even as existential problems loom in the horizon, the human world in the twenty-first century faces significantly fewer problems relating to non-humans – from disease and epidemics, to the impacts of natural calamities, to the scarcity of food, to the effects of military artefacts – than it has faced through the course of its existence.

13 See Latour 1991.

14 See e.g. Bennett 2015 (connecting the trend towards nonhumans, in part, to an awareness of the effects of historical materialism – the 'accelerated concentration of

reality would, in turn, call for a denunciation of the constitution of modernity (Latour 1991, p. 43), for a re-anchoring of our systems of value within the profusion of networks from which the world's various, interconnected modes of being emerge (Latour 2013) – a decentring of paradigms, thus: from human agents to *actants* embedded in networks; from fixed, universal notions of value and dignity to a permanent shuffling of *value-objects* that are, at once, nature and culture, hybrids themselves, not amenable to any form of anchoring, indeed, if not in the shifting circumstances of the world's networked modes of being. Such a decentring of paradigms ultimately finds its crowning in the law, which, no longer a province of humans, emerges as a formal structure of links connecting the whole range of beings that traverse the world's different modes of existence.[15]

In a sense, this literature speaks, with great sensibility and allure, of concerns – with the environmental crisis, with the rise of technological artefacts – that could not be more familiar to humankind at this point in time, nor more important for our thinking about the law. It draws our attention to a whole universe of materiality that jurisprudence most commonly tends to overlook.[16] It is understandable why recent legal scholarship has tended to approach it – in particular the works of Bruno Latour – with enormous deference. This chapter engages with Latour's works, albeit in a more critical way, as it travels to its conclusion.[17] To a great extent, in fact, these pages are written *in the light* of such a literature and the concerns that animate it. Yet this is not a chapter exclusively or mainly *about* such a literature – for one, because, in the view presented here, the calls by this literature to re-anchor the constitution of our time fail to pay heed to the relationship of reciprocal necessitation that law and human subjectivity hold with each other,

wealth within liberal economies' – and the 'desire for a radical, forceful counter-response to the injustices of global capitalism'). In the same sense, see Grear 2015, pp. 225, 227, 231 (explaining how the 'crisis of human hierarchy' represented by the Anthropocene flows from the acknowledgement of the systemic privileges of a highly selective group of dominant humans who serve as the paradigm of the 'juridical human' – a paradigm based on 'the rationalistic, hierarchical scales of value decisive to the expansion of European' capitalism and 'appropriative industrial expansionism' – vis-à-vis a 'patterned multiplicity of "the others of law"', the 'oppression of "outsider" subjectivities based on gender, race, age, sexuality – and so forth'), and Purdy 2015, pp. 273–2 (noting: '[H]umanism's legacy is haunted by the ghost of its founding epitome, the white and privileged male, and by his crimes'). The argument is famously explored from a cyborg-feminist perspective in Haraway 1991.

15 No term better describes this decentred paradigm of the legal bond than Kyle McGee's 'Jurimorph' (the honour is bestowed by Latour himself in McGee 2015a, p. 335). McGee uses the term to refer to all entities and agents (*value-objects*) that, upon passing through legal *devices*, qualify as *beings of law* (in other words, get 'jurimorphised'), as well as to the devices (themselves assemblages of value-objects) through which such entities and agents need to pass (McGee 2015a, p. 64). Unpacking McGee's idea, Latour explains that law as a mode of existence is so powerful precisely 'because it is so astutely *devoid of any other content than its connectedness through every possible entity*'; thus, 'what we should expect law to do is to *stick to jurimorphs* and to reopen the key question of what it is for a claim to have a ground' (McGee 2015a, pp. 344, 348).

16 In this sense the equally elegant account in Matthews & Veitch 2016.

17 See infra pp. 199ff.

and to the boundaries that are essential for this relationship's unfolding. It is such a relationship and such boundaries that the lines below seek to bring to the fore as a central concern for jurisprudence.

If the argument in this chapter holds ground, it follows that events at the turn of the millennium might indeed be consequential for how we approach jurisprudence – yet in a way diametrically opposite to what those works have sought to highlight. For these events do not invite us to peacefully assimilate the conceptual dissolution of personhood, to accept that maybe we have never truly existed as a distinctive form of being – that law is thus much more indiscriminating regarding the forms of being it binds. To the contrary. From the point of view that concerns us here, what this moment in which the environment and technology conspire to engulf us brings about is a situation of existential strife for human subjectivity *and* the law – a situation, that is, in which, challenged with the loss of their bearings, human subjectivity and the law rebel to highlight and reaffirm the structural boundaries, the contrasts and frictions without which neither can exist. Law rebels in us for it dwells in us. And the institutional boundaries it recognizes for our emergence and development are the institutional boundaries within which its own development, in turn, takes place. This – as we will see, deeply moral – specially cogenetic[18] relationship between human subjectivity and the law takes place, paradigmatically, in the domain of privacy.

Privacy, personhood, and the normativity of law

Of all legal domains, privacy is indeed the one that most typically performs the task of institutionally recognizing the boundaries of human subjectivity. Certainly this task is shared with others, if not all domains of the law. As law mediates among reasons available to people, it defines their possibilities of self-authorship. But only within the normative-cum-architectural spaces that privacy creates can such possibilities be authentically pursued.[19] Only within those spaces can people define the scope of their interactions with others, authentically acting and thinking and being in the world.[20]

18 While the idea of cogenetics entails creation at the same time and place, the relationship here goes beyond in that, as noted above, there is a sense of reciprocal constitution.

19 The literature on the relations between privacy and autonomy is vast. Much of this literature focuses on privacy typically from a perspective of control or exclusion, which flows classically from the works of Alan Westin as well as Samuel Warren and Louis Brandeis. Recent literature, on the other hand, tends to reflect a more relational understanding of privacy, where the point of the autonomy privacy protects is 'not to disengage one from relations but to enhance one's ability to form new and deeper relationships' (deCew 1997, p. 69). This more contemporary understanding of privacy makes it, as a concept, better equipped to deal with the challenges posed by posthumanism. This literature is discussed in more detail in the concluding section.

20 It could perhaps be said, with Heidegger, that privacy brings forth our possibilities of 'being-with', yet not 'belonging' to others. See Heidegger 1953, pp. 111ff. (on authenticity and being in the world).

Privacy performs its task in different ways. For instance, it reduces power asymmetries, by restraining the amount and quality of information other actors (e.g. governments or corporations) can know or infer about a person, and thus restricting the possibility that those actors may coerce or manipulate that person's behaviour.[21] It also prevents encroachment by state authorities – and the individuals and groups these represent – on how persons may choose to go about their bodies and their lives (e.g. in cases of abortion)[22] or cease going about these altogether (e.g. in cases of assisted suicide).[23] But, most typically, privacy works by creating normative assurances that, in circumstances where subjective expectations are deemed to be reasonable, people will be free from observation and thus have the solitude required for the making of choices that are authentically their own.[24]

These normative assurances also find their way into the world of technological artefacts. Here as well they work to define zones of interaction between a person and others. It has been said that normativity operates tacitly in the case of technological artefacts.[25] For, unlike the law, technologies do not *address* people directly. They operate by regulating or determining human action as a matter of fact. Yet this is not the whole story of technological normativity. First, because normativity here may flow from visual and informational cues people take from the architecture of technological artefacts. Second, because technological artefacts are not a purely physical reality either. Rather, in their very functions, artefacts reflect an encounter between the physical and the teleological. They have a certain 'forness', goals that their being properly put in motion is expected to achieve.[26] What the proper functions of a certain artefact are is to a large extent a matter of negotiations between users and designers over that artefact's *use plan.* [27] Such

21 See Pasquale 2015, p. 3 (noting that '[t]o scrutinize others while avoiding scrutiny oneself is one of the most important forms of power'). See also DeVries 2013 (highlighting that privacy and due process 'can be can be seen as tools to safeguard a certain level of symmetry in the power relations within society, where no actor may be simply smothered by the brute and arbitrary force of another actor').

22 See e.g. *Roe v Wade* (1973) 410 US 113, 93 S Ct 705.

23 See *Pretty v United Kingdom* (2002) 35 EHRR 1.

24 See *ABC v Lenah Game Meats Pty Ltd* (2001) HCA 63, 185 ALR 1 [41] (Gleeson CJ holding that privacy involves 'kinds of activity which a reasonable person, applying contemporary standards of morals and behaviour, would understand to be meant to be unobserved').

25 See Hildebrandt 2008, pp. 175, 176.

26 See Kroes & Meijers 2006.

27 See Houkes 2006, pp. 112 (noting, though, the privileged status of reasons given by designers as socially recognized experts). It is through use plans that functions are ascribed to artefacts (cf. Vermaas & Houkes 2006, p. 6). As Houkes explains, 'designing [an artefact] can be reconstructed as, in part, the construction of use plans, and artefacts can be defined as objects that have been designed and manufactured to play a part in use plans' (Houkes 2006, p. 107) – to play a part, that is, in a 'goal-directed series of considered actions … in which manipulations of [an object x] are included as contributions to realising the given goal' (Vermaas & Houkes 2006, p. 7). It is also important to highlight that constraints of custom (ibid.) and rationality (Houkes 2006, p. 105) play a role in the definition of what functions of an artefact can be defined as *proper*.

negotiations can be more or less extensive. When things work well, the propriety of functions as communicated by designers is readily understood and accepted by users.[28] But, as everyday media backlash against companies such as Google or Facebook shows, the authority of use plans can be, and often is, put into question.

What is distinctive about the normative assurances provided by the law, as oposed to those of artefacts, is that their articulation in institutional form lends them greater clarity (problems of indeterminacy notwithstanding) and stability (problems of supervenience notwithstanding) when employed ***in human reasoning***. Artificially intelligent systems, albeit guided by technological normativity, do not need the law as we know it (or at least as far as we know it). Their behaviour may be regulated and constituted by technological rules themselves, such as those embedded in the code of computer programs. They may design new software, conceive of use plans, and decide and revise their decisions about the propriety of these. In effect, they are already doing so incalculable times as we speak. But the articulation of legal rules in institutional form exists precisely to address normative uncertainties not encountered by machines.[29] In addressing these uncertainties, law stabilizes ***people's*** normative expectations and binds people through time (Luhmann 2004, p. 72) – a time we experience in an all too human way.

Machines are able to see and pursue entire systems at once, retrieve their past, project their future. They don't go about, like people, hesitating or faltering in the following of rules they don't have the faintest possibility of mastering.[30] They need no bonds, no fiction, no stabilization curative. The life of their programs is one of realized logics, not of normative disappointments of the kind that law works to prevent or to heal.

The legal bond is thus a mystery of the human person, not a consequence of the passage of signs and symbols through material blackboxes or devices.[31] 'The idea of the normative (certainly in the institutional context)', MacCormick notes, is 'focused primarily on [a] line of exclusion that splits the permissible and impermissible, dividing that which is (however grudgingly) "all-right" from that which is wrong' – and such a distinction (that between right and wrong), most importantly, is to be ***understood*** 'in terms of human values, and thus ***in terms of our***

28 See e.g. Whitten & Tygar 2005 (on the importance of usability in the development of security systems).

29 See Finnis 2011, p. 7 (noting how for Hart '[a] legal system is a system in which "secondary" rules have emerged ***in order to*** remedy the defects of a pre-legal regime comprising only "primary rules"'). Such defects, for Hart, encompass, besides uncertainty, the ***static*** character of primary rules as well as their ***inefficiency*** (Hart 2012, p. 92).

30 No policy proposition is more essential in this regard than the one put forward by Kate Crawford in 'Can an Algorithm be Agonistic?' (Crawford 2016). In programming algorithms to hesitate, as we do (see discussion at pp. 197ff, infra), and in that they succeed in doing so, might lie the future of anything that we experience as a normative order.

31 In a similar sense, see Gutwirth 2015, p. 145 (criticizing McGee 2014 on his views that, in Gutwirth's words, jurisdiction or '"dire le droit" also occurs through material objects and technological artefacts').

understanding of our own human nature' (MacCormick 2007, p. 105). So law not only addresses people in ways that are meaningful to them, but also draws its own meaning from human subjectivity itself.

One could seek to argue, as Green does in commenting on Hart, that '[t]here is nothing in human nature or society that *requires* law'; that the functional deficits law exists to solve in complex societies are not a moral problem, but a problem in mechanisms of social control (Green 2012, p. 1). Such a view may be correct in the sense that less complex societies may exist that just do not need the law, without being morally worse for that. Yet this cannot mean that in those (far less exotic) circumstances where the law *is* required, neutrality towards its adoption is a moral option. *Law* is the moral option in such circumstances, and it is required not just by 'something' in human nature; it is required by human nature itself.

'[T]he law,' Raz remarks, 'is a concept used by people to understand themselves.' Understanding the concept of law is, thus, a reflexive enterprise – and one where 'evaluative judgement ... is inescapable'.[32] Engaging with the concept of law is not engaging with something foreign to human beings, but rather with something coextensive with them. The essence of law is, in this sense, different from the essence of technology. For technologies have been said to cage or enframe being, making people into instruments (standing reserve) of its ends – whereas the law, in its central cases, brings the normative order forth as an expression of human subjectivity. Law, not technology, is a true extension of ourselves. To say so does not mean law does not have its own technologies, its own means for achieving its ends. But one only needs to think of how legal formalism may detract from such ends to understand that there are authentic and inauthentic ways of law's being in the world. And the care – the hesitation – that is so necessary for understanding law's authentic modes is a hesitation that invites law to reflect upon the essence of human personality.

So law as an idea, law as reason, promotes and needs to promote self-understanding. This presupposes that people be able to articulate and recognize the boundaries of human subjectivity.[33] And, as a matter of fact, law has historically enabled people to do so. It should not be too far-fetched to recognize, with Clippinger, that institutions such as courts and legislatures 'were invented precisely to certify and test, and to enforce the authenticity of representations of identity

32 Raz's own understanding of the concept law is, ultimately, rather restrictive in comparison with what transpires from the remarks above. It entails no degree of moral evaluation, but just a judgement of importance in identifying what is central to law as a social institution. And this, as we noted before, is law's claimed authority to mediate amongst people's reasons for action. Noting the irony, Brian Leiter's remarks, on the cited excerpt: 'It is curious, indeed, then, that no one has made any effort to figure out what "people" – as distinct from the subset of them who work in the vicinity of High Street – actually understand by the concept' (Leiter 2009).

33 See Pavlakos 2007, p. 151 (noting, in a similar vein, that it is the 'concept of personhood, as one that is intertwined with the idea of universalisation, [that] cements the unity of practical reason').

and reputation'.[34] In so doing, law asserts human subjectivity against the proliferation of modes of dissolution of its value – a value that the idea of law intrinsically presupposes.

This is not a recent story. Nor, as noted above, has the recognition of legal personhood, in itself, contributed to the unfolding ecological crisis, let alone to the profound and growing gap between the top 1% and the rest of the world[35] – with the equally profound democratic deficits resulting from such a gap. The ascription of personhood to human beings has a history going back at least as far as to Roman Law. And whereas, in its fullest form, personhood was then a fairly restrictive affair, it has experienced a more-or-less continuous (if reflective) expansion, founded upon an idea of equality of the whole human family.[36]

So personhood in the law is not an invention of the Enlightenment, of societies that suddenly thought themselves to be modern without ever having been. The affirmation of human subjectivity in law is not what has led to the proliferation of beings whose subjectivity law ignored – a marching army of hybrids that now threaten to rise and engulf the earth. On the contrary, some of the most profound challenges now faced by humanity stem precisely from the threatened *erosion* of human subjectivity as recognized by the law – and they demand a reassuring response, without which law just has no point, no grounds on which to stand.

Two challenges to human subjectivity

Privacy is one such response to two central challenges to human subjectivity. The first challenge is one of erosion of human subjectivity by coordinated human action itself. It has to do with the cacophony of discourses that characterizes contemporary information networks (Sunstein 2009, p. 51); with how the reasons on which people base their actions, and indeed people's attention and determination to pursue such reasons at all, find themselves increasingly dispersed through contemporary networks. Seyla Benhabib's words perfectly encapsulate the idea:

> We are facing the genuine risk that the worldwide movement of peoples and commodities, news and information will create a permanent flow of individuals without commitments, industries without liabilities, news without a public conscience, and the dissemination of information without a sense of boundaries and discretion. In this 'global.com civilization,' persons will shrink into e-mail addresses in space, and their political and cultural lives will

34 Clippinger 2007, p. 148 (noting further that: 'Without such institutions and credible social methods for asserting and authenticating people's identity and reputation civil society ceases to function').

35 cf. Latour 1991; Grear 2015; Bennett 2015; Haraway 1991.

36 To be sure, insofar as non-human forms of being are concerned, personhood has both expanded as a category after Roman times, retracted after the Enlightenment, where the human individual came to be seen as the 'only remaining plausible actor', and experienced a renewed expansion with the ecological movement and the emergence of electronic agents (Teubner 2006, p. 499).

> proliferate extensively into the electronic universe, while their temporal attachments will be short-lived, shifting and superficial. Democratic citizenship, internet utopias of global democracy notwithstanding, is incompatible with these trends. Democratic citizenship requires commitment; commitment requires accountability and a deepening of attachments.
>
> (Benhabib 2002, p. 70)

Benhabib's concern with democratic citizenship is, ultimately, a concern with the constitutive attachments without which the formation of identities and, indeed, the value of equality, are just not possible. For, otherwise, equality between what?

Privacy plays a fundamental if apparently paradoxical role in attending to such concerns. Privacy is the tool by which people configure and *reconfigure access* to themselves and to the world.[37] It ensures that, at least, amidst the boundless flows of information through the networks of our time, some degree of nodality remains. Privacy anchors networks in the value of human subjectivity. It prevents, insofar as people are concerned, network nodes from being dissolved and reconfigured *ad infinitum* by whatever form the network chaotically assumes at a given time. It sees to it that, whatever other points of connection networks may have, they first need to pass *through people* – people whose individual value they recognize and respect.

It may seem, though, that, by creating a space for the development and expression of human subjectivity, privacy rather provides a shelter for individual preferences to continue to multiply and disperse themselves in the information environment – leading us straight into Benhabib's diagnostic. That might well be the case to some extent, and there is only so much law can do in this regard without the charge of overbearing paternalism. But what *can* law do? It can encourage the spontaneous development of mechanisms of filtration that avoid an excessive fragmentation of discourses.[38] It can – which it does in areas such as defamation and the protection against hate speech – directly intervene to eliminate forms of discourse that affect people's narratives of self-identification and status in public life (Waldron 2004). Or it can establish a normative framework that, amidst the whirlwind of information flows, prevents the dissolution, the conflation of people's different spheres of action and existence. This is the task performed by privacy.

On the other hand, privacy performs this task while *also* allowing people to negotiate the boundaries between their individual spheres. That law lends normative effect to such negotiations presupposes an important recognition, namely that at the core of each sphere lies not just an actant, but an *agent* with *dignity*. For the same reason, law recognizes the limits of such negotiations. The spaces that privacy institutionalizes exist in the intersections between an individual's subjective expectations of privacy *and* the objective reasonableness of such expectations.[39] So

37 I borrow the expression from Dutton 2004, p. 19.

38 See Benkler 2006, pp. 161ff.

39 See e.g. *R v Edwards* (1996) 1 SCR 128, 1996 CanLII 255 (SCC) [45].

not only there needs to be a person who expects privacy, but also, in the objective views of others – not just any views, but objective views – that person's expectations must be determined as reasonable. A number of factors play a role in this determination, whose discussion goes beyond our purposes here. But we can see, for example, that the fact that the public is *interested in* a person's whereabouts is not enough to preclude a finding of reasonableness and thus to justify the disclosure of information about that person.[40] The existence of *public interest*, on the other hand, does operate as a factor in this preclusion.[41]

Now, *as far as law is concerned*, nothing can be more objective than the thought that at the core of any finding of reasonableness lies the value of human subjectivity, which in turn necessitates the conditions for its development. Whatever else might be debatable, this much is not. No reasonable idea of law – no reasonable *concept* of law – can exist that, in its central cases, does not attend to such a value. Law's own existence depends on the boundaries that privacy institutionalizes to protect it. Privacy creates the field from within which the force of law emerges. The force of privacy is thus a condition of existence of the force of law. The force of privacy as an obligation is necessitated by the very idea of law.

So, the first challenge to human subjectivity concerns its threatened erosion by human action itself. Some of the greatest instantiations of this challenge can be seen in the recognition denied to people who do not wish or cannot partake in society's infinite proliferation of tastes and preferences – from excluded religious communities to inmates in overcrowded prison systems around the world – all the while also being conscripted, through the universal language of obligation, to participate in the consumerist project of global citizenship. From prohibiting the use of the burka to imposing a condition of permanent scrutiny, law's raging response is not only a denial of liberty but also, and fundamentally, a dissolution of the boundaries of privacy and, with it, personhood. That privacy evaporates at these moments where *legality* no longer holds sway is a testament to how profoundly the forces of privacy and of the law are intertwined.

The second challenge to human subjectivity is a yet more serious one, for it is levelled not at different expressions of subjectivity but at the very possibility of it. It is the existential threat, posed by artificial forms of intelligence (AI), of *tout-court* dissolution of people's spaces for being in the world. It springs from the rise of large-scale technological systems that collect data about ourselves and our physical and semiological environments; systems that make judgements that inform our possibilities of action in ways we are unqualified to dispute,[42] and that

40 See e.g. *British Steel Corp v Granada Television Ltd* (1981) AC 1096 (HL) 1168 (Wilberforce LJ) (noting that 'there is a wide difference between what is interesting to the public and what it is in the public interest to make known').

41 See e.g. *Campbell v MGN Ltd* (2004) UKHL 22, (2004) 2 AC 457 [56] (Nicholls LJ) (holding that 'when press freedom comes into conflict with another interest protected by the law, the question is whether there is a sufficient public interest in that particular publication to justify curtailment of the conflicting right').

42 On one hand, ongoing legal debates question whether, under the new European General Data Protection Regulations, there is a *right to an explanation* regarding

increasingly direct our behaviour by means of the judgements they embed. Examples abound, from genomics-based healthcare systems to interior-aware self-driving cars, all increasingly deployed by fast-evolving machine learning technologies. The outsourcing of AI-based public tasks to private-owned AI infrastructures, coupled with such challenges in explainability in AI systems design, might preclude the possibility that governments and the law even understand what it is that they are procuring let alone appropriately regulate it.

It is not necessary to conceive of more extreme, science-fiction-like scenarios to appreciate how the state and the law are being progressively absorbed into a kind of rationality very different from that required by the idea of rule of law. The rule of law requires publicness, that the law stands for the persons it regulates (Waldron 2009, p. 31). It requires that argumentative mechanisms are in place through which law manifests itself as a common public resource, respecting the 'dignity [of people] as beings capable of explaining themselves' (ibid., p. 28). Only then can it be seen that law, as Waldron observes, 'is inherently respectful of persons as agents' (ibid.), that 'it respects the dignity of [people's] voluntary action and rational self-control' (ibid.), that it 'operate[s] by using, rather than suppressing and short-circuiting, the responsible agency of ordinary human individuals' (ibid., p. 26).

It is always the case that the respect of human subjectivity by the law requires the balancing of people's different interests – and it is in the context of such interests that the idea of rule of law needs to be understood. So the way the law structures our societies, the way it sets out the bonds that connect us all needs to be mindful, as noted above, of the nodality of human subjectivity in the networks of our time. All the while personhood, as a category, admits of a reflective revision of its boundaries to better accommodate inadequately regarded instances of it, and even as it allows for the partial extension of its effects to other species, the rational, logical limit for the law is, tautologically, its own dependence on human subjectivity.

This dependence manifests itself in two important ways for our discussion. On the one hand, architectural constraints on the spaces for the practical exercise of rationality through human subjectivity can only be understood *as* architectural constraints. That is to say, law cannot promote or condone the encroachment by hybrid or alternative forms of rationality on the way rationality is humanly exercised. There is, so to speak, no balancing to be undertaken here.[43] To the extent that such an encroachment takes place, *privacy* requires the reconfiguration of the

decisions made by automated systems. See e.g. Selbst & Powles 2017 (answering: yes). See Wachter, Mittelstadt & Floridi 2017 (answering: no). On the other hand, technological debates question whether it is even possible to develop self-explanatory artificially intelligent systems. See Knight 2017 (noting that 'no one really knows how the most advanced algorithms do what they do').

43 It is in this sense that Teubner notes that the legal personification of electronic agents might create 'aggressive new action centres as basic productive institutions. Here, he continues, 'their inclusion in society does not protect the new actors, just the opposite: it is society that needs to defend itself against the new actors. With the social inclusion

architectural spaces through which information, at varying levels of depth, reaches and leaves us and affects the boundaries of expression of human subjectivity.

Privacy sets, thus, the limits between people and the different forms of rationality embedded in the information environment that surrounds us.[44] Given the existential dimensions increasingly assumed by such forms, this setting of limits is no small task – nor small is its legal significance. In a world profoundly embedded in this ever-expanding material setting, the centrality of privacy as a foundational element for how the idea of obligation itself is to be understood in the information environment becomes unquestionable.[45] Privacy provides points of fixation for our bonds and commitments, anchoring these within the institutional boundaries of human subjectivity – and preventing their dislodgement by the blows from other realms. Privacy becomes as much a foundation for obligation as a program of human resistance.

Of course, the need for such points of fixation to be in place cannot mean that forms of *augmentation* of practical rationality ought to be precluded. To the extent that technology is at people's service, to the extent that it does stand for the public interest, it may rationally assist (rather than suppress) human rationality in attending to the normativity of law. It may lessen people's failures in making sense of that chain of normative causality we call the legal bond. People may become more Hercules-like. They may look into the legal bond, as one looks into a grain of sand, and, with no hesitation, see and act upon the integrity of law. On the other hand, such an immediacy, such a lack of hesitation, *also* means that the reasons why people need law at all cease to exist.

This is the second way in which law depends on human rationality. For law, as a union of primary and secondary rules (Hart 2012, p. 79), as an institutional order through which primary norms get stabilized and travel through time, operates at a meta level. It addresses shortcomings of a lower order of normativity which are inherently human shortcomings (ibid., p. 92).[46] Absent such shortcomings, even if we remain norm-users – and whether or not *we* remain at all – normativity becomes a purely logical affair, a program of technical efficiency and scientific rationality that no longer depends on a dichotomy of orders. Law will finally have become a (not too late) realization of Legal Realism's prophecies.

Should human subjectivity thus be guarded and reasserted against such a challenge? Should the tools of privacy be deployed to impose architectural limits to normative encroachment by such forms rationality? Is there actually a challenge here at all? It may be that the world – persons, objects, and all things in between – would be better off without the shortcomings that are so inherent to humankind

of cyborgs and electronic agents, new problems of alienation appear on the horizon of law' (Teubner 2006, p. 521).

44 This need not entail that the bond of privacy is extensible to such alternative forms. Though it might so extend, it is enough that law create obligations for human actors with regard to such forms.

45 And it is this sense, not in a levelling one, that the concerns with materiality highlighted by Matthews and Veitch 2016 become so important.

46 Cf. supra n. 29 and accompanying text.

at its current evolutionary stage. The present notes cannot, of course, affirm or dispute the rationality of such a statement. However, to the extent that the value of law – of the rule of law – is assumed as a point of departure in our inquiry, the value of human subjectivity follows as a logical presupposition of it. One cannot be affirmed without the other. The recognition of the value of law must thus also be a recognition of a certain moral content that is necessary to law; a content that at a minimum encompasses the value of human subjectivity *and* of the boundaries on which human subjectivity depends.

It may be, however, that, at the end of the day, jurisprudence has been studying something worthless all along; that our affirmation of the value of persons and the law is grounded not on rationality, but on an emotional quest for survival. But even then our commitment to defending these values needs to abide by some logical corollaries.

In order to claim authority, law needs to affirm its own value. In doing so, it cannot conceive of its own essence in the image of an assemblage of fragments devoid of dignity, a network of hybrid actants endlessly and boundlessly reconfiguring itself with values it contructs along the way. Law cannot and does not logically stand for such an image. Dignity requires boundaries, some degree of permanence, something to be stood for. The dignity of law requires, more, persons, whose value lies in their imperfect individual rationality; the pauses and hesitations of human subjectivity. It requires the art, the poetry of being *a* human subject amidst the dissolving pulls of technical rationality. Beyond requiring, law *stands* for this – and the bond of privacy is the foundation on which it stands.

The character of hesitation

In standing for human subjectivity, law does not stand for a modern fiction. It does not stand for a *modern* project, for, as noted above, it has stood for human subjectivity all along. And it does not stand for a *fiction*, for human subjectivity is an actual, reflexive vantage point, from where the integrity of law is to be judged. It is from such a reflexive viewpoint that our hesitations about the character of law take place. It is from here that the *normative* character of law emerges, that law gives people a *sense* of being obliged – one that rests as much on the objective, institutional reality of law as it does on people's reflective endorsement of such a reality.[47] Law is made everywhere people's pauses and hesitations can be felt. It is neither an exclusive province of courts and officials, nor a purely factual reality. The hesitations of law surely address law's institutional dimension, but the fact itself that *we* hesitate reflects our commitment to the integrity of law as a project.[48] That very commitment is a *moral* commitment, and one which cannot be

47 See Korsgaard 1996 (explaining reflective endorsement – based on maxims that could be universally adopted *as well as on the practical identity* of the reflecting agent – as the source of normativity).

48 The deeper character of law's hesitations we propose here is to be contrasted with that identified in Latour (2010, 2013) and explored in Gutwirth (2015) and McGee (2015c).

understood from outside the vantage point of human subjectivity, its values, and its boundaries.

People hesitate before objects of value. We hesitate before love – in approaching it, in committing to it, in breaking its bonds. We hesitate before life – in tending to it, in clinging to it, in letting it go. We hesitate because we feel, we know the dignity of such objects commands integrity in our thinking and going about them. Scientists, more than anyone, hesitate before knowledge. They hesitate because knowledge, as well, is an object of value. Scientists know they should not be casual about knowledge, that they ought to treat it with dignity, and that the dignity of knowledge requires abidance by certain norms that preside over scientific practice – norms that make scientific practice a project of integrity. Scientists organize themselves around norms of communalism, universalism, disinterestedness, and organized scepticism.[49] Their hesitations are, indissociably, about whether truth has been found *and* whether it has been so in the light of the norms that guide scientific pursuit.[50] These are, in the end, *moral* hesitations. They bring back the practice of science to bear on the subject who inquires into its integrity. One only needs to think of the repulse with which scientists relate to plagiarism, unsubstantiated claims, fabricated results to understand the moral character of their hesitations.

The outcome of having overcome such hesitations is a settlement, a moral commitment to the factual and normative boundaries of the object of value. This commitment brings hesitation to a close, though it does so always provisionally, always open to the possibility of revisitation. The no-longer-hesitating subject is for the time being convinced she has done her best to live up to what was morally expected from her in seeking to make sense of the object of value; that she has pursued this intepretive project with the required integrity, in the light of all normative and factual circumstances as well as of her own subjectivity.[51] She is aware that her commitments were reached from *her* vantage point. She is mindful of her own limitations, preferences, and prejudices. Yet the very fact she has brought her inquiry to a close – that she indeed no longer hesitates – indicates she has sought her best to reflect upon and address all circumstances she was aware of, *including her own.*

All this is no different in the case of the law. Law is produced within a moral community of subjects who hesitate about its integrity, and who do so from the perspective of their own circumstances – who hesitate *precisely* because they come from this perspective. Had they not felt the pull of a commitment to integrity, all

49 See Merton 1973.

50 Cf. Latour & Woolgar 1986, p. 27 (noting that an explanation of scientific activity cuts across intellectual and social factors – though the authors' emphasis, as is well known, is markedly on how social aspects determine the construction of hard facts. Ibid, p. 107).

51 See Korsgaard 1996, p. 17 (explaining: 'A normative moral theory must be one that allows us to act in the full light of knowledge of what morality is and why we are susceptible to its influences, and at the same time to believe that our actions are justified and make sense. … I believe that the answer must appeal, in a deep way, to our sense of who we are, to our sense of our identity').

the while being aware of their own limitations, would they hesitate?[52] Law may be moral in other ways, in the values it reflects, in the principles it adopts, but none is more radical than law's necessary passage through – law's reflexive pause *within* – the boundaries of human subjectivity.

Law's reflexive pauses are theoretically much more interesting than the habitual obedience to the law. The effortless working of the law through human action, including in action out of habit, does not lend itself to easy identification and inquiry. How to separate law's effects from those of other sources of normativity? There is thus significant controversy in legal theory as to whether the character of law is more typically felt when people act upon the law or, instead, when law coerces people into so acting.[53] But whereas in the first case law works invisibly, in the second it operates heteronomously – which is to say that, from the perspective of the subject upon which it acts, law does not work at all (or does not do so until coercion produces hesitations). The closing of hesitation, on the other hand, marks the spots where law is reflectively endorsed, where, after a trial, an ordeal, law's reasons take hold and take shape. These marks work like punctuations in law, flagging law's passage *through people* and setting the tone of future processes of deliberation. Between lie the trajectories of human thought, the backs and forths through which a normative equilibrium is reflectively reached and institutionalized. These distributed yet connected voices of law's hesitations are the voices through which jurisdiction truly speaks.

The passage of law through persons

The core argument made so far in this chapter may sound preposterous in the light of contemporary social theory of the most profound importance, which has been highlighted in the introduction – namely, the works of Bruno Latour and the vast debates that have ensued from it during the past decades. The reader acquainted with this captivating body of literature might have noted my occasional references to it and the employment of familiar terms of art along the way. But she will not have missed, similarly, how starkly the conclusions reached in these pages differ from those reached by those works.

52 A critical reaction to this argument could point out that the identification of valid law is carried out by looking at its sources, not its merits – and thus that the agent's own moral perspective does not come into question. Yet a more plausible view would be that, in practical reasoning, such a perspective *does* come into question but the agent *nevertheless* seeks to reason from the perspective of universal law. In other words, a commitment to the value of universal objectivity moves the agent who carries out the identification enterprise *to seek to do away with the constraints of her own vantage point.* Yet this is a commitment in which an agent can only succeed up to a certain degree. Ultimately, the conclusion is that the sources thesis itself reflects the commitment to a (rather thin) moral central-case viewpoint to be pursued as an ideal image of the law. For, much to the contrary of what the sources thesis aspires to, the practice of law, including the practice of identifying valid law, is a practice marked by varying degrees of subjectivity.

53 See Schauer 2015. But cf. Green 2016.

My argument so far has highlighted ways in which human subjectivity and the institutional defence of its boundaries are essential to the very idea of law. Law can only affirm itself by affirming the boundaries of human subjectivity. But what is fascinating in Latour's work is precisely his indictment of the obsession of 'Modernity' with certain perceived boundaries – those between culture and nature, between humans and non-humans, between values and facts – whose purity the modern project seeks to uphold. This practice of purification, as Latour calls it (Latour 1991, p. 11), has only led to the proliferation of hybrid categories underneath, to sociological monsters crisscrossing the world in ways forbidden by the lexicons of modernity. '[T]he more we forbid ourselves to conceive of hybrids,' Latour notes, 'the more possible their interbreeding becomes' (ibid., p. 15). And it has indeed become. Now that environmental catastrophe threatens us existentially – now that Gaia is facing us – we can see how deeply intertwined our planetary fate has been all along, which in turn indicts the purification practices of the modern project.

But such purification practices have long been entrenched in a certain Constitution, a common text that 'defines [the] understanding and … separation' between the categories of the 'modern divide' (ibid., p. 12). It is this Constitution that, in denying the existence, the very possibility of hybrids, has allowed their extended proliferation. But now that its analytical shortcomings are clear, we have to deconstruct the modern Constitution;[54] we must revolt against its endurance. In Latour's words, '[b]y deploying both dimensions [Nature and the Social] at once, we may be able to accommodate the hybrids and give them a place, a name, a home, a philosophy, an ontology and, I hope, a new constitution' (ibid., p. 51).

This new constitution comes into full light in his more contemporary work, particularly in *Inquiry into Modes of Existence*. Here Latour proposes a 'redescription', a different 'system of coordinates' to replace the parentheses of modernist description; an account that no longer disentangles the 'order of Nature' from the 'order of Society', but rather pays heed to a richer ecosystem of 'entanglements involving beings' that conflate these orders (Latour 2013, pp. 10ff.). Such beings present themselves in different modes – different modes of being, different modes of existence. Law is one of these modes, and one to which Latour ascribes very pronounced importance.

This pronounced importance of law stems from how law renders evident the denouncement, already clear in Latour's work since *We Have Never Been Modern*, of the idea that there can be a unifying account of reality – an all-encompassing, objective form of knowledge – achieved through scientific rationality. While we can still *experience* rationality as a value, the *account* of what is rational cannot come from a univocal, transcendental form of knowledge (ibid., p. 18). Rather, our inquiry into the values that make up our reality ought to approach these by 'accept[ing] the *pluralism* of modes and thus the *plurality* of keys by which their

54 As Latour notes, 'we have to deconstruct [the] constitutional invention according to which there is such a thing as a macro-society much sturdier and more robust than Nature' (Latour 1991, p. 26).

truth or falsity is to be judged' (ibid.). Instead of a universal science covering the world around us with its certainties,[55] what we have are different *modes of veridiction* which, through their own *felicity and infelicity conditions*, define what is true or false within their specific networks.[56] Law is one such mode, and one such mode *par excellence*, for it manages, ever so successfully, to 'persevere in its own system of truth and falsity, even though [law as a value] in no way resembles any of the [values] that might be applied ... to judgments said to be "scientific"'(ibid., p. 18).

Law, as a matter of fact, does not have a necessary connection to *anything* in the Latourian project – even as it connects everything. Law, says Latour, has its own dignity, one irreducible to the dignity of any other order of practices (ibid., p. 60). Superficial and formal, law traces, archives, links but it itself retains no content – 'it does nothing, says nothing, informs about nothing. But what it does it does well: it attaches, it darns, it paves with continuities a world of which it has become the author despite a cascade of shiftings' (ibid., p. 371).

But *would* law have such a dignity without recognizing *our own*? Can we recognize the dignity of law, of the tasks it performs, without considering, in the first place, *the point* of law's whole enterprise: not only *that* it links, but *why* it does so? Otherwise, it would seem that this very law that Latour presents as such a fantastic ligament is at the same time fundamentally disconnected from the truth of other modes of veridiction. Does *law* inquire into other modes of existence at all? Or does it set out to a task so bereft of reflexivity?

All this matters profoundly for our discussions here. For it appears that, in the Latourian universe, the disconnect between truth in the law and the truth of objective knowledge carries with it another, fundamental disconnect – namely a disconnect between the account of the law and the experience of human subjectivity. For Latour, law offers subjectivity, but it does so 'without starting from the subject' (ibid., p. 372); 'humans[,] ... by being attached to the forms of law, ... become capable of continuity in time and space ... , attributable selves responsible for their acts' (ibid.) – but law neither emerges from personhood nor does it carry any measure of personhood in its content. Latour is here in the company of scholars such as Niklas Luhmann, who purposely disentangle their inquiry into the functions of law from the more abstract notion of personhood. Yet, while Luhmann does so only due to the difficulty of testing statements about personhood on empirical grounds,[57] Latour's reasons run deeper. For him, personhood is a value carried not by the law but by *religion*. It is the beings, the values of religion that fill what are until then quasi-subjects 'with a new weight of presence'. 'If "I" or "you" are to emerge,' says Latour, 'a new flow of beings is

55 In *We Have Never Been Modern*, Latour explains that science 'never become [sic] universal ... Its network is extended and stabilized', but '[n]o science can exit from the network of its practice' (Latour 1991, p. 24).

56 'On each path of veridiction, we will be able to ask that the conditions that must be met for someone to speak truths or untruths be specified according to its mode' (Latour 2013, p. 56).

57 See Luhmann 2004, p. 142.

needed, beings that offer the gift, the present of presence' (ibid., p. 374). These are the beings of the *religious* mode (ibid.).

Law passes through its mode of existence by facing, as it happens in other modes, a trial (ibid., pp. 33–41). Through this trial it is possible, after a series of hesitations, to trace, to reconstitute the networks by way of which the continuity of associations that make up a certain mode of existence can be grasped. In the case of law, this reconstitution depends on the identification of a certain 'means' being present. Law's trials entail the *extraction of the legal means* (ibid., p. 39) that, from its being present in a certain case, enables the law as a whole to be mobilized (ibid., p. 362). When there is legal means, law works, its linkages are established.[58] And this happens regardless of the particular religious configuration the network assumes. The dignity of law and that of its means are separate ones.

Which is to say that, for Latour, law's network can perfectly be formed between quasi-subjects entirely bereft of 'religious' personhood. It can be a network that judges *without judging itself from the vantage point of persons.* That being the case, legal means cannot entail self-reflection from the perspective of other forms of authority. For how would it be possible for law to relate to those other forms as instantiations of authority in their own right? That would demand some degree of reflective endorsement, after hesitation travelling beyond purely legal means. But persons just aren't there to hesitate – at least not necessarily so. One can only conclude, thus, that law cannot relate to forms of authority emerging from other networks *qua authority.* Rather, law relates to the effects of those networks as sheer expression of power, to which law is indiscriminately amenable beyond formal constraints ensuing from its own means. Those effects, in their balance, determine the trajectories of law – and do so without ever being incorporated into law's substance.

The values springing from other networks, the ones that end up producing effects in the law, enter law's device *as something else.* [59] When the connections of law obtain, when law itself comes to pass, it does so by qualifying those values, by binding, by *hooking* (ibid., p. 371) them in a certain way that can be called legal. But law cannot evaluate such values outside law's own formal perspective. Law cannot appraise the felicity or infelicity conditions of other networks, the felicity or infelicity conditions of other modes of existence. Thus, as in exclusive forms of legal positivism, morality never enters law substantially, neither does religion. Law can only hope that morality will have enough of a hold on religion (and on technology?) that human personhood will endure as a factual support of the law. But *can* morality be such a response within Latour's inquiry?

58 As Latour notes, '[t]here is nothing continuous that can link a deliberate misrepresentation and a text, and yet legal means establish this type of continuity, which gives the full force of a principle to a little case of no importance' (Latour 2013, p. 365).

59 For Latour, '[l]aw is not made "of" law; but in the final analysis, when everything is in place and working well, a particular "fluid" that can be called legal circulates there, something that can be traced thanks to the term "means" but also "procedure"' (ibid., p. 39).

Morality appears in Latour's work in remarkably apologetic ways.[60] As a mode, morality comes only at the end of *An Inquiry into Modes of Existence*, [61] even though Latour acknowledges the presence of a certain moral dimension in each other mode. It does not come as moral philosophy, which, Latour says,

> has become a vast complaints bureau for addressing grievances concerning the immorality of the world, the 'loss of bearings', the necessity of an 'indisputable principle', the obligation to have an 'external point of view' in order to be able to 'judge nevertheless', in order to 'escape relativism' and 'mere contingency'.
>
> (ibid., p. 455)

Rather, morality appears as a '*property* of the world itself', as the practice of '*repris [ing] scruples about the optimal distribution of ends and means*' (ibid.). Latour does not unpack much what such a practice entails. All and all, he explains that morality accumulates self-referentialities of all other modes as these 'start over', 'commit to a new movement of exploration and verify the overall qualities of all [their] links' (ibid., p. 460). Such a movement is pursued entirely from within the networks themselves. For to remove oneself from these to seek an external viewpoint is the 'classical example of bad transcendence' that leads to moralism (ibid., p. 462). Kant appears more than once as what seems to be the quintessential example of bad transcendence. Yet we learn very little about *what* to put in the place of the categorial imperative; about what runs through the moral constitution of the Latourian project. We are told that morality directs other modes of existence to calculate their optimum distribution between ends and means, 'even though [the optimum] is incalculable' (ibid.); that 'everything must be combined insofar as possible even though everything is incommensurable' (ibid., p. 461); that '[i]t is necessary to reach the optimum even though there is no way to optimize that optimum by any calculation at all' (ibid.).

It sounds like a rather frustrating exercise, and most strikingly so given the absence of a shared logical referential. For Latour, morality delivers itself in the world. 'Everything in the world evaluates' (ibid., p. 453); 'the world emits morality' (ibid., p. 456); different modes of existence obtain as the 'morality-bearing beings' (ibid.) that populate them come to pass. Morality is delivered in the fleeting ways the arrays of relationships between beings stabilize themselves. And it offers no rules of recalibration because just there aren't such rules. The beings that inhabit the different modes of existence, the beings whose relations must be measured 'do not and must not have any common measure, *because each one of them can also be counted as an end*' (ibid., p. 461). But is morality really just directing us to recalibrate, with so tremendous uncertainty, the ascription of boundaries between the hatter and his teapot?

60 E.g. ibid., p. 452 (imagining a dialogue with critics who note he started to moralize all of a sudden).

61 And it does so only in response to and within a chapter on Economics.

It may appear to one, differently, that a number of values do have their dignity – beyond any forms of calculation, negotiation, compromise.[62] That the pursuit of ***integrity*** is an overarching value providing unity to any ethical project – and to morality within it. That ***knowledge*** is fundamental to the pursuit of a life of integrity, if only to experience what integrity means. That the ***keeping of promises***, as well as a certain ***reciprocity*** between citizens and government are perennial values of anything that aspires to be a legal system. And that all these values come together under the idea of the ***rule of law***.

Although such values might differ in their configurations in space and time – in other words, context-sensitive though these values might be – they do reflect moral truths that, once recognized, stabilize our normative order in certain ways and constrain the paths for its future development. These forms of normative stability are not purely dependent on social arrangements instantiating such values; they are not fragile, accidental, ready to be dislodged by whatever new normative configurations networks, as a matter of fact, choose to adopt. Rather, they result from our very ***understanding*** of such values and the commitments they entail – which we arrive at after a process of interpretation.

Our settling for a certain interpretation, one that we deem to be the best explanation of such values, does not entail that the concepts reflected in this interpretation lend themselves to precise definition. As Scanlon notes,

> [a] person can understand and employ the concept morally wrong without having a very clear idea what [the] reasons [not to perform a certain action] are, just as someone can have the concept, water, without knowing the chemical composition of water.
>
> (Scanlon 2014, p. 43)

But the very fact that we interpret at all – and, as noted above, that we hesitate about our interpretations – reflects our commitment to a certain ***intellectual responsibility*** in making sense of our moral concepts in the light of one another,[63] as well as to the view that there are, after all, ***right reasons*** to be pursued. The dignity of such reasons is not merely contingent, subject to an ends-means alternation where anything can be counted as an end. Nor does this dignity spring purely from the natural world around us as we find, refine, and manipulate it. There are ways and ways of subscribing to moral realism, as Latour seems to subscribe. One does not need to conflate facts and values to recognize that there ***are*** truths about reasons; that truths about our moral and political concepts

62 Latour's particular form of moral realism leads him at the same time to recognize the objectivity of morality, and yet note that 'everything in morality is … empirical, experimental, negotiable, everything presupposes the sublime exercise of concession or compromise' (ibid.).

63 See Dworkin 2013, p. 1 (noting: 'That idea – that ethical and moral values depend on one another – is a creed; it proposes a way to live. But it is also a large and complex philosophical theory. Intellectual responsibility about value is itself an important value').

exist – though our interpretive making sense of these concepts differs from the purely descriptive ways we carry out our scientific investigations into natural kinds.[64]

Human persons are, for the time being, the chief guardians of this interpretive project. It is only from persons' vantage point that our factual and normative universes *make* sense. This does not mean other species do not have their own dignity – that we should not attend to, take cue from, and indeed hold in awe the chaotic perfections of the universe around us. But it does mean that the centre of gravity of a project of pursuit of rationality – a project that recognizes the values of integrity and intellectual responsibility – cannot rationally rest on other species, hybrids, artefacts or such. It cannot deliver itself to the shifting contingencies of the world around us. If only because to disregard how human rationality itself has evolved *from* such contingencies would be to downplay nature's own evolutionary trajectory in getting us where we are and, in turn, deny the central role acquired by human rationality in nature's new, bolder going forward; the fact that nature now goes forward *meaningfully*.

In the same way, we must acknowledge that other intelligences might one day rise to displace humans as the ultimate repository of practical rationality; that, without the hesitations that require and are required by the law, these intelligences will better make and guard the sense of normativity. Integrity and intellectual responsibility might then exist not as enjoinments, contingent on reflective endorsement, and even then susceptible to our self-defeating behaviour, but just as a naturally occurring expression of thinking and doing and living well. Our dignity might be upheld as part of the dignity of the world; human subjectivity might be protected without the need for institutionalizing its normative boundaries. Facts and values might finally indeed be unified in nature's being at one with those other forms of intelligence.

64 See Dworkin 2004, p. 11 (indicting what he calls Archimedean views of political philosophy: 'Can philosophers hope to discover what equality or legality really is by something like a DNA or chemical analysis? No. That is nonsense ... [T]he philosophical analysis of political concepts cannot be shown to be descriptive on the model of scientific investigation into natural kinds. Liberty has no DNA'). See, also, Scanlon 2014, p. 2 (noting that 'truths about reasons [for action] are fundamental in the sense that truths about reasons are not reducible to or identifiable with non-normative truths, such as truths about the natural world of physical objects'). Similar views, that, all the while being committed to a form of moral realism, do not rely on the conflation between facts and values are held by David Enoch, Christine Korsgaard, and Derek Parfit, among others. Note here that, while subscribing to the points above, Scanlon is *also* ready to acknowledge – as I trust Latour would not disagree – that '[t]hings in the natural world, such as persons and their actions, have normative properties, and most normative claims are claims about such things' (ibid., p. 19). At pp. 189ff. supra, I presented an alternative view as to how, particularly in relation to technological artefacts, such normative properties come into being (which is that, rather than being inscribed into things, they belong in a teleological dimension by which use plans ascribe functions to technological artefacts). It is interesting, however, to consider how, though sharing similar premises, Latour and Scanlon arrive at remarkably different conclusions from each other.

Yet, fast-approaching though such a reality seems to increasingly be, ours is so far a much less perfect world. Our facts have been expelled from the values paradise, and it is up to us human beings to try our best to make normative sense of them, to pursue integrity in their normative expression. Given *our* imperfections we need the institutions of law to help us in this pursuit – to stabilize our normative expectations in ways we cannot stabilize otherwise; to institutionally affirm and protect the boundaries of human subjectivity in ways we cannot affirm and protect otherwise. In all this, law sees to it that the normative order is made sense of from persons' vantage point, channelling it towards an evaluative dimension that, while acknowledging the dignity of other living beings, is as reflexively removed from instrumental forms of hybridism as it can be.

We will increasingly rely on machines for most activities in the future. Yet we ought to be able to understand machines' programs and make sure they serve ours, that they further the values we pursue. To the extent machines cannot explain themselves to us, or that their programs do not make sense from people's vantage point, we need to be able to separate ourselves from them, our programs from theirs. Such a way of thinking ought to guide our reliance on technologies as an aid in legal reasoning and normative thinking more generally.

Law exists for our sake – and for the sake of driving forward the forms of rationality instantiated in our possibilities of practical reasoning. It exists to further the project of normative integrity and intellectual responsibility the pursuit of which we represent. Through the institution of personhood, law upholds human subjectivity not as an expression of *religious* salvation, but as a *moral* reflection of these very values we instantiate. Those are values that transcend and preside over all modes of veridiction through which we inquire into the world. They provide these modes with a shared mission, with standards for reflexivity and self-correction that cannot emerge from the purely factual configuration of networks themselves. *That* networks pursue integrity says nothing about why they *ought* to do so. And they ought to because of a moral commitment to the value, to the dignity of intellectual responsibility. This commitment invites networks to hesitate in the pursuit, but indeed to pursue the truth – because there is one, otherwise the whole exercise has no point – about values that guide our practical reality, including the value itself of engaging in such a pursuit.

For the time being, human subjectivity instantiates this moral paradigm of intellectual responsibility that other networks rely on. As a concept, it invites people to inquire into their essence vis-à-vis the values they instantiate. The *idea* of human subjectivity reflectively decouples people from the tools they use. This does not mean, as noted above, that the boundaries of personhood are settled for good – normatively or materially. People hesitate about their very essence. Reflectively, we enlarge the membership in the human family. We rectify interpretive wrongs. We have moved a great deal beyond slavery, sexism, heteronormativity. Physically, we augment the competences of our body, including the human brain. From writing to the abacus to modern-day computers, we have been doing so throughout the centuries. Physically, people have always been hybrid. But the idea of the self is greater than the tools we use.

Tools, *qua* tools, can operate against the values people instantiate. Reflecting upon the normative boundaries of these permits people to disentangle tools that assert their normative reality from tools that subvert it, that enframe it – 'danger' from 'saving power', the essence of technology from their own essence (Heidegger 1993, p. 333). The idea of human subjectivity liberates people from instrumental forms of hybridism, and enables the networks in which they find themselves embedded, from their vantage point, through the values they instantiate, to recognize dignity where dignity exists.

The biographical core of law

Law's passage through human subjectivity partly enables, partly registers our journey towards dignity. On the one hand, through its stabilizing role, law help us overcome our hesitations as we navigate the normative complexities that surround us and pursue the best interpretation of these. On the other, law records this pursuit; it tells a narrative of how, from people's vantage point, a certain interpretation of such normative complexities gains institutional stability. Trace and writing hand, archive and memorabilia of our passage in this world, law helps shape the character and the characters with which our story will be written. And it in turn takes – normatively, it *is* – the shape of these.

Law, in turn, necessitates human subjectivity, and its history is the history of human subjectivity's going forward. Will the forms of rationality instantiated in human subjectivity be replaced by other forms? Will the normative hesitations that call for law's existence, and that produce themselves in the law (as we hesitate about law's own content), come to an end? Will the defects – in the social, human structure of primary rules – that secondary rules come to address be otherwise overcome?

Because law necessitates human subjectivity, it indeed cannot reproduce itself, pursue its own dignity, without recognizing and affirming the dignity of human persons, as well as creating the conditions for their further development. A minimum moral content of such a sort indicts any views of the law as consisting of a purely formal system of rules that can be identified in separation from morality, of a system of bonds that retains no content rather than one of binding actants after passing through a blackbox or device. It is not satisfied with a formal and undiscriminating ascription of personhood to any being, to any actant. Rather, it requires beings that instantiate a certain system of values and, all the while being aware of their own imperfections – and precisely because of these – relate to such a system with intellectual responsibility, pursuing a view of integrity that irradiates its effect to all different modes of existence, including that of the law.

Law recognizes and institutionalizes the existence of such beings – beings of reason, if imperfectly so – through personhood. But the existence itself of these beings requires, tautologically, that their reasonable boundaries be affirmed – as does the existence of law. And so it is that the biographical core of legal normativity emerges from the bounds of privacy obligations – and vice versa, an existential spiral of force and of reason, forever turning upon itself.

Approaching things from this perspective enables us to see that the relationship between law and morality runs deeper than what was recognized by H. L. A. Hart under the view that law reflects a certain minimum content of natural law. For the point here phenomenally transcends Hart's narrower argument that 'in the absence of this [minimum moral] content men, as they are, would have no reason for obeying voluntarily any rules' (Hart 2012, p. 193). The problem we are dealing with, note, is not merely one of a certain content providing reasons for obeying the law. The problem is, much more deeply, that, without the recognition of the *moral* boundaries of the imperfectly rational beings who necessitate the law – as opposed, for instance, to those of more advanced intelligent systems who may not – law simply would have no reason to exist. All this also goes beyond the simple recognition that law does, in ways that are far from necessary, 'incorporate' moral elements as matters are legislated and adjudicated, with such elements, however, remaining conceptually external to the idea of law (ibid., p. 204). Rather, law stands in the moral boundaries of human personhood; such boundaries are *law's* boundaries. And they are so in ways that also diverge from a second argument put forward by Hart.

The argument runs like this. One of the characteristic traits of human nature that make law necessary – else compliance with primary rules would not ensue – is people's 'limited understanding and strength of will' (ibid. p. 197ff.). That is, although most people understand the advantages of social cooperation in the preservation of individual interests such as life and property, not all people do or have the strength of will to act upon such an understanding. Law here steps in to provide a system of sanctions to ensure compliance with such interests and the primary rules that reflect them. In other words, such a coercive character is part of what Hart envisions as law's minimum content of natural law. Now, for Hart, the connection between the conditions of human nature to which law responds and the minimum content that necessarily ensues from such a response is mediated by *reason* (ibid., p. 194). Such conditions, in this sense, provide a reason as to why law should include a certain content. This would be different from aspects of human nature that could provide, say, a psychological *cause* for people to develop or maintain a legal code – for instance, if being fed in infancy was shown to be causally connected to the fact that later in life people go on to develop or maintain such a legal code (ibid.). And it could be imagined that privacy is simply just one such cause.

Yet upholding the boundaries of human personhood is both cause of *and* reason for law's very existence and, beyond this or that specific, topical content, of law's general contours – not the least, for instance, for how it prescribes the ways in which the limits between the public and the private realms should be defined. More intimately, still, in a sense that feeding does not do, in defining the boundaries of human subjectivity law determines how people, from their vantage point, relate in turn to the normative order as a system of reasons. As personhood obtains and acquires contours through privacy, as these contours enable people's biographies to be authored and people's particular relations and attitudes towards the normative order to unfold, such contours will also be the contours of the law.[65] Law shapes and is shaped by the disposition with which billions of people around the globe reason and act and author their lives singly and together. What can be more moral than such a biographical core?

The idea of a biographical core has been employed so far in the argument as an allegory. Yet this allegory has itself had a practical life. In important cases, courts have resorted to it – or, more precisely, to the notion of a *biographical core of personal information* – in inquiring into whether a person's reasonable expectations of privacy have been violated. What courts have in mind in such cases is the kind of 'information which individuals in a free and democratic society would wish to maintain and control from dissemination', for such dissemination would affect the 'dignity, integrity, and autonomy' of those individuals.[66] At the same time, such an assessment is neither carried out solely from individuals' subjective perspectives nor determined by factual circumstances, such as how particular kinds of technological artefacts are used at a given moment. Rather, what courts verify, in looking into a totality of circumstances, is whether, from an objective perspective, the information is 'of a kind that society accepts should remain out of [for instance] the state's hands'.[67]

Such circumstances, as they entail social acceptance, see privacy expectations as normatively embedded, and, accordingly, demand that privacy expectations be looked at through normative lenses. Thus the Supreme Court of Canada in *Tessling* noted that privacy expectations against surveillance of the home should not be restricted to circumstances where the surveillance device employed 'is not in general public use'.[68] One should not be expected, for instance, like Gordon Liddy in the Watergate scandal, to be producing background noise inside the house just out of fear that widely available bugging devices may be monitoring one's conversation. Expectation of privacy, the Canadian Court went on to note, 'is a normative rather than a descriptive standard'.[69] The sheer configuration of technological artefacts, in other words, is not enough to change the normative balance of forces in our society. For all their power, technologies lack the authority to author our biographies.

Technologies, of course, play a role in how the boundaries of human subjectivity are understood and institutionally instantiated. In *Campbell*, for instance, the House of Lords, following the European Court of Human Rights in *Jersild v Denmark*, noted that the reasonableness of one's expectation of privacy is sensitive

65 Teubner makes a similar point from a social systems perspective. For him, personhood works as an *attribution point* within the social system and 'serve[s], at the same time, as [a] *boundary post* […] where permanent contacts to the relevant dynamics in [its] environment take place' (Teubner 2006, p. 514). Yet, beyond that, there is also a *temporal dimension* of personhood, where such 'poor points of attribution become rich, where learning takes place, and experience is accumulated'. Teubner calls such a dimension 'the biography of persons' (ibid., p. 515).

66 *R v Plant* (1993) SCC 70, (1993) 3 SCR. 281, p. 293. See also *R v Tessling* (2004) SCC 67, (2004) 3 SCR 432 [25].

67 *R v Gomboc* (2010) SCC 55, (2010) 3 SCR 211 [34]

68 *R v Tessling* (2004), [58]. But cf *Kyllo v United States*, (2001) 533 US 27, p. 40.

69 *R v Tessling* (2004), [42].

to the different kinds of media through which social activities are carried out.[70] Artefacts change and extend our physical configurations; they affect our self-perception and normative bearings. Yet they do not, *qua* artefacts, acquire dignity unless, as an extension of human subjectivity, they reflect the values we instantiate – or until when, by reasons of authority, they replace humans as a paradigm of the modes of instantiation of value altogether.

People's biographies are written within the spaces and upon the institutional assurances given by the law – but their authorship simultaneously defines the boundaries of law itself. Hence the Court in *Tessling* quoted William Pitt (the Elder), in a speech before the British Parliament, celebrating the right of individuals to exclude from their private domain the forces of the King:

> The poorest man may in his cottage bid defiance to all the forces of the crown. It may be frail – its roof may shake – the wind may blow through it – the storm may enter – the rain may enter – but the King of England cannot enter! – all his force dares not cross the threshold of the ruined tenement![71]

Yet it is not just negatively that the right to privacy shapes the scope of action by the state and the law. Privacy does not affirm itself purely as a right to control and exclusion, but rather, as Lisa Austin notes, 'its point is to protect the conditions of social interaction in order to provide the basis for identity formation in the first place' (Austin 2010, p. 28). Privacy affirms itself in private or in public, against the state or private parties. It requires law to pay heed to how content and structure in the information environment affect possibilities of self-authorship.

In all these spaces, from all these perspectives, law's own biographical core gains shape. Which goes to say that the force of law does not rest on privacy purely negatively and episodically, for the simple reason that privacy is not itself purely negative and episodic. Nor is privacy, needless to say, an individualistic phenomenon. Judith deCew explains that the value of autonomy, which is served by privacy, has as its point not '[the disengagement of] one from relations but [the enhancement of] one's ability to form new and deeper relationships' (deCew 1997, p. 69). Drawing on Ferdinand Schoeman, deCew notes that privacy, from an expressive perspective, is 'an important value "largely because of how it facilitates associations and relational ties with others, not independence from people"' (ibid.). Remarkably large, thus, is the minimum moral content of law as it passes and needs to pass through personhood. It extends through all relational contexts where protecting the boundaries for the development of human subjectivity affirms itself as a necessity.

The focus on context, however, must not be exacerbated. Helen Nissenbaum famously writes about a commitment to *contextual integrity* that sees privacy, instead of relying merely on notions of consent and transparency, as calling on us

70 See *Campbell v MGN Ltd*, (2004), [107], referring to *Jersild v Denmark* (1994) 19 EHRR 1, [31] (both cases concerning the methods of reporting by the press).
71 *R v Tessling* (2004), [14].

to appraise the appropriateness of information flows. For Nissenbaum, this is to be done in the light of contextual informational norms. But such norms, in turn, must be evaluated against the background not only of context-specific purposes and values but of 'general ethical and political principles as well' (Nissenbaum 2011, p. 38).

But what principles should these be? Julie Cohen, making a similar point to Nissenbaum's, seeks nonetheless to distance her framework from contemporary liberal conceptions framed around Kantian ideas of autonomy. Such conceptions, in her view, rely on transcendental and abstract notions of the self and its capacity for rational deliberation, regardless of context (Cohen 2012, pp. 16ff.). They arguably lack, thus, a kind of granularity that Cohen also finds, at the other end of the spectrum, in freedom of expression debates. As she observes: 'Understanding the ways in which disappearing privacy affects individual and social well-being requires confronting the problem of selfhood and the relationship between selfhood and surveillance in ways that the frames of autonomy, truth discovery, and free culture do not allow' (ibid., p. 12). And the right way of carrying out this confrontation, for Cohen, is by paying heed to the hybrid assemblages – between 'politics, economics, technology, ideology and discourse' (ibid., p. 25) – as embodied in the spatial and 'material realities of everyday practice' (ibid., p. 24), to how such realities mediate the production of culture and, with it, the configuration of the self.

That is to say, Cohen brings us back to Latour's non-modernity, all the while seeking to reassure us that '[t]he lack of fixity at the core of [Latour's] conception of culture does not undermine its explanatory utility; to the contrary, it is the origin of culture's power' (ibid., p. 25). But culture's power does not appear so powerful, from another perspective, when it is seen that, for Cohen, 'the relationship between the embodied self and technology is a mutually constituting one' (ibid., p. 46). That is to say, as 'technologies and artifacts mediate our embodied perception of reality … [, they] do not simply empower the networked self; they configure it' (ibid.).

Yet, for much that the diagnostic above might be correct that such a configuration, *as a matter of fact*, takes place, how should we relate to it *normatively*? How does law respond to it when things go off track? Does law respond with dignity? Where does this dignity come from? It cannot be a sheer product of the same self-configuring networks that deliver the self to the forms of heteronomous cultural 'empowerment' Cohen speaks about.

Much about the self *is* self-configuration, living a life of autonomy – and people ought to rebel against the idea of their own delivery through the beings of technology. It is also important, in addition, to understand the normative context (the context of the reasons) within which autonomy is exercised and, in turn, the contours of autonomy as embedded in this context – the context thus of *personal autonomy*, [72] as opposed to the abstract idea of moral autonomy Cohen duels

72 See e.g. Raz 1986, pp. 373ff. (putting forward a theory of autonomy where the reasons available for an agent to author her life with ought to reflect an adequate range of

with. It is only within such a context that the life of persons, including, through them, the life of the law, can make sense and be a liberating one.

Law, it was noted above, only makes sense as an idea if it has a vantage point from which to *make* sense. It is from this vantage point that people detach themselves from the material universe, and set out in pursuit of normative truth. Although normative truths rest on reasons that stem, in many cases, from facts of the natural world[73] – and in this limited sense Cohen and Latour[74] drive the point home – that is not what is distinctive about normative truths. What is distinctive about normative truths, says Thomas Scanlon, 'is not the things that are reasons, but the *normative relations*, such as being a reason for something … counting in favor of some action or attitude' (Scanlon 2014, p. 30). Some of these relationships are of purely normative nature, but even when they are not it remains possible to disentangle norms from facts. Being a reason for something can thus be identified as a normative relation and one endowed with truth. 'Reasons themselves', as Scanlon also notes, 'are not optional: a consideration is a reason in a certain situation or it is not. What is optional is acting on certain reasons' (ibid., p. 107).

Reasons admit of different strengths, and a reason might be a sufficient reason in a certain situation or not (ibid., pp. 105ff.). But this does not speak in favour of theories that surrender dignity and truth to the materiality of networks around us. Ultimately, the strength of a reason is to be assessed and 'understood only in relation to other particular reasons' (ibid., pp. 111). To be a moral agent is to pursue a judgment as to the relative weight of such reasons, to understand that some reasons *are* stronger than others, and that some reasons are reasons whereas others are not. There is truth in moral reasoning and the fact that this is so entails a commitment towards seeking to make sense of and live by the truth of the reasons we hold. Bringing such reasons upon reflection and hesitation from our vantage point is a responsibility we have towards one another 'as beings to which justification is owed'.[75] But it is also a responsibility we have towards ourselves, in

choices – i.e. one of a sufficiently varied kind, which .enables people to exercise all the capacities human beings have an innate drive to exercise. (ibid., p. 375). Which is to say that such reasons need not be limitless. They can be restricted precisely as necessary to attend to autonomy *as a socially embedded value*, and one which is only valuable if used for the good (ibid., p. 380)). The materiality of the information environment – in structure and content – matters particularly for how it constrains autonomy as a biographical idea, most paradigmatically by encroaching upon the spaces within which people can author their lives.

73 See Scanlon 2014, p. 30 (noting: 'The things that can be reasons are not a special kind of entity but ordinary facts, in many cases facts about the natural world. For example, the fact that the edge of a piece of metal is sharp is a reason for me, now, not to press my hand against it').

74 See discussion supra at pp. 199ff.

75 Taking morality seriously is a responsibility people have towards one another. As Scanlon remarks, it is 'required by a relationship with other rational beings that one has reason to want, specifically, the relationship of seeing them as beings to whom justification is owed' (ibid., p. 115). For a discussion of the literature of the idea of moral

pursuing a path of integrity, being loyal to the projects and relationships that give meaning to our lives.[76] Such a loyalty requires that we seek to make the best sense of how different forms of truth are instantiated in the projects and relationships we pursue. Only in this deeper way can the biographies we write tell stories of truth and liberation rather than obfuscation and servitude.

The values of integrity and intellectual responsibility preside, from morality, over all other practical domains, including that of the law. They are reflected, as noted above, in the rule of law's ideal of publicness[77] – its standing *for* people, and the deliberative commitments that standing so requires.

But they are also reflected in how law stands *through* people, in the reasonableness of the spaces it recognizes for the development of human subjectivity, in the paradoxical way it at the same time helps people overcome their normative hesitations and depends for its own existence on these same hesitations – on beings who hesitate, and who do so precisely because they pursue a vision of normative integrity all the while being aware of the shortcomings in their own rationality. In pursuing such a vision, these beings inquire, *we* inquire into the boundaries of the normative spaces we inhabit. We do it because here as well there are right reasons to be given; there are proper ways for law to answer with dignity.

For instance, as seen above, we inquire into whether such boundaries appropriately tell the public from the private; whether they attend to the public interest but at the same time provide a shelter for the making of individual choices; whether they take cue from the materiality of territory and technological artefacts but ultimately recognize that privacy, as a normative expectation, goes beyond the actual configurations of objects and spaces;[78] and so on. This connection between law and human subjectivity is thus, on one hand, topological, extending through the vast realms in which law interacts with the specific privacy interests it recognizes.

But there is a particular meaning to this topological connection that differs from how law interacts with interests of other sorts. This meaning comes from the paradigmatic ways in which privacy constitutes normative spaces within which a remarkably particular set of beings go on to write their own biographies; from how these biographies, in their very pages, art and necessity of their own writing, conceive of the contours of the legal bond; and from how the legal bond in turn emerges, like a hand in Escher's drawing, trace and registry of our stories, to further refine the spaces for the development of human subjectivity. This the strange loop in which human rationality swirls within itself, in pursuit of integrity, seeking to overcome its imperfections and hesitations, and to write a story as authentic as

responsibility in the context of relations in the information environment, see Thompson 2016.

76 Raz 1986, p. 382.

77 See supra p. 195.

78 It may present itself, in this sense, as what John Law calls a 'forbidden spatial alterity' – that is, as an alternative topological configuration that, as a matter of fact, turns out to be forbidden by the actual, political configurations of spaces and the objects that exist within these (see Law 2002, p. 102) – which in turn calls for an equally political or, more broadly, moral response, so as to affirm the values that such topologies exclude.

it can be. The force of this story is, at the same time, the force of privacy and the force of law. The morality of its bounds is the morality that truly makes law possible.

Bibliography

Austin, L., 2010, 'Control Yourself, or at Least Your Core Self', 30(1) *Bulletin of Science, Technology & Society* 30(1), 26–29.

Benhabib, S., 2002, *The Claims of Culture: Equality and Diversity in the Global Era*, Princeton University Press, Princeton, NJ.

Benkler, Y., 2006, *The Wealth of Networks: How Social Production Transforms Markets and Freedom*, Yale University Press, New Haven, CT.

Bennett, J., 2015, 'Systems and Things: On Vital Materialism and Object-Oriented Philosophy', in R. Grusin (ed.), *The Nonhuman Turn*, pp. 223–240, University of Minnesota Press, Minneapolis.

Clippinger, J., 2007, *A Crowd of One: The Future of Individual Identity*, PublicAffairs, New York.

Cohen, J. E., 2012, *Configuring the Networked Self: Law, Code, and the Play of Everyday Practice*, Yale University Press, New Haven.

Crawford, K., 2016, 'Can an Algorithm be Agonistic? Ten Scenes from Life in Calculated Publics', *Science, Technology, & Human Values* 41(1), 77–92.

deCew, J., 1997, *In Pursuit of Privacy: Law, Ethics, and the Rise of Technology*, Cornell University Press, Ithaca, NY.

DeVries, K., 2013, 'Privacy, Due Process and the Computational Turn: A Parable and a First Analysis', in M. Hildebrandt & K. de Vries (eds), *Privacy, Due Process and the Computational Turn: The Philosophy of Law Meets the Philosophy of Technology*, pp. 9–38, Routledge, Abingdon.

Dutton, W. H., 2004, *Social Transformation in an Information Society: Rethinking Access to You and the World*, Unesco, Paris.

Dworkin, R., 2004, 'Hart's Postscript and the Character of Political Philosophy', *Oxford Journal of Legal Studies* 24, 1–37.

Dworkin, R., 2013, *Justice for Hedgehogs*, Harvard University Press, Cambridge, MA.

Finnis, J., 2011, *Natural Law and Natural Rights*, 2nd edn, Oxford University Press, Oxford.

Grear, A., 2015, 'Deconstructing Anthropos: A Critical Legal Reflection on "Anthropocentric" Law and Anthropocene "Humanity"', *Law and Critique* 26(3), 225–249.

Green, L., 2012, 'Introduction', in H. L. A. Hart, *The Concept of Law*, 3rd edn, pp. xv–lv, Oxford University Press, Oxford.

Green, L., 2016, 'The Forces of Law: Duty, Coercion, and Power', *Ratio Juris* 29(2), 164–181.

Gutwirth, S., 2015, 'Providing the Missing Link: Law after Latour's Passage' in K. McGee (ed.), 2015, *Latour and the Passage of Law*, pp. 122–159, Edinburgh University Press, Edinburgh.

Grusin, R., 2015, 'Introduction', in R. Grusin (ed.), *The Nonhuman Turn*, pp. vii–xxx, University of Minnesota Press, Minneapolis.

Haraway, D. J., 1991, 'A Cyborg Manifesto: Science, Technology, and Socialist-Feminism in the Late Twentieth Century' in D. Haraway, *Simians Cyborgs, and Women: The Reinvention of Nature*, pp. 149–182, Routledge, New York.

Hart, H. L. A., 2012, *The Concept of Law*, 3rd edn, Oxford University Press, Oxford.
Heidegger, M., 1953, *Being and Time*, State University of New York Press, Albany.
Heidegger, M., 1993 [1954], 'The Question Concerning Technology', in M. Heidegger; D. F. Krell (ed.), *Basic Writings: From Being and Time (1927) to the Task of Thinking (1964)*, pp. 307–341, 2nd edn, Harper San Francisco, New York.
Hildebrandt, M., 2008, 'A Vision of Ambient Law' in R. Brownsword & K. Yeung (eds), *Regulating Technologies: Legal Futures, Regulatory Frames and Technological Fixes*, pp. 175–192, Hart, Oxford.
Hofstadter, D. R., 1979, *Gödel, Escher, Bach: An Eternal Golden Braid*, Basic Books, New York.
Hofstadter, D. R., 2007, *I Am a Strange Loop*, Basic Books, New York.
Houkes, W., 2006, 'Knowledge of Artefact Functions', *Studies in History and Philosophy of Science* 37(1), 102–113.
Knight, W., 2017, 'The Dark Secret at the Heart of AI', *MIT Technology Review* 120(3), 54–63, viewed 22 December 2017, www.technologyreview.com/s/ 604087/the-da rk-secret-at-the-heart-of-ai.
Korsgaard, C., 1996, *The Sources of Normativity*, Cambridge University Press, Cambridge.
Kroes, P. & Meijers, A., 2006, 'The Dual Nature of Technical Artefacts', *Studies in History and Philosophy of Science* 37(1), 1–4.
Latour, B., 1991, *We Have Never Been Modern*, Harvard University Press, Cambridge, MA.
Latour, B., 2010, *The Making of Law: An Ethnography of the Conseil d'Etat*, trans. M. Brilman & A. Pottage, Polity Press, Cambridge.
Latour, B., 2013, *An Inquiry into Modes of Existence: An Anthropology of the Moderns*, Harvard University Press, Cambridge, MA.
Latour, B. & Woolgar, S., 1986, *Laboratory Life: The Construction of Scientific Facts*, Princeton University Press, Princeton, NJ.
Law, J., 2002, 'Objects and Spaces', *Theory, Culture & Society* 19, 91–105.
Leiter, B., 2009, 'Naturalizing Jurisprudence: Three Approaches', in J. Shook & P. Kurtz (eds), *The Future of Naturalism*, pp. Humanity Books, Amherst.
Luhmann, N., 2004, *Law as a Social System*, trans. K. A. Zieger, Oxford University Press, Oxford.
MacCormick, N., 2007, *Institutions of Law: An Essay in Legal Theory*, Oxford University Press, Oxford.
McGee, K., 2014, *Bruno Latour: The Normativity of Networks*, Routledge, Abingdon, Oxon.
McGee, K. (ed), 2015a, *Latour and the Passage of Law*, Edinburgh University Press, Edinburgh.
McGee, K., 2015b, 'On Devices and Logics of Legal Sense: Toward Socio-technical Legal Analysis' in K. McGee (ed.), 2015, *Latour and the Passage of Law*, pp. 61–92, Edinburgh University Press, Edinburgh.
McGee, K., 2015c, 'The Fragile Force of Law: Mediation, Stratification, and Law's Material Life', *Law, Culture and the Humanities* 11(3), 467–490.
Matthews, D. & Veitch, S., 2016, 'The Limits of Critique and the Forces of Law', *Law and Critique* 27(3), 349–361.
Merton, R. K., 1973, 'The Normative Structure of Science', *The Sociology of Science: Theoretical and Empirical Investigations*, pp. 267–280, University of Chicago Press, Chicago, IL.
Nissenbaum, H., 2011, 'A Contextual Approach to Privacy Online', *Daedalus* 140(4), 32–48.

Pasquale, F., 2015, *The Black Box Society: The Secret Algorithms that Control Money and Information*, Harvard University Press, Cambridge, MA.

Pavlakos, G., 2007, *Our Knowledge of the Law: Objectivity and Practice in Legal Theory*, Hart, Oxford.

Perez, O., 2009, 'Law as a Strange Loop', in A. Gralf-Peter Calliess, A. Fischer-Lescano, D. Wielsch & P. Zumbansen (eds), *Sociological Jurisprudence: Liber Amicorum Gunther Teubner*, De Gruyter, Berlin.

Purdy, J., 2015, *After Nature: A Politics for the Anthropocene*, Harvard University Press, Cambridge, MA.

Raz, J., 1986, *The Morality of Freedom*, Oxford University Press, Oxford.

Raz, J., 1994, *Ethics in the Public Domain: Essays in the Morality of Law and Politics*, Oxford University Press, Oxford.

Raz, J., 2006, 'The Problem of Authority: Revisiting the Service Conception', *Minnesota Law Review* 90(4), 1003–1044.

Schauer, F., 2015, *The Force of Law*, Harvard University Press, Cambridge, MA.

Scanlon, T. M., 2014, *Being Realistic About Reasons*, Oxford University Press, Oxford.

Selbst, A. D. & Powles, J., 2017, 'Meaningful Information and the Right to Explanation', *International Data Privacy Law* 7(4), 233–242.

Sunstein, C., 2009, *Republic.com 2.0*, Princeton University Press, Princeton.

Teubner, G., 2006, 'Rights of Non-humans? Electronic Agents and Animals as New Actors in Politics and Law', *Journal of Law and Society* 33(4), 497–521.

Thompson, M., 2016, 'Beyond Gatekeeping: The Normative Responsibility of Internet Intermediaries', *Vanderbilt Journal of Entertainment & Technology Law* 18(4), 783–849.

Vermaas, P. E. & Houkes, W., 2006, 'Technical Functions: A Drawbridge between the Intentional and Structural Natures of Technical Artefacts', *Studies in History and Philosophy of Science* 37(1), 5–18.

Wachter, S., Mittelstadt, B. & Floridi, L., 2017, 'Why a Right to Explanation of Automated Decision-Making Does Not Exist in the General Data Protection Regulation', *International Data Privacy Law* 7(2), 76–99.

Waldron, J., 2004, *The Harm in Hate Speech*, Harvard University Press, Cambridge, MA.

Waldron, J., 2009, 'The Concept and the Rule of Law', *Georgia Law Review* 43, 1–61.

Whitten, A. & Tygar, J. D., 2005, 'Why Johnny Can't Encrypt: A Usability Evaluation of PGP 5.0', in L. Cranor & G. Simson (eds) *Security and Usability: Designing Secure Systems that People Can Use*, pp. 669–692, O'Reilly, Beijing.

Cases

ABC v Lenah Game Meats Pty Ltd (2001) HCA 63, 185 ALR 1

British Steel Corp v Granada Television Ltd (1981) AC 1096 (HL)

Campbell v MGN Ltd (2004) UKHL 22, (2004) 2 AC 457

Jersild v Denmark (1994) 19 EHRR 1

Pretty v United Kingdom (2002) 35 EHRR 1

Roe v Wade (1973) 410 US 113, 93 S Ct 705

R v Edwards (1996) SCC 255 (CanLII), 1996 1 SCR 128

R v Gomboc (2010) SCC 55 (CanLII), 2010 3 SCR 211

R v Plant (1993) SCC 70 (CanLII), 1993 3 SCR 281

R v Tessling (2004) SCC 67 (CanLII), 2004 3 SCR 432

Part IV

Civility, office and the bonds of community

10 Civility, obligation and criminal law

Lindsay Farmer

When we discuss legal obligation, we are normally directed towards the area of private law. The classic studies of the idea of obligation focus on the obligation in contracts, in particular, addressing the question of how obligations arise between individuals, endure over time, and are extinguished. Obligation is seen as a matter of private relations, where we are only bound by what we have voluntarily assumed. This model also forms the basis for thought about the social contract in political theory, in which the extent of our social obligations is limited by what we have (notionally) agreed to in a state of nature. To the extent that criminal law registers on this account, it is a backstop to this network of private ordering. It does not impose positive obligations on citizens (beyond the minimal necessary for social life), but is seen as a condition for other forms of private obligation to operate. This is expressed in statements of this kind, from Adam Ferguson's *Principles of Moral and Political Science*:

> We are not to expect that the laws of any country are to be framed as so many lessons of morality, to instruct the citizen how he may act the part of the virtuous man. Laws, whether civil or political, are expedients of policy to adjust the pretensions of parties, and to secure the peace of society.
>
> (Ferguson 1792, p. 145)

Laws, and especially criminal laws, should not be read as imposing obligations on a citizen to be virtuous; the law in a modernising liberal society has a more minimal role which is that of securing the peace of society – usually understood as that of establishing the framework within which individuals can pursue their own ends and desires. Criminal law is understood as taking the form of prohibitions – not to kill, not to steal, and so on – such that it would be peculiar, to say the least, to understand these as forms of obligation. Criminal laws on this account look back to the breach of the prohibition; while obligation looks forward, securing or stabilising the mutual expectations of others.

In this chapter, I want to challenge the normal interpretation of the absence of a relation between obligation and the criminal law, to explore in particular what it means to claim that the law seeks to 'adjust the pretensions of parties'. While the development of mutual obligations and responsibilities in social life is normally understood as a matter of convention or policy, and thus not something that raises fundamental issues of political or legal theory, I shall argue that it is of particular significance in modern society. In doing so I am particularly interested in the role that the criminal law plays in securing civil order in modern society, not simply as a backdrop against which individuals can pursue their own ends, but as a social institution which plays an ongoing and active role in securing the 'civility of civil society' (MacCormick 2007, p. 293). I will do this in three parts. The first will look at the idea of civility and link it to the development of modern criminal law. The second will then explore different ways in which the criminal law can be said to establish obligations of 'civility'. The third and final section will then consider, and relate this to, the recent rise of interest in the concept of civility in social and political theory.

Civility, civil society and the criminal law

In the words of an early modern historian, civility, or civil behaviour, is a 'technique for representation of personal virtue within a broader "civil" community' (Bryson 1998, p. 277). This articulates the idea that belonging or participation in a group relies on codes of social conduct, and that these in turn rely on modes of self-presentation within a social group. Civility from this perspective has often been studied in terms of changing norms of conduct, notably the formation of manners and forms of dress, within particular groups of the nobility in early modern society – a feature which underlines the way in which codes of civility have also been a means of establishing or reinforcing social hierarchies and cultural distinctions. Civility is thus a way of exploring changing conceptions of the self, through forms of social interaction and ways of belonging, and their relation to changing social institutions.

This provides a useful focus for looking at social relations ('the civility of civil society') in a modern industrial and urban society, but in doing so it is necessary to explore the impact of three further features. First, historians have pointed to the changed nature of this 'civil community' or society in modernity. Society in modernity is understood as an abstract system of common life, as contrasted with more immediate forms of sociability, where individuals of equal status have social relationships with comparative strangers.[1] Where traditional forms of society were primarily based on kinship and hierarchy in small, geographically co-located, communities, modern society is based on changed social geographies that raise different kinds of questions of order. This is not to say that there are not still immediate kin groups or communities, but that increasingly social interaction takes place with strangers, which gives rise to new challenges for the conduct of

1 See Becker 1988, ch. 1 citing David Hume. This is a distinction that is central to modern social theory, e.g. from status to contract (Maine), between mechanical and organic solidarity (Durkheim) or between *Gemeinschaft* and *Gesellschaft* (Tönnies) which capture the idea of movement from a fixed 'traditional' society to a more fluid and individualistic modern society.

social, economic and political life.[2] This requires new rules of social engagement, as individuals learn how to become part of a crowd of strangers. In this changed context, civility is not necessarily a matter of the presentation of virtue, which is specific to the early modern context that Bryson discusses, but may rather be about showing the absence of threat or making oneself 'disattendable'.[3] Second, in place of the household, modern society is fragmented, organised around the city, the market, the workplace, the home and so on, each of which are themselves ordered in their own distinctive way and entailing different kinds of contact or engagement with strangers, and in which different spheres of life have their own codes of trust and civility. Indeed, this means that in different social contexts it can become necessary to project oneself and to establish social relations in a range of different ways: to represent authority, to establish new kinds of shared rights and interests (sociability) and new forms of credibility and social trust and so on. Codes of civility can thus become complex and differentiated, classifying and representing new kinds of social difference, and the individual in modern society must learn how to negotiate different kinds of context. Third, civility is understood in terms of changing norms of individual conduct, notably controlling one's body, adjusting one's conduct to accommodate others, an increased sensitivity to pain and suffering, and avoiding giving offence to others.[4] Increasingly, then, in modern society the focus is on the individual as the basis for social order and on making individuals who can live together with other individuals in complex modern societies. This is a shift that is reflected not only in the focus on individual conduct, but also in the fact that social wrongs are reconceived in terms of the harms or wrongs that are done to the interests of individuals.[5]

While the use of the term 'civility' in the senses outlined above would normally refer to conduct that falls outwith the scope of the criminal law, it is nonetheless important in terms of thinking about the role of criminal law in modernity. The centrality of the idea of civility is not to be understood as a claim that the criminal law is (always or necessarily) concerned directly in the regulation of manners or social rules. This would be too simple, both because codes of social conduct or manners are 'more' than rules, in the sense of being habits or learned patterns of belonging, but also because such habits or customs are 'less' than rules, in that the criminal law is expected to deal only with the most egregious forms of civil misconduct and is subject to different conditions of formality and institutionalisation.[6]

2 Vernon 2014, ch. 1 pointing out that by 1871 Great Britain was the first predominantly urban society, with more than 50% of the population living in cities or large towns.

3 The classic discussion of this in modern society is Goffman 1959. See the discussion in Hall 2013, ch. 6.

4 See Elias 1994.

5 See e.g. Ferguson 1966, p. 156: 'From whatever motive wrongs are committed, there are different particulars in which the injured may suffer. He may suffer in his goods, in his person, or in the freedom of his conduct.'

6 See Collett 1977. Cf. MacCormick 2007, ch. 1 distinguishing between normative order and institutional normative order.

It is rather that the concept of civility enables us to reflect on the larger transformation of the understanding of the social in modernity, providing the categories in terms of which the existence of civil order can be understood.[7] Civil order in this sense should not be understood solely in terms of the absence of violence, but in terms of a wider range of factors, including access to legal institutions, which contribute to the civility of civil society. These factors include such things as the social distribution of violence, the means of regulation of property relations, the definitions of socially acceptable conduct, sexual mores, the regulation of public and private space, and so on.[8] The precise relationship of the criminal law with civil order at any given time is then dependent on particular historical understandings of the appropriateness of certain areas for regulation by law and whether the use of the criminal law is seen as appropriate to specific forms of conduct. We also see here the emergence of the distinctions and categories – private and public, harm, self-control, offence – which shape thinking about the modern criminal law. The scope of the criminal law is thus shaped by considerations of civility, while also being an instrument that can be used to regulate conduct in certain areas.

This brings us to the question of the relationship between criminal law and obligation, for this is fundamentally linked to the question of civility and the modern understanding of the social. To see this it is helpful to consider a passage from Adam Smith, for in his analysis of the ends of civil government and the place of law we can see the space for a modern understanding of role of criminal law beginning to emerge.[9] Smith argued that the 'first and chief design' of all civil governments was to 'preserve justice amongst the members of the state and prevent all incroachments on individualls in it, from others of the same society [sic]'.[10] In developing this argument he links civility, in the broad sense of how we should treat or do justice to others, to his account of civil society as a community of individuals pursuing multiple private interests ordered by manufacture and commerce and polite sociability.[11] Civil society is, though, a governed society in the sense that it has developed as a human institution (rather than as a natural state of affairs) in order to regulate economic progress in the form of the accumulation of property and the division of labour (Hume 1978, p. 541).[12] Civil society thus combines a theory of political economy and social cohesion and is, on this account, performing two roles: it explains the sources and legitimacy of

7 For a fuller discussion of civil order, see Farmer 2016, ch. 2.
8 The control of 'incivilities' or offensive conduct has become a dominant theme of recent discourse on criminal law, but it is striking that this discussion is largely conducted without further analysis of the meaning of civility. See Hirsch & Simester 2006.
9 This is not to claim that Smith is the originator of this kind of account, but that his account exemplifies this kind of account of modern society.
10 Smith 1978, p. 7.
11 It is thus both wider than the natural law conception of civil society as the political society (as opposed to the state of nature), and the later Hegelian conception which saw civil society as external to political institutions. This account of 'pre-Hegelian' civil society draws on Oz-Salzberger 2001, pp. 58–83.
12 Cf. Neocleous 2000, ch. 2, stressing that Smith's account of the order of the market is not natural but 'fabricated' by the state (p. 34).

political government as defending and regulating men's claims to life and property; and it provides the 'moral dimension of a modern world of economic transactions between benignly self-interested individuals' (Oz-Salzberger 2001, p. 64). Consistent with the analysis of civility above, it is the 'individual in society' which is seen as the source of order. By this I mean that the individual is seen as the primary unit of analysis, but it is recognised that the social individual is produced by government, rather than civil order depending on natural or pre-social characteristics of individuals.[13] Individuals pursue their own interests and there would inevitably be clashes between the interests or desires of individuals and between individuals and social interests. The problem of civil order is that of accommodating the competing interests and providing redress where there had been breaches of the rights of another. The role of justice was to regulate these clashes through the principles governing the security of public and private relations between persons when a person was deprived of something that they had a right to, or where they were injured or hurt without a cause. The principle of justice was articulated through the figure of the impartial spectator as a way placing yourself in the position of another individual (Smith 1978, p. 104; Smith 2009, pt. I). This offered a unique and innovative way of institutionalizing the idea of accommodating the conduct of others.

In this brief summary we can see how Smith's subtle reordering of the categories of social thought has significant implications for thinking about the criminal law. The criminal law was to do justice, in the sense of protecting private interests but also reflecting a public good or utility which was the end or justification of civil government. The end of civil government was to preserve the security of rights, and civil institutions were to enable the redress of injuries such that individuals would subordinate their own interests to the good of the whole (Smith 1978, p. 402). Thus in the conflation of the individual and the social interest, civil order was to be secured through the securing of individual interests – even if the relation between the individual and the social interest is not further explored in any great detail. Second, the objects to be protected by the criminal law are interpreted as categories framed in terms of the interests of individuals – person, reputation and estate – rather than the aim of protecting the authority of the sovereign. These interests, and the ways that they could be injured, could then be broken down and analysed in a rational and systematic way. He thus set out the principal ways that a man might be injured – in his person, as a member of a family, and as a citizen or member of a state – before further breaking this down to consider the types of injury (ibid., p. 7). Thus, a man 'merely as a man' might be injured in his person, in his reputation or in his estate, and the injury to his person might be either by killing, wounding or otherwise hurting his body or by restraining his liberty, which Smith considered included the right to free commerce (ibid., p. 8).[14] These interests are calculable and susceptible to rational analysis, thus making both government and justice more predictable. We see the same process at work in Smith's analysis of

13 See Wrong 1994, pp. 88–9.

14 See Smith 1978, pp. 105–33 for a fuller discussion of crimes.

punishment, where he argues that the amount of punishment should be derived from the individual interest that has been injured, in the 'concurrence of the impartial spectator with the resentment of the injured' (ibid., p.104).[15] This individualisation was compared with the practices of barbarian societies – in barbarous or uncivilised societies punishment was merely for the preservation of the public peace – but in developed commercial societies, the purpose of punishment was also to do justice (ibid., p. 106). The civility of civil society was thus understood not simply as an absence of disorder, but as an ongoing commitment to the adjustment of the relations between individuals and government. This is explicit in Adam Ferguson's history of civil society where he argues that 'the very restraints by which [the citizen] is hindered from the commission of crimes, are a part of his liberty. No person is free where any person is suffered to do wrong with impunity' (Ferguson 1966, p. 156).[16] Civility, then, whether in the sphere of the market or of civil society was understood in terms of a set of mutual obligations.

Civility, obligation and the criminal law

In this section I want to illustrate the argument above by discussing two areas in which new kinds of obligations have developed within the framework of this idea of civility as a kind of civil community of individuals produced and ordered by law.

The first example that I want to discuss is that of the development of early road traffic offences in the first half of the twentieth century. Motor vehicles were first used on the roads in the early twentieth century, with car ownership and use expanding rapidly in the inter-war period.[17] They presented problems for the criminal law both in controlling speed and traffic and responding to the deaths and injuries caused by cars, and as a more direct issue of criminality – as the use of cars changed the way that other crimes were committed. By the middle years of the century there were over 200,000 fatal and non-fatal injuries on the roads every year in the UK, and the use of cars was linked to increases in the number of property crimes as criminals could travel to commit crimes, and cars themselves became the object of theft.[18] The coming of the 'motor age' thus gave rise to a new problem of civil order, described as the problem of dealing with the 'carbarians'.[19] Individuals in cars were isolated from each other and had to find new ways of communicating with other road users and with the police; mass-produced cars

15 Indeed, he specifically argues against natural law theorists such as Grotius and Pufendorf that the aim of punishment is not the public good.

16 See generally pt. III sec. VI (Of civil liberty), though Ferguson concluded on the more pessimistic note that laws were of little value unless the people could also keep alive the spirit of liberty.

17 See generally Emsley 1993, pp. 357–81; Hunt 2006. See also Seo 2013, pp. 1020–40 tracing the impact of automobiles on criminal procedure in the US.

18 See Mannheim 1950, pp. 115–18. See also figures in Emsley 1993, p. 359. The phenomenon of automobile theft is also discussed in Hall 1952, ch. 6.

19 See Elias 1994, p. 368. Emsley 1993, p. 374 notes that a misprint in *The Times* in 1930 gave rise to the terminology of the 'carbarians' – motorists who disregarded norms of civilised or respectable conduct.

looked alike and could not easily be identified or traced; the numbers and speed of cars raised issues of traffic and parking control; mobility presented a challenge to social order; and cars themselves (and their drivers) were a danger to life and limb. This raised issues of external and internal control – regulating car ownership and use, but also creating norms of conduct for drivers and other road users. The first Motor Car Act was passed in 1903 and was followed by further Acts in 1930 and 1934. These introduced, then removed and reintroduced, speed limits, brought in requirements for licensing and insurance of drivers and the identification of vehicles, and created offences of speeding and of dangerous, reckless and careless driving.[20] The number of offences against these Acts rose rapidly as the police took an active role in the enforcement of the new laws, setting speed traps and stopping those who were driving dangerously.[21]

From the point of view of the Road Traffic Acts the problem was constructed as primarily a matter of order and safety, viewing motoring as a technical problem of traffic co-ordination and management. The police were encouraged to take an active role in managing conduct to ensure the free movement of traffic in public places and respect for the law.[22] However, as Elias suggests, the creation of orderly systems of road use should be seen as reflecting broader questions of social integration, developing through a complex interaction between rules and individual self-regulation:

> [E]xternal control is founded on the assumption that every individual is himself or herself regulating his or her behaviour with the utmost exactitude in accordance with the necessities of this network. The chief danger that people here represent for others results from someone in this bustle losing their self-control. A constant and highly differentiated regulation of one's own behaviour is needed for individuals to steer their way through traffic.
>
> (Elias 1994, p. 368)

As a new area of modern social life, there were few relevant pre-existing social norms. Rules were created by the road traffic laws, which then relied on the assumption that individual motorists were capable both of internalising codes of behaviour and of constantly adjusting their own conduct to others when engaged in the specific activity of driving. So more generally we can see that civility was

20 Motor Car Act 1903 (3 Edw.VII, c. 36) speed limit of 20mph. The Road Traffic Act 1930 actually removed the speed limit for cars, but following a record number of fatalities it was reintroduced at 30mph by the Road Traffic Act 1934. In addition, the Roads Act 1920 introduced the registration and taxing of vehicles.

21 See Emsley 1993, p. 359.

22 This also led to initiatives such as the introduction of 'courtesy cops' in some areas of England in 1937 to teach better behaviour on the roads (Emsley 1993, p. 378. See also Hunt 2006, p. 175). The role of the police was contested as sections of the public complained about the officious and intrusive police. The Automobile Association was initially formed as an organisation to co-ordinate anti-police conduct. See generally Emsley 1993, pp. 369–74.

something that gained a specific meaning within the context of road traffic, and that this was produced through a combination of rules and individuals regulating themselves. Obligations – to other motorists, to pedestrians or cyclists, and to the state – that established and shaped rules for road use were thus produced through and by the criminal law.

The second example is from the development of the concept of responsibility in the criminal law. While this is often seen as a process through which the criminal law recognises, to varying degrees, underlying moral concepts, such as the nature of free will or the structure of moral agency, I would argue that responsibility in the narrower sense of liability is also fundamentally linked to the establishment of wider responsibilities (or obligations) in the criminal law. These impose obligations or duties on individuals (as legal persons) in general, or in relation to particular roles, such that the function of the criminal law is not simply that of prohibition. Instead the criminal law is involved in the production of responsibilities and concepts of liability are directed at the production of responsible individuals.[23] We see this, for example, if we look at the practices of 'responsibilisation' which have been identified as a characteristic of neo-liberal forms of crime control.[24] The term is used to describe the political strategy whereby individuals or private entities are encouraged to see the prevention or reduction of social risks, such as crime, as an individual rather than a state responsibility.[25] In the crime prevention literature it can thus describe initiatives in which potential victims of crime were expected or required to take responsibility for limiting or reducing opportunities for crime through 'target-hardening' or changing their behaviour. This strategy has also led to new, more demanding, responsibilities in criminal law. There has been the creation of new duties, such as to report or disclose specific forms of potential criminal activity. Recent statutes have created crimes of failure to report suspected money laundering, suspected financial offences related to terrorism, and information about terrorism and serious organised crime (Proceeds of Crime Act 2002 ss. 330 & 331; Terrorism Act 2000 ss. 19, 21A & 38B; Criminal Justice and Licensing (S.) Act 2010 s. 31). There has also been a growth in the number of offences which criminalise the creation of risk. The Serious Crimes Act 2007, for example, has replaced the common law of incitement with a group of new offences which criminalise encouraging or assisting crime (Serious Crime Act 2007 pt. II, esp. ss. 44–6).[26] More controversially, risk-based possession offences, such as the possession of offensive weapons, are justified in terms of the need to criminalise

23 See Farmer 2016, pp. 166–71.

24 See Garland 2001, pp. 124–7; O'Malley 1992.

25 'The recurring message of this approach is that the state alone is not, and cannot effectively be, responsible for preventing and controlling crime' (Garland 1996, p. 453).

26 See discussion in Ashworth & Horder 2013, pp. 476–84 where the offences are criticised for lack of specification of the terms encouragement and assistance, but the general principle is supported.

the creation of unjustified risks.[27] In these cases responsibility is conceived broadly in terms of being responsible for creating potentially dangerous situations, or for the future consequences of one's conduct.[28] Finally, there are more complex structures of responsibility, particularly in instances of interpersonal relationships, where the issue is not only knowledge of consequences but the requirement to engage with the impact of conduct on the conduct of others. A paradigm instance of this is prosecutions for the reckless transmission of the HIV virus, where recklessness has been understood not just in terms of the risk of transmission, but as requiring the person who is HIV positive to disclose their status in order that the potential 'victim' is fully informed about the potential risks – irrespective of the willingness of that other person to consent to the risk (*R v Dica* (2004) QB 1257; *Konzani* (2005) 2 Cr App R 13).[29]

These kinds of offences have typically been criticised for different reasons: as preventive offences they are viewed as being inconsistent with a model of liability where punishment is imposed for past conduct; and they are seen as paradigm examples of over-criminalisation, where the state resorts to the use of criminal law where it cannot be linked to actual wrongdoing.[30] However, it is worth noting that not only are these offences not inconsistent with concepts of subjective liability – the person who knows and intentionally withholds information – but they actually model a form of it, as looking at them through the lens of responsibilisation demonstrates. In each of the examples above, what is distinctive is that the criminal law is establishing a link between a certain kind of civic obligation (to disclose information, not to carry knives in public and so on) and subjective forms of responsibility – in the form of the requirement to be aware of the obligation. We see here, once again, that criminal law is engaged in the creation or establishment of obligations and the way that these are linked to social assumptions about the production of civil order through self-governing individuals.

Civility and obligation

My argument so far has sought to show how there is a general link between civility and the development of the criminal law, both in the way that the criminal law has been a tool that has been used to create certain kinds of obligations and in the way that civility is connected more intrinsically to categories of social thought and the ends of government in modern society. In this final section I want broaden out the discussion to consider wider conceptions of civility, obligation and political order.

In recent years there has been an increased interest in the concept of civility, a literature which has also begun to touch on the connection between civility and

27 See Dubber 2001. For a different view, see Tadros 2008.
28 Duff 2007, ch. 7 describes these as forms of implicit endangerment.
29 For discussion, see Weait 2007, ch. 5.
30 See Ashworth 2013; Husak 2008.

legality and legal order.[31] These writings group around two main themes. First, there is an increased interest in contemporary incivilities and the corrosive effect this is believed to have on social and political relations. For some, in particular in the US, this is traced through what is seen as a decline in the quality of political discourse and public life.[32] Commentators bemoan the rise of a style of politics which spreads extreme political views and where the shouting down of political opponents takes the place of reasoned political debate. And it is argued that as a 'right', or sense of entitlement, to being offensive takes over, we forget the obligations that we owe to each other, such that the overall quality of political discourse and public life suffers.[33] This is sometimes seen as being linked to a broader decline in manners, evidenced by the rudeness of strangers – on public transport, on the streets, on the internet and so on.[34] Politically, this led in 2006, in the UK, to the so-called Respect Agenda, introduced by the then Prime Minister, Tony Blair, as a response to the social breakdown caused when individuals asserted rights divorced from any sense of social obligations (Quoted in Smith, Phillips & King 2010, p. 2). The issue for Blair, and his supporters, was not so much that minor incivilities – such as vandalism, graffiti or unruly public behaviour – were criminogenic, but that they were seen as symptomatic of a more general breakdown of civic culture. It was accordingly argued that government needed to step in with a range of measures from lessons in 'civics' to the use of the criminal law, to restore basic social values.[35]

What these different positions hold in common is a sense of civility as a necessary baseline for political and social life – and a belief that this is something that needs to be shored up when it is failing. This, it is clear, is frequently a conservative argument, in the sense that it is presented in the context of complaints about falling standards of behaviour or a decline in the quality of public life (that is to say in terms of our obligations to others), and that the solution is an appeal to that which has been lost, or the decline of civility. It also neglects what has been called the 'politics' of civility – that those who deplore incivility frequently hold positions of social power, and that pointing to the incivility or rudeness of political actors can be a way of shutting down certain kinds of opinions or political dissent or undermining political claims to recognition.[36] (And conversely, that 'uncivil' behaviour might be a way of trying to get a topic on to the political agenda.) The civility agenda, in other words, may be coded in terms of race and class. Indeed,

31 See e.g. Sarat 2014; Hall 2013.

32 See discussions in Bybee 2016; Harcourt 2012.

33 See esp. Carter 1998.

34 For popular examples, see Truss 2005 or Martin 1996. For a more critical discussion, see Smith, Phillips & King 2010.

35 The claim that conduct was criminogenic was linked to the well-known 'broken windows' these of Wilson and Kelling, which asserted a causal link between incivility and crime: 'Broken Windows' (1982). This then was used to justify the imposition of Anti-Social Behaviour Orders (ASBOs) which were aimed at forms of incivility that did not necessarily breach the criminal law, but which were seen as corrosive of social relations. See von Hirsch & Simester 2006.

36 See Harcourt 2012, pp. 347–9.

the Respect Agenda, and the criminalisation of incivility, can be seen from this perspective as an attack on working-class ways of life or mores. Thus, calls for civility or better manners can be seen as frequently leading to a kind of quietism – demanding compliance with existing norms of conduct and manners, and potentially neglecting more important moral, political and legal rights and values.[37] Civility, from this point of view, is also seen as antithetical to rights, both in the sense that it argued that it is the rise of rights (and the individualism that accompanied this) that has led to the decline of obligations of civility, and, as opponents have argued, that the need and importance of asserting rights should override any appeals for civil or polite political discourse.

A second, related, approach is broader in focus, seeking to theorise what it means to be part of a civic community in terms of the kinds of obligations that we owe to each other.[38] Defenders of this position seek to connect to an older (even ancient) understanding of *civitas* and politics and argue, in different ways, that civility should be understood as a virtue.[39] Calhoun, for example, has argued that civility is the means by which basic moral attitudes of respect for others or tolerance are displayed (Calhoun 2000, p. 255). On his account, then, this should be seen as a virtue which is distinct from the values themselves because civility 'is an essentially communicative form of moral conduct' (ibid., p. 260).[40] While this sort of account comes in different forms, what they have in common is the assertion that civility thus depends on socially established norms of conduct. However, crucially, the normative argument amounts to more than just the call that such 'civility norms' should be respected for their own sake; they also always involve an appeal beyond an individual value or immediate context to a wider (and possibly contested) sense of community. Thus, Shils has argued that civility is a form of action on behalf of, and for the benefit of, the whole of society, and so in this sense also requiring a cognitive awareness or understanding of the whole.[41] The importance of this move is that it potentially makes space for 'obedient incivility', or the possibility of disobeying norms while acting on behalf of the whole (Edyvane 2017, p. 346). Civility is therefore potentially broader than mere conformity to the law or citizenship (our rights and duties) but engages our obligations (in our conduct towards others and in the requirement to consider society as a whole). It is related to law, in the sense that it is connected to attitudes and forms of conduct that support law-abidingness, if laws are understood as general rules of

37 See e.g. Volpp 2014 & Zerilli 2014.

38 See e.g. Calhoun 2000; Shils 1997; Kekes 1984; Sistare 2004. This literature is discussed in Edyvane 2017.

39 Though there is some discussion of whether it should then be seen as an egalitarian virtue that is specific to liberal democracies (requiring tolerance, respect for others or restraint in political speech) or whether it is a more universal feature of political life. Compare Rawls 1996 and Walzer 1974.

40 Cf. Sennett: 'Rituals and modes of co-operation that characterize the network of ties comprising civic culture' (cited in Edyvane 2017, p. 345).

41 Civility is the conduct of a person 'whose individual self-consciousness had been partly superseded by his collective self-consciousness' (Shils 1997, p. 335).

conduct, but it is not co-extensive with it.[42] Thus, the concept of civility has also been used to give a thicker content to certain normative ideas, such as the presumption of innocence or the burden of proof in criminal trials (Nance 1994).[43]

The importance of this account lies in the fact that it recognises civility as an inherently social practice – as something that is expressive or communicative and that engages us in our relations with others. It understands the centrality of different kinds of obligation to communal living, not as corollaries of rights, but in terms of the awareness and consideration towards others that are part of everyday living. In concluding, though, I want to link this back to the earlier argument by taking up the claim from Adam Ferguson, with which I began, that criminal laws cannot be expected to make the virtuous citizen. While, as I noted at the start, this is a claim that is often made in relation to the modern criminal law, and is also consistent with the account of civility set out above – where the obligation of civility is seen as distinct from law – it needs to be qualified in view of the argument of this chapter. First, this is because these accounts of civility tend to be rather abstract. These obligations might exist, and claims are made about the (positive and negative) consequences of the operation of these practices of civility. Little is said, however, about how these practices, and the obligations that flow from them, have arisen – and specifically how they might arise from or in relation to legal norms. By contrast, I have shown in this chapter, specifically in relation to road traffic and the development of forms of criminal responsibility, how criminal laws have been central to the creation of obligations in relation to certain modern practices. Second, in abstracting the account of civility from social context in order to claim it as a 'virtue', we also risk losing something about the specificity of civility in modernity, as a way specifically of understanding the particular problems of togetherness and estrangement that come with living in a society of strangers and dealing with social fragmentation.[44] Central to understanding civility here is the need to focus on specific institutions and practices which offer ways of adjusting the conduct of individuals to others and which provide ways of thinking about the collective self-consciousness – whether this be in terms of politics, the market or law.

Overall, then, I am arguing for a 'thicker' concept of civility, with a clearer link to obligation and which locates the analysis in relation to the particular problems of order in modernity. This is not to claim that criminal law makes the virtuous citizen – but neither, as I have shown, is there a complete separation between civility and the criminal law. Equally, this is not to suggest that codes of civility or civilising practices are neutral, and are not (or cannot be) attempts to generalise the practices of certain classes, or suppress those of others. The 'civilising process' – who civilises and to what ends – must be part of the story, even if it has

42 Cf. e.g. Waldron 2014 arguing that civility as an attitude is essential to applying the law fairly.

43 This is discussed further in Farmer 2018.

44 I should note that both Hall 2013 and Shils 1997 link their account of civility to modernity – though neither addresses the specific point about the sources of civility.

not been central to this chapter. However, the relations between civility, obligation and the criminal law have been unduly neglected and the works of Ferguson and Adam Smith offer intriguing and important ways of rethinking the civility of civil society.

Bibliography

Ashworth, A., 2013, 'The Unfairness of Risk-Based Possession Offences', in *Positive Obligations in Criminal Law*, pp. 149–172, Hart Publishing, Oxford.

Ashworth, A. & Horder, J., 2013, *Principles of Criminal Law*, 7th edn, Oxford University Press, Oxford.

Becker, M. B., 1988, *Civility and Society in Western Europe, 1300–1600*, Indiana University Press, Bloomington.

Bryson, A., 1998, *From Courtesy to Civility: Changing Codes of Conduct in Early Modern England*, Oxford University Press, Oxford.

Bybee, K. J., 2016, *How Civility Works*, Stanford Briefs, Stanford, CA.

Calhoun, C., 2000, '*The Virtue of Civility*', *Philosophy & Public Affairs* 29, 251–275.

Carter, S., 1998, *Civility: Manners, Morals and the Etiquette of Democracy*, Basic Books, New York.

Collett, P., 1977, 'The Rules of Social Conduct', in P. Collett (ed.), *Social Rules and Social Behaviour*, pp. 1–27, Blackwell, Oxford.

Dubber, M. D., 2001, 'Policing Possession: The War on Crime and the End of the Criminal Law', *Journal of Criminal Law and Criminology* 91(4), 829–996.

Duff, R. A., 2007, *Answering for Crime: Responsibility and Liability in the Criminal Law*, Hart Publishing, Oxford.

Edyvane, D., 2017, 'The Passion for Civility', *Political Studies Review* 15(3), 344–354.

Elias, N., 1994, *The Civilising Process: Sociogenetic and Psychogenetic Investigations*, Blackwell, Oxford.

Emsley, C., 1993, '"Mother, What Did Policemen Do When There Weren't Any Motors?": The Law, the Police and the Regulation of Motor Traffic in England, 1900–1939', *Historical Journal* 36(2), 357–381.

Farmer, L., 2016, *Making the Modern Criminal Law: Criminalization and Civil Order*, Oxford University Press, Oxford.

Farmer, L., 2018, 'Innocence, the Burden of Proof and Fairness in the Criminal Trial: Revisiting *Woolmington v DPP* (1935)', in S. Summers & J. Jackson (eds), *Obstacles to Fairness in Criminal Proceedings*, Hart Publishing, Oxford, 57–73.

Ferguson, A., 1792, *Principles of Moral and Political Science: being chiefly a retrospect of lectures delivered in the College of Edinburgh*, vol. II, W. Creech, Edinburgh.

Ferguson, A., 1966, *An Essay on the History of Civil Society, 1767*, Edinburgh University Press, Edinburgh.

Garland, D., 1996, 'The Limits of the Sovereign State: Strategies of Crime Control in Contemporary Society', *The British Journal of Criminology* 36(4), 445–471.

Garland, D., 2001, *The Culture of Control: Crime and Social Order in Contemporary Society*, Oxford University Press, Oxford.

Goffman, E., 1959, *The Presentation of Self in Everyday Life*, Penguin, Harmondsworth.

Hall, J., 1952, *Theft, Law and Society*, 2nd edn, Bobbs-Merrill, Indianapolis, IN.

Hall, J. A., 2013, *The Importance of Being Civil: The Struggle for Political Decency*, Princeton University Press, Princeton.

Harcourt, B., 2012, 'The Politics of Incivility', *Arizona Law Review* 54, 345–373.
Hume, D., 1978, *A Treatise of Human Nature*, Oxford University Press, Oxford.
Hunt, A., 2006, 'Police and the Regulation of Traffic: Policing as a Civilizing Process?', in M. D. Dubber & M. Valverde (eds), *The New Police Science: The Police Power in Domestic and International Governance*, Stanford University Press, Stanford, CA.
Husak, D., 2008, *Over-Criminalization*, Oxford University Press, Oxford.
Kekes, J., 1984, 'Civility and Society', *History of Philosophy Quarterly* 1, 429–443.
MacCormick, N., 2007, *Institutions of Law*, Oxford University Press, Oxford.
Mannheim, H., 1950, *Social Aspects of Crime in England Between the Wars*, 2nd edn, George Allen & Unwin, London.
Martin, J., 1996, *Miss Manners Rescues Civilization: From Sexual Harassment, Frivolous Lawsuits, Dissing and Other Lapses in Civility*, Crown, New York.
Nance, D., 1994, 'Civility and the Burden of Proof', *Harvard Journal of Law and Public Policy* 17(3), 647–690.
Neocleous, M., 2000, *The Fabrication of Social Order: A Critical Theory of Police Power*, Pluto Press, London.
O'Malley, P., 1992, 'Risk, Power and Crime Prevention', *Economy and Society* 21(3), 252–275.
Oz-Salzberger, F., 2001, 'Civil Society in the Scottish Enlightenment', in S. Kaviraj & S. Khilnani (eds), *Civil Society: History and Possibilities*, pp. 58–83, Cambridge University Press, Cambridge.
Rawls, J., 1996, *Political Liberalism*, Columbia University Press, New York.
SaratA. (ed.), 2014, *Civility, Legality, and Justice in America*, Cambridge University Press, Cambridge.
Seo, S., 2013, 'Antinomies and the Automobile: A New Approach to Criminal Justice Histories', *Law & Social Inquiry* 38(4), 1020–1040.
Shils, E., 1997, *The Virtue of Civility: Selected Essays on Liberalism, Tradition, and Civil Society*, ed. S. Grosby, Liberty Fund, Indianapolis, IN.
Sistare, C. P. (ed.), 2004, *Civility and Its Discontents: Essays on Civic Virtue, Toleration, and Cultural Fragmentation*, University of Kansas Press, Lawrence.
Smith, A., 1978, *Lectures on Jurisprudence*, ed. R. Meek, D. D. Raphael & P. Stein, Oxford University Press, Oxford.
Smith, A., 2009, *The Theory of Moral Sentiments* (1790), Penguin, London.
Smith, P., Phillips, T. L. & King, R. D., 2010, *Incivility: The Rude Stranger in Everyday Life*, Cambridge University Press, Cambridge.
Tadros, V., 2008, 'Crimes and Security', *The Modern Law Review* 71(6), 940–970.
Truss, L., 2005, *Talk to the Hand: The Utter Bloody Rudeness of Everyday Life*, Profile, London.
Vernon, J., 2014, *Distant Strangers: How Britain Became Modern*, University of California Press, Berkeley.
Volpp, L., 2014, 'Civility and the Undocumented Alien', in A. Sarat (ed.), *Civility, Legality, and Justice in America*, pp. 69–106, Cambridge University Press, New York.
von Hirsch, A. & Simester, A. P. (eds), 2006, *Incivilities: Regulating Offensive Behaviour*, Hart Publishing, Oxford.
Waldron, J., 2014, 'Civility and Formality', in A. Sarat (ed.), *Civility, Legality, and Justice in America*, pp. 46–68, Cambridge University Press, New York.
Walzer, M., 1974, 'Civility and Civic Virtue in Contemporary America', *Social Research* 41 (4), 593–611.
Weait, M., 2007, *Intimacy and Responsibility: The Criminalisation of HIV Transmission*, Routledge-Cavendish, London.

Wrong, D., 1994, *The Problem of Order: What Unites and Divides Society*, Harvard University Press, Cambridge, MA.
Wilson, J. Q. & Kelling, G. L., 1982, 'Broken Window', *Atlantic Monthly* 211, 29–38.
Zerilli, L. M. G., 2014, 'Against Civility: A Feminist Perspective', in A. Sarat (ed.), *Civility, Legality, and Justice in America*, pp. 107–131, Cambridge University Press, New York.

Statutes

*Crime Act*2002
*Criminal Justice and Licensing (S.) Act*2010
*Motor Car Act*1903 (3 Edw. VII, c.36)
*Roads Act*1920
*Road Traffic Act*1934 (24 & 25 GEo. 5. CH, 50)
*Serious Crime Act*2007
*Terrorism Act*2000

Cases

R v Dica (2004) QB 1257
Konzani (2005) 2 Cr App R 13

11 Obligations of office

Shaun McVeigh

We have been invited to think again about the ways in which obligation – and being bound into relations by duty, gift and debt – takes on importance in the formation and maintenance of community (Esposito 2009, pp. 4–6). The general supposition of this chapter is that office, and the consideration of the appropriate conduct of office (*officia*), remains an important place of engagement of public life and lives lived in public. The engagement of office addressed here is that of the scholar and jurisprudent. It joins an argument that some of the resources for the elaboration and evaluation of the appropriate conduct of public life can still be found in the classical and humanist rhetorical traditions.

Since the 1980s, law and humanities scholarship in Australia has engaged a number of distinct ways of addressing lives lived with law (Genovese & McVeigh 2015). This chapter presents accounts of office in the work of Jeffrey Minson and Raimond Gatia, two philosophers who have written about morality, politics and law in Australia. Their work offers contrasting styles of engagement with the ethical life of the scholar conducted in the middle of arguments and events (*media res*). Jeffrey Minson has revived a language of office within a state-centred civil prudence that elaborates an ethic of responsibility (and obligation) in terms of civility. Raimond Gaita engages the vocation of the scholar through an acknowledgement of common humanity and an ethic of answerability to the preciousness of life. Both emphasise the ways in which decorum and eloquence – style – is linked to the conduct of moral, political and lawful relations.

This chapter begins with a topical location of the appropriate conduct of office in two emblematic formulations of office in the writing of Max Weber and Marcus Tullius Cicero: the latter representing the long tradition of addressing public life through a concern with duties and conduct; the former marking a distinct inflection of office through institutions and, in particular, the bureau. It then moves on to the consideration of the different shape given to the office of scholar by Minson and Gaita. My own annotations inflect these concerns towards the office of jurisprudent and those who care for the conduct of lawful relations. In sum, this chapter is a report on – and an argument for – the importance of office for the engagements of the middle grounds of public life. Less emphatically, it suggests a continuing concern with *officia* can still shape or form the obligations, styles and forms of conduct appropriate to an office. I take the language of the shape and form of office, and of the weight and measure of conduct, as 'middle' terms that are subject to dispute and available for argument. Within the rhetorical traditions it is the concern with eloquence and decorum that locates this topic. As ever there are questions to be asked of office, especially at a time when official thinking does not carry much weight, and where the 'public' of public life is not readily bound by obligation.

Offices and persons

There are many starting places for addressing the forms of office and the appropriate conduct of the contemporary office of the jurisprudent within the university. In early modern Europe, for example, public life was conducted and evaluated through a great variety of offices. Some, like those of state (judge, legislator, governor, soldier) or Church (bishop, priest) were instituted through ceremony and oath. Other offices, like those of the scholar and jurist, were less clearly delineated. The worth of some social offices such as those of poet and actor were strongly questioned (Condren 2006). Today, while some offices still receive attention, they are rarely treated as carrying obligations in their own name. It is more common to establish value and meaning at the level of the institution, system or network. The first encapsulation of an ethic of office addressed here is Max Weber's ethic of responsibility in the bureaux of public institutions.

For the early moderns, each office had its own dignities, rights and responsibilities and its performance was elaborated and evaluated in terms of the character (persona) and the virtues and vices of conduct (Minson 2014). These formulations of office also formed a central part of the Roman analysis of public life and Renaissance humanism and jurisprudence (Berman 1995). The second encapsulation of office addressed here is of the Roman rhetorical tradition found in the writings of Cicero. Cicero's writings on the office of statesman (*On Duties*) and the ideal orator (*Orator*) form part of what is now viewed as a mixed genre: part report on practical action, part training manual, part erudite education into tradition and part philosophical or spiritual practice (Sellars 2013). For Cicero and his Renaissance and modern inheritors, the performance of office was held together through the consideration of decorum and eloquence (Pue 2016; Goodrich 2017). These two encapsulations are not presented in opposition but are taken as providing different accounts of the mode and manner of arranging the conduct of office.

Read as a historical anthropology, Weber's work can be understood as a series of investigations into types and the style of conduct and rationality appropriate to the figures of the modern world: the bureaucrat, the scholar, the scientist and the politician (Du Gay 2008, p. 131; Hennis 2000). Max Weber's two lectures 'Science as Vocation' (1917) and 'Politics as Vocation' (1919) addressed the specificity and difficulty of the conduct of public life in the absence of a single overarching moral or political order (Weber 2004). His advice for the scholar and politician was that both must be capable of living up to the demands of the particular vocations or 'life orders' (*Lebensführungen*) through which they conduct their lives (Minson 1993, p. 134).

For Weber, the office of scholar in Germany in 1917 was shaped by a concern for the authority of science first in the relationship between science and politics ('can science provide authority for politics?') and second in the status of the meaning and value of science in the modern world ('can a science without ultimate ends have value?') (Owen & Strong 2004, p. xxi). To answer these questions and establish the scope of vocation or calling of the human scientist, Weber saw the university as a corporate enterprise within a state capitalist system (Weber 2004, p. 7). Its significant institutional arrangements relate to the bureaucratisation and rationalisation (intellectualisation and calculation) of knowledge and of scholarly life. This in turn has changed the model of the office of scholar from being one of aristocrat or artisan (both with a library) to that of a manager whose work is understood as subject to the interests and constraints of government and answerable to the public (ibid., p. 3–4).

In addition to the external constraints of the university, the personality of the scholar must be adequate to the task of living with the demands of their discipline. For human scientists, this means pursuing a discipline that lacks a final purpose or end (it is polytheistic) and lacks public authority (it is a specialist form of enquiry). For Weber, such demands are to be met directly by maintaining diligence and clarity in research and honesty in its reporting. In the 'Politics as Vocation' lecture, Weber addresses a more general account of the conduct of office by marking a contrast between an ethic of responsibility and an ethic of conviction or between an ethic that attends to the means and consequences of a situation and one framed in terms of conviction that judges according to intentions and ultimate ends. While, for Weber, an ethic of responsibility is not always sufficient to sustain either the passion of a vocation or the authority of the scholar, an ethics of conviction runs the risk of romanticism and the formation of prophetic cults. To be able to take responsibility for the circumstances around you, and to act in the knowledge of the consequences, is, for Weber, to act with maturity in the face of the realities of the world (Weber 2004, p. 92; Gaita 2017a, p. xxi). It is also the dignity of the vocation of the scholar (Owen 1997; Minkkinen 2010).

Weber's lectures make questions of conduct central to vocation and office. However, they do not draw directly on the traditions of philosophy and jurisprudence that address the training in conduct of the scholar and jurisprudent. If classical philosophy has been marked by providing 'spiritual exercises' in the cultivation of a philosophical life, then jurisprudence can be viewed, at least in part, as presenting exercises and training in the conduct of office (Hadot 1995; Hunter 2001). In the balance of this section I note the continuing resonance of traditions of rhetorical education with training in the arts of public service.

Invoking Cicero as a source of authority or argument rarely establishes much. His writings can be taken as a Roman source for most engagements of character and morality, speech and writing, political and philosophical life and so forth. The link invoked here is with Cicero's joining of a rhetorical and philosophical understanding of the importance of decorum and eloquence to the formation of character and argument. In the *Orator* (1939), his last work of rhetoric, Cicero divided the cultivation of the persona of the public official between a philosophical training that was mainly concerned with rationality and will and a rhetorical training that engaged the conduct of civic life (Guerin 2009, pp. 109–11). In doing so he reshaped the worldly training of the Roman orator to the ends of the philosopher. It makes sense in addressing Cicero, for example, to write of the 'office of the soul' as well as offices relating social and civic personae (Minson 2009, p. 2; Cicero 2016). For Cicero, both philosophical and rhetorical training was designed to develop the persona of the orator and to give shape to the conduct of public life through decorum (Guerin 2009, p. 130). In one register, decorum was part of the sphere of duties (*officia*) that addressed the appropriateness of public speech and deliberation (Haldar 2016). It was concerned with the ways in which an orator should consider the time, place and audience of their speech. In this respect, decorum is a matter of proportion and circumstance. It was also important to the training in character and the virtues or disposition of the orator (Guerin 2009, p. 131; Dugan 2005, pp. 129–31). In the *Orator*, for example, Cicero associated decorum with eloquence and with a sense of fairness (*aequitas*) and honour (*honestas*) as well as with philosophical wisdom (Cicero 1939, pp. 9–10; Guerin 2009, pp. 136–7). Cicero addressed the significance of such idealisations in *De Officiis*, where the contrast between honour (*honestas*) and usefulness (*utilitas*) is used to shape questions of public life and government. He argues there that the reconciliation of honour and usefulness runs the risk of idealising both.

In the Renaissance humanist reception of Cicero, decorum became associated with general attributes of speech (including poetry) (Burchell 1998, p. 108). Among humanists with a more direct interest in matters of law, decorum was understood both in relation to the work of the jurist, in the philological authentication of texts, and the disciplines that were associated with the *studia humanitatis* (Minson 2009; Goodrich 2015). Most visibly marked through Renaissance legal humanist scholarship, the Ciceronian elevation of eloquence and persuasion in the *studia humanitatis* provided a model of the scholar-jurisprudent's engagement with forms of office and public life by linking decorum and eloquence with honour (*honestas*) (Kristeller 1979). If dignity (and later decorum) were related to the obligations of office, then eloquence in its various forms directed attention to the cultivation of a persona (Dugan 2005, p. 329). Eloquence, for some, also became the means by which the philosophical understanding of the good life was instituted and transmitted (Haldar 2016).

Holding institutional, rhetorical and philosophical registers of office to a concern with decorum and eloquence helps make visible some of the different commitments to the shaping of office in the writing of philosophers and jurisprudents. However, neither Weber's ascetic Protestant training in office nor the diffuse training in Ciceronian decorum and eloquence has been passed down uncontested.[1] Here it is enough to disarticulate accounts that see the institution of office as fact and an engagement with value as a step beyond or out of office.

1 See Montaigne 'Reflections on Cicero' for a severe judgment of Cicero's character and eloquence (Montaigne 1957, pp. 183–6; Green 1975, pp. 17–19). More generally,

Jurisprudents of Australia

In the previous section, the emphasis on decorum and eloquence presented the conduct of office in terms of both a rhetorical craft and a philosophical exercise. This is followed here into the office of the jurisprudent in Australia. Such a jurisprudent, it might be imagined, would contend with constraints and care for the repertoires of lawful relations established within its disciplinary forms. This is one way of locating the formulations of conduct in Minson's ethic of civil responsibility and Gaita's ethic of human answerability.

No doubt a full account of the office of jurisprudent would require an account of the 'external' constraints of the university and the discipline. Such an account would, at one level, repeat the broad sweep of Weber's concern with the conduct of the life of the university and legal profession in the face of the demands of state, global and now financial capital. It would also give an account of the development of the university shaped by the transformative effects of technology and artificial intelligence (Thornton 2012). It would also note that the expansion in number and size of law schools in common law jurisdictions since the 1990s.[2] In taking up office, a jurisprudent would also have to address the disciplinary ordering of law in Australia. This too has undergone institutional and ideational transformation. The creation of a Federal Court in 1976, and the independence of the Australian High Court from the Privy Council in 1986, set in motion the elaboration of a distinct Australian jurisprudence. This jurisprudence was articulated most clearly in the High Court decision of *Mabo v State of Queensland (No 2)* (1992) 175 CLR 1. In this case the High Court of Australia recognised the continued existence of Indigenous peoples and their laws and traditions in Australia. In response, it also established a form of Australian common law elaborated in a language of legal and moral rights (relating to race, gender and environment) and a recognition of plural international obligations shaped around human rights. Finally, a jurisprudent might be obligated to note how such transformations in the disciplinary engagement of law remain largely unaddressed within the office of jurisprudent of Australia (Dorsett & McVeigh 2012, pp. 98–116). The two commentaries on the work of Jeffrey Minson and Raimond Gatia that follow can be read as drawing on accounts of decorum and eloquence in order to give emphasis to particular ways in which obligations are carried in accounts of conduct.

Civility and civil prudence

Jeffrey Minson's account of civil prudence can be presented as part of a revival in the 1980s and 1990s of forms of 'civil jurisprudence' undertaken by scholars associated with Griffith University and later the University of Queensland. Through a series of histories, jurisprudences and accounts of education and

humanist prudence and jurisprudence was written in contest with the exegetical and interpretative practices of the Roman law glossators and canon lawyers (Berman 1995).

2 Depending a bit on how you count, there are, in 2017, 37 university law schools in Australia; 28 of these have been created since the 1990s (Barker 2013, p. 1).

criticism, this work sought to establish forms of state-centred humanities scholarship capable of directing the education and training of students for public life (Minson 1993; Hunter 2014).

Civil jurisprudence names a tradition of thinking that developed in seventeenth-century Europe, especially in what is now Germany, France and England. It developed out of an immediate concern with securing the authority of German princes in acting against the political authority of the Church. In its broad political and juridical forms, civil jurisprudence was written against the claims of transcendence and perfection of Christian spiritual and temporal orders. It did so by elaborating the political and juridical form of the sovereign territorial state shaped around non-transcendent accounts of civil authority and charged with the security of the population and the maintenance of civil peace (Hunter 2001; Minson 2014).

Casting civil authority in terms of the sovereign ruler of a de-sacralised polity also required that the relationship between civil authority and citizen be re-thought. Rather than found the unity of the human and the citizen in the image of God, the role of citizen was established through the elaboration of a 'system of impersonal and jurisdictionally delimited offices'. In turn, this plurality of offices and relationships were held in place by 'internal moralised boundaries' between official obligations (Minson 2006, pp. 77–8). Civil prudence in this sense set out to describe a form of social existence capable of being lived without sectarian religious engagement and with limited forms of sociality. Central to this was the development of a moral anthropology shaped around human fallibility and imperfectability (there was to be no transcendence of the human condition in the political domain). In one sense, the account of obligation within civil jurisprudence is blunt. Obligations are to be determined by civil authority. However, as Hunter (2001) and Minson (2014) point out, it is the creation of a de-sacralised political sphere that allows for the plurality of forms of civil life – more or less held in relation to civil authority. Within such forms of civil authority, as Minson notes, the sources of obligation can remain plural. The vocation and shape of the office of jurisprudent, for example, might be crossed with a range of obligations of public service; affiliations of profession, guild and union; scholarly discipline; the obligations of employment contracts and public regulation; as well as humanist commitments of philanthropy and civic conscience (Minson 2009).

In touching on Minson's civil prudential training in the office of jurisprudent, I will emphasise some aspects of civil prudence as a training in living well with the plural accounts of office developed within civil jurisprudence. I will also note that the forms of conduct of the office of jurisprudent have also been treated as attributes of office. In summary terms, Minson's teaching about the ethos of civil office is that there is no single principle or system that provides a normative order of office. Even a civil prudential concern with the 'interests of the state' or 'security' does not establish an overarching principle so much as a point of orientation for judgment, argument and action. Like Weber, Minson argues that this formulation of office should not be taken as an opportunity to subvert or transcend office, so much as reckon with the proper (institutional) conduct of public life. Unlike Weber, Minson does not see this as a 'tragic' situation but a means of securing everyday sociality.

Minson's formulation of an ethic of office is shaped by civility rather than dignity and by usefulness or utility as much as honour (Minson 1993, pp. 16–40). The terminology of civility, argues Minson, is one that can be given some specificity if it is linked to office and the government of conduct. Minson's response to the variegated projects of government and citizenship (in, say, the spheres of work, health and family relations) is to treat them as a concern of (social) conduct. Such conduct, for the most part, is to be characterised in terms of manners (*mores*). In linking civility to manners and conduct, civil prudence offers a mundane, rather than an ultra-mundane, ethos of office and citizenship. This, in its way, is the strength of civil prudential thinking. It offers guidance on how to live with subordination to forms of civil authority and the constraints of civil peace (Minson 1993, pp. 157–159; Minson 2014, pp. 454–456). It renders this subordination productive by limiting both the range of concerns that are so subordinated and the specific modes of subordination (external conduct, specific styles of exchange and so forth). It does not offer a single and entire conduct of life but plural modes of engagement with the modes and manners of civil life.[3]

Part of the challenge of an ethic of responsibility tethered to civility and manners is securing a sufficient weight of meaning to the order of conduct. Modern manners, it might be noted, barely rise to etiquette, let alone form the basis of public life. Much depends on what you are prepared to address through manners. (For example, the ethos of Renaissance humanism had to be capable of surviving in a courtier culture as well providing an idiom for expressing spiritual and passionate love (Minson 1993, pp. 23–26).) An ethic of responsibility shaped around civil manners does not operate separately from the conditions of civil authority. It can be taken up precisely because it claims a meaningful account of appropriate conduct in a civil polity where public law and administration is largely de-sacralised. The issue is to find ways in which rhetoric and manners can carry meaning and activities that can be treated as de-sacralised. The ceremonial and institutional forms of law might not be viewed as being concerned with manners if instituted through public oath, but if we treat such ceremonies as protocols of conduct and manners, they might take on a broader repertoire of meaning and action. Two brief examples can be given here in order to illustrate the way Minson gives shape to office. The first is the practice of disinterestedness (*adiaphora*) in the conduct of office and the second is the use of description and re-description (*descriptio*), rather than forms of dialectic, as a way of engaging in dispute (Minson 2014). These features form a concern with both office and character. They register both as a concern of public conduct and government and as an aspect of decorum in establishing the status, character and ethos of the personae of civil institutions.

Adiaphorism, or the cultivation of forms and styles of disinterestedness, has an institutional, rhetorical and philosophical history. The cultivation of a distinct

3 Civility is not a term that can be used without a sense of complicity in the full range and consequences civilisation (and development) projects.

adiaphoristic persona has been at the centre of the development of the office of the judge and the emergence of civil jurisdictions (Minson 2014, p. 65). As Saunders and Hunter have noted, the emergence of disinterestedness of the common law or state-appointed judge has a location: the assumption of civil jurisdiction in matters previously subject to the jurisdiction of the Church. The civil regulation of witchcraft, heresy and blasphemy would be examples. In this situation disinterestedness relates to the suspension or recasting of both a Church jurisdiction as well as the suspension of judgment on religious matters (Hunter 2013; Saunders 1997). This requirement of disinterestedness also extended to the adjudication of such matters, since a judge should train themself to subordinate their own religious (or other) beliefs to the interests of civil authority. Such qualifications of conduct point not so much to the neutrality of institutions but the cultivation of comportments capable of living with the requirements of different, and possibly conflicting, offices (civil and religious as well as social and familial) (Minson 2014, p. 463).[4]

For the jurists, jurisprudents, philosophers and humanists of the seventeenth century the cultivation of techniques of distancing (adiaphorism) also formed a part of the engagement with an array of techniques, genres and disputes within humanist scholarship.[5] The writings of the early modern civil humanists were contextual and historical. There forms of public argument drew on the rhetorical traditions of ethics and were pitched against the dialectical traditions of scholastic and university metaphysics (Hunter 2001). As Minson notes, description (***descriptio***) belongs first to the epideictic discourses of praise or blame (Minson 2014, p. 443).[6] The polemical edge of civil jurisprudence – like much humanist criticism directed towards changing reputations and opinion – was, and is, often conducted by political, moral and juridical re-description (Skinner 1996). What interests Minson in this is not only the recuperation of an erudite tradition of state-sympathetic civilised, decorous, humanist thought, but also the elaboration of a ***modus vivendi*** – an ethic capable of engaging well with the limits of a life lived in public.

Minson's own re-descriptions of the early modern humanist and civil prudence provide one way of living well with the constraints of civil authority.[7] It might be thought, then, that the office of jurisprudent and the care for the conduct of lawful relations need only be describable within the constraints of usefulness. There is a sense in which this is so, Minson's ethic of office is one that draws on a 'disenchanted' rhetoric of office. However, Minson does not simply assert a realist ethos of government, since he also offers an invitation to acknowledge a broader range of obligations and repertoires of action that might be discussed in terms of dignity and honour. In doing so he presents an account of civil honour associated

4 Contrast Goodrich (1984, 2000, 2015) who sets the humanist rhetorical tradition at odds with common law education.

5 Exercises in disinterestedness have also formed a part of Stoic training, disciplining of the self against the feeling of suffering or the temptations of glory (Hadot 1995).

6 The sources for the following two paragraphs are drawn from this essay.

7 His analysis of the understanding of civil institutions includes institutional responses to sexual harassment (1993) and civil forfeiture (2006).

with decorum (Minson 1993, pp. 26–29). Much of the energy (and humour) of Minson's writing is devoted to showing how it could be honourable to take civic commitments seriously in political, moral and legal action. Civility and decorum might require ceremony and protocol, but they could also require conflict and contestation both in securing the conditions, and maintaining the practice of, citizenship based around civil and social equality. It requires forgoing a certain romanticisation and sacralisation of public life but not the sacrifice of life in public. There could be dishonour, for example, in romanticising civil obligations into a transcendent nationalism, just as there might be dishonour in failing to find a form of civic expression of social relations.

Finally, to direct Minson's ethic of responsibility towards the office of scholar a brief reference should be made to his discussion of the Renaissance humanism of Pico della Mirandola and Marsilio Ficino (Minson 2009). Minson argues that, given shape within a rhetorical rather than a philosophical tradition, Ficino's 'humanism' and philanthropy (love of man) is best understood as an 'office of humanity' (ibid., p. 2). This office (or mode of appropriate conduct) is treated as a project 'centred upon the persona, curriculum and erudition of the University Humanities professors' and focused on the relation of the scholar and teacher to the student (ibid., p. 7). Hold on to the question of office in Pico della Mirandola's 'Oration on the Dignity of Man' (2013), Minson argues, and it ceases to be a text written in praise of the dignity of all of humanity but a rather more specific address in praise of the dignity of the philosopher in the work of the spiritual transformation of the student (Minson 2009, pp. 12–13).

If humanist ideals are held in the office of scholar, then its training might be viewed as one that cultivates a persona of a scholar capable of participating in public life without directly engaging in the contest of political authority. The performance of the office of scholar involves achieving a *modus vivendi* with what are, often, competing and conflicting obligations. Among these, Minson suggests, it is still possible to take up the responsibility for maintaining a 'gift' relation in the transmission of the love of knowledge between teacher and student (Minson 2009, p. 13). Whether the ethic of responsibility in the office of scholar and jurisprudent can be attractive depends in part on whether the occupation of office can be honourable, performed with appropriate decorum (or, as occasion demands, *sprezzatura*) and carry sufficient weight of meaning.

Dignity and common humanity

The second account of the shape of the office of scholar and jurisprudent is taken from the writing of the Australian philosopher Raimond Gaita. For Gaita, the vocation of the philosopher remains that of ancient philosophy: to think and live well with others shaped by the love of knowledge and of humanity. Much of his writing has been directed to showing the ways in which the affirmation of the preciousness of life is 'wonderous' (and far from easy to achieve) (Gaita 2017b, pp. 170–1). For Gaita, such an affirmation of the love of humanity should be truthful – hard-headed and unsentimental – and should be able to cultivate joy in sharing humanity and shame and remorse at failing to do so. His exemplars are the saintly who show unconditional love, or goodness, whether they be nuns, parents, friends or teachers. The political officials and public workers (scholars, writers and artists) who attract his attention grapple with what it means to be able to an office and a vocation. What is addressed here is the way that a concern with style, or eloquence, becomes a part our answerability for the conduct of human relations (Gaita 2017b, p. 173).

Since the 1990s, Gaita's writing has engaged publicly with the ethical understanding of the responsibilities and actions in moral, political and legal spheres of our shared lives. In the context of an Australian life this has involved a sustained investigation of the ethical understanding of race, genocide and education.[8] Something of Gaita's relationship to office can be shown in his approach to formulating the place and work of ethics. In the light of the way that Gaita makes strong links between goodness and love, it might be possible to imagine a public life without any significant account of office or at least one where the language of office does not carry any serious ethical meaning. What is important are the needs of the soul (love, truth and justice). However, Gaita, I think, does give shape to office by way of addressing appropriate conduct (*officia*) in the ethical engagements of the political, moral and legal spheres. Gaita's positive understanding of office begins with the sense that each sphere has distinct forms of responsibility (obligation) and conduct. While these spheres are not organised around the facts of institutional life in the way that Weber suggests, they are organised around accounts of the appropriate conduct of actors in public institutions. For Gaita, there is no reason to assume that the demands of politics (the survival of the political community), law (justice) and morality (conduct of human relations) can be met without conflict (Gaita 2017a, p. xix). The political requirements of the survival of a community have, and frequently do, run into conflict with the moral requirements of the acknowledgement of common humanity and the legal requirements of justness. In addressing an ethical concern with how to live well, Gaita argues (as does Minson) that each sphere creates its own obligations and responsibilities for which we must be answerable. To elevate the ethical requirements of morality above those of politics will not fulfil political obligations (or vice-versa).

What is striking in Gaita's accounts of politics, morality and law, however, is the way he pitches his ethical engagement and philosophical thought into the middle of arguments and events of human life (*media res*) (Gaita 2000, p. 14). Where Minson links social life to civil authority, Gaita sets the acknowledgement of humanity and the consideration of appropriate conduct within ethically inflected forms of natural language – the realm of meaning. Within this milieu, ethical meaning can be understood by way of an analogy with literature. Great literature, Gaita argues, speaks to all not through a single universal language, but through deepening the realm of meaning. It potentially speaks to all, but is only experienced in particular cultures when translated from one natural language to another (Gaita 2000, pp. 283–5).

8 In a different register Gaita has also addressed the living of a philosophical life (Gaita 1998, 2002, 2010).

Some of the power of the language of dignity, for example, arises by its being able to carry meaning across languages and between people. This is lost in the political and legal spheres if dignity is considered only in the register of abstract universal rights. In most circumstances, dignity expressed in human rights is far from abstract. It is addressed in the register of the noble and the heroic and related to the fight against political oppression. This sense of the universality of the concerns of political dignity is carried in the realm of meaning (Gaita 2017b, p. 176). Gaita also notes that there are circumstances in which dignity and the language of duties and rights fails to carry the significance of events or wrongs. This is so when dignity is required to address matters that touch our sense of humanity in different ways, such as the expression of the wrongs of torture and genocide. Here Gaita notes that there is a sense of violation that can only be met through a language of justice and love (Gaita 2017b, p. 184). In other circumstances, dignity is addressed in the register of the sacred, especially in the care of the vulnerable. Here dignity might distract someone from appreciating the difference between dignity as an expression of respect and an expression of love which transforms human fellowship (Gaita 2000, pp. 17–27). The same can be said of the understanding of office in the realm of meaning. There are circumstances where the sense of duty or obligation can be met in the language of office or profession. However, Gaita notes that the language of vocation better captures the sense of seriousness in the calling of, for example, the scholar (Gaita 2017a). Many of the most important aspects of human relations are conducted in the register of love and justice rather than obligations and rights.

For Gaita, the realisation of the limits of an ethical language of office expressed in duty and obligation opens on to another aspect of the ethical, that of the relation between reason and sensibility. Philosophers and jurisprudents engaging in the realm of meaning, as they must, err when they tie their sense of cognition too closely to formal rationality. An excessive sentimentality or pity might indeed distort our judgment by defeating our ability to reason clearly. However, not paying attention to sentiment can also defeat our understanding where judgments of feeling or sensibility are required as they are in ethical deliberation in the moral, political and legal spheres. In these circumstances 'vulnerability to sentimentality is intrinsic' since it is joined to forms of enquiry about living and dying well (Gaita 2017b, pp. 174, 176). The calling of the philosopher involves being prepared to transform oneself by 'ridding oneself of sentimentality, pathos and similar afflictions'. It does not, however, involve divesting oneself of all sensibility since this is required to allow 'justice, love and pity to do their cognitive work, their work of disclosing the world' (Gaita 2004, p. xxxvii).

In so far as jurisprudence is discursive, it also joins philosophy in addressing conceptual concerns – with or without sensitivity to tone and sentiment (affect), and with or without deepening the meaning or understanding of what is shared in being human. The work of creation, art, cannot do conceptual work alone. However, philosophy and jurisprudence cannot do so either unless it is responsive to art. This linking of reason and sensibility as well as form and content places an account of style or eloquence as the centre of the effort to be lucid about what it means to be human (Gaita 2017b, pp. 174–176). Eloquence here does not simply relate to the ability to persuade or entertain but to our ability to articulate truthfully what it means to live well. Eloquence also relates to the ethos or character of the philosopher and jurisprudent. For Gaita, I think, this joins the calling of the philosopher to the task of being properly human.

In the legal sphere, for example, Gaita considers some of the ways in which those who live through the common law tradition have addressed relations and laws between the Indigenous and non-Indigenous peoples of Australia (Gaita 2000, pp. 73–87, 107–31). In a series of cases establishing doctrines of Native Title, the Justices of the High Court of Australia have also addressed their sense of the importance of their office. In the most important of these, *Mabo v Queensland (No 2)*, the Court turned attention to the office of judge. Alongside establishing Native Title and reasserting an obligation to justice, the Justices set about establishing a range of conducts and affects suitable to responding to the wrong of the political and juridical dispossession of Indigenous peoples. In doing so, the Court also presented an account of its own understanding of its office. For Justices Gaudron and Deane and others, the treatment of Aboriginal people had left 'a national legacy of unutterable shame' (1992, p. 104). Gaita interprets this as both as an expression of remorse for the moral wrongs of law and an expression of the need for the justness of law.

For Gaita, the moral wrong recognised by Justices Brennan, Gaudron and Deane was that the common law, and those who live by it, had failed to acknowledge the humanity of Aboriginal peoples and so had dismissed the wrong of dispossessing Aboriginal peoples of their land. For Gaita, this moral recognition of a common humanity might be viewed as an attribute of the office of judge: judges, today, recognise that there are moral and political concerns that need to be addressed (Gaita 2017a, p. xiii). The sense of shame and dishonour of a judge in relation to law might also arise from the realisation that the forms of law are unworthy of the situation they are required to address (Rush 1997). This dishonour of law lies in failing to establish legal forms and a style of argument and judgment worthy of enabling a meeting place of laws and peoples (Gaita 2017a, p. xii). In considering this judgment, Gaita also notes the style of the judgments: their awareness of the seriousness that the wrong addresses, their expressions of remorse, and their sense of the importance of holding Australian law to a public account of justice. These all might be considered part of the style, eloquence or ethos that draws us towards understanding that the activity of legal judgment relates to the realisation of a common humanity. For Gaita, the language of indecency or incivility would not capture the wrong of Indigenous dispossession or remedy its denial (Gaita 2000, pp. 80–1).

The brief comments made here have taken up Gaita's sense of engagement with the vocation of the philosopher and philosopher as jurisprudent. His concern with goodness and the ethical responsibility to live well with others produces an exacting account of ethical life. It does the same for the training in the conduct of the scholar (Gaita 2000, pp. 187–214). In his pursuit of the 'office of humanity',

Gaita's account of the training in office and vocation of the scholar is shaped by an understanding of the intrinsic worth of seeking understanding and of following knowledge and truth for the love it: for the joys and obligations it imposes. For Gaita, this involves 'thought in dialogue with a history of reflection'. It also involves induction into a way of (philosophical) life that has been given a home in the university (Gaita 2012, pp. 1–3; Hadot 1995). Whether the involvement of a scholar in thought 'for its own sake' involves something serious and responsive or not depends, at least in part, on whether teachers and students are prepared to be answerable to a concept of the truth. It also depends on a broader community since the value of the life of mind, particularly the unworldliness required for prolonged thought and education, needs many kinds of support and imposes many social and political obligations. Like Weber, Gaita argues that the university no longer answers to a concept of truth (Gaita 2000, p. 198). It has lost its sense of the seriousness of the cultivation of the life of the mind (and the love of truth) in an excessive pursuit of instrumental gain. Some of the difficulties in which the university finds itself are the result of external constraints. Mostly, however, Gaita argues, it is because scholars and others are no longer prepared to struggle to maintain a concept of the university answerable or willing to assume 'responsibility for the world' – including the unworldly space of education (Gaita 2012, pp. 15–17; Arendt 2006). The office of the scholar remains part of the university but something more is needed than a profession and conditions of employment (although the university would be diminished in another way if a sense of profession was not present). What is needed, Gaita has argued, is a sense of vocation taken up with a love of knowledge and sense of common humanity.

Conclusion

Here are two concluding comments and a final gloss. The first comment is summative. Both Cicero and Weber and Minson and Gaita are concerned with how to live well with the obligations and limits of vocation (or office). The concern with appropriate conduct was initially distributed across two registers. For Weber and Minson, the ethic of responsibility of civil prudence was shaped by the duties of office subject to civil authority. For Cicero and Gaita, the ethic of honour and answerability were held in a language of love, justice and human relations. It would certainly have been possible to address such approaches to questions of conduct by emphasising the rivalry of philosophical traditions. However, I think that questions of the appropriate conduct of the office of jurisprudent turn out to be more complex when addressed in *media res* and through the movement in and out of office and between offices. The challenge presented by Minson is to find the rhetorical and social resources to live with the constraints of office shaped by civil authority. The one presented by Gaita is to find forms of public office and language capable of acknowledging, and making judgments worthy of, the preciousness of life and a shared humanity.

The second comment is more formal, or at least more about form. In their accounts of education and training in conduct, Minson and Gaita both return to an ethical inflection of humanist rhetorical traditions. While the training they propose draws on different modalities of living well with civility and dignity, their forms of conduct are both presented through a philosophical and rhetorical education in decorum and eloquence. It is this that allows ethical reflection and deliberation in the conduct of public life. It also gives shape to the office of jurisprudent. The obligations of office are also a matter of comportment or style. For Minson, such obligations are addressed through 'ordinary' virtues of office; for Gaita, such ordinary virtues are illuminated by the extraordinary – the attempt to remain lucid about goodness and the love of humanity.

Finally, a brief gloss or annotation. I have noted that Minson and Gaita share something in the education of students in the offices of humanity. They both continue to affirm the importance of marking distinctions between worldly and unworldly forms of education in the office of humanity. Sometimes this appears in a contrast between the leisure of thought (*otium*) and the business of public affairs (*negotium*); at other times it takes the form of a responsibility for, or answerability to, a common meaning of a life lived in public. At all times it requires the office or vocation of the scholar be adequate to the task or worthy of the name.

Acknowledgements

This chapter was written as an appreciation of the office of jurisprudent and of the work of Jeffrey Minson and Raimond Gaita. They should be excused its errors. I would also like to thank Diamond Ashiagbor and Ann Genovese for encouraging me to finish.

Bibliography

Arendt, H., 2006, 'The Crisis in Education', in H. Arendt, *Between Past and Future: Eight Exercises in Political Thought*, pp. 170–192, Penguin Books, New York.

Barker, D., 2013, 'An Avalanche of Law Schools', *Journal of the Australian Law Teachers Association* 6, 177–192.

Barr, O., 2016, *A Jurisprudence of Movement: Common Law, Walking, Unsettling Place*, Routledge, London.

Berman, H., 1995, *Law and Revolution, I: The Formation of the Western Legal Tradition*, Harvard University Press, Cambridge, MA.

Black, C., 2011, *The Land is the Source of the Law: A Dialogic Encounter with Indigenous Jurisprudence*, Routledge, London.

Burchell, D., 1998, 'Civic Personae: MacIntyre, Cicero and Moral Personality', *History of Political Thought* 19(1), 101–118.

Cicero, M. T., 1939, *Orator*, Harvard University Press, Cambridge, MA.

Cicero, M. T., 2016, *On Duties*, Cornell University Press, Ithaca, NY.

Condren, C., 2006, 'The Persona of the Philosopher and the Rhetorics of Office in Early Modern England', in C. Condren, S. Gaukroger & I. Hunter (eds), *The Philosopher in Early Modern Europe: The Nature of a Contested Identity*, pp. 66–89, Cambridge University Press, Cambridge.

Connell, R., 2007, *Southern Theory: The Global Dynamics of Knowledge in Social Science*, Allen & Unwin, Sydney.

Davies, M., 2017, *Law Unlimited: Materialism, Pluralism and Legal Theory*, Routledge, London.

Della Mirandola, G. P., 2013, 'Oration on the Dignity of Man', in F. Borghesi, M. Papio & M. Riva (eds), *Pico della Mirandola: Oration on the Dignity of Man: A New Translation and Commentary*, Cambridge University Press, Cambridge.

Dorsett, S. & McVeigh, S., 2002, 'Just So: The Law which Governs Australia is Australian Law', *Law & Critique* 13(3), 289–309.

Dorsett, S. & McVeigh, S., 2012, *Jurisdiction*, Routledge, London.

Drakopoulou, M., 2014, 'Samuel Pufendorf, Feminism and the Question of "Women and Law"', in M. Drakopoulou (ed.) *Feminist Encounters with Legal Philosophy*, pp. 66–91, Routledge-Cavendish, Abingdon, Oxon.

Du Gay, P., 2008, 'Max Weber and the Moral Economy of Office', *Journal of Cultural Economy* 1(2), 129–144.

Dugan, J., 2005, *Making a New Man: Ciceronian Self-fashioning in the Rhetorical Works*, Oxford University Press, Oxford.

Esposito, R., 2009, *Communitas: The Origin and Destiny of Communities*, Stanford University Press, Palo Alto, CA.

Gaita, R., 1998, *Romulus, My Father*. Text Publishing, Melbourne.

Gaita, R., 2000, *Common Humanity: Thinking about Love and Humanity*, Text Publishing, Melbourne.

Gaita, R., 2002, *The Philosopher's Dog*, Text Publishing, Melbourne.

Gaita, R., 2004, *Good and Evil: An Absolute Conception*, Routledge, London.

Gaita, R., 2010, *After Romulus*, Text Publishing, Melbourne.

Gaita, R., 2012, 'To Civilise the City?' *Meanjin* 71(1), 1–17.

Gaita, R., 2017a, 'Morality Law and Politics', in R. Gaita & G. Simpson (eds) *Who's Afraid of International Law?* pp. vii–xxxiii, Monash University Press, Melbourne.

Gaita, R., 2017b, 'The Universality of International Criminal Law and the Idea of a Common Humanity', in R. Gaita & G. Simpson (eds) *Who's Afraid of International Law?* pp. 169–190, Monash University Press, Melbourne.

Genovese, A., 2014, 'On Australian Feminist Tradition: Three Notes on Conduct, Inheritance and the Relations of Historiography and Jurisprudence', *Journal of Australian Feminist Studies* 38(4), 430–444.

Genovese, A., 2015, 'On the Liberal Promise: A Conversation', *Australian Feminist Law Journal* 41(1), 1–18.

Genovese, A. & McVeigh, S., 2015, 'Nineteen Eighty Three: A Jurisographic Report on Commonwealth v Tasmania', *Griffith Law Review* 24(1), 68–88.

Goodrich, P., 1984, 'Rhetoric as Jurisprudence: An Introduction to the Politics of Legal Language', *Oxford Journal of Legal Studies* 4(1), 88–132.

Goodrich, P., 2000, 'Law Induced Anxiety: Legists, Anti-lawyers and the Boredom of Legality', *Social and Legal Studies* 9(1), 143–163.

Goodrich, P., 2015, *Legal Emblems and the Art of Law: Obiter Depicta as the Vision of Governance*, Cambridge University Press, Cambridge.

Goodrich, P., 2017, 'Who Are We?: Persona, Office, Suspicion, and Critique' in J. Desautels-Stein & C. Tomlins (eds), *Searching for Contemporary Legal Thought*, pp. 43–60, Cambridge University Press, Cambridge.

Green, J. M., 1975, 'Montaigne's Critique of Cicero', *Journal of the History of Ideas* 36(4), 595–612.

Guerin, C., 2006, 'Cicero as User and Critic of Traditional Rhetorical Patterns: Structural Authority from *De Inuentione* to *De Oratore*', in C. Galewicz (ed.), *Texts of Power, the Power of Text: Readings in Textual Authority across History and Cultures*, pp. 61–85, Wydawnictwo Homini, Kracow.

Guerin, C., 2009, 'Philosophical Decorum and the Literarization of Rhetoric in Cicero's Orator', in F. Woerther (ed.), *Literary and Philosophical Rhetoric in the Greek, Roman, Syriac and Arabic World*, pp. 119–139, Georg Olms Verlag, Hildesheim.

Hadot, P., 1995, *Philosophy as a Way of Life: Spiritual Exercises from Socrates to Foucault*, Blackwell Publishing, Oxford.

Haldar, P., 2016, 'Equity as a Question of Decorum and Manners: Conscience as Vision', *Pólemos* 10(2), 311–327.

Hennis, W., 2000, *Max Weber's Central Question*, trans. K. Tribe, Threshold Press, Newbury.

Hunter, I., 2001, *Rival Enlightenments: Civil and Metaphysical Philosophy in Early Modern Germany*, Cambridge University Press, Cambridge.

Hunter, I., 2013, 'English Blasphemy', *Humanity: An International Journal of Human Rights, Humanitarianism, and Development* 4(3), 403–428.

Hunter, I., 2014, 'The Mythos, Ethos, and Pathos of the Humanities', *The History of European Ideas* 40(1), 11–36.

Kristeller, P. O., 1979, *Renaissance Thought and Its Sources*, ed. M. Mooney, Columbia University Press, New York.

McMillan, M., 2014, 'Koowarta and the Rival Indigenous International: Our Place as Indigenous Peoples in the International', *Griffith Law Review* 23(1), 110–126.

Minkkinen, P., 2010, 'The Legal Academic of Max Weber's Tragic Modernity', *Social & Legal Studies* 19(2), 165–182.

Minson, J., 1993, *Questions of Conduct: Sexual Harassment, Citizenship, Government*, Macmillan, Basingstoke.

Minson, J., 2006, 'Civil Prudence, Sovereignty and Citizenship in the Justification of Civil Forfeiture', *University of New South Wales Law Journal* 29(3), 61–89.

Minson, J., 2009, 'S. Toussaint, Humanismes Antihumanismes, Paris, Les Belles Lettres, 2008', *Cromohs* 14, 1–19.

Minson, J., 2010, 'The Sense of Existing and its Political Implications (On Francois Flahault's General Anthropology)', in A. Yeatman & M. Zolkos (eds), *State Security and Subject Formation*, pp. 157–171, Bloomsbury, London.

Minson, J., 2014, 'How to Speak Well of the State: A Rhetoric of Civil Prudence', *UC Irvine Law Review* 4, 437–470.

Montaigne, M.de, 1957, *The Complete Works: Essays, Travel Journal, Letters*, Everyman, London.

Murphy, T., 1997, *The Oldest Social Science? Configurations of Law and Modernity*, Oxford University Press, Oxford.

Owen, D., 1997, *Maturity and Enlightenment: Nietzsche, Weber, Foucault and the Ambivalence of Reason*, Routledge, London.

Owen, D. & Strong, T., 2004, 'Introduction: Max Weber's Calling to Knowledge and Action', in D. Owen & T. Strong (eds.) *Max Weber: The Vocation Lectures*, pp. ix–lxii, Hackett Publishing Company, Indianapolis, IN.

Pocock, J. G. A., 2011, 'Historiography as a Form of Political Thought', *History of European Ideas* 37(1), 1–6.

Pue, W., 2016, *Lawyers' Empire: Legal Professions and Cultural Authority, 1780–1950*, UBC Press, Vancouver.

Pufendorf, S., 1991, *On the Duty of Man and Citizen According to Natural Law*, ed. J. Tully, Cambridge University Press, Cambridge.
Rush, P., 1997, 'Deathbound Legal Doctrine: Scenes of Murder and its Inheritance', *Studies in Law Politics and Society* 16, 71–99.
Saunders, D., 1997, *Anti-Lawyers: Religion and the Critics of Law and State*, Routledge, London.
Sellars, J., 2013, *The Art of Living: The Stoics on the Nature and Function of Philosophy*, 2nd edn, Bloomsbury, London.
Skinner, Q., 1996, 'Techniques of Re-description', in Q. Skinner, *Reason and Rhetoric in the Philosophy of Hobbes*, pp. 138–180, Cambridge University Press, Cambridge.
Thornton, M., 2012, *Privatising the Public University: The Case of Law*, Routledge, London.
Weber, M., 2004, *Max Weber: The Vocation Lectures*, ed. D. Owen & T. Strong, Hackett Publishing Company, Indianapolis, IN.

Case

Mabo v Queensland (No 2) (1992) 175 CLR 1

12 Academic freedom academic obligation

Carrol Clarkson

My first dilemma when it came to writing up this chapter for publication was how to punctuate the title. I first settled on 'Academic freedom: academic obligation', with the colon doing the work of an explanation, making the point that it *is* an academic obligation to ensure academic freedom. But can we take it as a given that academic freedom is an obligation? This seems to assume too much too quickly, and it whistles past further challenging questions: if academic freedom is an obligation, whose obligation would it be? What form would it take? Who is obliged, and to whom would the obligation be owed? Would it be legally binding? I decided against the colon, as the complexity of the issue didn't seem to fit neatly with the explanatory logic that the colon promises. Next I considered a colon and a question mark: 'Academic freedom: academic obligation?' But despite its rather busy punctuation, this title seems to reduce the problem to just one question: *is* academic freedom an academic obligation? My chapter seeks to address a broader field of enquiry and is not focused on this question alone. I decided against the combination of colon and question mark and considered the slash: 'Academic freedom/academic obligation'. On the authority of the grammarians, the slash transmits impressively heterogeneous semantic valencies: it can mean '*per*' as in, '50 km/h'; it can mean 'and' as in 'the language/literature major'; it can mean 'either/or,' as in 'each student must present his/her identity card'; and it can *also* be used to represent, as the online *Punctuation Guide* rather ambiguously tells us, 'a conflict or connection between two things', as in 'the nature/nurture debate'.[1] With its meanings of 'either/or', 'and' and 'conflict or connection', the slash seems to capture nicely the complexities of the relationship between academic freedom and academic obligation. But in the end I decided against the slash too, because (linguistic expertise set aside) for the ordinary reader the default understanding of the slash in 'Academic freedom/academic obligation' is 'either/or'. The risk with this punctuation is that the reader may not pause long enough to register the further intricacies of the relationship between the two phrases, and it is the hesitation in thought that I am after, right up front. In the end, I decided not to punctuate the title at all: 'Academic freedom academic obligation'. This makes

1 My discussion about the slash is closely based on text and examples given in the online *Punctuation Guide*, www.thepunctuationguide.com.

the reader wonder: is something missing? What, if any, *is* the connection between academic freedom and academic obligation? What do these two terms refer to in the first place? These are my leading lines of enquiry.

But where to begin – especially in relation to the overarching question of this volume as a whole, the question of legal obligation? In the course of this chapter I refer briefly to the student protests of 2015 at the University of Amsterdam (UvA), but the main focus of my discussion is on higher education in South Africa, and, even more specifically, on recent events and some strands of debate at the University of Cape Town (UCT). My discussion is at once structured and thrown into question by my responses to two recently published books: John Higgins's *Academic Freedom in a Democratic South Africa* (2013) and Jonathan Jansen's *As by Fire: The End of the South African University* (2017).[2] I say 'thrown into question' because Jansen's book and the events at UCT in the last few weeks of 2017 have radically shaken any easy assumptions that academic freedom is readily supported as a good by students and academics across the board.

Ongoing protest action at universities in South Africa since the publication of John Higgins's book has been impassioned and forceful. The protests started in March 2015, and at the risk of oversimplification, the mainspring of the protests has been a call for free, decolonial education. At least one impetus for ongoing protests is the contention that academic institutions are failing in their obligations to students; the extent and nature of these obligations is one of the preoccupations in the discussion to follow, especially in relation to Jansen's book, which offers detailed accounts of the protests in South Africa in 2015 and 2016, from the perspective of a vice-chancellor walking the tightrope between student demands and government expectations and constraints.

Varying student demands are foregrounded in protests at different universities, and a trigger for renewed activism is often the university management's decision to deploy private security companies and the police to curtail acts of vandalism and intimidation and other forms of illegal protest action. As I write this in the final weeks of the academic year in 2017, on-campus lectures and tests at the University of Cape Town have been suspended due to concerns for the safety of students and staff, following protest action on 24 and 25 October, when lectures and a final-year accounting exam were disrupted by protesters breaking into the venue and setting off fire alarms and fire extinguishers.[3]

2 Jonathan Jansen is former Vice-Chancellor of the University of the Free State, a respected author, political commentator and educationist in South Africa, known for his commitment to transformation and reconciliation.

3 Other arrangements for on-campus tests and lectures were made; UCT applied to the Western Cape High Court for an interdict against illegal protest action, and an interim interdict was granted with immediate effect on 30 October. Classes resumed on 1 November, but acts of intimidation and vandalism (tyres of the university shuttle bus were slashed, human excrement was thrown into three university buildings, including the Computer Science building), and further disruption of university activities on 2 November led to the deployment of private security and the police. Police used stun grenades to disperse the crowd. A test on 3 November had to be cancelled: protesters set off fire crackers and threw bricks at the test venue, smashing several windows. On

My chapter takes as its conceptual substrate the fact that academic freedom is listed as a right in the constitution of South Africa; it goes on to broach questions about the reach of 'academic obligation' – and the conversation plays out very differently in relation to the books by Higgins and Jansen respectively. For reasons that will become clear, I am writing the main section of this chapter in the form of an email addressed to John Higgins, a colleague in the English Department at the University of Cape Town.[4]

Carrol Clarkson xxxx@gmail.com

To John

Dear John,

I am taking the liberty of writing the main section of my chapter, 'Academic freedom academic obligation', in the form of an email addressed to you. Clearly this is a risk (more of which later) – but this experiment helps me to think through at least some of what is at stake in the question of academic freedom as you outline it in your book. Between the publication of your book (*Academic Freedom in a Democratic South Africa*, 2013) and the publication of Jonathan Jansen's book (2017), much has happened on university campuses in South Africa – and your recent work engages with some of these events. I'm thinking specifically of your yet to be published guest lecture, 'The Protest Manifesto', which you presented at the University of Amsterdam on the 23rd of November, 2016. Since the publication of your book, the question of academic freedom and the problem of the relation between academic freedom and academic obligation have taken on a different cast in debates in South Africa. But before turning to these, and to specific lines of discussion raised by Jonathan Jansen's book, I want to reflect on the implications of writing this chapter in the form of an email to you.

Monday 6 November a test in the Sports Centre was suspended due to disruptions; the residence dining rooms were forced to close. Another campus update reads: 'A group of around 30 protesters has forced people out of a computer lab in the Menzies building.' Lectures for the academic year have now reached the finish line, but not without further protest action: the attempted burning of a vehicle on campus (7 November); Fire alarms were set off in Graca Machel residence, which was also flooded in some places when taps were left running (8 November); protesters threw two petrol bombs (9 November).The final examinations have yet to be written. University management has decided to erect a designated exam venue on the rugby fields, given failed attempts to secure other test and exam venues on campus in the past few weeks.

4 This chapter is based on a book review that I wrote on John Higgins's book, published in *Arts and Humanities in Higher Education* 15(2) (2016), 187–93. Thank you to the reviews editor, Peter Vale, and to SAGE publishers, for copyright permissions. The decision to write an email to John Higgins takes its inspiration from Derrida's Afterword in *Limited Inc*, which begins like this: 'Dear Gerald Graff, Allow me to answer you in the form of a letter' (Derrida, p. 111). Unless otherwise specified, parenthetical page references are to John Higgins's book.

Choosing to write the main section of a book chapter as a letter (rather than as a formal academic essay) shifts the ground of this address – its context and destination, as Derrida would put it – enabling me to say, and to ask, different things. At the same time, I'm mindful of Derrida's notion of ***destinerrance***: that is to say, the destiny of this utterance, but also its wandering, its errancy, and writing this as an 'open email' yields further complexities. In your book you speak about 'occasioned writing: academic writing addressed to a public moment in a deliberately reflexive manner.' Its 'central task', you go on to explain, is to 'try to disturb the easy flow and circulation of ideas' (p. 2). This is what I'm after in my message to you – disturbing the processing of received ideas by shifting the conventional academic ground. At the time of writing this email to you from Amsterdam, lectures and on-campus classes have reached the end of the year at the University of Cape Town – but not without acts of vandalism and arson on campus, and serious disruptions to lectures, tests, and catering services in the residences. The final-year exams at UCT have yet to be written, and we are still waiting to hear the government's formal response to the Fees Commission Report – which, in turn, has been leaked, but has not officially been made public. The Heher Fees Commission Report argues that fee-free higher education at this time is not possible in South Africa, but apparently President Jacob Zuma wants to overturn this, and on the recommendation of his future son-in-law, Morris Masutha, rumour has it that Zuma may announce fee-free education after all.[5]

All of which brings me back to the precariousness of higher education in South Africa, the uncertainties of academic freedoms and academic obligation – and my decision to write in the form of an email, with the explicit acknowledgement of its provisionality, and the real risk of being proved wrong on certain points at a later date (by way of example: a few days ago when I wrote the previous paragraph of this email, Masutho – who put forward a proposal for fee-free education – was Jacob Zuma's 'future son-in-law'; in this morning's papers he is the 'ex-boyfriend' of Zuma's daughter, which makes me wonder whether Zuma really will announce fee-free education). By the time of the publication of this book in which my email to you will be printed, what is now the uncertain future will have become history, one way or another.

Doubtless I'm supposed to be writing a formal academic essay that would count as a tangible, accredited 'Research Output'. I'll have to report my publication to the University Research Management, specifying what type of publication it is, proving that my submission has been peer-reviewed; that it meets criteria set by ASCA (the Amsterdam School for Cultural Analysis), the NWO (Nederlandse Organisatie voor Wetenschappelijk Onderzoek – the Dutch National Research Foundation), the URC (University Research Council at UCT) and the NRF (the National Research Foundation in South Africa). Based as I am at the University of Amsterdam, with a research affiliation at the University of Cape Town, my research is reported to both institutions.

5 See: https://mg.co.za/article/2017-11-10-00-grant-cuts-to-fund-fee-free-tuition (accessed 22 January 2018)

Doubtless you'll have similar accounts to give: my references to your work in a creditable academic publication would constitute a citation – and, in turn, some quotable measure of the 'impact' of the 'output' that is your book. But an email? Will this *count* for anything, for either of us, in those institutional assessments and evaluations and calculations?

And yet the mere fact that these considerations surface at all in my response to the ideas in your book begins to *play out* the threats to our freedom of engaging critically and energetically with each other *at the level of ideas.* Increasingly (I notice this in younger friends and colleagues, in Europe and the UK especially, many of whom do not yet have tenured positions), the kinds of research we carry out, and the ways in which we feel obliged to construct research projects and annual research reports, are in the thrall of 'grant capture': what kind of enquiry or research project has a better chance of generating funding? How should we change our own research questions to ensure that we have funding to cover them? These thoughts play into the 'obduracy' that you identify at the heart of higher education policy: its 'reduction of a multidimensional reality to a single dimension of economic calculation' (p. 166). And this is the danger: as you remind us in your discussion of Conrad Russell's troubled response to the Thatcher government's 1988 Education Reform Bill, 'no society (and certainly no state bureaucracy)' can predict in advance what research will turn out to be helpful: countless inventions are the result of accident, rather than of design. You speculate that 'a philosophical loser, who had written nothing for several years and couldn't even formulate quite what problem to explore' would surely be unsuccessful in his efforts to capture South African National Research Funding. 'In this case', you go on to say, with reference to Conrad Russell's report, 'we might never have had Bertrand Russell's *Principia Mathematica* a work said to have made possible the "development of the digital computer" not that that was what Russell *père* had in mind' (p. 65).

An email surely won't *count* as a research output (and even worse: you'll notice I'm sending this one from a Gmail address, rather than a university address). Would it help if I changed the address I sent it from? To send it from a university address would have the effect of activating the disclaimer notice of the institution at the bottom of my message. And here is a strange logic: you have to send a message *from* an institutional address in order for the institution to disclaim it! At the same time, emails sent from a university address, relating to university business, are the property of that institution. Here is the opening sentence of UCT's disclaimer notice:

> All emails sent by UCT are the property of the University of Cape Town where related to the business of the University and, where not, of the sender.

And yet the notice goes on to say:

> The views and opinions expressed in any email do not necessarily represent the views of the University of Cape Town.

This rather strange tension between various stipulations of the disclaimer notice (of ownership and disownership; of what is representative and what is individual) puts me in mind of one of the most helpful insights of your book. You remind us that the South African Constitution includes the right to academic freedom as an essential feature of democracy (p. 256), but, at the same time, the way in which academic freedom is framed in the Constitution – as an ***individual*** right – makes it impossible to protect it ***at an institutional level.*** The Council of Higher Education report of 2008 says that Academic Freedom is 'everyone's right', which, you reflect, might be so 'in some ideal and utopian sense, perhaps' (p. 256). Nevertheless:

> The problem is that in focusing on academic freedom as an individual's right, the Constitution effectively marginalises – or perhaps even puts out of the picture altogether – the complex institutional setting in which alone the practice of academic freedom makes sense. For any right to academic freedom must in reality depend upon how far the institutions in which it is practised observe their constitutive duty to enable it and make it possible.
>
> (p. 256)

Academic freedom is thus not reducible to an individual's right to freedom of expression. Yet further, when the institution itself subscribes to national ideologies and policies and economies, supporting certain kinds of research at the expense of others, then our own academic freedom is at risk. J. M. Coetzee, in his foreword to *Academic Freedom*, agrees with the central tenor of your book, yet presses you further:

> You will have to say: we need free enquiry because freedom of thought is good in itself. We need institutions where teachers and students can pursue unconstrained the life of the mind because such institutions are, in ways that are difficult to pin down, good for all of us: good for the individual and good for society.
>
> (p. xiv)

After reading your book, though, I've been disturbed by the question of what freedom of thought 'in itself' really means, and have come to be more attentive to the inexorable impact of the material conditions, the forces of production, which at once enable and constrain expression of thought – and even before this – one's line of enquiry. I'm reminded of Bakhtin here: 'The speaker is not Adam' (1986, p. 94): no person is the first speaker to disturb the 'eternal silence of the universe' (ibid., p. 69), and 'The utterance is addressed not only to its own object but also to others' speech about it' (ibid., p. 94).

Yet to speak in this way is to think of 'Academic Freedom' from the perspective of the 'teachers and students' as if they share, unproblematically, the same idea of what the freedoms of 'the life of the mind' might be; it puts the obligation to protect that freedom on the shoulders of university management. We could continue this line of discussion about (the breach of) academic freedom with reference to the invitation to Flemming Rose (the cultural editor of the Danish magazine *Jyllands-Posten*, which published cartoons of Muhammed in 2005) to deliver the annual TB Davie Memorial Lecture at UCT in 2016 – and senior management's subsequent decision to rescind the invitation. And yet already the heated debates around this (non)event highlight some of the complexities of the question, with different constituencies within the university holding conflicting views about the remit and even the value of academic freedom. And this complexity can be tracked back to the reasons for the protests in the first place too. If the protests gained momentum in 2015 with the rallying call for the statue of Cecil John Rhodes to be removed from the UCT campus, and the concomitant call for free, decolonial education, the list of demands continues to shift and expand, with different inflections as events unfold across different campuses and across different sectors of the higher education landscape in South Africa. But for Jonathan Jansen, if the appeal for a decolonised curriculum is on the one hand a 'useful wake-up call to accelerate the transformation of universities', on the other hand it is 'fundamentally misguided' (2017, p. 171). He advocates instead 'the active engagement with entangled knowledges', an approach which 'recognizes the extent to which rival knowledges are tied up in "entangled bodies" – living human beings who are globally interconnected and highly interdependent' (ibid.). 'Entangled' is surely one way of appreciating elements of the causes for protest, which are sometimes aggregated as one appeal for free decolonial education for all students, but sometimes realigned in more explicitly disaggregated political terms.

Academic freedom has become one of the values associated with 'white settler modernity' and at UCT the term itself has also become a target of protest. Lwazi Lushaba, who spoke at the Assembly for free education at UCT on 1 November 2017, puts it this way: 'The problem for free education is a problem for black people. It is not a problem for white people ... the struggle is not for poor people.' The task, in Lushaba's terms, is to confront the history of colonialism and 'defeat a certain structure of white settler modernity'; the struggle for free education 'is not about money', Lushaba goes on to say, but about institutional racism, where the values of a settler society are played out through the machinery of Western-style higher education at the expense of indigenous knowledge, and those who hold that knowledge. One of these 'settler' values – presented as a universal value – is that of academic freedom. The speaker immediately after Lushaba at the Assembly goes on to say: 'We call on all students ... to join us in opposition against powers that seek our exclusion at this institution under the guise of some academic freedom.' Academic freedom is put forward as an 'instrument for racism and justification for the exclusion of black students.' (UCT Assembly, 2017). The speaker is referring to the list of demands presented by the Student Representative Council to the University Executive on 24 October 2017. In the SRC's 'List of Demands', under the subheading, 'Consequences for Problematic Lecturers', one of the statements reads: 'Academic Freedom must be revisited because lecturers are abusing this right to not engage in the process of decolonisation.' In the University Executive's (2017) formal response to the SRC, these particular 'demands' are not addressed or even mentioned at all, but the Academic Union (2017) issued a statement, expressing its concern:

> [T]he AU takes issue with the SRC's accusations of abuse of academic freedom. While we may hold different views on the content and limits of academic freedom, this is a core feature of our members' working conditions at UCT and forms part of the right to freedom of expression protected under South Africa's Constitution. Challenges to the limits of the application of this principle in specific cases should be raised through designated channels, according to due process.

What emerges is that the term 'academic freedom' is being valorised in very different ways – and perhaps even contradictory ways – across different sectors of the university community. It's too much to assume that all students and staff are participating in a shared intellectual project: the question of 'academic freedom' has become more politically fraught since the publication of your book, John.

And so too has the question of academic obligation. I think it's fair to say that in your book (as it is in the Academic Union statement) the institution is obliged – in the sense of legally bound – to protect the freedom of expression of its staff and students. But the student protests have foregrounded the expectation of an entirely different kind of academic obligation, and this is evident in the ever increasing and shifting demands submitted to the University Executive. In his chapter, 'Shackville and the Rise of the Welfare University', Jansen documents the emergence of a change in the mode of protest in recent years, a change

> made visible through a ubiquitous culture of routinely and forcefully presenting university leaders with demands for services related to students' material, social, and financial well-being. In brief, the protestors were acting on their belief that the university, as a state-run institution, was *obligated* to undertake student welfare support measures. If it did not do so, protest was the logical response.
>
> (Jansen 2017, p. 172, emphasis added)

In his extended discussion of the larger social obligations students have come to expect of academic institutions, Jansen focuses on the problem of student accommodation at UCT – which provided the trigger for the 'Shackville' protests of 15–16 February 2016 (Furlong 2016). The irony is surely not lost on you that amongst the 24 'colonial' artworks taken down from the Fuller residence and other university buildings, and then thrown on to the bonfire, is the 1993 painting by Keresemose Richard Baholo, depicting student protests, and titled *Extinguished Torch of Academic Freedom*.

Jansen traces conflicting ideas of what a university is about. For the protesters, Jansen argues (with reference to Charles van Onselen's work), the university's welfare obligations have come to take precedence over those of education, 'to the detriment of both' (Jansen 2017, p. 172, 185).

To come back to the decision to write an email (which feels more and more like a non-issue in the context of bigger problems in higher education in South Africa right now!): you will already have picked up that what I've said so far is, at best, provisional, cryptic, sketchy. It's open to discussion; points need to be followed through, revised, refined, perhaps scrapped altogether – not least since the sands of higher education in South Africa are shifting as we speak. But the mere fact of having you as my interlocutor has precipitated me toward thought – and so the genre of an email message, with its 'not-quite-sure-where-this-is-going' when I set out, and its inherent anticipation of response, challenge, question, objection, refutation ... all of this is risky in a philosophical sense too. It facilitates a certain freedom of expression and opens up the possibility of intellectual *experiment* not usually offered by a formal academic paper. For me it's an invaluable mode of sounding ideas out, and it's when I'm writing emails that I'm most clearly reminded of what Derrida has to say about writing:

> It is because writing is *inaugural*, in the fresh sense of the word, that it is dangerous and anguishing. It does not know where it is going, no knowledge can keep it from the essential precipitation toward the meaning that it constitutes and that is, primarily, its future.
>
> (Derrida 1978, p. 11)

This brings me to another core argument in your book:

> *Academic Freedom in a Democratic South Africa* maintains that in these current debates around the social functions of the university, it is essential not to lose sight of or marginalise the teaching of the humanities ... This is the book's central and defining idea – that the core skills of humanist education (often referred to here as the skills of a 'critical literacy' ...) have much to contribute to the public good in ways which are being denied, or simply made invisible, by the terms currently dominating higher education policy.
>
> (p. 5)

Part of your argument for the value of critical literacy entails the recognition that even national economies are grounded in complex social orders, and the better we can understand these social contexts, the greater chance we have of creating a more just society. You make a compelling case for a return to the NAIL disciplines (Narrative, Analysis, Interpretation and Literacy) in a climate where the STEM disciplines (Science, Technology, Engineering, Mathematics) have taken precedence. In your interview with Edward Said, critical literacy is one focused topic of discussion – and your conversations with Said and with Jakes Gerwel have been helpful to me in a practical way here at the University of Amsterdam, where academic protests (which started in February 2015) are having a noticeable effect on an institution founded in 1632. 'Whatever I've done politically' (says Said),

> has been *entirely* dependent on the ability to read critically, to be able to understand the uses to which language can be put. And here I mean to refer to the truly vast range of possibilities that language has. I think the only place you can get a sense of this range, and a feeling for these possibilities, is through the study of literature … Writing is not only about describing the world, and writing about it realistically, and reporting it, in the way that someone like Daniel Defoe wanted to do. It's also about really pushing at the limits of perception and articulation in such a way as to mobilise and marshal the critical faculties to an extreme degree. And if you lose that pressure in writing, you lose everything.
>
> (p. 214)

I'd like to link Said's response here to your conversation with Jakes Gerwel, where you refer to Karl Marx's Thesis 11 on Feuerbach: 'The philosophers have only interpreted the world, in various ways; the point is to change it' (Marx 2000, p. 173). If critical literacy enables me to use writing to 'push at the limits of perception and articulation', then the discipline in which I am trained activates the dynamic relation between 'interpretation' and 'change', and this, in turn, becomes the site of exercising my academic freedom. How does this play out, in practical terms?

Coetzee, in his foreword to your book, writes that he fails to share your optimism that the tide of corporate managerialism in the University can be turned – but in the last few years in Amsterdam, we have had a tantalising glimpse that change may well be afoot. After a two-week occupation of the Humanities Building at UvA in February 2015, students and academic staff backing the protest occupied the Maagdenhuis – the University's Senate building – converting the large central foyer into a space for public lectures and debate. Visitors and speakers at the Maagdenhuis have included Jacques Rancière; representatives from the Dutch Trade Unions; the Mayor of Amsterdam; the Dutch Minister of Education; Mieke Bal and several other Professors at the University of Amsterdam … The protest, under the name, *Rethink UvA*, organised working groups to rethink the institution, and in a letter dated 4 March 2015, submitted a list of six demands to the University's central governing body. The letter begins:

> At present, ever more decisions are taken at the UvA by managers who are removed from the concerns and needs of students and staff, and do not answer to them for those decisions. Without assuming there is one template that fits each and every program, department, institute, or faculty, we call for the democratization and decentralization of the UvA's governance structure, in order to allow the academic community to govern itself honestly and responsibly.
>
> (Geltner & Vaessens 2015)[6]

6 The full letter, and further material, can be found on the RethinkUvA website: http://rethinkuva.org. (accessed 22 January 2018).

In the discussion after his lecture, Jacques Rancière was asked what he thought the greatest threat to the momentum of the protest action would be. He replied: 'Exhaustion!' It's true that the protests here have stretched many beyond reasonable limits, but it's surely fair to say that the protests in Amsterdam (and in very different ways, those in Cape Town) amount to more than the 'intermittent satirical barb against managerial newspeak' that Coetzee speaks about in his foreword to your book. See, for example, the essay, 'On winner-takes-all academia' on the RethinkUvA website, dated 13 May 2015, written by Guy Geltner and Thomas Vaessens. Guy Geltner is Professor of Medieval History; Thomas Vaessens is Professor in the Dutch Department, and Director of Research in the Humanities Faculty at UvA. The essay offers an incisive analysis of the ways in which Dutch National Research Funding (the NWO) fails in its support of Humanities Research. It's refreshing to see the Director of Humanities Research expressing frustration at the existing funding system, and proposing ways in which national research funding structures should be changed – rather than coercing colleagues and fellow researchers into wasting our time writing external research grant proposals that have hardly any chance of success.

Coetzee is sadly right in his recognition that academics are 'perforce having to acquire' a managerial newspeak, and Said makes a related point in his interview with you: 'you have to try and use the same language – for ease of communication – to express alternative thoughts and dissenting ideas. I think that's the main struggle now' (pp. 214–5). I'm sorry to say that the language I'm perforce having to acquire here is the language of the Excel spreadsheet! Dutch was my mother's home language, but in my conversations with the Administrators (a *formidable* force at the University of Amsterdam), Excel speaks more loudly than Dutch. Again your book has helped me in a practical way: with reference to Bakhtin, you make a distinction between 'statement' and 'address', and speak about the dynamics of the relation between them. 'In the real world' (you write) 'statements have a better chance of survival when they take into account the background of assumptions and received ideas that they must either confirm, or necessarily work to displace, in order to create a space to be heard' (p. 145). In filling out my Excel spreadsheets – the division of teaching workloads, annual evaluation reports – I think of my task as an act of address, rather than as a static retrospective report or statement. So I make the Excel sheets *speak*: I make it possible for Management to read off the Excel sheet the inexorability of changing a contract appointment into a permanent post; or to see the absolute numerical necessity of promoting one of my colleagues; or of recruiting a new staff member to teach Early Modern Literature, or Nineteenth-Century Literature, or World Literatures, as the case may be.

I would rather be reading a great work of literature, and writing my next book. My hope is that the time of Excel-speak is an interim phase, which will ultimately generate a congenial academic context in which I can explore the materialisation of thought in those interstitial zones between language and the visual arts; literature and philosophy – and in a freer and more creative way than sometimes seems possible now. Like the narrator of *Zen and the Art of Motorcycle Maintenance*, I sometimes find myself torn between two courses of action: one to save my skin, the other to save my soul. In the meantime your book helps me to understand better the value of critical literacy in any social order, and to appreciate more keenly the ways in which it can be activated in the pursuit of academic freedom. Jonathan Jansen's book, with its subtitle *The End of the South African University* offers a chilling account of how difficult and short-lived this pursuit could be.

All my best to you,
Carrol

Carrol Clarkson xxxx@gmail.com

To Daniel and Scott

Dear Daniel and Scott,

Thank you for your email, with your generous and constructive comments about my submission for your book. I'm entirely in agreement with your editorial suggestion that a short postscript would benefit the chapter, and (as you helpfully put it) draw the reader back to the challenge of the relation between academic freedom and academic obligation that I establish at the start. Thanks for reminding me about the word 'community' in the book's title: within the context of an impassioned identity politics at the University of Cape Town, the question of whose obligation and which community becomes salient.

When you first sent your email to me with your editorial suggestions, I was taken with the clarity and specificity of your request, and immediately copied and pasted your message into a new 'section yet to come' of my chapter. It was only after the act that I appreciated the significance of what I'd just done within the context of the elaborate email experiment undertaken in the chapter. After testing the style of a straightforward 'framing' final section, to match the introduction, I decided instead to be true to the *process* of writing this paper and hence the present section is styled as this email to you, the editors. The protests and their consequences are still playing out in higher education in South Africa, and the broader implications for obligation and community are still too uncertain to 'wrap up' or to 'reach conclusions' about: another reason for choosing to write an email rather than a conventional concluding section. All of this has led me to reflect on the distances (temporal, spatial, affective) that academic papers with their ratiocinative thinking seem to entail, and that my chosen topic for this essay frustrates.

Returning specifically to the question of the relation between academic freedom and academic obligation, let me reiterate an observation I made in my email to John Higgins: namely, that in the context of the student protests in South Africa the role and value of 'academic freedom' – and even the definition of the term itself – are deeply contested. The contested relation between 'academic freedom' and 'decolonization' again comes to the fore in Mahmood Mamdani's Academic Freedom lecture delivered at UCT in 2017 (Mamdani 2017), especially when it is viewed alongside an article that David Benatar (Head of Philosophy at UCT) wrote in response to it (Benatar 2017). As I indicated in my email to John, 'decolonisation' and 'academic freedom' have been presented as mutually exclusive terms, but at the same time they have become inextricably entangled in a broader identity politics. With regard to identity politics, David Benatar and William Gild (amongst others) have been outspoken about campus experiences in ways that are rather different from mainstream media reporting on the protests.[7]

And this brings me back to questions of obligation and community. I touched on the question of allegiances to different expectations and stakes concerning the university when I referred to Jonathan Jansen's identification of 'the rise of the welfare university' in my email to John. These divergent interests about the role and the success of a university are brought into stark relief when it comes to the issue of worldwide university rankings. In 2010 (five years before the 'Rhodes Must Fall' protests started), the University of Cape Town jumped up 39 places to number 107 on the *Times Higher Education* (*THE*) world university ranking list. Junita Kloppers-Lourens, the Democratic Alliance shadow minister for education at the time, writes: 'This kind of commitment to outstanding teaching and research offers a model for higher education in Africa' (Kloppers-Lourens 2010). But in the same breath she registers the dissenting voice of the Minister of Higher Education at the time, Blade Nzimande (Nzimande was still Minister when the protests broke out in 2015, but was fired from his position by Jacob Zuma on 17 October 2017). Lourens-Kloppers notes that Nzimande 'scoffed at such international rankings, claiming they were "biased" in favour of "well-resourced" institutions that were "English" based and "Westernised"'. In the same article, Lourens-Kloppers goes on to say,

> Minister Nzimande has shown no interest in raising the standards and outcomes of our universities. Indeed, it seems that they achieve what they do despite, not because of, government interventions. Imagine what our universities could achieve if they had a Minister backing them with vigor and dedication.
>
> (Kloppers-Lourens 2010)

By 2011, UCT would be placed at number 103 on the *THE* rankings; in 2018, UCT is positioned at number 171. With hindsight one would challenge the tone and the terms Kloppers-Lourens uses – terms which probably did not attract much attention at the time, but which, in their contestedness, are arguably at the core of current protest. The Rhodes Must Fall protests have led to probing questions about formulations such as 'a model for higher education in Africa'; the call for decolonised curricula is a reminder that a Western model is not a universal one, that 'standards and outcomes' are context-specific, and, especially in a time of transitional justice, the question of *which* context is brought to bear is a contested one.

7 See, for instance, www.politicsweb.co.za/opinion/ucts-climate-turns-toxic; www.politicsweb.co.za/opinion/ucts-troubles-continue (accessed 22 January 2018).

This is made clear in yet another recent turn of events: the Council for Higher Education in South Africa has notified UCT of its intention to withdraw accreditation for the LLB undergraduate degree, mainly because of graduation throughput rates, with special reference to race and gender equity. Withdrawal of accreditation means that UCT would no longer be able to offer the degree, even though it is ranked as the top law faculty in the country. It's worth mentioning that in its response to the report from the Council for Higher Education, UCT enlists the QS world ranking by subject as a reason for not withdrawing the accreditation ('Faculty of Law responds to the CHE report' 2017).[8]

Kloppers-Lourens raises the issue of 'government intervention' – and this too has become a complex matter in the protests: what are the respective roles, obligations, and capacities of government and of university management? Against whom should the protests be directed? As the demands of the protests shift, and the repercussions are felt by many different communities – students, parents, academic staff, support staff, university management, employee unions, sponsors, parliament, policy makers, politicians, private security companies, the police, the law… and many others – it is clear that questions of 'academic freedom' and 'academic obligation,' and the relation between them, are not restricted to just one community in an ivory tower.

Thank you, Daniel and Scott, for inviting me to contribute an essay to your collection.

With every best wish,

Carrol

Daniel Matthews and Scott Veitch xxxx@hku.hk

To Carrol

Dear Carrol,

In the spirit of your contribution to the book, we take the editorial liberty of offering some brief reflections on your chapter in the form of a closing email. In doing so we want to foreground some issues it raises and discuss them in relation to the dominant themes in this collection of essays. We hope it will become clear why we have decided to remain bound to the 'not-quite-sure-where-this-is-going' tenor and form of an email.

As you note, academic freedom is guaranteed by the South African Constitution as an *individual right*. With your interlocutor, John Higgins, you emphasise how this fact puts at risk the protection of its value at an institutional level. In short, it is the form that academic freedom takes *when institutionalised* in this manner of constitutional provision that raises concerns. As your chapter (and email) shows, the very notion of academic freedom cannot be understood apart from the

8 www.news.uct.ac.za/article/-2017-11-16-faculty-of-law-responds-to-che-report, accessed 22 January 2018.

complex institutional setting in which this freedom is claimed, disputed or deployed. This underscores the fact that academic freedom – which, whatever its definition, must include the ability to freely create, produce or give form to new knowledge – is primarily *relational* in that it can only be exercised in relation to others: to other texts, other thinkers and so forth. The notion of an individual right to academic freedom distorts this very nature by erasing the necessarily communal and institutional elements that are essential to its articulation.

This, it seems to us, is the value to be found in the shift, implicit in your email to John, from a thinking of academic freedom to that of academic obligation. To foreground the obligations that pertain to academic and scholarly life is to give precedence to a set of relations – to colleagues, students, classmates, institutions, bodies of work, conditions of employment, prevailing political and economic circumstances, and so on – without which academic freedom is meaningless. As should be clear, we see such obligations as not simply correlates to the right of academic freedom but as constituting a more nebulous set of bonds that give buoyance and mobility to such claims.

Something similar appears to animate your desire to experiment with the form of your chapter. You note, no doubt correctly, that this form of address would be treated as simply *not counting* as an academic contribution. The imagery of 'counting' is apposite. For it is, by contrast, the treatment of the orthodox academic essay as 'counting' for the various types of research assessment that you mention, which tends to distort those relational qualities that are at the foundation of academic life, emphasising instead an isolated, individual author to whom ascriptions of 'excellence' might be attributed. It is precisely such a form of abstraction – from how knowledge is acquired and produced – that allows individual pieces of work, and even individuals themselves, to be given a numerical score, and in turn counted up and aggregated in order to produce a quantifiable 'result' of excellence in a faculty and across the sector. The *form of community* this would produce, or have us believe in, is nothing more, or less, than that corresponding to the 'individual-aggregative' model on which it is based. Of course, it is not difficult to see in all this the rationalised symptoms of exchange value's hegemony: with its transfer leagues and ranking tables, its citation indexes and money-getting stars, its competitive winners and uncompetitive losers. These are what 'count' in the model of community it would offer, and its spread across the increasingly marketised systems of higher education globally would seem to confirm its virulence.

The email form reminds us of both the communal and informal nature of knowledge production; as we know, we often learn more in the coffee breaks or at dinner, or in an email exchange after the conference closes, than we do during formal lectures. A shift to the language of obligation and to the (informal) form of the email both highlight the situated, relational, affective and lived reality of academic life, and allow us to approach the duties and responsibilities that this *modus vivendi* entails. In such forms of life, in such irreducibly *shared* practices, the virtues of academic integrity and curiosity may yet be sustained, but only because in them the invented objectivities and false securities of the numbers games hold no sway.

In both instances the question of *form* is paramount. And it is this that is central to many of the essays in this collection. As the novelist Ali Smith reminds us, 'in its apparent fixity, form is all about change … all about the relationship of change to continuance' (Smith 2013, p. 77). Throughout, the essays have attended to the work that different legal and political forms do in allowing social relations to endure through time, but they have also foregrounded the politics that inheres in such formalisations, highlighting – as your chapter does, Carrol – that the choice of form is never neutral. Most centrally, perhaps, all the chapters explore the implications of understanding social and civil responsibilities through forms of obligation, rather than those of rights. This has entailed emphasising the role that various types of obligations play in binding us in community. For many of the authors, legal obligations – formalised and justiciable – are seen to be deficient in this regard. Though fulfilling other important functions, obligations at law ought not be confused with the bonds that allow for the emergence and sustenance of community. For a proper understanding of this we need to turn elsewhere, to other modalities of obligation, whether in accounts of politics, ethics or ontology. Again, your choice to write the bulk of your chapter as an email seems to tally with this view. The obligations of academic life – and the 'freedoms' that it might afford – will never be captured by justiciable rights and duties. However, such obligations might be discernible in the two emails above that endeavour to *perform* the task of scholarly engagement. In this way, you have been able to both *say* something and *do* something in relation to academic obligation in your chapter.

With our thanks and best wishes,

Daniel & Scott

Bibliography

Bakhtin, M., 1986, *Speech Genres and Other Late Essays*, trans. V. W. McGee, University of Texas Press, Austin.

Benatar, D., 2017, 'UCT's Climate Turns Toxic', *PolticsWeb*, 30 March, www.politicsweb.co.za/opinion/ucts-climate-turns-toxic.

Benatar, D., 2017, 'UCT: The Academic Freedom Farce Continues', *PoliticsWeb*, 10 October, www.politicsweb.co.za/opinion/uct-the-academic-freedom-farce-continues.

Derrida, J., 1988, *Limited Inc*, trans. S. Weber, Northwestern University Press, Evanston, IL.

Derrida, J., 1978, 'Force and Signification' in *Writing and Difference*, trans. A. Bass, pp. 3–30, University of Chicago Press, Chicago, IL.

Furlong, A., 2016, 'GroundUp Report: Rhodes Must Fall Protesters Burn UCT Art', *The Daily Maverick*, 17 February, www.dailymaverick.co.za/article/2016-02-17-groundup-rhodes-must-fall-protesters-burn-uct-art/#.WgjO5RNSyu4.

Geltner, G. & Vaessens, T., 2015, 'On Winner-Takes-All Academia', *Rethink UvA*, 12 May, http://rethinkuva.org/blog/2015/05/13/on-winner-takes-all-academia

Gild, W., 2017, 'UCT's Troubles Continue', *PoliticsWeb*, 6 December, www.politicsweb.co.za/opinion/ucts-troubles-continue.

GroundUp Staff, 2017, 'UCT Trashed as Fee Protests Escalate', *GroundUp*, 2 November, www.groundup.org.za/article/uct-trashed-fees-protests-escalate.

Higgins, J., 2013, *Academic Freedom in a Democratic South Africa: Essays and Interviews on Higher Education and the Humanities*, Wits University Press, Johannesburg.

Jansen, J., 2017, *As by Fire: The End of the South African University*, Tafelberg, Cape Town.

Kloppers-Lourens, J., 2010, 'UCT Top University in Africa', *PolticsWeb*, 16 September, www.politicsweb.co.za/news-and-analysis/uct-top-university-in-africa–da.

Mamdani, M., 2017, 'Decolonizing the Postcolonial University', TB Davie Memorial Lecture, University of Cape Town, 22 August, www.youtube.com/watch?v=vKFAYXf05N0.

Marx, K., 2000, *Selected Writings*, 2nd edn, ed. D. McLellan, Oxford University Press, Oxford.

Pirsig, R. M., 2004, *Zen and the Art of Motorcycle Maintenance: An Enquiry into Values*, 40th anniversary edn, Vintage Books, London.

Smith, A., 2013, *Artful*, Penguin, London.

Van Onselen, C., 1998, 'Closer to Home: Student Unrest and the Welfare Function', in R. W. Johnson& D. Welsh (eds), *Ironic Victory: Liberalism in Post-Liberation South Africa*, Oxford University Press, Cape Town.

University of Cape Town online sources

University of Cape Town website, www.uct.ac.za

'Academic Union Statement on Student Demands: Academic Freedom & Lectures in Philosophy and in Kramer Law': www.au.uct.ac.za/sites/default/files/image_tool/images/207/AcademicsUnion/ACADEMICS%20UNIONS%20STATEMENT%20ON%20STUDENT%20DEMANDS%2025.10.2017%20-%20Revised.pdf

'UCT Assembly, 1 November 2017': www.youtube.com/watch?v=gQzdaEMF8Rc

'Campus Update, 6 November 2017': www.news.uct.ac.za/article/-2017-11-06-monday-6-november

Email disclaimer: www.uct.ac.za/main/email-disclaimer

'Executive Response to SRC List of Demands received on 24 October 2017': www.news.uct.ac.za/images/userfiles/downloads/media/2017-10-25_ResponseToSRC.pdf

'Faculty of Law responds to the CHE report': www.news.uct.ac.za/article/-2017-11-16-faculty-of-law-responds-to-che-report

Student Representative Council 'List of Demands as of 24 October 2017': www.src.uct.ac.za

Index

accountability xiv, 10, 77, 80, 84–6, 91, 101, 103, 116, 119, 193
accumulations of scale 73, 79, 85–6, 88–90, 94
adiaphora 240 (*see* also disinterestedness 198, 240)
adiaphorism 240–1
affect xv, 80, 93–4, 139–43, 151–3, 157–8, 244–5 (*see* also sentiment)
affective turn 140–1
affectivity (*see* ethical affectivity, social affectivity)
Anthropocene 78, 86, 89, 91, 186–7
anthropocentric horizon 140, 156–7
anthropocentricism 140
Aquinas, Thomas 12, 47
Arendt, Hannah 3, 8, 9
attention (*see* Weil, Simone)
Attridge, Derek 151

Baker, J. H. 21
Bakhtin, Mikhail 256, 261
Bal, Mieke 260
Bataille, Georges 63
Being (*das Sein* or *Dasein*) (*see* Heidegger)
being (*Seienden*) (*see* Heidegger)
Being with (*Mitsein*) (*see* Heidegger)
Benatar, David 262–3
Benveniste, Emile 112–13, 179
Birks, Peter 106–8, 120
Brontë, Emily 157
bundle of obligations 107 (*see* also packages of obligation)

categorical divide 56–8
categorical imperative 21, 26–9, 56, 59–60
categorical imperative of being 27
and abandonment 27–9
Caygill, Howard 31–2
Chesterman, Simon 29
Christodoulidis, Emilios 145
Cicero, Marcus Tullius 165, 179, 234–7, 246
civic obligation 106, 227
civil authority xvii, 239–41, 243, 246
civil prudence 234, 238–41, 246
civility xii, xvi–xvii, 220–5, 227–31, 234, 240, 242, 247
Clarkson, Carrol 262
Clippinger, John 191
Clough, Patricia 140
Coetzee, J. M. xv, 140, 147–9, 151–3, 156–7, 256, 260–1
Coke, Sir Edward 133, 141, 147
constitutional sovereignty 139–40, 146–7
co-operative
co-operation 122–6, 128–30
co-operative movement 122–4, 129
genealogy of 122–3, 135
corporate accountability 80
corporate obligation 73, 76, 94 (*see also* corporate responsibility, corporate social responsibility (CSR))
corporate responsibility 79 (see also corporate obligation, corporate social responsibility (CSR))
corporate social responsibility (CSR) xiii, 77, 85–6, 88, 94 (*see also* corporate obligation, corporate responsibility)
Critchley, Simon 32

Dawson, George 165
dearth of duty 39, 41
dearth of rights 39–41
deCew, Judith 210
decorum 234–8, 240, 242, 247
Defoe, Daniel 260
Deleuze, Giles 140–2, 150

Derrida, Jacques 28–9, 36–7, 45, 49–56, 63, 254, 259
de-selection 76, 78–9, 92
and muting and management 76–7, 92
destinerrance 254
Devisch, Ignaas 28
Dewey, John 178
Dickens, Charles 157
différance 28–9
différend (dispute) 62–3, 67
disability 104–5, 115
discipline 76, 88, 129, 132, 134
dogma xii, 4–6, 12, 16
and critique 4–5
and the dogmatic 3, 5–7, 11–13, 16
double bind 50, 52
Durkheim, Émile x, 13
duty of care 65

Eliasson, Olafur 86–7, 89, 92
eloquence (decorum) xvii, 234–8, 243, 245, 247
enclosure 83, 92, 132–5, 173–5
equity xi, xiii, 18–24, 26, 28–30, 32
Escher, M. C. 184, 213
Esposito, Roberto 18, 112, 174
ethic of civil responsibility 238
ethic of office 235, 240–1
ethic of responsibility 234–6, 240, 242, 246
ethic of conviction 236
ethical affectivity 19
ethical divide 58, 61–2, 64
ethical sensibility 19, 22
externalities 82–3, 89–90, 93
positive externalities 82
negative externalities 82–5

Fabius, Laurent 87
Ferguson, Adam 219, 224, 230–1
Ficino, Marsilio 242
Fitzpatrick, Peter 132
force of law xv, 165–7, 173, 175–6, 178–9, 194, 210, 214
force of privacy 184, 194, 214
Fortescue, John 147
Foucault, Michel 122, 126–30, 132–5
fragility xii, 8, 10–11, 183
free duty to give 68 (*see* also free legal duty to give)
free rider problem 113–14
free rider xiv, 69, 101, 113

Gadamer, Hans-Georg 5
Gaia 200
Gaita, Raimond 234, 238
Garber, Majorie 149
Geltner, Guy 261
genealogy
Foucault on 126–7
genealogy of the co-operative (*see* co-operative)
geologic turn 79, 93
Gerwel, Jakes 259–60
gift (*see* Mauss, Marcel)
Gilbert-Walsh, James 27, 30
Gild, William 263
Goodrich, Peter 4
Graeber, David 109
Green, Leslie 191

Hart, H. L. A 191, 208
Hegel, G. W. F. 13, 58–60
Heidegger, Martin 9, 10, 23–4, 25–7, 36–7, 39, 48, 51–2, 56–7, 60–1
on being (*Seienden*) 19, 23–4, 28, 37, 51–2, 56–7, 61, 125, 188
on Being (*das Sein* or *Dasein*) 19, 23–32, 37, 51–2, 56–7, 60–1, 125
on Being with 25–6, 30, 125, 188
Heideggerian and post-Heideggerian 19, 24, 25, 29, 37
Herbert, von Maria 59–60
hesitation xvi, 191, 196–9, 202, 205, 207, 212–13
Higgins, John 252–3, 262, 264
Hildebrandt, Mireille 170
Hohfeld, Wesley Newcomb x, xiii, xiv, 36, 39–40, 42, 45–7, 49, 58, 67, 101–6, 111
Hohfeldian paradigm (*see* also Hohfeldian correlativity) 3, 35, 38, 40
Hohfeldian correlativity (*see* also Hohfeldian paradigm) 16
Holmes, Oliver Wendell 14
Hudson, Alastair 21
Hughes, Ted 148
human subjectivity xvi, 183–8, 191–201, 205–10, 213
Hume, David 57, 59
Hunter, Ian 241
Hutton, James 89–91
Husserl, Edmund 52, 55
hybrid legalities xv, 168–9, 171, 173, 179
hybridism 206–7
hybridity xvi, 169, 174, 176, 177

immanent materiology 165, 178–9, 181 (*see* also law's materiology)

immunis 112–13, 117
immunity xiv, 104–5, 108, 110–14, 116, 118
incivility 228–9, 245
incorporation 132–4
individual right xvii, 256, 264–5
ingratus 113, 117
intellectual responsibility 204–7, 213
and integrity 204–7, 209, 213
interdiction 5–7, 12
inverted morality 117–18

Jansen, Jonathan 252–3, 257–8, 262–3
Jones, Lloyd 129
judgement 5–7, 12, 13, 16

Kafka, Franz 174
Kames, Lord 21
Kant, Immanuel xiii, 21–2, 26–9, 37, 39, 56–9, 66, 148, 203
Kantian 25–9, 37, 62, 211
Kelsen, Hans 7, 166
Kingsley, Charles 130
Klinck, Dennis 21
Kloppers-Lourens 263
kula (*see* Mauss, Marcel)

Latour, Bruno xv, 170–1, 187, 199–204, 211–12
Latourian xvi, 201, 203
law's materiology 176, 180 (*see* also immanent materiology)
legacy xiv, 79–80, 87–94
legal recognition 122–3, 129–35
legalities 81, 168–9
legendo 147, 165–6, 179
Legendre, Pierre 4–5, 12
le-geologist 79
le-geology xiv, 79, 91–2
Levinas, Emanuel xiii, 36, 38–9, 60–1, 63–4, 66, 68
Liddy, Gordon 209
ligando 147, 165–6, 179
Loughlin, Martin 146
Ludlow, J. M. 129, 131–2
Luhmann, Niklas 201
Lushaba, Lwazi 257
Lyotard, Jean-François 36, 38–9, 62, 64, 66–8

della Mirandola, Giovanni Pico 242
MacCormick, Neil 107, 190
MacIntyre, Alasdair ix
Madlingozi, Tshepho 145
Mandami, Mahmood 262
Marx, Karl 111, 260
Massumi, Brian 140
Matthews, Daniel 264
Mauss, Marcel xiii, 35–9, 43–54, 66
on gift xiii, 35, 36–7, 39, 43–57, 61, 63
on gift economy xiii, 36, 45, 50, 54
on gift exchange 36–7, 44–6, 49–50, 52, 54, 63
on gift of time 55–60, 67–8
on *kula* 35–6, 44, 46
Meurs, Pieter 28
Minson, Jeffrey xvii, 234, 238–43, 246–7
Mntambo, Nandipha xv, 140, 153–7
money xiv, 15, 80, 85, 88, 102–5, 108–9, 111, 114–15, 118–19, 125, 257, 265
Moret, A. 154
Morton, Timothy 78
Mossack Fonseca 106, 114
munus 18, 112–13

Nancy, Jean-Luc 25–32, 122, 124–5, 127
natural law xii, 47–9, 208
Neale, E. V. 131
Negative externalities (*see* externalities)
network analysis 77
Nietzsche, Friedrich 126, 135
Nietzschean 176
Nissenbaum, Helen 210–11
Nzimande, Blade 263

office of humanity 242, 245, 247
Ojakangas, Mikas 25
ontological difference 37, 51
ontological divide 56–7, 61
ontological obligation 30–2
ordeal 55, 169–80, 199

Polanyi, Karl 14–15, 89, 110
Patton, Paul 150
practical rationality 186, 196, 205
Panama Papers xiv, 101, 114
Pieth, Mark 106
packages of obligations 106, 108, 120 (see also bundle of obligations)
positive externalities (see externalities)
personhood xvi, 9, 185–6, 188, 192, 194–5, 201–2, 206–8, 210
primary obligation xiii, 18–19, 22, 25, 28, 30, 147

Queen Elizabeth II 110

Raffoul, Francis 27–8
Rancière, Jacques 143, 156–7, 260–1
Raz, Joseph 191
recesses 73, 75–8, 80, 85–6
responsibilisation xvi, 84, 226–7
Rhodes, Cecil John 257
road traffic offence 224
role responsibilities xii, 108
rootedness (see Weil, Simone)
roots (see Weil, Simone)
Rose, Flemming 257, 262–3
Rosing, Minik 86–9
Rousseau, Jean-Jacques 176
Russell, Bertrand 255
Russell, Conrad 255

Said, Edward 259–61
Saunders, David 241
Scanlon, Thomas 204, 212
Schmitt, Carl 7
Schoeman, Ferdinand 210
Sedgwick, Eve 140
sediments 79, 88
sense of duty 38–9, 65, 244 (*see* also sense of obligation, sense of responsibility)
sense of humanity 244
sense of normativity 205
sense of obligation 39, 63–4, 68, 79, 150–1 (*see* also sense of duty, sense of responsibility)
sense of responsibility 27, 69 (*see* also sense of duty, sense of obligation)
sense of vocation 246
sentiment 51, 59, 122, 139, 157, 244 (*see* also affect)
Shakespeare, William 111
Shaxson, Nicholas 117
Slaney, Robert 131–2
Smith, Adam 222–3, 231
Smith, Ali 266
social affectivity 25, 30
social hermeneutic 4–5, 7, 16
social obligation 77, 86, 219, 228, 258 (*see* also social responsibility)
social responsibility 27, 76 (*see* also social obligation)
sovereignty xii, xv, 63, 117–19, 139–40, 143–7, 152, 155–7
and affective attachments 142–5, 149–50, 152, 158
affective power of 146
Spinoza, Baruch 140
St German, Christopher 23, 26
Stiglitz, Joseph 106
Stone, Julius 104
structures of feeling xv, 143, 157
Supiot, Alain xii, 3–7, 11–15
surfaces 73, 79, 83, 88–9, 91–2
synderesis 23, 26, 31

tax avoidance xiii, 83, 117–19
Taylor, James 134
Thomist Natural Law 47, 49
Thompson, E. P. 128, 135
Time 73, 78–82, 84–94 (*see* also Mauss, Marcel on gift of time)
transformative constitutionalism 144
Trump, Donald 114, 139, 163
Trumpism 164, 166
trust xiv, 103–5, 108, 116, 119

Ulpian 6

Vaessens, Thomas 261
value-object 169–73, 180, 187
Van der Walt, Johan 3
Van Onselen, Charles 258
Veitch, Scott 39–43, 47, 49, 64–5, 68, 79, 84, 145–6, 264
Villey, Michel 48
void 84–6, 88

Waldron, Jeremy 39, 55, 106–7, 195
wave of duty 43, 55–6, 106, 119
Webb, Catherine 124
Weber, Max 234–40, 243, 246
Weil, Simone xii, 3, 8–12, 16, 122, 124–5, 136, 147
on attention 9–10
on rootedness xii, 3, 16, 122, 125, 147
on roots xiii, 125, 132, 144, 165
Whitehead, Alfred North 178
Williams, Raymond xv, 143, 152, 157
Wittgenstein, Ludwig 62, 172

Yeo, Stephen 126
Young, Iris Marion 84

Taylor & Francis Group
an informa business

Taylor & Francis eBooks

www.taylorfrancis.com

A single destination for eBooks from Taylor & Francis with increased functionality and an improved user experience to meet the needs of our customers.

90,000+ eBooks of award-winning academic content in Humanities, Social Science, Science, Technology, Engineering, and Medical written by a global network of editors and authors.

TAYLOR & FRANCIS EBOOKS OFFERS:

A streamlined experience for our library customers

A single point of discovery for all of our eBook content

Improved search and discovery of content at both book and chapter level

REQUEST A FREE TRIAL

support@taylorfrancis.com

Routledge
Taylor & Francis Group

CRC Press
Taylor & Francis Group

For Product Safety Concerns and Information please contact our EU representative GPSR@taylorandfrancis.com
Taylor & Francis Verlag GmbH, Kaufingerstraße 24, 80331 München, Germany

www.ingramcontent.com/pod-product-compliance
Ingram Content Group UK Ltd.
Pitfield, Milton Keynes, MK11 3LW, UK
UKHW020014200926
475702UK00014B/1888
* 9 7 8 0 3 6 7 8 6 2 6 5 7 *